Finding **YOUR** Place in the World

JOE WILLIAMSON

ISBN: 1450557392
ISBN-13: 9781450557399
Library of Congress Control Number: 2010901479
CreateSpace Independent Publishing Platform
North Charleston, South Carolina

TABLE OF CONTENTS

About the author:

Joe Williamson lives in Carmel, Indiana with his wife Maureen. He is the father of three sons, Andy, Aaron and Owen and one daughter, Anne. He currently manages a financial consulting practice in Indianapolis. He has served the church for more than 40 years in capacities that include teacher, deacon, elder, and financial counselor. His primary ministry in the past several years has been discipleship; much of the content of this book came from this ministry. All profits from sales of this book are used to help fund discipleship initiatives in financially impoverished areas of the world.

In addition to the contents of the book, there are tools you may find helpful in the Appendix. If you have questions on their use or any discipleship related questions fee free to email Joe at tSOARMinistries@live.com or visit the website at www.tSOAR.org.

Introduction

If you've picked up this book with the thought that you will read it and suddenly know your place in the world, you are mistaken. Hopefully what you will find is a process to help you discover your place, but even then you will find it is not a place but an ongoing relationship with Jesus. Our hope is that this book will provide you with the tools you need for that journey.

The purpose of the workbook (the first 12 weeks) is to prepare one for the next section, a 24-week set of readings that includes everything that Jesus taught. In the workbook you will learn the basic concepts that a disciple must understand as well as gain insight into hearing God as he speaks through his written word as well as through experiences.

The workbook is written in a way to be useful for a new believer as well as a mature believer who may be using it for mentoring. For this reason, the 3 daily questions from the 24-week set is included as the last 3 questions in the workbook each day mainly for use by the person already familiar with the hearing God. (You can see the questions with instructions on using them on page 97.) Those new to listening to God may not feel comfortable answering these questions until week 10; if so, omit them until then.

Final Thoughts in the Appendix provides some suggestions for the first few times through the 24-week section. While all scripture is God breathed and useful in teaching, rebuking, correcting and training in righteousness, Jesus' teaching is assigned to you in the Great Commission. Continue to use these readings until you not only know what Jesus commanded but have learned to obey it consistently.

As you gain familiarity with what he commanded and have learned the discipline of spending time before him daily to listen to him speak into your life, not only through the scriptures but the circumstances he allows in your life, you should begin to see your place in the world, why you are where you are now at this point in time in history.

The basic discipleship concepts taught in the workbook can be remembered by the acronym tSOAR, keeping in mind there are 3 t's (time, truth, trust, Surrender, Obey, Abide, and Reconcile). Once understood they can also be used to gain insight into the overall teaching of the Bible to better understand it. There are questions on page 98 that can be used as a weekly review of one's life in the context of these concepts. They can be used to work through acute issues of life using the format in the Appendix under Anxiety, Temptations and Issues of Life.

As you begin to hear God and he inspires you to certain actions, do them. The Appendix includes a Personal Organization system to keep track of what the Lord wants you to do. Should you have difficulty understanding it email us at tSOARMinistries@live.com with questions.

All quoted scriptures are from the public domain World English Bible (WEB).

Other (seed) fell amid the thorns, and the thorns grew with it, and choked it. That (seed) which fell among the thorns, these are those who have heard, and as they go on their way they are choked with cares, riches, and pleasures of life, and bring no fruit to maturity. (Luke 8:7,14)

The greatest barrier to a deepening spiritual life is time. Many things compete for time including the obligations of our life roles, our desire for more, and our desire to enjoy what we have.

What keeps you from spending time with the Lord on a consistent basis each day?

"Hypocrites! You know how to discern the appearance of the sky, but you can't discern the signs of the times!" (Matt. 16:3)

We become proficient at what we need to do to live day to day, but may be oblivious to what God wants to do. We need spiritual wisdom to understand what he is doing in our midst at this time and place in history and what he is calling us to do. It requires a combination of biblical revelation to understand what God wants to do in the world generally and a growing relationship with him (time).

"Mankind have a great aversion to intellectual labor; but even supposing knowledge to be easily attainable, more people would be content to be ignorant than would take even a little trouble to acquire it" according to Samuel Johnson. We must have sufficient desire for spiritual wisdom to stay disciplined.

Do you understand what God wants to do generally? Can you relate your knowledge of God's purposes to your present time and circumstances? Do you know what God is calling you to do?

What are you presently doing to increase your knowledge of scripture?

Lord, what are you teaching me?

Lord, what else have you said to me through thoughts, circumstances, conversations, emotions, or the work of the enemy?

Lord, what do you want me to do today?

At home: At work: In ministry:

"I came that they may have life, and may have it abundantly." (John 10:10)

"Again, the Kingdom of Heaven is like a treasure hidden in the field, which a man found, and hid. In his joy, he goes and sells all that he has, and buys that field." (Matt. 13:44)

One passage tells us Jesus came so that we might have abundant life. The other one tells us the cost for abundant life; we must give up all else to receive it. Before that sort of decision can be made, one must completely trust the one who makes the offer.

Do you trust God completely? If no, what is the cause of your lack of complete trust?

Lord, what are you teaching me through today's readings?

Lord, what else have you said to me through thoughts, circumstances, conversations, emotions, or the work of the enemy?

Lord, what do you want me to do today?

At home: At work: In ministry:

"So therefore whoever of you who doesn't renounce all that he has, he can't be my disciple." (Luke 14:33)

Yesterday we learned we must have complete trust in order to give up all we have to receive the abundant life that Jesus offers. Today's passage makes it clear that discipleship is costly; it costs all that we have. This implies our possessions of course, but from others of Jesus' teaching we know that it includes our relationships, our time, and our right to ourselves: all.

He said you **can't** be his disciple without giving up everything. He didn't say it was optional. Why do you think this is true?

Lord, what are you teaching me through today's readings?

Lord, what else have you said to me through thoughts, circumstances, conversations, emotions, or the work of the enemy?

Lord, what do you want me to do today?

At home: At work: In ministry:

TODAY'S DATE: _____

"If you remain in my word, then you are truly my disciples. You will know the truth, and the truth will make you free." (John 8:31-32)

We often want to know why we should do something before doing it. Jesus asks his disciples to *"remain in my word"* or obey his teaching first, **then** they will know the truth and be set free.

Are you familiar with the full body of Jesus' teaching?

Are you making a consistent effort to obey his teaching? If so, how?

Lord, what are you teaching me through today's readings?

Lord, what else have you said to me through thoughts, circumstances, conversations, emotions, or the work of the enemy?

Lord, what do you want me to do today?

At home: At work: In ministry:

"Remain (abide) in me, and I in you. As the branch can't bear fruit by itself, unless it remains in the vine, so neither can you, unless you remain in me." (John 15:4)

Jesus assures us that he is with us to the end of the age and at all times, but his command here implies that we may not be "in him."

What do you think he means by being "in him?"

What do you think he means by not being able to bear fruit unless we remain in him?

Lord, what are you teaching me through today's readings?

Lord, what else have you said to me through thoughts, circumstances, conversations, emotions, or the work of the enemy?

Lord, what do you want me to do today?

At home: At work: In ministry:

"All authority has been given to me in heaven and on earth. Go, and make disciples of all nations, baptizing them in the name of the Father and of the Son and of the Holy Spirit, teaching them to observe all things that I commanded you. Behold, I am with you always, even to the end of the age." (Matt. 28:18-20)

As disciples we have the "ministry of reconciliation" as Paul put it. Being a disciple implies that we are obeying all Jesus commanded as well as actively teaching others to obey. Are you?

If not, what implications would it have for your life if you began?

Lord, what are you teaching me through today's readings?

Lord, what else have you said to me through thoughts, circumstances, conversations, emotions, or the work of the enemy?

Lord, what do you want me to do today?

At home: At work: In ministry:

Lord, what have you taught me this week?

What areas do I need to work on?

What specifically will I do and when will it be done?

Lord, what else have you said to me about time through thoughts, circumstances, conversations, emotions, or the work of the enemy?

Lord, what do you want me to do today?

At home: At work: In ministry:

WEEKLY REVIEW

TIME: Lord, did I spend adequate time truly listening to you each day?

TRUTH: Lord, what truths did you reveal to me this past week?

TRUST: Lord, did I trust that you were in control of all of the circumstances of my life this week, or did I worry, become anxious or reflect lack of trust in another way?

SURRENDER: Lord, did my thoughts and actions reflect that I have surrendered all to you? Did I practice spiritual disciplines daily? Did I ask your forgiveness and forgive others?

OBEY: Lord, was I obedient in the attitudes of my mind (humility and servanthood rather than pride, etc.)? Did I do the things I sensed you wanted me to do?

ABIDE: Lord, was I aware of your presence and of you speaking to me throughout the week?

RECONCILE: Lord, did I disciple other Christians or share the gospel with non-believers as you provided opportunities?

TIME – DAY 1   **TODAY'S DATE:** _____

When it was day, he departed and went into an uninhabited place. (Luke 4:42)

Deepening of our spiritual life begins with time alone with God, time spent with him receiving the truth he reveals. How does one get to know God and develop a love relationship with him? As with any meaningful relationship, it begins with time spent with that person getting to know their mind and heart. Love develops and deepens over time. As one grows in understanding God and learns to live in the truth that he is always present, can always be spoken to, and can always be heard, the time spent with him expands and the relationship goes to greater depths.

What are the greatest challenges that keep you from a more committed life in Christ?

Do you often let urgent matters crowd out important ones?

Record how larger amounts of time were spent in the past 24 hours.

Lord, what are you teaching me?

Lord, what else have you said to me through thoughts, circumstances, conversations, emotions, or the work of the enemy?

Lord, what do you want me to do today?

At home: At work: In ministry:

After he had sent the multitudes away, he went up into the mountain by himself to pray. When evening had come, he was there alone. (Matt. 14:23)

Jesus had a regular practice of rising early in the morning to spend time alone with the Father. Sometimes he spent time with the Father at the end of the day or even left in the midst of ministry as he felt the need. We tend to get so caught up in the urgent demands of life that we allow the important aspects to be crowded out.

How much "impulse spending" of time did you expend on unscheduled activities yesterday (do not include time diverted when God interrupts)?

Jesus seemed to never hurry. It seems logical that there is always time to do God's will yet most people do not seem to have enough hours in the day to do all they want to do. What are you allowing in your life that is likely not God's will?

Record how larger amounts of time were spent in the past 24 hours.

Lord, what are you teaching me through today's readings?

Lord, what else have you said to me through thoughts, circumstances, conversations, emotions, or the work of the enemy?

Lord, what do you want me to do today?

At home: At work: In ministry:

"I came that they may have life, and may have it abundantly." (John 10:10)

"I am the vine. You are the branches. He who remains in me, and I in him, the same bears much fruit, for apart from me you can do nothing." (John 15:5)

Everyone who understands the 'abundant life' Jesus offers desires to have it. At times we experience it or what we think it is, but too soon we are back into our normal experience of life. We are burdened and stressed by the never-ending series of responsibilities and appointments. Demands come upon us from home, from work, from church, from school and from civic duties. There are also the more distant claims for attention from crises around the world regularly brought to our attention. Surely God understands that with such a busy life he is lucky to get our occasional devotion as we are on our way to the next thing on our busy schedules.

How would you describe 'abundant life'?

What would Jesus do in your current calling (family, employment, ministry) that is different from what you do that might change how time is spent?

Record how larger amounts of time were spent in the past 24 hours.

Lord, what are you teaching me through today's readings?

Lord, what else have you said to me through thoughts, circumstances, conversations, emotions, or the work of the enemy?

Lord, what do you want me to do today?

At home: At work: In ministry:

"You search the Scriptures, because you think that in them you have eternal life; and these are they which testify about me. Yet you will not come to me, that you may have life." (John 5:39-40)

We may feel guilty that we do not spend more time in Bible study or that we do not know the word of God better. But as the verses above suggest, there is something even more fundamental we lack: we refuse to come to Jesus to have life. We must get to know the One the Bible speaks of in order to understand it. We overstate the complexity of our lives. We give the Lord a very low priority in our schedules even though we may affirm with our lips he is top priority. A review of how we spend our time and what we think about will reveal the priority we give him.

Record how larger amounts of time were spent in the past 24 hours.

Is modern technology (e.g. cell phones, email, etc.) a help or hindrance to your time? What changes might you make to become more effective or efficient?

Lord, what are you teaching me through today's readings?

Lord, what else have you said to me through thoughts, circumstances, conversations, emotions, or the work of the enemy?

Lord, what do you want me to do today?

At home: At work: In ministry:

"However when he, the Spirit of truth, has come, he will guide you into all truth, for he will not speak from himself; but whatever he hears, he will speak. He will declare to you things that are coming." (John 16:13)

We must change our schedules and give top priority to time apart with God each day in order to listen and learn from the only one who knows what *our* life is to be about, why *we* are here. This can only be revealed to us by God and for him to communicate with us we must spend time listening.

Record how larger amounts of time were spent in the past 24 hours.

Review your notes of time usage for the past 5 days.

    a.   What do you see that is surprising or revealing about how your time is spent?

    b.   What areas are missing or seem deficient?

Do your priorities need to be reordered? If so, how? What changes will you make to your daily schedule to give top priority to the Lord each day?

Lord, what are you teaching me through today's readings?

Lord, what else have you said to me through thoughts, circumstances, conversations, emotions, or the work of the enemy?

Lord, what do you want me to do today?

At home: At work: In ministry:

"My Father is still working, so I am working, too." (John 5:17)

"Most certainly, I tell you, the Son can do nothing of himself, but what he sees the Father doing. For whatever things he does, these the Son also does likewise." (John 5:19)

Jesus understood that the Father is always at work and that circumstances are not random. He paid attention to what the Father allowed in his life and surely much of his time alone with the Father was spent discussing the significance of his circumstances.

We must increasingly realize that the Father is at his work to **this** very day and learn to recognize what he is doing in our lives to understand what he is calling us to. Our lives will become less busy and more purposeful. We will learn to see him in the midst of daily life. Then we will begin to experience the fullness of life he came to give us. The daily question about circumstances is meant to help you stay connected with what the Lord is saying to you through them.

What is the Father doing in your home?

      At work?

      In your ministry?

What is the Father calling you to in your home?

      At work?

      In your ministry?

Lord, what are you teaching me through today's readings?

Lord, what else have you said to me through thoughts, circumstances, conversations, emotions, or the work of the enemy?

Lord, what do you want me to do today?

At home: At work: In ministry:

Lord, what have you taught me this week about time?

What areas of time do I need to work on?

What specifically will I do and when will it be done?

Lord, what else have you said to me about time through thoughts, circumstances, conversations, emotions, or the work of the enemy?

Lord, what do you want me to do today?

At home: At work: In ministry:

WEEKLY REVIEW

Time: Lord, did I spend adequate time truly listening to you each day?

Truth: Lord, what truths did you reveal to me this past week?

Trust: Lord, did I trust that you were in control of all of the circumstances of my life this week, or did I worry, become anxious or reflect lack of trust in another way?

Surrender: Lord, did my thoughts and actions reflect that I have surrendered all to you? Did I practice spiritual disciplines daily? Did I ask your forgiveness and forgive others?

Obey: Lord, was I obedient in the attitudes of my mind (humility and servanthood rather than pride, etc.)? Did I do the things I sensed you wanted me to do?

Abide: Lord, was I aware of your presence and of you speaking to me throughout the week?

Reconcile: Lord, did I disciple other Christians or share the gospel with non-believers as you provided opportunities?

"I am the way, the truth, and the life. No one comes to the Father, except through me." (John 14:6)

For I rejoiced greatly, when brothers came and testified about your truth, even as you walk in truth. (3 John 1:3)

Jesus says that he is the truth, so truth is personal. John tells of his joy of hearing that the church he is writing to continues to walk in the truth so truth is also relational. From these truths proceeds the general understanding that Christianity is not a religion as is often understood, but is meant to be a living, personal relationship with God, the source of all truth.

How personal is your relationship with God?

What can you do to make your relationship with God more personal and intimate?

Lord, what are you teaching me?

Lord, what else have you said to me through thoughts, circumstances, conversations, emotions, or the work of the enemy?

Lord, what do you want me to do today?

At home: At work: In ministry:

Jesus answered, *"If I glorify myself, my glory is nothing. It is my Father who glorifies me, of whom you say that he is our God. You have not known him, but I know him. If I said, 'I don't know him,' I would be like you, a liar. But I know him, and keep his word. Your father Abraham rejoiced to see my day. He saw it, and was glad."* **The Jews therefore said to him, "You are not yet fifty years old, and have you seen Abraham?" Jesus said to them,** *"Most certainly, I tell you, before Abraham came into existence, I AM."* (John 8:54-58)

Moses said to God, "Behold, when I come to the children of Israel, and tell them, 'The God of your fathers has sent me to you;' and they ask me, 'What is his name?' What should I tell them?" God said to Moses, "I AM WHO I AM," and he said, "You shall tell the children of Israel this: 'I AM has sent me to you.'" God said moreover to Moses, "You shall tell the children of Israel this, 'Yahweh, the God of your fathers, the God of Abraham, the God of Isaac, and the God of Jacob, has sent me to you.' This is my name forever, and this is my memorial to all generations. (Ex. 3:13-15)

Jesus' words in John 8:58, *"before Abraham came into existence, I AM"* seem obscure unless one is familiar with the passages in Exodus where God tells Moses that his name is "I AM." Jesus Christ is God. This truth is central to all that follows and must become the central truth of our lives. Only then will we be able to trust enough to surrender our lives to him completely. Only then will we desire to learn to obey him with all our heart, soul, mind and strength. Only then will we believe in his abiding presence even though we cannot see him physically. And only then will we continually desire to reconcile others to him.

What reservations do you have in believing Jesus Christ is God?

Lord, what are you teaching me through today's readings?

Lord, what else have you said to me through thoughts, circumstances, conversations, emotions, or the work of the enemy?

Lord, what do you want me to do today?

At home: At work: In ministry:

Pilate therefore said to him, "Are you a king then?" Jesus answered, *"You say that I am a king. For this reason I have been born, and for this reason I have come into the world, that I should testify to the truth. Everyone who is of the truth listens to my voice."* **Pilate said to him, "What is truth?"** (John 18:37-38)

"Everyone therefore who hears these words of mine, and does them, I will liken him to a wise man, who built his house on a rock. The rain came down, the floods came, and the winds blew, and beat on that house; and it didn't fall, for it was founded on the rock. Everyone who hears these words of mine, and doesn't do them will be like a foolish man, who built his house on the sand. The rain came down, the floods came, and the winds blew, and beat on that house; and it fell—and great was its fall." (Matt. 7:24-27)

Jesus therefore said to those Jews who had believed him, *"If you remain in my word, then you are truly my disciples. You will know the truth, and the truth will make you free."* (John 8:31-32)

Like Pilate, many believe truth cannot be known or that truth is relative. We have learned that truth is personal and relational. Jesus says that a wise man puts his teaching into practice to withstand the storms of life. He also says that those who hold to his teaching will know the truth, and by knowing the truth will be set free. Since Jesus is God, he knows the best way to live an earthly life. He knows what obedience to his teaching brings.

Are you trying to put Jesus' teaching into practice? If no, why not?

If yes, a) how do you go about it?

      b) What are your results?

      c) What area is giving you the most difficulty?

Lord, what are you teaching me through today's readings?

Lord, what else have you said to me through thoughts, circumstances, conversations, emotions, or the work of the enemy?

Lord, what do you want me to do today?

At home: At work: In ministry:

"However when he, the Spirit of truth, has come, he will guide you into all truth, for he will not speak from himself; but whatever he hears, he will speak. He will declare to you things that are coming." (John 16:13)

All things were made through him. Without him was not anything made that has been made. (John 1:3)

The heavens declare the glory of God. The expanse shows his handiwork. (Psalm 19:1)

Jesus Christ is the revealer of physical or natural truth. As creator of all, he knows all things, how they are held together and how they work whether they are his creation or man's. There is no situation or problem in life that he does not know the solution to. He may not provide the answer we *want* each time we ask, but he will provide the answers we *need*.

What truth do you need God to reveal to you now?

Ask the Lord if recent circumstances provide information related to the truth needed above. Write down what comes to your mind.

Lord, what are you teaching me through today's readings?

Lord, what else have you said to me through thoughts, circumstances, conversations, emotions, or the work of the enemy?

Lord, what do you want me to do today?

At home: At work: In ministry:

"I will pray to the Father, and he will give you another Counselor, that he may be with you forever,—the Spirit of truth, whom the world can't receive; for it doesn't see him, neither knows him. You know him, for he lives with you, and will be in you." (John 14:16-17)

Jesus Christ is the revealer of spiritual truth through the Holy Spirit. He reveals spiritual truth throughout the Bible. He also reveals it in nature and in the circumstances of life. In the gospels Jesus often used nature, current events, and even the work of the enemy to reveal truth. Through the Holy Spirit, he continues to reveal truth in these same ways as one abides in him.

What spiritual truth has God revealed to you through the Bible recently?

What spiritual truth has God revealed to you through circumstances including thoughts, emotions, conversations and the work of the enemy recently?

Lord, what are you teaching me through today's readings?

Lord, what else have you said to me through thoughts, circumstances, conversations, emotions, or the work of the enemy?

Lord, what do you want me to do today?

At home: At work: In ministry:

"Remain in me, and I in you. As the branch can't bear fruit by itself, unless it remains in the vine, so neither can you, unless you remain in me. I am the vine. You are the branches. He who remains in me, and I in him, the same bears much fruit, for apart from me you can do nothing. If a man doesn't remain in me, he is thrown out as a branch, and is withered; and they gather them, throw them into the fire, and they are burned." (John 15:4-6)

"For everyone who does evil hates the light, and doesn't come to the light, lest his works would be exposed. But he who does the truth comes to the light, that his works may be revealed, that they have been done in God." (John 3:20-21)

We will cover this truth again under abide, but it is important enough to cover more than once. We must live in the truth ("remain in me") if we are to have fruitful lives. Once we stop living by the truth we slip into darkness, and once in darkness may slip further into evil. We must take care to remain in the light, to walk by the truth as best we understand it. And we must take the time to increasingly understand the truth so we may walk more consistently in it.

Most who begin to follow Jesus intend to continue following him, but something happens. We get busy. Circumstances go against us. The cares and concerns of this life pull us away from our relationship with God. We must be vigilant to stay on course, to remain in him.

What most often distracts you from a consistent relationship with God?

How can you prevent this from happening?

Lord, what are you teaching me through today's readings?

Lord, what else have you said to me through thoughts, circumstances, conversations, emotions, or the work of the enemy?

Lord, what do you want me to do today?

At home: At work: In ministry:

TRUTH – SUMMARY   **TODAY'S DATE:** _____

Lord, what have you taught me this week about truth?

What aspects of truth do I need to explore further?

What specifically will I do and when will it be done?

Lord, what else have you said to me through thoughts, circumstances, conversations, emotions, or the work of the enemy?

Lord, what do you want me to do today?

At home: At work: In ministry:

WEEKLY REVIEW

Time: Lord, did I spend adequate time truly listening to you each day?

Truth: Lord, what truths did you reveal to me this past week?

Trust: Lord, did I trust that you were in control of all of the circumstances of my life this week, or did I worry, become anxious or reflect lack of trust in another way?

Surrender: Lord, did my thoughts and actions reflect that I have surrendered all to you? Did I practice spiritual disciplines daily? Did I ask your forgiveness and forgive others?

Obey: Lord, was I obedient in the attitudes of my mind (humility and servanthood rather than pride, etc.)? Did I do the things I sensed you wanted me to do?

Abide: Lord, was I aware of your presence and of you speaking to me throughout the week?

Reconcile: Lord, did I disciple other Christians or share the gospel with non-believers as you provided opportunities?

"When the strong man, fully armed, guards his own dwelling, his goods are safe. But when someone stronger attacks him and overcomes him, he takes from him his whole armor in which he trusted, and divides his spoils." (Luke 11:21-22)

Jesus answered him, *"If a man loves me, he will keep my word. My Father will love him, and we will come to him, and make our home with him. He who doesn't love me doesn't keep my words. The word which you hear isn't mine, but the Father's who sent me."* (John 14:23-24)

We must trust in something trustworthy or we will live lives of perpetual fear. In the first passage above, the man trusted in his armor. Many trust in their wealth, ability, intelligence, another person or some other aspect of their lives. Only God is completely trustworthy. Anything or anyone else leaves the possibility that stronger forces will remove our object of trust.

We must trust Jesus' teaching that is faithfully preserved for us in the gospels for it to become the guide for our lives. Jesus Christ, God incarnate visited earth and gave us the words of life. Many times he referred specifically to his teaching, his words, and his commands. His teachings are the focus of this discipleship program because they were his focus. His last command was Matthew 28:20 (*teaching them to observe all things that I commanded you*) and was said after *"All authority has been given to me in heaven and on earth."* (Matt. 28:18)

What do you trust in?

What reservations do you have that the gospels have faithfully preserved Jesus' basic teaching?

What reservations do you have that Jesus' teaching as informed by the rest of scripture is a sufficient guide for your life?

Lord, what are you teaching me?

Lord, what else have you said to me through thoughts, circumstances, conversations, emotions, or the work of the enemy?

Lord, what do you want me to do today?

At home: At work: In ministry:

When he got into a boat, his disciples followed him. Behold, a violent storm came up on the sea, so much that the boat was covered with the waves, but he was asleep. They came to him, and woke him up, saying, "Save us, Lord! We are dying!" He said to them, *"Why are you fearful, O you of little faith?"* **Then he got up, rebuked the wind and the sea, and there was a great calm. The men marveled, saying, "What kind of man is this, that even the wind and the sea obey him?"** (Matt. 8:23-27)

Life often involves storms that arise without warning like the one in this scripture. Unexpected and unpredictable circumstances of life take us by surprise. Often this leads to a natural response of fear yet here Jesus rebukes the disciples for their lack of faith. When the storms of life come to us without warning we must remember that God is always with us and allows all things. After the initial surprise we must learn to respond in faith by asking God what he is saying to us through the circumstances or how he is calling us to respond.

What recent circumstances caught you by surprise causing you to fear or have anxiety?

How did you respond to these circumstances?

Lord, what are you teaching me through today's readings?

Lord, what else have you said to me through thoughts, circumstances, conversations, emotions, or the work of the enemy?

Lord, what do you want me to do today?

At home: At work: In ministry:

Behold, one came to him and said, "Good teacher, what good thing shall I do, that I may have eternal life?" He said to him, *"Why do you call me good? No one is good but one, that is, God. But if you want to enter into life, keep the commandments."* **He said to him, "Which ones?" Jesus said,** *"'You shall not murder.' 'You shall not commit adultery.' 'You shall not steal.' 'You shall not offer false testimony.' 'Honor your father and mother.' And, 'You shall love your neighbor as yourself.'"* **The young man said to him, "All these things I have observed from my youth. What do I still lack?" Jesus said to him,** *"If you want to be perfect, go, sell what you have, and give to the poor, and you will have treasure in heaven; and come, follow me."* **But when the young man heard the saying, he went away sad, for he was one who had great possessions. Jesus said to his disciples,** *"Most certainly I say to you, a rich man will enter into the Kingdom of Heaven with difficulty."* (Matt. 19:16-23)

This man was interested in spiritual things. He was ready to take the next step in his spiritual walk until he found out what it entailed. He had a good life. He was wealthy so he had all his needs provided for but apparently felt something was still lacking which is why he sought Jesus. He was not ready yet to give up his life to receive what Jesus had to offer. He didn't trust that what Jesus offered was better than what he already had.

Is anything so important to you that it that keeps you from completely following Jesus?

Do you trust that God's will is better than your own? If so, how do your actions reflect that belief?

Lord, what are you teaching me through today's readings?

Lord, what else have you said to me through thoughts, circumstances, conversations, emotions, or the work of the enemy?

Lord, what do you want me to do today?

At home: At work: In ministry:

In the fourth watch of the night, Jesus came to them, walking on the sea. When the disciples saw him walking on the sea, they were troubled, saying, "It's a ghost!" and they cried out for fear. But immediately Jesus spoke to them, saying *"Cheer up! It is I! Don't be afraid."* Peter answered him and said, "Lord, if it is you, command me to come to you on the waters." He said, *"Come!"* Peter stepped down from the boat, and walked on the waters to come to Jesus. But when he saw that the wind was strong, he was afraid, and beginning to sink, he cried out, saying, "Lord, save me!" Immediately Jesus stretched out his hand, took hold of him, and said to him, *"You of little faith, why did you doubt?"* (Matt. 14:25-31)

This was not the first act of faith Jesus asked of Peter. Another time Jesus asked him to cast his net on the other side of the boat after he had spent all night fishing without success; his net was filled to the breaking point. Here Jesus asks for more faith to be exercised. Expect him to do the same with you as you grow in maturity.

We must trust that God will enable us to obey his will, however impossible it seems to us. If we trust God and are obedient to him, we will know no fear or anxiety even in circumstances we do not comprehend. He may use times of fear and anxiety to reveal our lack of trust in order that we know this truth about ourselves. We must first be aware of our need to grow in faith so we may be set free from fear.

What has God called you to do in the past that seemed beyond your ability at the time?

What is God calling you to do now that seems beyond your ability to obey?

Lord, what are you teaching me through today's readings?

Lord, what else have you said to me through thoughts, circumstances, conversations, emotions, or the work of the enemy?

Lord, what do you want me to do today?

At home: At work: In ministry:

"Aren't two sparrows sold for a small coin? Not one of them falls on the ground apart from your Father's will, but the very hairs of your head are all numbered. Therefore don't be afraid. You are of more value than many sparrows. (Matt. 10:29-31)

God is our refuge and strength, a very present help in trouble. Therefore we won't be afraid, though the earth changes, though the mountains are shaken into the heart of the seas; though its waters roar and are troubled, though the mountains tremble with their swelling. (Psalm 46:1-3)

We must trust that nothing happens apart from the will of the Father. When disaster strikes, often the work of the enemy, this is a difficult truth. Jesus does not say the Father causes the sparrows to fall, but that they do not fall apart from his will. The Father did not cause airliners full of passengers to fly into the World Trade Center towers, sinful man did. Natural disasters such as earthquake, hurricanes or tsunamis, so-called 'acts of God' may also present a challenge to trust. In ways we cannot understand, these things also seem part of the Father's will. Trust accepts this and asks in the midst of life's mysteries "What are you revealing to me through this?" It is helpful to keep in mind that God's main purpose is to reconcile the world to himself so they might know him and be conformed to the image of Christ. Often "bad things" are useful for that.

What types of circumstances or things cause you to fear or have anxiety?

What may God be teaching you or calling you to in these circumstances?

Lord, what are you teaching me through today's readings?

Lord, what else have you said to me through thoughts, circumstances, conversations, emotions, or the work of the enemy?

Lord, what do you want me to do today?

At home: At work: In ministry:

Then Jesus came with them to a place called Gethsemane, and said to his disciples, *"Sit here, while I go there and pray."* **He took with him Peter and the two sons of Zebedee, and began to be sorrowful and severely troubled. Then he said to them,** *"My soul is exceedingly sorrowful, even to death. Stay here, and watch with me."* **He went forward a little, fell on his face, and prayed, saying,** *"My Father, if it is possible, let this cup pass away from me; nevertheless, not what I desire, but what you desire."* **Again, a second time he went away, and prayed, saying,** *"My Father, if this cup can't pass away from me unless I drink it, your desire be done."* (Matt. 26:36-39,42)

We must trust that God's will, as it is revealed to us, is better than what we prefer (our will). Sometimes we may need to spend extended time in prayer, perhaps with close friends as with Jesus in Gethsemane, before we know with certainty the will of the Father. Once we know his will we must surrender our will to his. How we live our lives makes a difference in what we experience; we can only be certain that our life is unfolding as he desires if we are surrendered, obedient and abiding in him.

Do you **really** trust that God's will is better than your own – enough to surrender your life completely to him and go to your personal cross? If not, what are your concerns?

Lord, what are you teaching me through today's readings?

Lord, what else have you said to me through thoughts, circumstances, conversations, emotions, or the work of the enemy?

Lord, what do you want me to do today?

At home: At work: In ministry:

TRUST – SUMMARY   TODAY'S DATE: _____

Lord, what have you taught me this week about trust?

What circumstances give me the most difficulty in trusting God?

What specifically will I do to try to increase my ability to trust?

Lord, what else have you said to me through thoughts, circumstances, conversations, emotions, or the work of the enemy?

Lord, what do you want me to do today?

At home: At work: In ministry:

WEEKLY REVIEW

Time: Lord, did I spend adequate time truly listening to you each day?

Truth: Lord, what truths did you reveal to me this past week?

Trust: Lord, did I trust that you were in control of all of the circumstances of my life this week, or did I worry, become anxious or reflect lack of trust in another way?

Surrender: Lord, did my thoughts and actions reflect that I have surrendered all to you? Did I practice spiritual disciplines daily? Did I ask your forgiveness and forgive others?

Obey: Lord, was I obedient in the attitudes of my mind (humility and servanthood rather than pride, etc.)? Did I do the things I sensed you wanted me to do?

Abide: Lord, was I aware of your presence and of you speaking to me throughout the week?

Reconcile: Lord, did I disciple other Christians or share the gospel with non-believers as you provided opportunities?

Jesus said to her, "Woman, believe me, the hour comes, when neither in this mountain, nor in Jerusalem, will you worship the Father. You worship that which you don't know. We worship that which we know; for salvation is from the Jews. But the hour comes, and now is, when the true worshippers will worship the Father in spirit and truth, for the Father seeks such to be his worshippers. God is spirit, and those who worship him must worship in spirit and truth." (John 4:21-24)

We come to Jesus with baggage: our will, our prejudices, our worldview, our view of what we need to have the life we want, our view of what God should be like and so forth. In A Grief Observed C.S. Lewis called God the Great Iconoclast who continually destroys every false image we have of him. We must abandon anything that is false, so he can renew our minds to conform us into his image. Before he can do that we must surrender all we have to him, including false views of God.

For example, I used to believe all my problems would be solved when I made a commitment to Jesus Christ. In a sense this is true, but not in the way I thought. I wanted everything to go well, every decision I made to be the correct one and no harm to befall me. When things didn't turn out that way my confidence in God was shaken, but I persevered and God used that time of questioning to give me a more mature and correct understanding of who he is.

The Samaritan woman had an inadequate view of God that Jesus clarified. Can you recall a false view of God that you once held which he clarified? If so, what was it and how did he do it?

Ask the Lord to reveal any prejudice, worldview, or view of him that you must surrender. Record anything that he brings to mind.

Lord, what are you teaching me through today's readings?

Lord, what else have you said to me through thoughts, circumstances, conversations, emotions, or the work of the enemy?

Lord, what do you want me to do today?

At home: At work: In ministry:

"Or what king, as he goes to encounter another king in war, will not sit down first and consider whether he is able with ten thousand to meet him who comes against him with twenty thousand? Or else, while the other is yet a great way off, he sends an envoy, and asks for conditions of peace. So therefore whoever of you who doesn't renounce all that he has, he can't be my disciple." (Luke 14:31-33)

Discipleship is costly – receiving the fullness of life promised to a disciple costs everything you have! If you choose to be a disciple of Jesus Christ, there must be a one-time decision to surrender everything to God. Surrender everything??? Yes, but before you literally give away all you have, begin with this approach: Imagine Jesus is physically present. He asks for your money and you give it all to him. He asks for your house, car, and all your other possessions including the clothes on your body, and you give them. He asks for your family members, and you give them. He asks for your time and you surrender it as well. He asks if you have anything left; you say only your life. He says "I will give you a new life and I am letting you have all these things you have just surrendered for now – just remember they are mine and I might ask you to surrender them forever, but you will know as you learn to live in me." He will make it clear when you are to give more as you grow.

In the scripture above, why do you think Jesus says one can't be his disciple unless he renounces all that he has rather than to say it would be difficult to be his disciple?

Have you come to the point of full surrender to God? If not, what prevents you? If so, have you taken anything back that you had previously surrendered (possessions, right to yourself, etc.)?

Lord, what are you teaching me through today's readings?

Lord, what else have you said to me through thoughts, circumstances, conversations, emotions, or the work of the enemy?

Lord, what do you want me to do today?

At home: At work: In ministry:

"Again, the Kingdom of Heaven is like a treasure hidden in the field, which a man found, and hid. In his joy, he goes and sells all that he has, and buys that field. Again, the Kingdom of Heaven is like a man who is a merchant seeking fine pearls, who having found one pearl of great price, he went and sold all that he had, and bought it." (Matt. 13:44-46)

"He who seeks his life will lose it; and he who loses his life for my sake will find it." (Matt. 10:39)

When we think of surrendering all that we have, we tend to think in terms of loss – what we no longer have. Yet today's readings imply that while we have given up our rights to ourselves, it is worth it. We gain much more than what we had, but we cannot receive it until we surrender all that we have. Having experienced it myself it seems like it is the best offer ever made to mankind, an offer only a fool would refuse. Yet many refuse.

What do you think prevents some Christians from surrendering all to God?

If you have "sold everything" for the kingdom, what is the most difficult part of the transaction and why?

If you have not "sold everything I have" for the kingdom, what prevents you?

Lord, what are you teaching me through today's readings?

Lord, what else have you said to me through thoughts, circumstances, conversations, emotions, or the work of the enemy?

Lord, what do you want me to do today?

At home: At work: In ministry:

"When you do merciful deeds" "When you pray" "If you forgive men their trespasses, your heavenly Father will also forgive you. But if you don't forgive men their trespasses, neither will your Father forgive your trespasses. Moreover when you fast." (Matt. 6:2, 5, 14-16)

Therefore I urge you, brothers, by the mercies of God, to present your bodies a living sacrifice, holy, acceptable to God, which is your spiritual service. Don't be conformed to this world, but be transformed by the renewing of your mind, so that you may prove what is the good, well-pleasing, and perfect will of God. (Rom. 12:1-2)

Surrender includes the practice of spiritual disciplines to remain surrendered. The book of Romans says we are to offer our bodies as living sacrifices; the problem with a living sacrifice is that it can crawl off the altar. The disciplines are designed to keep us on it.

Spiritual disciplines include prayer, solitude, fasting, giving, worship, confession, etc. While the surrender of everything to God is in one sense once for all, in another sense we must die daily. A life of complete surrender seems impossible to live and is without grace. It is not you, but Christ working in you who enables you to do all he commands. His grace is sufficient but it requires your cooperation and the disciplines enable his grace to be exhibited in our lives.

What spiritual disciplines do you find most meaningful? Which least?

Which spiritual disciplines do you feel God desiring you to practice more?

Lord, what are you teaching me through today's readings?

Lord, what else have you said to me through thoughts, circumstances, conversations, emotions, or the work of the enemy?

Lord, what do you want me to do today?

At home: At work: In ministry:

While he was at Bethany, in the house of Simon the leper, as he sat at the table, a woman came having an alabaster jar of ointment of pure nard—very costly. She broke the jar, and poured it over his head. But there were some who were indignant among themselves, saying, "Why has this ointment been wasted? For this might have been sold for more than three hundred denarii, and given to the poor." They grumbled against her. But Jesus said, *"Leave her alone. Why do you trouble her? She has done a good work for me. For you always have the poor with you, and whenever you want to, you can do them good; but you will not always have me. She has done what she could. She has anointed my body beforehand for the burying. Most certainly I tell you, wherever this Good News may be preached throughout the whole world, that which this woman has done will also be spoken of for a memorial of her."* (Mark 14:3-9)

Surrender includes the grace to let others love us, sometimes extravagantly like in the passage above. We know we are to love others. Many people like to be in control and be the ones loving others. It is often difficult to allow others to love us. We must allow them to do this so they will have the blessing of being able to love well.

How have you allowed others to love you at home, at work and in ministry?

How have you prevented others from loving you?

Lord, what are you teaching me through today's readings?

Lord, what else have you said to me through thoughts, circumstances, conversations, emotions, or the work of the enemy?

Lord, what do you want me to do today?

At home: At work: In ministry:

He began to teach them that the Son of Man must suffer many things, and be rejected by the elders, the chief priests, and the scribes, and be killed, and after three days rise again. He spoke to them openly. Peter took him, and began to rebuke him. But he, turning around, and seeing his disciples, rebuked Peter, and said, *"Get behind me, Satan! For you have in mind not the things of God, but the things of men."* (Mark 8:31-33)

Surrender includes acceptance of or surrender to divine providence. This is easy when God's providence includes blessing or pleasant circumstances. It is more difficult when it involves an unpleasant truth such as the death of someone close to you or serious illness. In the passage above, Peter's rebuke of Jesus immediately followed his confession of him as Christ, so in essence he knew he was rebuking God. We do the same thing when we react similarly to something unpleasant in our lives that God reveals. We must surrender to the truth God reveals including the unpleasant things and ask "What are you saying to me through this?"

What circumstances has God allowed in your life that you must surrender to?

What is your understanding of why God has allowed these circumstances?

What do you think he might want you to do as a result of it or what personal revelation is he making to you through it?

Lord, what are you teaching me through today's readings?

Lord, what else have you said to me through thoughts, circumstances, conversations, emotions, or the work of the enemy?

Lord, what do you want me to do today?

At home: At work: In ministry:

SURRENDER- SUMMARY

Lord, what have you taught me this week about surrender?

What aspects of surrender do I need most help with?

What specifically will I do and when will it be done?

Lord, what else have you said to me through thoughts, circumstances, conversations, emotions, or the work of the enemy?

Lord, what do you want me to do today?

At home: At work: In ministry:

WEEKLY REVIEW

Time: Lord, did I spend adequate time truly listening to you each day?

Truth: Lord, what truths did you reveal to me this past week?

Trust: Lord, did I trust that you were in control of all of the circumstances of my life this week, or did I worry, become anxious or reflect lack of trust in another way?

Surrender: Lord, did my thoughts and actions reflect that I have surrendered all to you? Did I practice spiritual disciplines daily? Did I ask your forgiveness and forgive others?

Obey: Lord, was I obedient in the attitudes of my mind (humility and servanthood rather than pride, etc.)? Did I do the things I sensed you wanted me to do?

Abide: Lord, was I aware of your presence and of you speaking to me throughout the week?

Reconcile: Lord, did I disciple other Christians or share the gospel with non-believers as you provided opportunities?

"'You shall love the Lord your God with all your heart, with all your soul, and with all your mind.' This is the first and great commandment. A second likewise is this, 'You shall love your neighbor as yourself.' The whole law and the prophets depend on these two command-ments." (Matt 22:37-40)

Jesus answered him, *"If a man loves me, he will keep my word. My Father will love him, and we will come to him, and make our home with him."* (John 14:23)

These verses sum up Jesus' teaching on obedience and life. Regardless of what specific action you believe Jesus to be calling you to, it must pass the tests of love of God and man.

How have you shown the love of God and man in your life during this past week at home?

b) At work?

c) In your ministry?

Lord, what are you teaching me through today's readings?

Lord, what else have you said to me through thoughts, circumstances, conversations, emotions, or the work of the enemy?

Lord, what do you want me to do today?

At home: At work: In ministry:

The scribes and the Pharisees brought a woman taken in adultery. Having set her in the midst, they told him, "Teacher, we found this woman in adultery, in the very act. Now in our law, Moses commanded us to stone such. What then do you say about her?" They said this testing him, that they might have something to accuse him of. But Jesus stooped down, and wrote on the ground with his finger. But when they continued asking him, he looked up and said to them, *"He who is without sin among you, let him throw the first stone at her."* Again he stooped down, and with his finger wrote on the ground. They, when they heard it, being convicted by their conscience, went out one by one, beginning from the oldest, even to the last. Jesus was left alone with the woman where she was, in the middle. Jesus, standing up, saw her and said, *"Woman, where are your accusers? Did no one condemn you?"* She said, "No one, Lord." Jesus said, *"Neither do I condemn you. Go your way. From now on, sin no more."* (John 8:3-11)

Obedience means avoiding behavior our conscience tells us is wrong (sin), even if it is something not wrong for others. As you listen to Jesus, your conscience will become more informed as he reveals more truth. Continue to be guided by the truth he reveals to you. Sin is the result of a life not fully surrendered or an occasional lapse in surrender.

What specific sin issue(s) do you feel the Lord wants you to address now?

Lord, what are you teaching me through today's readings?

Lord, what else have you said to me through thoughts, circumstances, conversations, emotions, or the work of the enemy?

Lord, what do you want me to do today?

At home: At work: In ministry:

"But I tell you, don't resist him who is evil; but whoever strikes you on your right cheek, turn to him the other also." (Matt. 5:39)

But it shall not be so among you, but whoever wants to become great among you shall be your servant. Whoever of you wants to become first among you, shall be bondservant of all. For the Son of Man also came not to be served, but to serve, and to give his life as a ransom for many." (Mark 10:43-44)

Obedience means not only doing the things (actions) that the Lord commands. Much of what the Lord commands is an attitude more than an action. For example, consider his teaching *"whoever strikes you on your right cheek, turn to him the other also."* Initially it seems to be an action (turn the cheek), but further reflection suggests it will more often be expressed as an attitude. (Being struck on the right cheek meant being hit by the person's left hand, which was degrading in Jesus' culture.) You may actually be struck on the cheek and have opportunity to turn the other, but more often you will be slighted (metaphorically struck on the cheek) and your attitude is the key to a proper response (by forgiving whether it is asked for or not). Sometimes the attitude he commands is stated more directly like in the second passage.

What ungodly attitude(s) are you most aware of in your life?

What do you think is the root cause of this attitude?

Lord, what are you teaching me through today's readings?

Lord, what else have you said to me through thoughts, circumstances, conversations, emotions, or the work of the enemy?

Lord, what do you want me to do today?

At home: At work: In ministry:

"Even so, let your light shine before men; that they may see your good works, and glorify your Father who is in heaven." (Matt. 5:16)

"Be careful that you don't do your charitable giving before men, to be seen by them, or else you have no reward from your Father who is in heaven." (Matt. 6:1)

Jesus teaches little in the way of direct commands except the Great Commission (Matt. 28:18-20). Instead he teaches truths we can apply to every aspect of our lives. The specific application of the general principle depends upon what the Holy Spirit reveals as we abide in him. For example, the passages above, both from the Sermon on the Mount seem to contradict each other. Are we to do our good deeds before men or not? Obviously in the second passage he is addressing wrong attitudes; the question is not whether to do our good deeds before men, but why are we doing what we are doing. Are we doing our good works out of obedience to God or so others will see what we are doing and will praise us? We must determine what he wants us to do and then obey out of loving obedience to Jesus whether we will be seen or not.

As you think of the ungodly attitude(s) you identified yesterday, do you sense any conviction from the Holy Spirit about your motives? If so, what is behind your motives?

Lord, what are you teaching me through today's readings?

Lord, what else have you said to me through thoughts, circumstances, conversations, emotions, or the work of the enemy?

Lord, what do you want me to do today?

At home: At work: In ministry:

"But what do you think? A man had two sons, and he came to the first, and said, 'Son, go work today in my vineyard.' He answered, 'I will not,' but afterward he changed his mind, and went. He came to the second, and said the same thing. He answered, 'I go, sir,' but he didn't go. Which of the two did the will of his father?" **They said to him, "The first."** (Matt. 21:28-31)

Once we know what the Lord wants us to do we should do it immediately. If we delay it may seem God has become silent because we may need to complete what we already know before He can tell us what we should do next.

What should you have already done at home?

b) At work?

c) In your ministry?

Lord, what are you teaching me through today's readings?

Lord, what else have you said to me through thoughts, circumstances, conversations, emotions, or the work of the enemy?

Lord, what do you want me to do today?

At home: At work: In ministry:

"Now after a long time the lord of those servants came, and reconciled accounts with them. He who received the five talents came and brought another five talents, saying, 'Lord, you delivered to me five talents. Behold, I have gained another five talents besides them.' His lord said to him, 'Well done, good and faithful servant. You have been faithful over a few things, I will set you over many things. Enter into the joy of your lord.'" (Matthew 25:19-21)

We must learn to be faithful to the Lord's call on our lives through consistent obedience. The specific acts of obedience required of us come through our daily lives. As we learn to hear him speak to us and learn to obey all that he commands, we will begin to see our lives much differently. We will begin to see opportunities for obedience to him in our homes, in our place of work, as well as in our place of ministry. In fact, we should see that wherever we are is our place of ministry and whatever we are doing is our work of ministry. Our only true job description or life purpose should be "disciple of Jesus Christ". There is no time when that is not true.

Have you begun to see that you are called to ministry as a disciple at all times and places?

When is it most apparent?

When least?

Lord, what are you teaching me through today's readings?

Lord, what else have you said to me through thoughts, circumstances, conversations, emotions, or the work of the enemy?

Lord, what do you want me to do today?

At home: At work: In ministry:

OBEY – SUMMARY

Lord, what have you taught me this week about obedience?

What aspects of obedience do I need most help with?

What specifically will I do and when will it be done?

Lord, what else have you said to me through thoughts, circumstances, conversations, emotions, or the work of the enemy?

Lord, what do you want me to do today?

At home: At work: In ministry:

WEEKLY REVIEW

Time: Lord, did I spend adequate time truly listening to you each day?

Truth: Lord, what truths did you reveal to me this past week?

Trust: Lord, did I trust that you were in control of all of the circumstances of my life this week, or did I worry, become anxious or reflect lack of trust in another way?

Surrender: Lord, did my thoughts and actions reflect that I have surrendered all to you? Did I practice spiritual disciplines daily? Did I ask your forgiveness and forgive others?

Obey: Lord, was I obedient in the attitudes of my mind (humility and servanthood rather than pride, etc.)? Did I do the things I sensed you wanted me to do?

Abide: Lord, was I aware of your presence and of you speaking to me throughout the week?

Reconcile: Lord, did I disciple other Christians or share the gospel with non-believers as you provided opportunities?

"Behold, I am with you always, even to the end of the age." (Matt. 28:20)

"In that day you will know that I am in my Father, and you in me, and I in you." (John 14:20)

"Remain (abide) in me, and I in you. As the branch can't bear fruit by itself, unless it remains (abides) in the vine, so neither can you, unless you remain (abide) in me." (John 15:4)

God is present in every believer through the Holy Spirit but since we cannot see him we often forget this vital truth. Once his abiding presence is real to us and regularly experienced through the eyes of faith, it is a great help in dealing with life's problems including sin. Just as we are more conscious of behavior when with fellow Christians, how much more so when aware of the Lord's presence!

Each of the elements is essential to discipleship, but abiding is the most important one in experiencing fullness of life because it involves being personally aware of Christ in your life and being united with him in thought, will and purpose. Abiding is not something that just happens; in the last reading above it is commanded. It can only happen if we trust enough to be surrendered and obedient.

How often do you experience Christ's presence and what usually prompts your awareness?

How can you better "remain in him" in the midst of your day?

Lord, what are you teaching me through today's readings?

Lord, what else have you said to me through thoughts, circumstances, conversations, emotions, or the work of the enemy?

Lord, what do you want me to do today?

At home: At work: In ministry:

"Father, I thank you that you listened to me. I know that you always listen to me, but because of the multitude that stands around I said this, that they may believe that you sent me." (John 11:41-42)

We encourage the discipline of listening to Jesus speak through your life every day to become more aware of his presence. One reason to read his words in the gospels is to get used to hearing his voice to assist with discernment. Since God is always with us, we can speak to him at any time. We should also expect God to speak to us; after all what kind of a relationship do we have if he does not speak? He will provide the wisdom we need if we listen to him. He will provide companionship as we live in his presence.

We must learn how he speaks to us and what he is saying. Look for recurring patterns or confirmation by subsequent events and scripture for what he seems to be saying to you. Regularly read the gospels and other scripture to see if what he seems to be saying is consistent with what he has revealed about himself. Discuss it with other believers; especially mature believers.

What recurring truth or message have you received recently and how have you received it?

Lord, what are you teaching me through today's readings?

Lord, what else have you said to me through thoughts, circumstances, conversations, emotions, or the work of the enemy?

Lord, what do you want me to do today?

At home: At work: In ministry:

"Whenever he brings out his own sheep, he goes before them, and the sheep follow him, for they know his voice. They will by no means follow a stranger, but will flee from him; for they don't know the voice of strangers." (John 10:4-5)

Then the devil took him into the holy city. He set him on the pinnacle of the temple, and said to him, "If you are the Son of God, throw yourself down, for it is written, 'He will put his angels in charge of you.' and, 'On their hands they will bear you up, so that you don't dash your foot against a stone.'" (Matt. 4:5-6)

We are individuals so God may speak to us in ways only we will understand. We must be careful to discern His voice. Whatever you understand God to say must be consistent with scripture, but keep in mind Satan quoted scripture when tempting Jesus, so scripture alone is not enough. We may have difficulty discerning whether a thought came from God, the enemy, or our imagination. Ask the Lord to clarify, especially if what he seems to be saying is unusual or different from how he normally speaks to us. As a general rule, what he says will come with peace, not urgency or condemnation. If we are uncertain, God will confirm his word to us.

Think of a time when you thought God might be speaking to you, but you were uncertain it was really God speaking. What do you think he might have been saying?

What caused you to be uncertain whether it was God?

What is the most unusual way God seems to have spoken to you?

Lord, what are you teaching me through today's readings?

Lord, what else have you said to me through thoughts, circumstances, conversations, emotions, or the work of the enemy?

Lord, what do you want me to do today?

At home: At work: In ministry:

He said to the multitudes also, *"When you see a cloud rising from the west, immediately you say, 'A shower is coming,' and so it happens. When a south wind blows, you say, 'There will be a scorching heat,' and it happens. You hypocrites! You know how to interpret the appearance of the earth and the sky, but how is it that you don't interpret this time?"* (Luke 12:54-56)

My experience is that God speaks mainly through scripture, thoughts, emotions, other people, and circumstances. Scripture reveals that he also speaks through angels, dreams, and even animals at times. A complete list cannot be made because God can speak in an infinite number of ways. Regardless of how we think he is speaking, we should try to discern it is him – the more unusual the "message", the more critical the discernment! Having fellow believers to discuss what we think God is saying to us aids in discernment and can keep us from error.

How does God most often speak to you?

How regularly have you "heard" God this past week outside of the Bible – several times each day, daily, occasionally or not at all? If you have heard him, what did he say?

Lord, what are you teaching me through today's readings?

Lord, what else have you said to me through thoughts, circumstances, conversations, emotions, or the work of the enemy?

Lord, what do you want me to do today?

At home:　　　　　　　　　At work:　　　　　　　　　In ministry:

Then six days before the Passover, Jesus came to Bethany, where Lazarus was, who had been dead, whom he raised from the dead. So they made him a supper there. Martha served, but Lazarus was one of those who sat at the table with him. Mary, therefore, took a pound of ointment of pure nard, very precious, and anointed the feet of Jesus, and wiped his feet with her hair. The house was filled with the fragrance of the ointment. Then Judas Iscariot, Simon's son, one of his disciples, who would betray him, said, "Why wasn't this ointment sold for three hundred denarii, and given to the poor?" (John 12:1-5)

There is a time to work and a time to rest. When we abide in Christ we know when it is time for each. In the scripture above, Jesus spent an evening as the honored guest of close friends and expensive perfume was poured on him. As Judas suggested, this indeed could have been sold and given to the poor. Whenever we spend money or time, it could always have been used for something different. We should carefully consider how we use our resources. They should always be used in service to God, but sometimes that service is for our needs.

Are you able to spend time and money on yourself and be at peace?

Describe a time when you spent too much time and money on yourself and how you felt?

What causes you to feel that too much time and money was spent in the previous question?

Lord, what are you teaching me through today's readings?

Lord, what else have you said to me through thoughts, circumstances, conversations, emotions, or the work of the enemy?

Lord, what do you want me to do today?

At home:　　　　　　　　　At work:　　　　　　　　　In ministry:

"I am the vine. You are the branches. He who remains in me, and I in him, the same bears much fruit, for apart from me you can do nothing. If a man doesn't remain in me, he is thrown out as a branch, and is withered; and they gather them, throw them into the fire, and they are burned. If you remain in me, and my words remain in you, you will ask whatever you desire, and it will be done for you. In this is my Father glorified, that you bear much fruit; and so you will be my disciples. Even as the Father has loved me, I also have loved you. Remain in my love. If you keep my commandments, you will remain in my love; even as I have kept my Father's commandments, and remain in his love. I have spoken these things to you, that my joy may remain in you, and that your joy may be made full. This is my commandment, that you love one another, even as I have loved you." (John 15:5-12)

Abiding is the most important element to experiencing fullness of life in Christ. As you begin to live in him, hear his voice and obey what you hear you will experience a profound difference in your life. The final element of discipleship, reconcile, will become second nature, as you want others to experience this fullness of life as well.

What evidence can you provide which suggests you are abiding?

What evidence can you provide which suggests you are not abiding?

What steps can you take to reduce the times you are not abiding?

Lord, what are you teaching me through today's readings?

Lord, what else have you said to me through thoughts, circumstances, conversations, emotions, or the work of the enemy?

Lord, what do you want me to do today?

At home: At work: In ministry:

ABIDE – SUMMARY   **TODAY'S DATE:** _____

Lord, what have you taught me this week about abiding?

What circumstances give me the greatest difficulty in abiding?

What specifically will I do and when will it be done?

Lord, what else have you said to me through thoughts, circumstances, conversations, emotions, or the work of the enemy?

Lord, what do you want me to do today?

At home: At work: In ministry:

WEEKLY REVIEW

Time: Lord, did I spend adequate time truly listening to you each day?

Truth: Lord, what truths did you reveal to me this past week?

Trust: Lord, did I trust that you were in control of all of the circumstances of my life this week, or did I worry, become anxious or reflect lack of trust in another way?

Surrender: Lord, did my thoughts and actions reflect that I have surrendered all to you? Did I practice spiritual disciplines daily? Did I ask your forgiveness and forgive others?

Obey: Lord, was I obedient in the attitudes of my mind (humility and servanthood rather than pride, etc.)? Did I do the things I sensed you wanted me to do?

Abide: Lord, was I aware of your presence and of you speaking to me throughout the week?

Reconcile: Lord, did I disciple other Christians or share the gospel with non-believers as you provided opportunities?

"All authority has been given to me in heaven and on earth. Go, and make disciples of all nations, baptizing them in the name of the Father and of the Son and of the Holy Spirit, teaching them to observe all things that I commanded you. Behold, I am with you always, even to the end of the age." (Matthew 28:18-20)

The verses above summarize the process for a disciple of Jesus Christ. It begins with repentance, the change of direction in one's life, moving toward God instead of away from him and is evidenced by baptism. It continues with discipleship, learning *'to observe all things that I commanded you'* which keeps that change of direction God-ward and the disciple growing more like Christ.

What can you do to increase your:

    a)   Knowledge of everything Jesus commanded?

    b)   Obedience of everything Jesus commanded?

Lord, what are you teaching me through today's readings?

Lord, what else have you said to me through thoughts, circumstances, conversations, emotions, or the work of the enemy?

Lord, what do you want me to do today?

At home: At work: In ministry:

"Not for these only do I pray, but for those also who believe in me through their word, that they may all be one; even as you, Father, are in me, and I in you, that they also may be one in us; that the world may believe that you sent me. The glory which you have given me, I have given to them; that they may be one, even as we are one; I in them, and you in me, that they may be perfected into one; that the world may know that you sent me, and loved them, even as you loved me. Father, I desire that they also whom you have given me be with me where I am, that they may see my glory, which you have given me, for you loved me before the foundation of the world. Righteous Father, the world hasn't known you, but I knew you; and these knew that you sent me. I made known to them your name, and will make it known; that the love with which you loved me may be in them, and I in them." (John 17:20-26) (Read OC May 22)

Reconcile was chosen because it implies the end result of bringing God and man together as originally intended, not just saving their souls for heaven, but experiencing eternal life with God now in the present moment. In chapter XV of The Screwtape Letters C. S. Lewis writes, "The present is the point at which time touches eternity…in it alone freedom and actuality are offered." The more you learn to live in the present with God, the more he is able to do in and through you. As the passage above implies, it is not just me and the Lord being one, but we are to be one with all those who have a personal relationship with Jesus Christ.

How often do you live in the present moment? What is your greatest challenge to being "in the moment?"

What are you doing to help those who know Christ (the church) to become one?

What are you doing that is bringing division among those who know Christ (the church)?

Lord, what are you teaching me through today's readings?

Lord, what else have you said to me through thoughts, circumstances, conversations, emotions, or the work of the enemy?

Lord, what do you want me to do today?

At home: At work: In ministry:

Now Simon Peter was standing and warming himself. They said therefore to him, "You aren't also one of his disciples, are you?" He denied it, and said, "I am not." One of the servants of the high priest, being a relative of him whose ear Peter had cut off, said, "Didn't I see you in the garden with him?" Peter therefore denied it again, and immediately the rooster crowed. (John 18:25-27)

So when they had eaten their breakfast, Jesus said to Simon Peter, *"Simon, son of Jonah, do you love me more than these?"* He said to him, "Yes, Lord; you know that I have affection for you." He said to him, *"Feed my lambs."* He said to him again a second time, *"Simon, son of Jonah, do you love me?"* He said to him, "Yes, Lord; you know that I have affection for you." He said to him, *"Tend my sheep."* He said to him the third time, *"Simon, son of Jonah, do you have affection for me?"* Peter was grieved because he asked him the third time, "Do you have affection for me?" He said to him, "Lord, you know everything. You know that I have affection for you." Jesus said to him, *"Feed my sheep."* (21:15-17)

Reconciliation to God is a one-time experience; you are reconciled to God when you first come to him in repentance. There is also an ongoing process similar to reconciliation called sanctification. Repentance turns you God-ward as you are reconciled to him. Sanctification is the ongoing process that conforms you to the image of Christ. Trials and other circumstances will reveal truth about yourself and areas of your life the Lord wants to deal with to make you more like him. Your God-like image has been marred by your sins and sins committed against you. You are forgiven for past sins after confession, but the Lord wants to work in your life to help you overcome the root cause and the damage it has upon you and others. As this happens, you will be able to experience the Lord more fully and increasingly experience fullness of life.

What trial or circumstance from your past has been significant in drawing you closer to God?

Think of a trial or circumstance from this past week; how did God use it in your life?

Lord, what are you teaching me through today's readings?

Lord, what else have you said to me through thoughts, circumstances, conversations, emotions, or the work of the enemy?

Lord, what do you want me to do today?

At home: At work: In ministry:

Walking by the sea of Galilee, he saw two brothers: Simon, who is called Peter, and Andrew, his brother, casting a net into the sea; for they were fishermen. He said to them, *"Come after me, and I will make you fishers for men."* **They immediately left their nets and followed him.** (Matt. 4:18-20)

Once you understand discipleship, it is apparent that a disciple is also a discipler. Having learned to obey all that Jesus commanded, there is a responsibility to make disciples. You could start discipling those who are already believers, but not yet disciples. You could disciple some who are not yet believers and bring them to the point where they are ready to make disciples. Anytime you bring someone closer to the Lord, you are involved in the process of reconciliation. It includes both evangelism and discipleship.

What concerns do you have about discipling others?

What steps can you take to overcome these concerns?

Lord, what are you teaching me through today's readings?

Lord, what else have you said to me through thoughts, circumstances, conversations, emotions, or the work of the enemy?

Lord, what do you want me to do today?

At home: At work: In ministry:

Jesus sent these twelve out, and commanded them, saying, *"Don't go among the Gentiles, and don't enter into any city of the Samaritans. Rather, go to the lost sheep of the house of Israel."* (Matt. 10:5-6)

But the man from whom the demons had gone out begged him that he might go with him, but Jesus sent him away, saying, *"Return to your house, and declare what great things God has done for you."* **He went his way, proclaiming throughout the whole city what great things Jesus had done for him.** (Luke 8:38-39)

We are called by the Lord to go where he commands. Assume he wants you to make disciples right where you are now unless he makes it clear to go elsewhere. You must listen to him on a regular basis (time) to clearly know what he wants you to do.

Try to maintain contact with those you disciple if possible, especially those who go on to disciple others. Your main task in discipling another is completed when the disciple has learned to abide in Christ; from that point on you can simply tell them to listen to Jesus and do whatever he tells them. Jesus asks us to lead people to him, to teach them to obey all that he commanded, but within that process he takes over their discipleship. This program covers everything Jesus taught us to obey; it serves as a starting point for discipleship and true life.

How do you rate your ability to listen to Jesus? What can you do to improve it?

Who is in your life now that he wants you to disciple?

Lord, what are you teaching me through today's readings?

Lord, what else have you said to me through thoughts, circumstances, conversations, emotions, or the work of the enemy?

Lord, what do you want me to do today?

At home: At work: In ministry:

"All authority has been given to me in heaven and on earth. Go, and make disciples of all nations, baptizing them in the name of the Father and of the Son and of the Holy Spirit, teaching them to observe all things that I commanded you. Behold, I am with you always, even to the end of the age." (Matthew 28:18-20)

We began the week with this verse and end with it as well. It is the most understandable command Jesus gave us: go and make disciples and teach them to obey everything he has commanded us.

What is your reaction to the Great Commission, to the Lord's call for you to go make disciples?

If you have been making disciples, what has it entailed?

Lord, what are you teaching me through today's readings?

Lord, what else have you said to me through thoughts, circumstances, conversations, emotions, or the work of the enemy?

Lord, what do you want me to do today?

At home: At work: In ministry:

Lord, what have you taught me this week about reconciliation?

What aspect of reconciliation do I need most help with?

What specifically will I do and when will it be done?

Lord, what else have you said to me through thoughts, circumstances, conversations, emotions, or the work of the enemy?

Lord, what do you want me to do today?

At home: At work: In ministry:

WEEKLY REVIEW

Time: Lord, did I spend adequate time truly listening to you each day?

Truth: Lord, what truths did you reveal to me this past week?

Trust: Lord, did I trust that you were in control of all of the circumstances of my life this week, or did I worry, become anxious or reflect lack of trust in another way?

Surrender: Lord, did my thoughts and actions reflect that I have surrendered all to you? Did I practice spiritual disciplines daily? Did I ask your forgiveness and forgive others?

Obey: Lord, was I obedient in the attitudes of my mind (humility and servanthood rather than pride, etc.)? Did I do the things I sensed you wanted me to do?

Abide: Lord, was I aware of your presence and of you speaking to me throughout the week?

Reconcile: Lord, did I disciple other Christians or share the gospel with non-believers as you provided opportunities?

Now David was the son of that Ephrathite of Bethlehem Judah, whose name was Jesse; and he had eight sons: and the man was very old in the days of Saul. The three eldest sons of Jesse had gone after Saul to the battle: and the names of his three sons who went to the battle were Eliab the firstborn, and next to him Abinadab, and the third Shammah. David was the youngest; and the three eldest followed Saul. Now David went back and forth from Saul to feed his father's sheep at Bethlehem. (I Sam 17:12-15)

God reveals his **character** that he wants us to imitate. God also reveals our **calling**, the things he wants us to do vocationally and in every other aspect of our life. Our calling is determined somewhat by the roles we occupy. We should strive to be competent in each role.

David's initial calling consisted of three things: Jesse's son, an Israelite, and a shepherd. As a son he learned obedience to his parents. As an Israelite he learned obedience to a loving and powerful God. We know from the Psalms David wrote later that he meditated about and prayed to God while shepherding (e.g., Psalm 23). He saw how God's care for Israel and for him was like his care for his sheep. As a shepherd he learned diligence in caring for his flock. He practiced long hours with his sling while tending the sheep to develop his competence as a shepherd, becoming so skilled he was not afraid to risk his life in protecting his flock from lions and bears. By Chapter 17 of I Samuel he had developed a God-like character and competence in his areas of calling.

What are your current callings (roles)?

What are you doing to exhibit diligence and develop competence in each role?

Lord, what are you teaching me through today's readings?

Lord, what else have you said to me through thoughts, circumstances, conversations, emotions, or the work of the enemy?

Lord, what do you want me to do today?

At home: At work: In ministry:

Jesse said to David his son, "Now take for your brothers an ephah of this parched grain, and these ten loaves, and carry them quickly to the camp to your brothers; and bring these ten cheeses to the captain of their thousand, and see how your brothers are doing, and bring back news." Now Saul, and they, and all the men of Israel, were in the valley of Elah, fighting with the Philistines. (I Sam 17:17-19)

Yesterday we learned that David had been to the battle lines on previous occasions (v.15), but was likely unaware of most of what is detailed about Goliath in the first 11 verses of I Samuel. In previous trips between the battle lines and his sheep David probably thought a lot about the battle, sure that God's army would be victorious. In verses 17-19 we find that David was at the battle lines earlier than usual that day in obedience to his father Jesse's request to hurry.

What circumstances do you find yourself in now as a result of obedience to your calling or roles?

Is there some issue that seems to continue unresolved in your life now? If so, what do you think God might want you to do or learn from it?

Lord, what are you teaching me through today's readings?

Lord, what else have you said to me through thoughts, circumstances, conversations, emotions, or the work of the enemy?

Lord, what do you want me to do today?

At home: At work: In ministry:

David rose up early in the morning, and left the sheep with a keeper, and took, and went, as Jesse had commanded him; and he came to the place of the wagons, as the army which was going forth to the fight shouted for the battle. Israel and the Philistines put the battle in array, army against army. David left his baggage in the hand of the keeper of the baggage, and ran to the army, and came and greeted his brothers. As he talked with them, behold, there came up the champion, the Philistine of Gath, Goliath by name, out of the ranks of the Philistines, and spoke according to the same words: and David heard them. All the men of Israel, when they saw the man, fled from him, and were terrified. (I Sam 17:20-24)

It is significant that David arrived at the time the battle lines were forming and heard the war cry from the Israelites. This may have been the first time he heard the war cry; since he left early that morning he probably arrived earlier than on previous trips. Hearing the war cry likely stirred his emotions much the same way that we are stirred when we hear the crowd cheer our favorite sports team. Imagine David's dismay when the Israelites ran in great fear from Goliath. In his mind any one of the Israelites could defeat Goliath because they had God on their side, however most of the men did not have David's character or trust in God.

Think back to key turning points in your life. What set of circumstances brought them about? Did they seem significant at the time?

Have you learned to connect God's providence with your daily circumstances? If so, what impact has it had?

Lord, what are you teaching me through today's readings?

Lord, what else have you said to me through thoughts, circumstances, conversations, emotions, or the work of the enemy?

Lord, what do you want me to do today?

At home: At work: In ministry:

The men of Israel said, "Have you seen this man who has come up? He has surely come up to defy Israel. It shall be, that the man who kills him, the king will enrich him with great riches, and will give him his daughter, and make his father's house free in Israel." David spoke to the men who stood by him, saying, "What shall be done to the man who kills this Philistine, and takes away the reproach from Israel? For who is this uncircumcised Philistine, that he should defy the armies of the living God?" The people answered him in this way, saying, "So shall it be done to the man who kills him." Eliab his eldest brother heard when he spoke to the men; and Eliab's anger was kindled against David, and he said, "Why have you come down? With whom have you left those few sheep in the wilderness? I know your pride, and the naughtiness of your heart; for you have come down that you might see the battle." David said, "What have I now done? Can't I even ask?" He turned away from him toward another, and spoke like that again; and the people answered him again the same way. When the words were heard which David spoke, they were repeated to Saul; and Saul sent for him. (I Sam 17:25-31)

David heard rumors of what King Saul would give to the man who defeated Goliath. He began asking around the camp to confirm the rumor. When his oldest brother Eliab asked him "Why have you come down?" perhaps David began to wonder, "Why am I here; what purpose does God have for me here?" His asking about the rewards for defeating Goliath was reported to Saul. At first glance this seems strange; all he did was ask what the rewards were — no evidence suggests he said he would be willing to face Goliath before he spoke to Saul. Apparently he was the only one expressing an interest in the reward; everyone else looked upon facing Goliath as the same as suicide. It is significant that David did not seek Saul; Saul sent for David. David let circumstances unfold until he knew what he was being called to.

Why do you think God has allowed your current circumstances?

What is he calling you to do in them?

Lord, what are you teaching me through today's readings?

Lord, what else have you said to me through thoughts, circumstances, conversations, emotions, or the work of the enemy?

Lord, what do you want me to do today?

At home: At work: In ministry:

David said to Saul, "Let no man's heart fail because of him. Your servant will go and fight with this Philistine." Saul said to David, "You are not able to go against this Philistine to fight with him; for you are but a youth, and he a man of war from his youth." David said to Saul, "Your servant was keeping his father's sheep; and when a lion or a bear came, and took a lamb out of the flock, I went out after him, and struck him, and rescued it out of his mouth. When he arose against me, I caught him by his beard, and struck him, and killed him. Your servant struck both the lion and the bear. This uncircumcised Philistine shall be as one of them, since he has defied the armies of the living God." David said, "Yahweh who delivered me out of the paw of the lion, and out of the paw of the bear, he will deliver me out of the hand of this Philistine." Saul said to David, "Go; and Yahweh shall be with you." (I Sam 17:32-37)

It is likely that only when David was being brought to Saul that he understood that God was confirming the reason he was there that day. Therefore he readily offered his services to Saul when he appeared before him. Saul's discouraging comments did not dissuade him because of his character and his certainty of God's calling.

As you think about your circumstances and what you know of God's general will through scripture, what do you think he is calling you to do?

Lord, what are you teaching me through today's readings?

Lord, what else have you said to me through thoughts, circumstances, conversations, emotions, or the work of the enemy?

Lord, what do you want me to do today?

At home: At work: In ministry:

Saul dressed David with his clothing. He put a helmet of brass on his head, and he clad him with a coat of mail. David strapped his sword on his clothing, and he tried to move; for he had not tested it. David said to Saul, "I can't go with these; for I have not tested them." David took them off. He took his staff in his hand, and chose for himself five smooth stones out of the brook, and put them in the shepherd's bag which he had, even in his wallet. His sling was in his hand; and he drew near to the Philistine. (I Sam 17:38-40)

David was aware of his area of competence in battle. He tried Saul's armor and weapons but had the wisdom to refuse them. Their use may have led to his defeat since he was unaccustomed to them. David later became proficient with the sword but could not have used it effectively when he faced Goliath. Instead he relied upon what God had prepared him with. As God reveals his calling to you, expect him to use your prior knowledge and experience to prepare you for the next step in your journey. He may call you to develop new knowledge and skill, but until it is developed rely upon what you already know.

What skills and competencies have you developed over your lifetime?

How are they being used in your current calling?

As you think about what God seems to be calling you to, can you see how what you already know might be useful?

Lord, what are you teaching me through today's readings?

Lord, what else have you said to me through thoughts, circumstances, conversations, emotions, or the work of the enemy?

Lord, what do you want me to do today?

At home: At work: In ministry:

HEARING GOD – SUMMARY   **TODAY'S DATE:** _____

Lord, what have you taught me this week about hearing you?

What do I need most help with?

What specifically will I do and when will it be done?

Lord, what else have you said to me through thoughts, circumstances, conversations, emotions, or the work of the enemy?

Lord, what do you want me to do today?

At home: At work: In ministry:

WEEKLY REVIEW

Time: Lord, did I spend adequate time truly listening to you each day?

Truth: Lord, what truths did you reveal to me this past week?

Trust: Lord, did I trust that you were in control of all of the circumstances of my life this week, or did I worry, become anxious or reflect lack of trust in another way?

Surrender: Lord, did my thoughts and actions reflect that I have surrendered all to you? Did I practice spiritual disciplines daily? Did I ask your forgiveness and forgive others?

Obey: Lord, was I obedient in the attitudes of my mind (humility and servanthood rather than pride, etc.)? Did I do the things I sensed you wanted me to do?

Abide: Lord, was I aware of your presence and of you speaking to me throughout the week?

Reconcile: Lord, did I disciple other Christians or share the gospel with non-believers as you provided opportunities?

John 8:31-32 *Jesus therefore said to those Jews who had believed him, "If you remain in my word, then you are truly my disciples. You will know the truth, and the truth will make you free."*

John 10:1-5 *"Most certainly, I tell you, one who doesn't enter by the door into the sheep fold, but climbs up some other way, the same is a thief and a robber. But one who enters in by the door is the shepherd of the sheep. The gatekeeper opens the gate for him, and the sheep listen to his voice. He calls his own sheep by name, and leads them out. Whenever he brings out his own sheep, he goes before them, and the sheep follow him, for they know his voice. They will by no means follow a stranger, but will flee from him; for they don't know the voice of strangers."*

To hear God you must become familiar with his voice by getting familiar with the teachings of scripture, beginning with Jesus' teaching but ultimately all of scripture. The devil can quote scripture **(Matt. 4:1-11)**, so we must draw close to God, knowing not only his word, but also his heart by spending time with him. As you spend time with Jesus learning to obey everything he commanded you will become increasingly familiar with his voice and the kinds of things he is likely to say. When you are unclear, ask someone in your group or a trusted pastor or elder. God also speaks through his church.

Do not become discouraged if you have difficulty discerning God's voice in your life. He has been speaking to you all of your life, but you have surely heard only a little of what he has said. Perhaps you have not even been aware God was speaking. Like learning a foreign language, understanding him will come gradually if you desire to learn and persist in your efforts.

Do you spend regular time each day with the Lord in expectation that he will speak to you?

Lord, what are you teaching me through today's readings?

Lord, what else have you said to me through thoughts, circumstances, conversations, emotions, or the work of the enemy?

Lord, what do you want me to do today?

At home: At work: In ministry:

John 14:8-14 *Philip said to him, "Lord, show us the Father, and that will be enough for us."*
Jesus said to him, "Have I been with you such a long time, and do you not know me, Philip?
He who has seen me has seen the Father. How do you say, 'Show us the Father?' Don't you
believe that I am in the Father, and the Father in me? The words that I tell you, I speak not
from myself; but the Father who lives in me does his works. Believe me that I am in the Father,
and the Father in me; or else believe me for the very works' sake." "Most certainly I tell you,
he who believes in me, the works that I do, he will do also; and he will do greater works than
these, because I am going to my Father. Whatever you will ask in my name, that will I do,
that the Father may be glorified in the Son. If you will ask anything in my name, I will do it."

The Lord knows where you are with him and where you should be. If you are a fairly new
disciple don't expect to be able to clearly hear and understand what God is saying at all times.
However, there is a point at which you should be able to hear him, to understand what he is
saying so you can begin to do what he is specifically calling you to do. This seems to be the
situation in the passage above where Jesus is instructing those who should have been better able
to understand what God was saying to them or calling them to. If you have been with him for
several years and are still unable to hear or understand, he will make the reason clear to you if
you take time to listen.

As you become increasingly aware of the Lord's presence and take time to listen to him as he
informs your mind, your life will change forever in ways you cannot now imagine. No matter
whether you have walked with the Lord for years or have just begun your journey, continue to
listen to him daily. He seeks to draw you into an increasingly intimate relationship with him.

If you are like Philip and have been with the Lord for a few years and are still unable to make
sense of what God is doing in your life, ask the Lord what changes you need to make.

Lord, what are you teaching me through today's readings?

Lord, what else have you said to me through thoughts, circumstances, conversations, emotions,
or the work of the enemy?

Lord, what do you want me to do today?

At home: At work: In ministry:

John 2:1-11 The third day, there was a marriage in Cana of Galilee. Jesus' mother was there. Jesus also was invited, with his disciples, to the marriage.

John 11:1-3 Now a certain man was sick, Lazarus from Bethany, of the village of Mary and her sister, Martha. It was that Mary who had anointed the Lord with ointment, and wiped his feet with her hair, whose brother, Lazarus, was sick. The sisters therefore sent to him, saying, "Lord, behold, he for whom you have great affection is sick."

God's will is sometimes mystical or otherworldly. More often it comes very naturally as a result of the family we are part of or the friends we have made. While the wedding at Cana was the scene of Jesus' first miracle, how he came to be there was a very normal thing – he was invited. Nothing suggests that he had any idea of anything special in his going. He went to be with Lazarus because his friend was ill. He was there for the same reason we are often at weddings or other special gatherings, simply an invitation or because a friend was is need.

Jesus found there were more reasons for him to be there than simply to witness a wedding or to comfort a friend. As we respond to the circumstances of our lives, we too should look for deeper reasons why the Father allowed them and what he is calling us to do. God has us where we are for a reason.

Think back on recent interactions with family and friends. What reasons can you see for God having you there?

What needs do your family or friends have that God is prompting you to meet?

Lord, what are you teaching me through today's readings?

Lord, what else have you said to me through thoughts, circumstances, conversations, emotions, or the work of the enemy?

Lord, what do you want me to do today?

At home: At work: In ministry:

Matt. 8:23-27 When he got into a boat, his disciples followed him. Behold, a violent storm came up on the sea, so much that the boat was covered with the waves, but he was asleep. They came to him, and woke him up, saying, "Save us, Lord! We are dying!" He said to them, *"Why are you fearful, O you of little faith?"* **Then he got up, rebuked the wind and the sea, and there was a great calm. The men marveled, saying, "What kind of man is this, that even the wind and the sea obey him?"**

Often God speaks through circumstances that are beyond our control. In some situations like the violent storm, we are tempted to fear. Perhaps our violent storms aren't acts of nature, but of a financial nature or family crisis. During these times we must recognize that Jesus is still "in the boat" with us so rather than responding in fear, we should turn to him in confidence that he is with us in each of our storms. Remember nothing happens apart from the will of the Father. The Father doesn't cause all things but allows them; sometimes things are caused by the work of the enemy.

God speaks through problems in our lives, when things don't go the way we expect. God knows all things, both in the spiritual and natural realms. We must learn to ask him questions in all aspects of our lives and listen for the answers he gives. Sometimes those answers come through thoughts, but often they will come through other people, other books, or seemingly random circumstances. Stay attuned to his Spirit to hear and understand.

What storm is God currently allowing in your life and do you sense his presence in it? What is he calling you to do in it?

Ask God about an issue of concern. Write down any thoughts that come to mind and pay particular attention to the events of the next few days and make notes of any relevant things in the 2nd to last question of each day.

Lord, what are you teaching me through today's readings?

Lord, what else have you said to me through thoughts, circumstances, conversations, emotions, or the work of the enemy?

Lord, what do you want me to do today?

At home: At work: In ministry:

John 4:1-6 Therefore when the Lord knew that the Pharisees had heard that Jesus was making and baptizing more disciples than John (although Jesus himself didn't baptize, but his disciples), he left Judea, and departed into Galilee. He needed to pass through Samaria. So he came to a city of Samaria, called Sychar, near the parcel of ground that Jacob gave to his son, Joseph. Jacob's well was there. Jesus therefore, being tired from his journey, sat down by the well. It was about the sixth hour.

John 7:1-13 After these things, Jesus was walking in Galilee, for he wouldn't walk in Judea, because the Jews sought to kill him. Luke 4:28-30 They were all filled with wrath in the synagogue, as they heard these things. They rose up, threw him out of the city, and led him to the brow of the hill that their city was built on, that they might throw him off the cliff. But he, passing through their midst, went his way.

Sometimes our actions are dictated by political or physical realities, like with Jesus in the passages above. God can use these realities to cause us to be in our circumstances as we respond to them. For example, Jesus meeting the woman at the well was a combination of being in the country because of political danger and resting at the well simply because he was tired. We must be aware of the practical realities and dangers of life and recognize that God also speaks through these. He can protect us when we are otherwise in danger as he did Jesus in the Luke passage, but we must first discern what God is calling us to out of our relationship with him rather than presume his will.

What current realities are impacting your actions?

What physical realities (tired, thirsty, hungry, etc.) did God use to determine your actions from yesterday? What stands out that might have been God speaking?

Lord, what are you teaching me through today's readings?

Lord, what else have you said to me through thoughts, circumstances, conversations, emotions, or the work of the enemy?

Lord, what do you want me to do today?

At home: At work: In ministry:

Mark 5:21-24 When Jesus had crossed back over in the boat to the other side, a great multitude was gathered to him; and he was by the sea. Behold, one of the rulers of the synagogue, Jairus by name, came; and seeing him, he fell at his feet, and begged him much, saying, "My little daughter is at the point of death. Please come and lay your hands on her, that she may be made healthy, and live." He went with him, and a great multitude followed him, and they pressed upon him on all sides.

Matt. 7:21-23 *"Not everyone who says to me, 'Lord, Lord,' will enter into the Kingdom of Heaven; but he who does the will of my Father who is in heaven. Many will tell me in that day, 'Lord, Lord, didn't we prophesy in your name, in your name cast out demons, and in your name do many mighty works?' Then I will tell them, 'I never knew you. Depart from me, you who work iniquity.'"*

You have a calling from God in each of the roles of life you currently occupy. As was the situation in the reading in Mark, your call from God will often come in the context of your vocational calling. Do not minimize the reality of God's calling from these roles; these are likely to be your primary ministry opportunities (the people you interact on a regular basis).

Your roles may seem insignificant to you, but Jesus teaches that only those faithful with little things can be trusted with much, so be faithful in what God has given you. Perhaps later he will expand it. Until then surrender your life to Jesus and begin learning from him, the only one who can reveal what will give fullness and meaning to your life. Guard against the presumption of those in the Matthew passage who took on their duties without having any real relationship with God; he is the one who calls. The decision of where we serve is not ours to make. Our responsibility is to obey when we are called.

What evidence do you see (if any) that God is leading you to a new calling or to a new expression in your current ones?

Lord, what are you teaching me through today's readings?

Lord, what else have you said to me through thoughts, circumstances, conversations, emotions, or the work of the enemy?

Lord, what do you want me to do today?

At home: At work: In ministry:

HEARING GOD II – SUMMARY   **TODAY'S DATE:** _____

Lord, what have you taught me this week about hearing you?

What do I need most help with?

What specifically will I do and when will it be done?

Lord, what else have you said to me through thoughts, circumstances, conversations, emotions, or the work of the enemy?

Lord, what do you want me to do today?

At home: At work: In ministry:

WEEKLY REVIEW

Time: Lord, did I spend adequate time truly listening to you each day?

Truth: Lord, what truths did you reveal to me this past week?

Trust: Lord, did I trust that you were in control of all of the circumstances of my life this week, or did I worry, become anxious or reflect lack of trust in another way?

Surrender: Lord, did my thoughts and actions reflect that I have surrendered all to you? Did I practice spiritual disciplines daily? Did I ask your forgiveness and forgive others?

Obey: Lord, was I obedient in the attitudes of my mind (humility and servanthood rather than pride, etc.)? Did I do the things I sensed you wanted me to do?

Abide: Lord, was I aware of your presence and of you speaking to me throughout the week?

Reconcile: Lord, did I disciple other Christians or share the gospel with non-believers as you provided opportunities?

When therefore it was evening, on that day, the first day of the week, and when the doors were locked where the disciples were assembled, for fear of the Jews, Jesus came and stood in the midst, and said to them, *"Peace be to you."* **When he had said this, he showed them his hands and his side. The disciples therefore were glad when they saw the Lord. Jesus therefore said to them again,** *"Peace be to you. As the Father has sent me, even so I send you."* **When he had said this, he breathed on them, and said to them,** *"Receive the Holy Spirit!"* (John 20:19-22)

Some of our time should be spent in the fellowship of other believers. After three years or so, plan to be part of two discipleship groups, one being your current group and the second being one you start to lead others into a deeper relationship with the Lord.

Who should you invite to be part of your initial group to help it grow? Perhaps others you are going through this workbook with or someone else you believe is ready for this step.

If you are not part of a group, when will you commit to become part of one?

Lord, what are you teaching me through today's readings?

Lord, what else have you said to me through thoughts, circumstances, conversations, emotions, or the work of the enemy?

Lord, what do you want me to do today?

At home: At work: In ministry:

"Go, and make disciples of all nations, baptizing them in the name of the Father and of the Son and of the Holy Spirit, teaching them to observe all things that I commanded you. Behold, I am with you always, even to the end of the age." (Matt 28:19-20)

Time together allows us to obey Jesus as we jointly learn, teach, admonish, encourage, rebuke and forgive one another. In this setting we are better able to express to each other how beloved we are by God as well as encourage one another to remain faithful in making disciples and growing spiritually.

What has been your experience with previous Christian groups that you have been a part of?

Did you find that a group setting helped you to grow spiritually? If so, how did it help?

Lord, what are you teaching me through today's readings?

Lord, what else have you said to me through thoughts, circumstances, conversations, emotions, or the work of the enemy?

Lord, what do you want me to do today?

At home: At work: In ministry:

When therefore it was evening, on that day, the first day of the week, and when the doors were locked where the disciples were assembled, for fear of the Jews, Jesus came and stood in the midst, and said to them, *"Peace be to you."* **When he had said this, he showed them his hands and his side. The disciples therefore were glad when they saw the Lord. Jesus therefore said to them again,** *"Peace be to you. As the Father has sent me, even so I send you."* **When he had said this, he breathed on them, and said to them,** *"Receive the Holy Spirit!"* (John 20:19-22)

We had these verses a couple of days ago, but let's look at them in a different light. Why were the disciples together? They feared the Jews. There is strength in numbers, especially as we face an uncertain future. Our future is always uncertain but we are more aware of it during trials. The fellowship of believers helps remind us of the truths of scripture when biblical characters faced similar trials. Often other believers will share personal trials that were similar when God showed Himself faithful. The testimony of other believers bolsters our trust in God.

What trial or circumstance from your past where God was faithful might you speak into the lives of others?

What trial or circumstance from this past week would it be helpful to hear from believers about to gain insight?

Lord, what are you teaching me through today's readings?

Lord, what else have you said to me through thoughts, circumstances, conversations, emotions, or the work of the enemy?

Lord, what do you want me to do today?

At home: At work: In ministry:

Then Peter came and said to him, "Lord, how often shall my brother sin against me, and I forgive him? Until seven times?" Jesus said to him, *"I don't tell you until seven times, but, until seventy times seven."* (Matt. 18:21-22)

Ideally believers would always love one another well, but the reality is they don't. Something is said or done which offends, often unintentionally. Problems arise because of personality differences. The problem might be in ourselves from a character defect of which we may be unaware. In Matthew 7:3-5 Jesus said, *Why do you see the speck that is in your brother's eye, but don't consider the beam that is in your own eye? Or how will you tell your brother, 'Let me remove the speck from your eye;' and behold, the beam is in your own eye? You hypocrite! First remove the beam out of your own eye, and then you can see clearly to remove the speck out of your brother's eye."* Regardless the cause, problems are bound to arise.

When you think of problems within the fellowship of believers, what specific conflict comes to mind? How was it resolved?

If you are not part of the conflict, but a witness to it, what should you do?

Lord, what are you teaching me through today's readings?

Lord, what else have you said to me through thoughts, circumstances, conversations, emotions, or the work of the enemy?

Lord, what do you want me to do today?

At home: At work: In ministry:

Jesus said to him, *"'You shall love the Lord your God with all your heart, with all your soul, and with all your mind.' This is the first and great commandment. A second likewise is this, 'You shall love your neighbor as yourself.' The whole law and the prophets depend on these two commandments."* (Matt. 22:37-39)

"This is my commandment, that you love one another, even as I have loved you. Greater love has no one than this, that someone lay down his life for his friends. You are my friends, if you do whatever I command you." (John 15:12-14)

Love is the greatest command and the heart of obedience. Everything we do should be out of love for God and man. As we become part of a group of believers our love for them will grow over time. Ideally it will grow to the level that Jesus refers to above, that we will lay our lives down for our brother. It is rare for someone to be called to lay their physical life down for another, but it has happened in church history. More likely our sacrifices will be of time, money or service. It also means that we have a group of believers who are willing to lay their lives down for us in our time of need.

Who is in your life now that would lay down their life for you?

Who is in your life now that you would lay down your life for?

Lord, what are you teaching me through today's readings?

Lord, what else have you said to me through thoughts, circumstances, conversations, emotions, or the work of the enemy?

Lord, what do you want me to do today?

At home: At work: In ministry:

"Not for these only do I pray, but for those also who believe in me through their word, that they may all be one; even as you, Father, are in me, and I in you, that they also may be one in us; that the world may believe that you sent me." (John 17:20-21)

Not only are we to become one with the Lord, we are also to become one with each other. This oneness of the church is to be a living testimony to the world. As we express the love of God to each other in true fellowship we are a witness more powerful than words.

Have you been part of a fellowship of believers that has exhibited this oneness?

Why do you think Jesus said that it was through oneness with God and each other that the world might believe?

Lord, what are you teaching me through today's readings?

Lord, what else have you said to me through thoughts, circumstances, conversations, emotions, or the work of the enemy?

Lord, what do you want me to do today?

At home: At work: In ministry:

GROUPS – SUMMARY

Lord, what have you taught me this week about groups?

What aspect of groups do I need most help with?

What specifically will I do and when will it be done?

Lord, what else have you said to me through thoughts, circumstances, conversations, emotions, or the work of the enemy?

Lord, what do you want me to do today?

At home: At work: In ministry:

WEEKLY REVIEW

Time: Lord, did I spend adequate time truly listening to you each day?

Truth: Lord, what truths did you reveal to me this past week?

Trust: Lord, did I trust that you were in control of all of the circumstances of my life this week, or did I worry, become anxious or reflect lack of trust in another way?

Surrender: Lord, did my thoughts and actions reflect that I have surrendered all to you? Did I practice spiritual disciplines daily? Did I ask your forgiveness and forgive others?

Obey: Lord, was I obedient in the attitudes of my mind (humility and servanthood rather than pride, etc.)? Did I do the things I sensed you wanted me to do?

Abide: Lord, was I aware of your presence and of you speaking to me throughout the week?

Reconcile: Lord, did I disciple other Christians or share the gospel with non-believers as you provided opportunities?

He said to all, *"If anyone desires to come after me, let him deny himself, take up his cross, and follow me."* (Luke 9:23)

The greatest barrier to a deepening spiritual life is time committed to it. This program grew out of my calling to discipleship in the late 1990's. I was married, had four children at home or in college, had a full-time job in the investment business and was active in my local church, so demands on my time were somewhat similar to what others might experience. Don't let your 'busyness' keep you from this vital ministry. It will give you a greater sense of purpose in life and will allow you to build a legacy which will reach future generations long after you have gone to be with the Lord.

My call came about 20 years into my spiritual walk. I had spent those years acquiring spiritual wisdom from an increasing understanding of biblical revelation to understand what God is wanting to do in the world generally, as well as a growing relationship with God (time) to understand what He was wanting to do at this time and place in history and what I was being called to. This week's meditations tell the story of how this program developed.

Don't expect to discover your life mission the first time through this program, or even the 7th time through, although it may become somewhat clearer if you are diligent and take time each day to add to your knowledge and experience with God.

Are you willing to commit time with the Lord daily, letting Him speaking to you through scripture?

Are you willing to commit time with the Lord daily, letting Him speaking to you through the events of your daily life? When each day?

Lord, what are you teaching me?

Lord, what else have you said to me through thoughts, circumstances, conversations, emotions, or the work of the enemy?

Lord, what do you want me to do today?

At home: At work: In ministry:

Jesus came to them and spoke to them, saying, *"All authority has been given to me in heaven and on earth. Go, and make disciples of all nations, baptizing them in the name of the Father and of the Son and of the Holy Spirit, teaching them to observe all things that I commanded you. Behold, I am with you always, even to the end of the age."* (Matt. 28:18-20)

Why did God use a layman rather than a pastor to initiate this ministry? I asked the Lord, "Why me?" and seemed to get the answer, "Why not you?" Perhaps it was to confirm that the ministry of discipleship is for all Christians, not just clergy.

Preparation for this ministry was much like many other Christ followers' might be. I had various experiences in ministry including serving as deacon, elder, and teaching the Bible for several years. The call to discipleship came from a member of a men's ministry leadership team of which I was a part to "mentor other men", a call I had heard twice before, but which resonated this time. It soon became apparent that the call was to discipleship rather than mentoring.

Do you have a sense of what God is calling you to now?

If so, what is it and what reasons or evidence can you give for this calling?

Lord, what are you teaching me through today's readings?

Lord, what else have you said to me through thoughts, circumstances, conversations, emotions, or the work of the enemy?

Lord, what do you want me to do today?

At home: At work: In ministry:

It happened in these days, that he went out to the mountain to pray, and he continued all night in prayer to God. When it was day, he called his disciples, and from them he chose twelve, whom he also named apostles. (Luke 6:12-13)

The expansion of this program throughout East Africa is primarily due to two African pastors. One is Rev. Mbusa Thaluliba who I met as a result of supporting a student at a seminary in Nairobi. His studies began just as the Listening to Jesus program had been developed; he agreed to try using it in Africa while I began using it in the U.S. Two years later we met in Nairobi. During this visit I met Rev. Felicien Nemeyimana who later provided the inspiration to train pastors and church leaders in discipleship.

Do not try to go alone in the Christian life. You should try to surround yourself with friends who are like-minded disciples so you can grow in your trust in them and benefit from their wisdom as well as allow them to speak truth into your life as you do the same for them. Often it is from such a group that God's vision becomes clear. As we learned yesterday, the initial call from which this program developed came from a group involved in men's ministry.

Who should be part of your core group?

Lord, what are you teaching me through today's readings?

Lord, what else have you said to me through thoughts, circumstances, conversations, emotions, or the work of the enemy?

Lord, what do you want me to do today?

At home: At work: In ministry:

"Everyone therefore who hears these words of mine, and does them, I will liken him to a wise man, who built his house on a rock. The rain came down, the floods came, and the winds blew, and beat on that house; and it didn't fall, for it was founded on the rock. Everyone who hears these words of mine, and doesn't do them will be like a foolish man, who built his house on the sand. The rain came down, the floods came, and the winds blew, and beat on that house; and it fell—and great was its fall." (Matt. 7:24-27)

There were many years and people involved in the process of this program's development. While the program was close to its current form in 2001, the part you are currently reading was added in 2009 as the result of input from others. I have come to the conclusion that the program will never be completed. It will continue to be modified and improved as time is taken to understand more truth of ways it can more effectively communicate with others.

Daily surrender over a long period of time is required to hear Jesus' words and to put them into practice. We will never be perfect in this life, but we should continue to strive for perfection. If we build our house on the Rock of Jesus Christ, we will stand firm.

Are you making a deliberate effort to put Jesus' teaching into practice? If so, how?

Lord, what are you teaching me through today's readings?

Lord, what else have you said to me through thoughts, circumstances, conversations, emotions, or the work of the enemy?

Lord, what do you want me to do today?

At home: At work: In ministry:

"One who has my commandments, and keeps them, that person is one who loves me. One who loves me will be loved by my Father, and I will love him, and will reveal myself to him." (John 14:21)

There were times when I was uncertain of the next step or even that there was a next step in this program's development. As early as 2001 or 2002, I often had a sense that the program was about done when the Lord would reveal another step, sometimes a significant one like the addition of Oswald Chambers' devotional to the daily readings. The gospel was the only scripture used initially to literally obey Jesus command to "teach them to obey all that I have commanded," but eventually at the request of Mbusa and others, parts of the New Testament were added and eventually the Old Testament.

I do not claim that I heard the Lord audibly in this process, but eventually each next step was clear. Once one step was completed, the next step could be revealed, but not always right away. There were weeks of rest when nothing new was revealed. God will reveal his will to you, but sometimes there may be periods of waiting patiently for him. None of the steps were overly difficult in themselves and usually I was unaware of where they would lead. Most of the process was simply doing what seemed the next simple thing to do, knowing only who I obeyed rather than why. As you sense God calling you to do something, seek only to obey once you clarify it is God calling rather than question why. This will allow you to abide with Him.

Do you think he is calling you to do something now?

Lord, what are you teaching me through today's readings?

Lord, what else have you said to me through thoughts, circumstances, conversations, emotions, or the work of the enemy?

Lord, what do you want me to do today?

At home: At work: In ministry:

"Go, and make disciples." (Matt. 28:19)

You are concluding this workbook which provides an introduction to discipleship. You understand more now than when you began 12 weeks ago. The 24-week Listening to Jesus program follows. However, after you have gone through the program in 24 weeks, you are not finished. We hope you continue to repeat the daily readings many times with increasing ability to understand what Jesus taught as well as greater obedience to his commands. We also hope that you will gain his vision that you "go and make disciples" of whoever he places in your life and on your heart.

Our vision is that you become part of an ongoing core group and that after a few years will form a second group of disciples and duplicate the same process with them. We hope members of your second group (their core group) will eventually form their own second group of disciples to continue the process.

What is your response going to be now to the call to "go and make disciples?"

Lord, what are you teaching me through today's readings?

Lord, what else have you said to me through thoughts, circumstances, conversations, emotions, or the work of the enemy?

Lord, what do you want me to do today?

At home: At work: In ministry:

CONCLUSION – SUMMARY   **TODAY'S DATE:** _____

Lord, what have you taught me this week?

What specifically will I do and when will it be done?

Lord, what else have you said to me about time through thoughts, circumstances, conversations, emotions, or the work of the enemy?

Lord, what do you want me to do today?

At home: At work: In ministry:

WEEKLY REVIEW

Time: Lord, did I spend adequate time truly listening to you each day?

Truth: Lord, what truths did you reveal to me this past week?

Trust: Lord, did I trust that you were in control of all of the circumstances of my life this week, or did I worry, become anxious or reflect lack of trust in another way?

Surrender: Lord, did my thoughts and actions reflect that I have surrendered all to you? Did I practice spiritual disciplines daily? Did I ask your forgiveness and forgive others?

Obey: Lord, was I obedient in the attitudes of my mind (humility and servanthood rather than pride, etc.)? Did I do the things I sensed you wanted me to do?

Abide: Lord, was I aware of your presence and of you speaking to me throughout the week?

Reconcile: Lord, did I disciple other Christians or share the gospel with non-believers as you provided opportunities?

Listening to Jesus: The Program

The purpose of the program is to help you continually examine your life and see it within the context of what God is saying to you through scripture and what he has allowed in the circumstances of your life. It covers the teachings of Jesus and other relevant scripture over 24 weeks. When you have completed it, go back through it again to understand it at a deeper level, hopefully with new disciples the Lord has put in your life. You should notice an improved ability to hear God and know with greater certainty what he is saying to you.

The first time through read only the gospel readings. The next time through you may wish to add one or more of the secondary readings. Include the readings that suit you; it is not necessary that you do more than the gospel reading, but you may find the other readings provide new insights.

Daily: Read the scripture for each day beginning with Week 1, Day 1. As you read, listen; let Jesus speak to you. Ask him how you should obey his teaching and whether it applies to your current circumstances. Write what you believe the Lord is saying to you in response to the question: **Lord, what are you teaching me?** Respond to the gospel separately from the secondary readings if you use them. If he reveals something specific to be acted upon now or something that should become routine in your life, note it in your answer to the third question.

After your scripture reading(s) journal your answer to the question: **Lord, what else have you said to me through thoughts, circumstances, conversations, emotions, or the work of the enemy?** Mentally replay the past day and note what God reveals to you. It may be spiritual truth or an answer you need to a current problem. Perhaps he used circumstances such as a setback or some other person to speak to you. Ask the Lord to reveal anything about your day or the past few days that he is using to communicate to you, often in non-routine events. Even if you are unsure what he is saying through a circumstance, make note of it; it may become clear later. Expect him to speak mostly about current needs with insights or things to do.

Finally journal your answer to the question: **Lord, what do you want me to do today? At home: At work: In ministry:** God is just as concerned about your physical well being as your spiritual well being. The Bible has a number of very practical directions God has given to his people, so expect him to speak in very practical ways to you. Record anything you sense that the Lord wants you to do now in any of these areas of your life. What should be listed is your "to do" list for that day. Everything you do each day should be what you believe God wants you to do. The list may help you be more intentional.

Weekly: On the 7th or meeting day, after noting what the Lord has revealed to you during the previous day, review your insights for the week to reinforce them. After your review, answer the 7 weekly questions, noting significant insights from each day for the past week in your answer to the second weekly question. See if a pattern emerges of something the Lord is teaching you or wanting you to do.

Weekly Meetings: Meet each week with a small group who are going through the same readings to share your insights and questions that may arise. You may be at different spiritual levels or have different views than other members. If you share differing views, do so in love with a desire to help each other as you seek to understand. Be discreet in what you share with others outside the group. You may hear personal information that should be kept private.

Daily Questions

Lord, what are you teaching me?

Lord, what else have you said to me through thoughts, circumstances, conversations, emotions, or the work of the enemy?

Lord, what do you want me to do today?

At home: At work: In ministry:

Weekly Review Questions

TIME: Lord, did I spend adequate time truly listening to you each day?

TRUTH REVEALED: Lord, what truths did you reveal to me this past week?

TRUST: Lord, did I trust that you were in control of all of the circumstances of my life this week, or did I worry, become anxious or reflect lack of trust in another way?

SURRENDER: Lord, did my thoughts and actions reflect that I have surrendered all to you? Did I practice spiritual disciplines daily? Did I ask your forgiveness and forgive others?

OBEY: Lord, was I obedient in the attitudes of my mind (humility and servant-hood rather than pride, etc.)? Did I do the things I sensed you wanted me to do?

ABIDE: Lord, was I aware of your presence and of you speaking to me throughout the week?

RECONCILE: Lord, did I disciple other Christians or share the gospel with non-believers as you provided opportunities?

Week 20

Part of being a disciple is making disciples, not just Christians but followers of Jesus Christ that seek to learn to obey everything he commanded. You are nearing the end of the Listening to Jesus Program. This is a good time to begin thinking and praying about inviting others to join your group.

During Week 21, make a list of all the people you know who you think may be ready to take this step. Pray over your list and with the Lord's leading select 3 names of those you will invite. During Week 23, invite the 3 people the Lord has put on your heart to join your group. Share the responses you get with your group at your next meeting.

Consider starting your own group, either by yourself or with one or two others in your current group especially as your current group becomes large. Try to continue to meet with your current group if possible to grow deeper with them by arranging for your new group to meet at a different time. A copy of the Listening to Jesus Leaders Guide can be obtained by emailing tSOARMinistries@live.com. You may also visit our website at www.tSOAR.org.

Perhaps you discern God leading you into a new area of ministry or vocation. Share these things with your group to help with discernment, confirmation or clarification of what you may be called to. Perhaps others in your group are receiving similar messages that could benefit other members or perhaps the whole group. The intent of Listening to Jesus is just that: that one learns to listen and over time becomes increasingly adept at hearing and more conscientious about obeying so the kingdom of God is advanced.

John 1:1-18 In the beginning was the Word, and the Word was with God, and the Word was God. The same was in the beginning with God. All things were made through him. Without him was not anything made that has been made. In him was life, and the life was the light of men. The light shines in the darkness, and the darkness hasn't overcome it. There came a man, sent from God, whose name was John. The same came as a witness, that he might testify about the light, that all might believe through him. He was not the light, but was sent that he might testify about the light. The true light that enlightens everyone was coming into the world. He was in the world, and the world was made through him, and the world didn't recognize him. He came to his own, and those who were his own didn't receive him. But as many as received him, to them he gave the right to become God's children, to those who believe in his name: who were born not of blood, nor of the will of the flesh, nor of the will of man, but of God. The Word became flesh, and lived among us. We saw his glory, such glory as of the one and only Son of the Father, full of grace and truth. John testified about him. He cried out, saying, "This was he of whom I said, 'He who comes after me has surpassed me, for he was before me.'" From his fullness we all received grace upon grace. For the law was given through Moses. Grace and truth were realized through Jesus Christ. No one has seen God at any time. The one and only Son, who is in the bosom of the Father, he has declared him.

1 Jo. 1:1-4 That which was from the beginning, that which we have heard, that which we have seen with our eyes, that which we saw, and our hands touched, concerning the Word of life (and the life was revealed, and we have seen, and testify, and declare to you the life, the eternal life, which was with the Father, and was revealed to us); that which we have seen and heard we declare to you, that you also may have fellowship with us. Yes, and our fellowship is with the Father, and with his Son, Jesus Christ. And we write these things to you, that our joy may be fulfilled.

Ge. 1:1-5 In the beginning God created the heavens and the earth. Now the earth was formless and empty. Darkness was on the surface of the deep. God's Spirit was hovering over the surface of the waters. God said, "Let there be light," and there was light. God saw the light, and saw that it was good. God divided the light from the darkness. God called the light "day," and the darkness he called "night." There was evening and there was morning, one day.

Ge. 1:26-27 God said, "Let us make man in our image, after our likeness: and let them have dominion over the fish of the sea, and over the birds of the sky, and over the livestock, and over all the earth, and over every creeping thing that creeps on the earth." God created man in his own image. In God's image he created him; male and female he created them.

Week 1 Day 2   20-Jan

John 3:1-8 Now there was a man of the Pharisees named Nicodemus, a ruler of the Jews. The same came to him by night, and said to him, "Rabbi, we know that you are a teacher come from God, for no one can do these signs that you do, unless God is with him." Jesus answered him, "Most certainly, I tell you, unless one is born anew, he can't see the Kingdom of God." Nicodemus said to him, "How can a man be born when he is old? Can he enter a second time into his mother's womb, and be born?" Jesus answered, "Most certainly I tell you, unless one is born of water and spirit, he can't enter into the Kingdom of God! That which is born of the flesh is flesh. That which is born of the Spirit is spirit. Don't marvel that I said to you, 'You must be born anew.' The wind blows where it wants to, and you hear its sound, but don't know where it comes from and where it is going. So is everyone who is born of the Spirit."

I Cor. 2:6-16 We speak wisdom, however, among those who are full grown; yet a wisdom not of this world, nor of the rulers of this world, who are coming to nothing. But we speak God's wisdom in a mystery, the wisdom that has been hidden, which God foreordained before the worlds for our glory, which none of the rulers of this world has known. For had they known it, they wouldn't have crucified the Lord of glory. But as it is written, "Things which an eye didn't see, and an ear didn't hear, which didn't enter into the heart of man, these God has prepared for those who love him." But to us, God revealed them through the Spirit. For the Spirit searches all things, yes, the deep things of God. For who among men knows the things of a man, except the spirit of the man, which is in him? Even so, no one knows the things of God, except God's Spirit. But we received, not the spirit of the world, but the Spirit which is from God, that we might know the things that were freely given to us by God. Which things also we speak, not in words which man's wisdom teaches, but which the Holy Spirit teaches, comparing spiritual things with spiritual things. Now the natural man doesn't receive the things of God's Spirit, for they are foolishness to him, and he can't know them, because they are spiritually discerned. But he who is spiritual discerns all things, and he himself is judged by no one. "For who has known the mind of the Lord, that he should instruct him?" But we have Christ's mind.

Ez. 36:24-28 For I will take you from among the nations, and gather you out of all the countries, and will bring you into your own land. I will sprinkle clean water on you, and you shall be clean: from all your filthiness, and from all your idols, will I cleanse you. I will also give you a new heart, and I will put a new spirit within you; and I will take away the stony heart out of your flesh, and I will give you a heart of flesh. I will put my Spirit within you, and cause you to walk in my statutes, and you shall keep my ordinances, and do them. You shall dwell in the land that I gave to your fathers; and you shall be my people, and I will be your God.

Week 1 Day 3   13-Mar

John 3:9-21 Nicodemus answered him, "How can these things be?" Jesus answered him, "Are you the teacher of Israel, and don't understand these things? Most certainly I tell you, we speak that which we know, and testify of that which we have seen, and you don't receive our witness. If I told you earthly things and you don't believe, how will you believe if I tell you heavenly things? No one has ascended into heaven, but he who descended out of heaven, the Son of Man, who is in heaven. As Moses lifted up the serpent in the wilderness, even so must the Son of Man be lifted up, that whoever believes in him should not perish, but have eternal life. For God so loved the world, that he gave his one and only Son, that whoever believes in him should not perish, but have eternal life. For God didn't send his Son into the world to judge the world, but that the world should be saved through him. He who believes in him is not judged. He who doesn't believe has been judged already, because he has not believed in the name of the one and only Son of God. This is the judgment, that the light has come into the world, and men loved the darkness rather than the light; for their works were evil. For everyone who does evil hates the light, and doesn't come to the light, lest his works would be exposed. But he who does the truth comes to the light, that his works may be revealed, that they have been done in God."

Rom. 8:1-4 There is therefore now no condemnation to those who are in Christ Jesus, who don't walk according to the flesh, but according to the Spirit. For the law of the Spirit of life in Christ Jesus made me free from the law of sin and of death. For what the law couldn't do, in that it was weak through the flesh, God did, sending his own Son in the likeness of sinful flesh and for sin, he condemned sin in the flesh; that the ordinance of the law might be fulfilled in us, who walk not after the flesh, but after the Spirit.

Num. 21:4-9 They traveled from Mount Hor by the way to the Red Sea, to compass the land of Edom: and the soul of the people was much discouraged because of the way. The people spoke against God, and against Moses, "Why have you brought us up out of Egypt to die in the wilderness? For there is no bread, and there is no water; and our soul loathes this light bread." Yahweh sent fiery serpents among the people, and they bit the people; and many people of Israel died. The people came to Moses, and said, "We have sinned, because we have spoken against Yahweh, and against you. Pray to Yahweh, that he take away the serpents from us." Moses prayed for the people. Yahweh said to Moses, "Make a fiery serpent, and set it on a standard: and it shall happen, that everyone who is bitten, when he sees it, shall live." Moses made a serpent of brass, and set it on the standard: and it happened, that if a serpent had bitten any man, when he looked to the serpent of brass, he lived.

Week 1 Day 4   18-Mar

John 5:16-30 For this cause the Jews persecuted Jesus, and sought to kill him, because he did these things on the Sabbath. But Jesus answered them, "My Father is still working, so I am working, too." For this cause therefore the

Jews sought all the more to kill him, because he not only broke the Sabbath, but also called God his own Father, making himself equal with God. Jesus therefore answered them, "Most certainly, I tell you, the Son can do nothing of himself, but what he sees the Father doing. For whatever things he does, these the Son also does likewise. For the Father has affection for the Son, and shows him all things that he himself does. He will show him greater works than these, that you may marvel. For as the Father raises the dead and gives them life, even so the Son also gives life to whom he desires. For the Father judges no one, but he has given all judgment to the Son, that all may honor the Son, even as they honor the Father. He who doesn't honor the Son doesn't honor the Father who sent him. "Most certainly I tell you, he who hears my word, and believes him who sent me, has eternal life, and doesn't come into judgment, but has passed out of death into life. Most certainly, I tell you, the hour comes, and now is, when the dead will hear the Son of God's voice; and those who hear will live. For as the Father has life in himself, even so he gave to the Son also to have life in himself. He also gave him authority to execute judgment, because he is a son of man. Don't marvel at this, for the hour comes, in which all that are in the tombs will hear his voice, and will come out; those who have done good, to the resurrection of life; and those who have done evil, to the resurrection of judgment. I can of myself do nothing. As I hear, I judge, and my judgment is righteous; because I don't seek my own will, but the will of my Father who sent me.

Rom. 8:5-11 For those who live according to the flesh set their minds on the things of the flesh, but those who live according to the Spirit, the things of the Spirit. For the mind of the flesh is death, but the mind of the Spirit is life and peace; because the mind of the flesh is hostile towards God; for it is not subject to God's law, neither indeed can it be. Those who are in the flesh can't please God. But you are not in the flesh but in the Spirit, if it is so that the Spirit of God dwells in you. But if any man doesn't have the Spirit of Christ, he is not his. If Christ is in you, the body is dead because of sin, but the spirit is alive because of righteousness. But if the Spirit of him who raised up Jesus from the dead dwells in you, he who raised up Christ Jesus from the dead will also give life to your mortal bodies through his Spirit who dwells in you.

Ez. 37:1-14 The hand of Yahweh was on me, and he brought me out in the Spirit of Yahweh, and set me down in the midst of the valley; and it was full of bones. He caused me to pass by them all around: and behold, there were very many in the open valley; and behold, they were very dry. He said to me, Son of man, can these bones live? I answered, Lord Yahweh, you know. Again he said to me, Prophesy over these bones, and tell them, you dry bones, hear the word of Yahweh. Thus says the Lord Yahweh to these bones: Behold, I will cause breath to enter into you, and you shall live. I will lay sinews on you, and will bring up flesh on you, and cover you with skin, and put breath in you, and you shall live; and you shall know that I am Yahweh. So I prophesied as I was commanded: and as I prophesied, there was a noise, and behold, an earthquake; and the bones came together, bone to its bone. I saw, and, behold, there were sinews on them, and flesh came up, and skin covered them above; but there was no breath in them. Then he said to me, Prophesy to the wind, prophesy, son of man, and tell the wind, Thus says the Lord Yahweh: Come from the four winds, breath, and breathe on these slain, that they may live. So I prophesied as he commanded me, and the breath came into them, and they lived, and stood up on their feet, an exceedingly great army. Then he said to me, Son of man, these bones are the whole house of Israel: behold, they say, Our bones are dried up, and our hope is lost; we are clean cut off. Therefore prophesy, and tell them, Thus says the Lord Yahweh: Behold, I will open your graves, and cause you to come up out of your graves, my people; and I will bring you into the land of Israel. You shall know that I am Yahweh, when I have opened your graves, and caused you to come up out of your graves, my people. I will put my Spirit in you, and you shall live, and I will place you in your own land: and you shall know that I, Yahweh, have spoken it and performed it, says Yahweh.

Week 1 Day 5   3-Apr

John 5:31-47 "If I testify about myself, my witness is not valid. It is another who testifies about me. I know that the testimony which he testifies about me is true. You have sent to John, and he has testified to the truth. But the testimony which I receive is not from man. However, I say these things that you may be saved. He was the burning and shining lamp, and you were willing to rejoice for a while in his light. But the testimony which I have is greater than that of John, for the works which the Father gave me to accomplish, the very works that I do, testify about me, that the Father has sent me. The Father himself, who sent me, has testified about me. You have neither heard his voice at any time, nor seen his form. You don't have his word living in you; because you don't believe him whom he sent. You search the Scriptures, because you think that in them you have eternal life; and these are they which testify about me. Yet you will not come to me, that you may have life. I don't receive glory from men. But I know you, that you don't have God's love in yourselves. I have come in my Father's name, and you don't receive me. If another comes in his own name, you will receive him. How can you believe, who receive glory from one another, and you don't seek the glory that comes from the only God? Don't think that I will accuse you to the Father. There is one who accuses you, even Moses, on whom you have set your hope. For if you believed Moses, you would believe me; for he wrote about me. But if you don't believe his writings, how will you believe my words?"

Rom. 8:12-17 So then, brothers, we are debtors, not to the flesh, to live after the flesh. For if you live after the flesh, you must die; but if by the Spirit you put to death the deeds of the body, you will live. For as many as are led by the Spirit of God, these are children of God. For you didn't receive the spirit of bondage again to fear, but you received the Spirit of adoption, by whom we cry, "Abba! Father!" The Spirit himself testifies with our spirit that we are children of God; and if children, then heirs; heirs of God, and joint heirs with Christ; if indeed we suffer with him, that we may also be glorified with him.

De. 18:15-18 Yahweh your God will raise up to you a prophet from the midst of you, of your brothers, like me. You shall listen to him. This is according to all that you desired of Yahweh your God in Horeb in the day of the assembly, saying, "Let me not hear again the voice of Yahweh my God, neither let me see this great fire any more, that I not die." Yahweh said to me, "They have well said that which they have spoken. I will raise them up a prophet from among their brothers, like you; and I will put my words in his mouth, and he shall speak to them all that I shall command him."

Week 1 Day 6   **14-Jan**

Luke 5:1-11 Now it happened, while the multitude pressed on him and heard the word of God, that he was standing by the lake of Gennesaret. He saw two boats standing by the lake, but the fishermen had gone out of them, and were washing their nets. He entered into one of the boats, which was Simon's, and asked him to put out a little from the land. He sat down and taught the multitudes from the boat. When he had finished speaking, he said to Simon, "Put out into the deep, and let down your nets for a catch." Simon answered him, "Master, we worked all night, and took nothing; but at your word I will let down the net." When they had done this, they caught a great multitude of fish, and their net was breaking. They beckoned to their partners in the other boat, that they should come and help them. They came, and filled both boats, so that they began to sink. But Simon Peter, when he saw it, fell down at Jesus' knees, saying, "Depart from me, for I am a sinful man, Lord." For he was amazed, and all who were with him, at the catch of fish which they had caught; and so also were James and John, sons of Zebedee, who were partners with Simon. Jesus said to Simon, "Don't be afraid. From now on you will be catching men." When they had brought their boats to land, they left everything, and followed him.

Acts 1:6-7 Therefore when they had come together, they asked him, "Lord, are you now restoring the kingdom to Israel?" He said to them, "It isn't for you to know times or seasons which the Father has set within his own authority."

Acts 2:1-4 Now when the day of Pentecost had come, they were all with one accord in one place. Suddenly there came from the sky a sound like the rushing of a mighty wind, and it filled all the house where they were sitting. Tongues like fire appeared and were distributed to them, and one sat on each of them. They were all filled with the Holy Spirit, and began to speak with other languages, as the Spirit gave them the ability to speak.

Is. 6:1-8 In the year that king Uzziah died, I saw the Lord sitting on a throne, high and lifted up; and his train filled the temple. Above him stood the seraphim. Each one had six wings. With two he covered his face. With two he covered his feet. With two he flew. One called to another, and said, "Holy, holy, holy, is Yahweh of Armies! The whole earth is full of his glory!" The foundations of the thresholds shook at the voice of him who called, and the house was filled with smoke. Then I said, "Woe is me! For I am undone, because I am a man of unclean lips, and I dwell in the midst of a people of unclean lips: for my eyes have seen the King, Yahweh of Armies!" Then one of the seraphim flew to me, having a live coal in his hand, which he had taken with the tongs from off the altar. He touched my mouth with it, and said, "Behold, this has touched your lips; and your iniquity is taken away, and your sin forgiven." I heard the Lord's voice, saying, "Whom shall I send, and who will go for us?" Then I said, "Here I am. Send me!"

Week 1 Day 7   9-Sep

Col. 1:15-23 He is the image of the invisible God, the firstborn of all creation. For by him all things were created, in the heavens and on the earth, things visible and things invisible, whether thrones or dominions or principalities or powers; all things have been created through him, and for him. He is before all things, and in him all things are held together. He is the head of the body, the assembly, who is the beginning, the firstborn from the dead; that in all things he might have the preeminence. For all the fullness was pleased to dwell in him; and through him to reconcile all things to himself, by him, whether things on the earth, or things in the heavens, having made peace through the blood of his cross. You, being in past times alienated and enemies in your mind in your evil works, yet now he has reconciled in the body of his flesh through death, to present you holy and without blemish and blameless before him, if it is so that you continue in the faith, grounded and steadfast, and not moved away from the hope of the Good News which you heard, which is being proclaimed in all creation under heaven; of which I, Paul, was made a servant.

Job 38:1-21 Then Yahweh answered Job out of the whirlwind, "Who is this who darkens counsel by words without knowledge? Brace yourself like a man, for I will question you, then you answer me! Where were you when I laid the foundations of the earth? Declare, if you have understanding. Who determined its measures, if you know? Or who stretched the line on it? Whereupon were its foundations fastened? Or who laid its cornerstone, when the morning stars sang together, and all the sons of God shouted for joy? Or who shut up the sea with doors, when it broke forth from the womb, when I made clouds its garment, and wrapped it in thick darkness, marked out for it my bound, set bars and doors, and said, 'Here you may come, but no further. Here your proud waves shall be stayed?' Have you commanded the morning in your days, and caused the dawn to know its place; that it might take hold of the ends of the earth, and shake the wicked out of it? It is changed as clay under the seal, and stands forth as a garment. From the wicked, their light is withheld. The high arm is broken. Have you entered into the springs of the sea? Or have you walked in the recesses of the deep? Have the gates of death been revealed to you? Or have you seen the gates of the shadow of death? Have you comprehended the earth in its breadth? Declare, if you know it all. What is the way to the dwelling of light? As for darkness, where is its place, that you should take it to its bound, that you should discern the paths to its house? Surely you know, for you were born then, and the number of your days is great!"

Week 2 Day 1   1-Jan

Luke 5:27-32 After these things he went out, and saw a tax collector named Levi sitting at the tax office, and said to him, "Follow me!" He left everything, and rose up and followed him. Levi made a great feast for him in his house. There was a great crowd of tax collectors and others who were reclining with them. Their scribes and the Pharisees murmured against his disciples, saying, "Why do you eat and drink with the tax collectors and sinners?" Jesus answered them, "Those who are healthy have no need for a physician, but those who are sick do. I have not come to call the righteous, but sinners to repentance."

Acts 13:42-52 So when the Jews went out of the synagogue, the Gentiles begged that these words might be preached to them the next Sabbath. Now when the synagogue broke up, many of the Jews and of the devout proselytes followed Paul and Barnabas; who, speaking to them, urged them to continue in the grace of God. The next Sabbath almost the whole city was gathered together to hear the word of God. But when the Jews saw the multitudes, they were filled with jealousy, and contradicted the things which were spoken by Paul, and blasphemed. Paul and Barnabas spoke out boldly, and said, "It was necessary that God's word should be spoken to you first. Since indeed you thrust it from you, and judge yourselves unworthy of eternal life, behold, we turn to the Gentiles. For so has the Lord commanded us, saying, 'I have set you as a light for the Gentiles, that you should bring salvation to the uttermost parts of the earth.'" As the Gentiles heard this, they were glad, and glorified the word of God. As many as were appointed to eternal life believed. The Lord's word was spread abroad throughout all the region. But the Jews stirred up the devout and prominent women and the chief men of the city, and stirred up a persecution against Paul and Barnabas, and threw them out of their borders. But they shook off the dust of their feet against them, and came to Iconium. The disciples were filled with joy with the Holy Spirit.

Am. 7:14-15 Then Amos answered Amaziah, "I was no prophet, neither was I a prophet's son; but I was a herdsman, and a farmer of sycamore figs; and Yahweh took me from following the flock, and Yahweh said to me, 'Go, prophesy to my people Israel.'"

Week 2 Day 2   14-Apr

Matt. 11:25-30 At that time, Jesus answered, "I thank you, Father, Lord of heaven and earth, that you hid these things from the wise and understanding, and revealed them to infants. Yes, Father, for so it was well-pleasing in your sight. All things have been delivered to me by my Father. No one knows the Son, except the Father; neither does anyone know the Father, except the Son, and he to whom the Son desires to reveal him. Come to me, all you who labor and are heavily burdened, and I will give you rest. Take my yoke upon you, and learn from me, for I am gentle and lowly in heart; and you will find rest for your souls. For my yoke is easy, and my burden is light."

Col. 3:1-17 If then you were raised together with Christ, seek the things that are above, where Christ is, seated on the right hand of God. Set your mind on the things that are above, not on the things that are on the earth. For you died, and your life is hidden with Christ in God. When Christ, our life, is revealed, then you will also be revealed with him in glory. Put to death therefore your members which are of the earth: sexual immorality, uncleanness, depraved passion, evil desire, and covetousness, which is idolatry; for which things' sake the wrath of God comes on the children of disobedience. You also once walked in those, when you lived in them; but now you also put them all away: anger, wrath, malice, slander, and shameful speaking out of your mouth. Don't lie to one another, seeing that you have put off the old man with his doings, and have put on the new man, who is being renewed in knowledge after the image of his Creator, where there can't be Greek and Jew, circumcision and uncircumcision, barbarian, Scythian, bondservant, freeman; but Christ is all, and in all. Put on therefore, as God's chosen ones, holy and beloved, a heart of compassion, kindness, lowliness, humility, and perseverance; bearing with one another, and forgiving each other, if any man has a complaint against any; even as Christ forgave you, so you also do. Above all these things, walk in love, which is the bond of perfection. And let the peace of God rule in your hearts, to which also you were called in one body; and be thankful. Let the word of Christ dwell in you richly; in all wisdom teaching and admonishing one another with psalms, hymns, and spiritual songs, singing with grace in your heart to the Lord. Whatever you do, in word or in deed, do all in the name of the Lord Jesus, giving thanks to God the Father, through him.

Pr. 1:1-7 The proverbs of Solomon, the son of David, king of Israel: to know wisdom and instruction; to discern the words of understanding; to receive instruction in wise dealing, in righteousness, justice, and equity; to give prudence to the simple, knowledge and discretion to the young man: that the wise man may hear, and increase in learning; that the man of understanding may attain to sound counsel: to understand a proverb, and parables, the words and riddles of the wise. The fear of Yahweh is the beginning of knowledge; but the foolish despise wisdom and instruction.

Week 2 Day 3   6-Sep

John 6:25-40 When they found him on the other side of the sea, they asked him, "Rabbi, when did you come here?" Jesus answered them, "Most certainly I tell you, you seek me, not because you saw signs, but because you ate of the loaves, and were filled. Don't work for the food which perishes, but for the food which remains to eternal life, which the Son of Man will give to you. For God the Father has sealed him." They said therefore to him, "What must we do, that we may work the works of God?" Jesus answered them, "This is the work of God, that you believe in him whom he has sent." They said therefore to him, "What then do you do for a sign, that we may see, and believe you? What work do you do? Our fathers ate the manna in the wilderness. As it is written, 'He gave them bread out of heaven to eat.'" Jesus therefore said to them, "Most certainly, I tell you, it wasn't Moses who gave you the bread out of heaven, but my Father gives you the true bread out of heaven. For the bread of God is that which comes down out of heaven, and gives life to the world." They said therefore to him, "Lord, always give us this bread." Jesus said to them, "I am the bread of life. He who comes to me will not be hungry, and he who believes in me will never be thirsty. But I told you that you have seen me, and yet you don't believe. All those whom the Father gives me will come to me. He who comes to me I will in no way throw out. For I have come down from heaven, not to do my own will, but the will of him who sent me. This is the will of my Father who sent me, that of all he has given to me I should lose nothing, but should raise him up at the last day. This is the will of the one who sent me, that everyone who sees the Son, and believes in him, should have eternal life; and I will raise him up at the last day."

Heb. 2:5-3:6 For he didn't subject the world to come, of which we speak, to angels. But one has somewhere testified, saying, "What is man, that you think of him? Or the son of man, that you care for him? You made him a little lower than the angels. You crowned him with glory and honor. You have put all things in subjection under his feet." For in that he subjected all things to him, he left nothing that is not subject to him. But now we don't see all things subjected to him, yet. But we see him who has been made a little lower than the angels, Jesus, because of the suffering of death crowned with glory and honor, that by the grace of God he should taste of death for everyone. For it became him, for whom are all things, and through whom are all things, in bringing many children to glory, to make the author of their salvation perfect through sufferings. For both he who sanctifies and those who are sanctified are all from one, for which cause he is not ashamed to call them brothers, saying, "I will declare your name to my brothers. In the midst of the congregation I will sing your praise." Again, "I will put my trust in him." Again, "Behold, here I am with the children whom God has given me." Since then the children have shared in flesh and blood, he also himself in the same way partook of the same, that through death he might bring to nothing him who had the power of death, that is, the devil, and might deliver all of them who through fear of death were all their lifetime subject to bondage. For most certainly, he doesn't give help to angels, but he gives help to the seed of Abraham. Therefore he was obligated in all things to be made like his brothers, that he might become a merciful and faithful high priest in things pertaining to God, to make atonement for the sins of the people. For in that he himself has suffered being tempted, he is able to help those who are tempted. Therefore, holy brothers, partakers of a heavenly calling, consider the Apostle and High Priest of our confession, Jesus; who was faithful to him who appointed him, as also was Moses in all his house. For he has been counted worthy of more glory than Moses, inasmuch as he who built the house has more honor than the house. For every house is built by someone; but he who built all things is God. Moses indeed was faithful in all his house as a servant, for a testimony of those things which were afterward to be spoken, but Christ is faithful as a Son over his house; whose house we are, if we hold fast our confidence and the glorying of our hope firm to the end.

Ex. 16:2-15 The whole congregation of the children of Israel murmured against Moses and against Aaron in the wilderness; and the children of Israel said to them, "We wish that we had died by the hand of Yahweh in the land of Egypt, when we sat by the meat pots, when we ate our fill of bread, for you have brought us out into this wilderness, to kill this whole assembly with hunger." Then Yahweh said to Moses, "Behold, I will rain bread from the sky for you, and the people shall go out and gather a day's portion every day, that I may test them, whether they will walk in my law, or not. It shall come to pass on the sixth day, that they shall prepare that which they bring in, and it shall be twice as much as they gather daily." Moses and Aaron said to all the children of Israel, "At evening, then you shall know that Yahweh has brought you out from the land of Egypt; and in the morning, then you shall see the glory of Yahweh; because he hears your murmurings against Yahweh. Who are we, that you murmur against us?" Moses said, "Now Yahweh shall give you meat to eat in the evening, and in the morning bread to satisfy you; because Yahweh hears your murmurings which you murmur against him. And who are we? Your murmurings are not against us, but against Yahweh." Moses said to Aaron, "Tell all the congregation of the children of Israel, 'Come near before Yahweh, for he has heard your murmurings.'" It happened, as Aaron spoke to the whole congregation of the children of Israel, that they looked toward the wilderness, and behold, the glory of Yahweh appeared in the cloud. Yahweh spoke to Moses, saying, "I have heard the murmurings of the children of Israel. Speak to them, saying, 'At evening you shall eat meat, and in the morning you shall be filled with bread: and you shall know that I am Yahweh your God.'" It happened at evening that quail came up and covered the camp; and in the morning the dew lay around the camp. When the dew that lay had gone, behold, on the surface of the wilderness was a small round thing, small as the frost on the ground. When the children of Israel saw it, they said one to another, "What is it?" For they didn't know what it was. Moses said to them, "It is the bread which Yahweh has given you to eat."

Week 2 Day 4   **17-Apr**

John 6:41-59 The Jews therefore murmured concerning him, because he said, "I am the bread which came down out of heaven." They said, "Isn't this Jesus, the son of Joseph, whose father and mother we know? How then does he say, 'I have come down out of heaven?'" Therefore Jesus answered them, "Don't murmur among yourselves. No one can come to me unless the Father who sent me draws him, and I will raise him up in the last day. It is written in the prophets, 'They will all be taught by God.' Therefore everyone who hears from the Father, and has learned, comes to me. Not that anyone has seen the Father, except he who is from God. He has seen the Father. Most certainly, I tell you, he who believes in me has eternal life. I am the bread of life. Your fathers ate the manna in the wilderness, and they died. This is the bread which comes down out of heaven, that anyone may eat of it and not die. I am the living bread which came down out of heaven. If anyone eats of this bread, he will live forever. Yes, the bread which I will give for the life of the world is my flesh." The Jews therefore contended with one another, saying, "How can this man give us his flesh to eat?" Jesus therefore said to them, "Most certainly I tell you, unless you eat the flesh of the Son of Man and drink his blood, you don't have life in yourselves. He who eats my flesh and drinks my blood has eternal life, and I will raise him up at the last day. For my flesh is food indeed, and my blood is drink indeed. He who eats my flesh and drinks my blood lives in me, and I in him. As the living Father sent me, and I live because of the Father; so he who feeds on me, he will also live because of me. This is the bread which came down out of heaven—not as our fathers ate the manna, and died. He who eats this bread will live forever." He said these things in the synagogue, as he taught in Capernaum.

I Cor. 10:1-13 Now I would not have you ignorant, brothers, that our fathers were all under the cloud, and all passed through the sea; and were all baptized into Moses in the cloud and in the sea; and all ate the same spiritual food; and all drank the same spiritual drink. For they drank of a spiritual rock that followed them, and the rock was Christ. However with most of them, God was not well pleased, for they were overthrown in the wilderness. Now these things were our examples, to the intent we should not lust after evil things, as they also lusted. Neither be idolaters, as some of them were. As it is written, "The people sat down to eat and drink, and rose up to play." Neither let us commit sexual immorality, as some of them committed, and in one day twenty-three thousand fell. Neither let us test the Lord, as some of them tested, and perished by the serpents. Neither grumble, as some of them also grumbled, and perished by the destroyer. Now all these things happened to them by way of example, and they were written for our admonition, on whom the ends of the ages have come. Therefore let him who thinks he stands be careful that he doesn't fall. No temptation has taken you except what is common to man. God is faithful, who will not allow you to be tempted above what you are able, but will with the temptation also make the way of escape, that you may be able to endure it.

Ps. 78:17-31 Yet they still went on to sin against him, to rebel against the Most High in the desert. They tempted God in their heart by asking food according to their desire. Yes, they spoke against God. They said, "Can God prepare a table in the wilderness? Behold, he struck the rock, so that waters gushed out, and streams overflowed. Can he give bread also? Will he provide flesh for his people?" Therefore Yahweh heard, and was angry. A fire was kindled against Jacob, anger also went up against Israel, because they didn't believe in God, and didn't trust in his salvation. Yet he commanded the skies above, and opened the doors of heaven. He rained down manna on them to eat, and gave them food from the sky. Man ate the bread of angels. He sent them food to the full. He caused the east wind to blow in the sky. By his power he guided the south wind. He rained also flesh on them as the dust; winged birds as the sand of the seas. He let them fall in the midst of their camp, around their habitations. So they ate, and were well filled. He gave them their own desire. They didn't turn from their cravings. Their food was yet in their mouths, when the anger of God went up against them, killed some of their fattest, and struck down the young men of Israel.

John 6:60-71 Therefore many of his disciples, when they heard this, said, "This is a hard saying! Who can listen to it?" But Jesus knowing in himself that his disciples murmured at this, said to them, "Does this cause you to stumble? Then what if you would see the Son of Man ascending to where he was before? It is the spirit who gives life. The flesh profits nothing. The words that I speak to you are spirit, and are life. But there are some of you who don't believe." For Jesus knew from the beginning who they were who didn't believe, and who it was who would betray him. He said, "For this cause have I said to you that no one can come to me, unless it is given to him by my Father." At this, many of his disciples went back, and walked no more with him. Jesus said therefore to the twelve, "You don't also want to go away, do you?" Simon Peter answered him, "Lord, to whom would we go? You have the words of eternal life. We have come to believe and know that you are the Christ, the Son of the living God." Jesus answered them, "Didn't I choose you, the twelve, and one of you is a devil?" Now he spoke of Judas, the son of Simon Iscariot, for it was he who would betray him, being one of the twelve.

Heb. 2:1-4 Therefore we ought to pay greater attention to the things that were heard, lest perhaps we drift away. For if the word spoken through angels proved steadfast, and every transgression and disobedience received a just recompense; how will we escape if we neglect so great a salvation—which at the first having been spoken through the Lord, was confirmed to us by those who heard; God also testifying with them, both by signs and wonders, by various works of power, and by gifts of the Holy Spirit, according to his own will?

Jos. 24:1-15 Joshua gathered all the tribes of Israel to Shechem, and called for the elders of Israel, for their heads, for their judges, and for their officers; and they presented themselves before God. Joshua said to all the people, "Thus says Yahweh, the God of Israel, 'Your fathers lived of old time beyond the River, even Terah, the father of Abraham, and the father of Nahor: and they served other gods. I took your father Abraham from beyond the River, and led him throughout all the land of Canaan, and multiplied his seed, and gave him Isaac. I gave to Isaac Jacob and Esau: and I gave to Esau Mount Seir, to possess it. Jacob and his children went down into Egypt. 'I sent Moses and Aaron, and I plagued Egypt, according to that which I did in its midst: and afterward I brought you out. I brought your fathers out of Egypt: and you came to the sea. The Egyptians pursued after your fathers with chariots and with horsemen to the Red Sea. When they cried out to Yahweh, he put darkness between you and the Egyptians, and brought the sea on them, and covered them; and your eyes saw what I did in Egypt: and you lived in the wilderness many days. 'I brought you into the land of the Amorites, that lived beyond the Jordan: and they fought with you; and I gave them into your hand. You possessed their land; and I destroyed them from before you. Then Balak the son of Zippor, king of Moab, arose and fought against Israel. He sent and called Balaam the son of Beor to curse you; but I would not listen to Balaam; therefore he blessed you still. So I delivered you out of his hand. 'You went over the Jordan, and came to Jericho. The men of Jericho fought against you, the Amorite, the Perizzite, the Canaanite, the Hittite, the Girgashite, the Hivite, and the Jebusite; and I delivered them into your hand. I sent the hornet before you, which drove them out from before you, even the two kings of the Amorites; not with your sword, nor with your bow. I gave you a land whereon you had not labored, and cities which you didn't build, and you live in them. You eat of vineyards and olive groves which you didn't plant.' Now therefore fear Yahweh, and serve him in sincerity and in truth. Put away the gods which your fathers served beyond the River, in Egypt; and serve Yahweh. If it seems evil to you to serve Yahweh, choose this day whom you will serve; whether the gods which your fathers served that were beyond the River, or the gods of the Amorites, in whose land you dwell: but as for me and my house, we will serve Yahweh."

Matt. 22:1-14 Jesus answered and spoke again in parables to them, saying, "The Kingdom of Heaven is like a certain king, who made a marriage feast for his son, and sent out his servants to call those who were invited to the marriage feast, but they would not come. Again he sent out other servants, saying, 'Tell those who are invited, "Behold, I have prepared my dinner. My cattle and my fatlings are killed, and all things are ready. Come to the marriage feast!"' But they made light of it, and went their ways, one to his own farm, another to his merchandise, and the rest grabbed his servants, and treated them shamefully, and killed them. When the king heard that, he was angry, and sent his armies, destroyed those murderers, and burned their city. "Then he said to his servants, 'The wedding is ready, but those who were invited weren't worthy. Go therefore to the intersections of the highways, and as many as you may find, invite to the marriage feast.' Those servants went out into the highways, and gathered together as many as they found, both bad and good. The wedding was filled with guests. But when the king came in to see the guests, he saw there a man who didn't have on wedding clothing, and he said to him, 'Friend, how did you come in here not wearing wedding clothing?' He was speechless. Then the king said to the servants, 'Bind him hand and foot, take him away, and throw him into the outer darkness; there is where the weeping and grinding of teeth will be.' For many are called, but few chosen."

Rom. 10:1-21 Brothers, my heart's desire and my prayer to God is for Israel, that they may be saved. For I testify about them that they have a zeal for God, but not according to knowledge. For being ignorant of God's righteousness, and seeking to establish their own righteousness, they didn't subject themselves to the righteousness of God. For Christ is the fulfillment of the law for righteousness to everyone who believes. For Moses writes about the righteousness of the law, "The one who does them will live by them." But the righteousness which is of faith says this, "Don't say in your heart, 'Who will ascend into heaven?' (that is, to bring Christ down); or, 'Who will descend into the abyss?' (that is, to bring Christ up from the dead.)" But what does it say? "The word is near you, in your mouth, and in your heart"; that is, the word of faith, which we preach: that if you will confess with your mouth that Jesus is Lord, and believe in your heart that God raised him from the dead, you will be saved. For with the heart, one believes unto righteousness; and with the mouth confession is made unto salvation. For the Scripture says, "Whoever believes in him will not be disappointed." For there is no distinction between Jew and Greek; for the same Lord is Lord of all, and is rich to all who call on him. For, "Whoever will call on the name of the Lord will be saved." How then will they call on him in whom they have not believed? How will they believe in him whom they have not heard? How will they hear without a preacher? And how will they preach unless they are sent? As it is written: "How beautiful are the feet of those who preach the Good News of peace, who bring glad tidings of good things!" But they didn't all listen to the glad news. For Isaiah says, "Lord, who has believed our report?" So faith comes by hearing, and hearing by the word of God. But I say, didn't they hear? Yes, most certainly, "Their sound went out into all the earth, their words to the ends of the world." But I ask, didn't Israel know? First Moses says, "I will provoke you to jealousy with that which is no nation, with a nation void of understanding I will make you angry." Isaiah is very bold, and says, "I was found by those who didn't seek me. I was revealed to those who didn't ask for me." But as to Israel he says, "All day long I stretched out my hands to a disobedient and contrary people."

Ps. 45 My heart overflows with a noble theme. I recite my verses for the king. My tongue is like the pen of a skillful writer. You are the most excellent of the sons of men. Grace has anointed your lips, therefore God has blessed you forever. Strap your sword on your thigh, mighty one: your splendor and your majesty. In your majesty ride on victoriously on behalf of truth, humility, and righteousness. Let your right hand display awesome deeds. Your arrows are sharp. The nations fall under you, with arrows in the heart of the king's enemies. Your throne, God, is forever and ever. A scepter of equity is the scepter of your kingdom. You have loved righteousness, and hated wickedness. Therefore God, your God, has anointed you with the oil of gladness above your fellows. All your garments smell like myrrh, aloes, and cassia. Out of ivory palaces stringed instruments have made you glad. Kings' daughters are among your honorable women. At your right hand the queen stands in gold of Ophir. Listen, daughter, consider, and turn your ear. Forget your own people, and also your father's house. So the king will desire your beauty, honor him, for he is your lord. The daughter of Tyre comes with a gift. The rich among the people entreat your favor. The princess inside is all glorious. Her clothing is interwoven with gold. She shall be led to the king in embroidered work. The virgins, her companions who follow her, shall be brought to you. With gladness and rejoicing they shall be led. They shall enter into the king's palace. Your sons will take the place of your fathers. You shall make them princes in all the earth. I will make your name to be remembered in all generations. Therefore the peoples shall give you thanks forever and ever.

Week 2 Day 7   19-Aug

Gal. 3:26-4:7 For you are all children of God, through faith in Christ Jesus. For as many of you as were baptized into Christ have put on Christ. There is neither Jew nor Greek, there is neither slave nor free man, there is neither male nor female; for you are all one in Christ Jesus. If you are Christ's, then you are Abraham's seed and heirs according to promise. But I say that so long as the heir is a child, he is no different from a bondservant, though he is lord of all; but is under guardians and stewards until the day appointed by the father. So we also, when we were children, were held in bondage under the elemental principles of the world. But when the fullness of the time came, God sent out his Son, born to a woman, born under the law, that he might redeem those who were under the law, that we might receive the adoption of children. And because you are children, God sent out the Spirit of his Son into your hearts, crying, "Abba, Father!" So you are no longer a bondservant, but a son; and if a son, then an heir of God through Christ.

Is. 40:1-12 "Comfort, comfort my people," says your God. "Speak comfortably to Jerusalem; and call out to her that her warfare is accomplished, that her iniquity is pardoned, that she has received of Yahweh's hand double for all her sins." The voice of one who calls out, "Prepare the way of Yahweh in the wilderness! Make a level highway in the desert for our God. Every valley shall be exalted, and every mountain and hill shall be made low. The uneven shall be made level, and the rough places a plain. The glory of Yahweh shall be revealed, and all flesh shall see it together; for the mouth of Yahweh has spoken it." The voice of one saying, "Cry!" One said, "What shall I cry?" "All flesh is like grass, and all its glory is like the flower of the field. The grass withers, the flower fades, because Yahweh's breath blows on it. Surely the people are like grass. The grass withers, the flower fades; but the word of our God stands forever." You who tell good news to Zion, go up on a high mountain. You who tell good news to Jerusalem, lift up your voice with strength. Lift it up. Don't be afraid. Say to the cities of Judah, "Behold, your God!" Behold, the Lord Yahweh will come as a mighty one, and his arm will rule for him. Behold, his reward is with him, and his recompense before him. He will feed his flock like a shepherd. He will gather the lambs in his arm, and carry them in his bosom. He will gently lead those who have their young. Who has measured the waters in the hollow of his hand, and marked off the sky with his span, and calculated the dust of the earth in a measure, and weighed the mountains in scales, and the hills in a balance?

Is. 40:27-31 Why do you say, Jacob, and speak, Israel, "My way is hidden from Yahweh, and the justice due me is disregarded by my God?" Haven't you known? Haven't you heard? The everlasting God, Yahweh, The Creator of the ends of the earth, doesn't faint. He isn't weary. His understanding is unsearchable. He gives power to the weak. He increases the strength of him who has no might. Even the youths faint and get weary, and the young men utterly fall; But those who wait for Yahweh will renew their strength. They will mount up with wings like eagles. They will run, and not be weary. They will walk, and not faint.

Week 3 Day 1   30-Jan

John 2:1-11 The third day, there was a marriage in Cana of Galilee. Jesus' mother was there. Jesus also was invited, with his disciples, to the marriage. When the wine ran out, Jesus' mother said to him, "They have no wine." Jesus said to her, "Woman, what does that have to do with you and me? My hour has not yet come." His mother said to the servants, "Whatever he says to you, do it." Now there were six water pots of stone set there after the Jews' way of purifying, containing two or three metretes apiece. Jesus said to them, "Fill the water pots with water." They filled them up to the brim. He said to them, "Now draw some out, and take it to the ruler of the feast." So they took it. When the ruler of the feast tasted the water now become wine, and didn't know where it came from (but the servants who had drawn the water knew), the ruler of the feast called the bridegroom, and said to him, "Everyone serves the good wine first, and when the guests have drunk freely, then that which is worse. You have kept the good wine until now!" This beginning of his signs Jesus did in Cana of Galilee, and revealed his glory; and his disciples believed in him.

Rev. 19:1-10 After these things I heard something like a loud voice of a great multitude in heaven, saying, "Hallelujah! Salvation, power, and glory belong to our God: for true and righteous are his judgments. For he has judged the great prostitute, who corrupted the earth with her sexual immorality, and he has avenged the blood of his servants at her hand." A second said, "Hallelujah! Her smoke goes up forever and ever." The twenty-four elders and the four living creatures fell down and worshiped God who sits on the throne, saying, "Amen! Hallelujah!" A voice came forth from the throne, saying, "Give praise to our God, all you his servants, you who fear him, the small and the great!" I heard something like the voice of a great multitude, and like the voice of many waters, and like the voice of mighty thunders, saying, "Hallelujah! For the Lord our God, the Almighty, reigns! Let us rejoice and be exceedingly glad, and let us give the glory to him. For the marriage of the Lamb has come, and his wife has made herself ready." It was given to her that she would array herself in bright, pure, fine linen: for the fine linen is the righteous acts of the saints. He said to me, "Write, 'Blessed are those who are invited to the marriage supper of the Lamb.'" He said to me, "These are true words of God." I fell down before his feet to worship him. He said to me, "Look! Don't do it! I am a fellow bondservant with you and with your brothers who hold the testimony of Jesus. Worship God, for the testimony of Jesus is the Spirit of Prophecy."

Num. 20:1-13 The children of Israel, even the whole congregation, came into the wilderness of Zin in the first month: and the people stayed in Kadesh; and Miriam died there, and was buried there. There was no water for the congregation: and they assembled themselves together against Moses and against Aaron. The people strove with Moses, and spoke, saying, "We wish that we had died when our brothers died before Yahweh! Why have you brought the assembly of Yahweh into this wilderness, that we should die there, we and our animals? Why have you made us to come up out of Egypt, to bring us in to this evil place? It is no place of seed, or of figs, or of vines, or of pomegranates; neither is there any water to drink." Moses and Aaron went from the presence of the assembly to the door of the Tent of Meeting, and fell on their faces: and the glory of Yahweh appeared to them. Yahweh spoke to Moses, saying, "Take the rod, and assemble the congregation, you, and Aaron your brother, and speak to the rock before their eyes, that it give forth its water; and you shall bring forth to them water out of the rock; so you shall give the congregation and their livestock drink." Moses took the rod from before Yahweh, as he commanded him. Moses and Aaron gathered the assembly together before the rock, and he said to them, "Hear now, you rebels; shall we bring you water out of this rock for you?" Moses lifted up his hand, and struck the rock with his rod twice: and water came forth abundantly, and the congregation drank, and their livestock. Yahweh said to Moses and Aaron, "Because you didn't believe in me, to sanctify me in the eyes of the children of Israel, therefore you shall not bring this assembly into the land which I have given them." These are the waters of Meribah; because the children of Israel strove with Yahweh, and he was sanctified in them.

Week 3 Day 2   12-Aug

Luke 8:22-25 Now it happened on one of those days, that he entered into a boat, himself and his disciples, and he said to them, "Let's go over to the other side of the lake." So they launched out. But as they sailed, he fell asleep. A wind storm came down on the lake, and they were taking on dangerous amounts of water. They came to him, and awoke him, saying, "Master, master, we are dying!" He awoke, and rebuked the wind and the raging of the water, and they ceased, and it was calm. He said to them, "Where is your faith?" Being afraid they marveled, saying one to another, "Who is this, then, that he commands even the winds and the water, and they obey him?"

Acts 4:23-31 Being let go, they came to their own company, and reported all that the chief priests and the elders had said to them. When they heard it, they lifted up their voice to God with one accord, and said, "O Lord, you are God, who made the heaven, the earth, the sea, and all that is in them; who by the mouth of your servant, David, said, 'Why do the nations rage, and the peoples plot a vain thing? The kings of the earth take a stand, and the rulers take council together, against the Lord, and against his Christ. "For truly, in this city against your holy servant, Jesus, whom you anointed, both Herod and Pontius Pilate, with the Gentiles and the people of Israel, were gathered together to do whatever your hand and your council foreordained to happen. Now, Lord, look at their threats, and grant to your servants to speak your word with all boldness, while you stretch out your hand to heal; and that signs and wonders may be done through the name of your holy Servant Jesus." When they had prayed, the place was shaken where they were gathered together. They were all filled with the Holy Spirit, and they spoke the word of God with boldness.

Ps. 104:1-7 Bless Yahweh, my soul. Yahweh, my God, you are very great. You are clothed with honor and majesty. He covers himself with light as with a garment. He stretches out the heavens like a curtain. He lays the beams of his rooms in the waters. He makes the clouds his chariot. He walks on the wings of the wind. He makes his messengers winds; his servants flames of fire. He laid the foundations of the earth, that it should not be moved forever.

You covered it with the deep as with a cloak. The waters stood above the mountains. At your rebuke they fled. At the voice of your thunder they hurried away.

Week 3 Day 3   18-Jun

Matt. 14:22-36 Immediately Jesus made the disciples get into the boat, and to go ahead of him to the other side, while he sent the multitudes away. After he had sent the multitudes away, he went up into the mountain by himself to pray. When evening had come, he was there alone. But the boat was now in the middle of the sea, distressed by the waves, for the wind was contrary. In the fourth watch of the night, Jesus came to them, walking on the sea When the disciples saw him walking on the sea, they were troubled, saying, "It's a ghost!" and they cried out for fear. But immediately Jesus spoke to them, saying "Cheer up! It is I! Don't be afraid." Peter answered him and said, "Lord, if it is you, command me to come to you on the waters." He said, "Come!" Peter stepped down from the boat, and walked on the waters to come to Jesus. But when he saw that the wind was strong, he was afraid, and beginning to sink, he cried out, saying, "Lord, save me!" Immediately Jesus stretched out his hand, took hold of him, and said to him, "You of little faith, why did you doubt?" When they got up into the boat, the wind ceased. Those who were in the boat came and worshiped him, saying, "You are truly the Son of God!" When they had crossed over, they came to the land of Gennesaret. When the people of that place recognized him, they sent into all that surrounding region, and brought to him all who were sick, and they begged him that they might just touch the fringe of his garment. As many as touched it were made whole.

Heb. 12:1-3 Therefore let us also, seeing we are surrounded by so great a cloud of witnesses, lay aside every weight and the sin which so easily entangles us, and let us run with patience the race that is set before us, looking to Jesus, the author and perfecter of faith, who for the joy that was set before him endured the cross, despising its shame, and has sat down at the right hand of the throne of God. For consider him who has endured such contradiction of sinners against himself, that you don't grow weary, fainting in your souls.

II Ki. 6:1-7 The sons of the prophets said to Elisha, "See now, the place where we dwell before you is too small for us. Please let us go to the Jordan, and every man take a beam from there, and let us make us a place there, where we may dwell." He answered, "Go!" One said, "Please be pleased to go with your servants." He answered, "I will go." So he went with them. When they came to the Jordan, they cut down wood. But as one was felling a beam, the axe head fell into the water. Then he cried, and said, "Alas, my master! For it was borrowed." The man of God asked, "Where did it fall?" He showed him the place. He cut down a stick, threw it in there, and made the iron float. He said, "Take it." So he put out his hand and took it.

Week 3 Day 4   13-Feb

John 11:38-44 Jesus therefore, again groaning in himself, came to the tomb. Now it was a cave, and a stone lay against it. Jesus said, "Take away the stone." Martha, the sister of him who was dead, said to him, "Lord, by this time there is a stench, for he has been dead four days." Jesus said to her, "Didn't I tell you that if you believed, you would see God's glory?" So they took away the stone from the place where the dead man was lying. Jesus lifted up his eyes, and said, "Father, I thank you that you listened to me. I know that you always listen to me, but because of the multitude that stands around I said this, that they may believe that you sent me." When he had said this, he cried with a loud voice, "Lazarus, come out!" He who was dead came out, bound hand and foot with wrappings, and his face was wrapped around with a cloth. Jesus said to them, "Free him, and let him go."

Acts 20:7-12 On the first day of the week, when the disciples were gathered together to break bread, Paul talked with them, intending to depart on the next day, and continued his speech until midnight. There were many lights in the upper room where we were gathered together. A certain young man named Eutychus sat in the window, weighed down with deep sleep. As Paul spoke still longer, being weighed down by his sleep, he fell down from the third story, and was taken up dead. Paul went down, and fell upon him, and embracing him said, "Don't be troubled, for his life is in him." When he had gone up, and had broken bread, and eaten, and had talked with them a long while, even until break of day, he departed. They brought the boy in alive, and were greatly comforted.

I Ki. 17:17-24 It happened after these things, that the son of the woman, the mistress of the house, fell sick; and his sickness was so severe, that there was no breath left in him. She said to Elijah, "What have I to do with you, you man of God? You have come to me to bring my sin to memory, and to kill my son!" He said to her, "Give me your son." He took him out of her bosom, and carried him up into the room where he stayed, and laid him on his own bed. He cried to Yahweh, and said, "Yahweh my God, have you also brought evil on the widow with whom I stay, by killing her son?" He stretched himself on the child three times, and cried to Yahweh, and said, "Yahweh my God, please let this child's soul come into him again." Yahweh listened to the voice of Elijah; and the soul of the child came into him again, and he revived. Elijah took the child, and brought him down out of the room into the house, and delivered him to his mother; and Elijah said, "Behold, your son lives." The woman said to Elijah, "Now I know that you are a man of God, and that the word of Yahweh in your mouth is truth."

Week 3 Day 5   21-Apr

John 14:5-11 Thomas said to him, "Lord, we don't know where you are going. How can we know the way?" Jesus said to him, "I am the way, the truth, and the life. No one comes to the Father, except through me. If you had known me, you would have known my Father also. From now on, you know him, and have seen him." Philip said to him, "Lord, show us the Father, and that will be enough for us." Jesus said to him, "Have I been with you such a long time, and do you not know me, Philip? He who has seen me has seen the Father. How do you say, 'Show us the Father?' Don't you believe that I am in the Father, and the Father in me? The words that I tell you, I speak not from myself; but the Father who lives in me does his works. Believe me that I am in the Father, and the Father in me; or else believe me for the very works' sake."

Acts 5:12-16 By the hands of the apostles many signs and wonders were done among the people. They were all with one accord in Solomon's porch. None of the rest dared to join them, however the people honored them. More believers were added to the Lord, multitudes of both men and women. They even carried out the sick into the streets, and laid them on cots and mattresses, so that as Peter came by, at the least his shadow might overshadow some of them. Multitudes also came together from the cities around Jerusalem, bringing sick people, and those who were tormented by unclean spirits: and they were all healed.

Ex. 3:1-15 Now Moses was keeping the flock of Jethro, his father-in-law, the priest of Midian, and he led the flock to the back of the wilderness, and came to God's mountain, to Horeb. The angel of Yahweh appeared to him in a flame of fire out of the midst of a bush. He looked, and behold, the bush burned with fire, and the bush was not consumed. Moses said, "I will turn aside now, and see this great sight, why the bush is not burnt." When Yahweh saw that he turned aside to see, God called to him out of the midst of the bush, and said, "Moses! Moses!" He said, "Here I am." He said, "Don't come close. Take your sandals off of your feet, for the place you are standing on is holy ground." Moreover he said, "I am the God of your father, the God of Abraham, the God of Isaac, and the God of Jacob." Moses hid his face; for he was afraid to look at God. Yahweh said, "I have surely seen the affliction of my people who are in Egypt, and have heard their cry because of their taskmasters, for I know their sorrows. I have come down to deliver them out of the hand of the Egyptians, and to bring them up out of that land to a good and large land, to a land flowing with milk and honey; to the place of the Canaanite, the Hittite, the Amorite, the Perizzite, the Hivite, and the Jebusite. Now, behold, the cry of the children of Israel has come to me. Moreover I have seen the oppression with which the Egyptians oppress them. Come now therefore, and I will send you to Pharaoh, that you may bring my people, the children of Israel, out of Egypt." Moses said to God, "Who am I, that I should go to Pharaoh, and that I should bring the children of Israel out of Egypt?" He said, "Certainly I will be with you. This will be the token to you, that I have sent you: when you have brought the people out of Egypt, you shall serve God on this mountain." Moses said to God, "Behold, when I come to the children of Israel, and tell them, 'The God of your fathers has sent me to you;' and they ask me, 'What is his name?' What should I tell them?" God said to Moses, "I AM WHO I AM," and he said, "You shall tell the children of Israel this: 'I AM has sent me to you.'" God said moreover to Moses, "You shall tell the children of Israel this, 'Yahweh, the God of your fathers, the God of Abraham, the God of Isaac, and the God of Jacob, has sent me to you.' This is my name forever, and this is my memorial to all generations."

John 20:24-31 But Thomas, one of the twelve, called Didymus, wasn't with them when Jesus came. The other disciples therefore said to him, "We have seen the Lord!" But he said to them, "Unless I see in his hands the print of the nails, and put my hand into his side, I will not believe." After eight days again his disciples were inside, and Thomas was with them. Jesus came, the doors being locked, and stood in the midst, and said, "Peace be to you." Then he said to Thomas, "Reach here your finger, and see my hands. Reach here your hand, and put it into my side. Don't be unbelieving, but believing." Thomas answered him, "My Lord and my God!" Jesus said to him, "Because you have seen me, you have believed. Blessed are those who have not seen, and have believed." Therefore Jesus did many other signs in the presence of his disciples, which are not written in this book; but these are written, that you may believe that Jesus is the Christ, the Son of God, and that believing you may have life in his name.

I Cor. 15:1-8 Now I declare to you, brothers, the Good News which I preached to you, which also you received, in which you also stand, by which also you are saved, if you hold firmly the word which I preached to you—unless you believed in vain. For I delivered to you first of all that which I also received: that Christ died for our sins according to the Scriptures, that he was buried, that he was raised on the third day according to the Scriptures, and that he appeared to Cephas, then to the twelve. Then he appeared to over five hundred brothers at once, most of whom remain until now, but some have also fallen asleep. Then he appeared to James, then to all the apostles, and last of all, as to the child born at the wrong time, he appeared to me also.

Jud. 6:13-22 Gideon said to him, "Oh, my lord, if Yahweh is with us, why then has all this happened to us? Where are all his wondrous works which our fathers told us of, saying, 'Didn't Yahweh bring us up from Egypt?' But now Yahweh has cast us off, and delivered us into the hand of Midian." Yahweh looked at him, and said, "Go in this your might, and save Israel from the hand of Midian. Haven't I sent you?" He said to him, "O Lord, how shall I save Israel? Behold, my family is the poorest in Manasseh, and I am the least in my father's house." Yahweh said to him, "Surely I will be with you, and you shall strike the Midianites as one man." He said to him, "If now I have found favor in your sight, then show me a sign that it is you who talk with me. Please don't go away, until I come to you, and bring out my present, and lay it before you." He said, "I will wait until you come back." Gideon went in, and prepared a young goat, and unleavened cakes of an ephah of meal. He put the meat in a basket and he put the broth in a pot, and brought it out to him under the oak, and presented it. The angel of God said to him, "Take the meat and the unleavened cakes, and lay them on this rock, and pour out the broth." He did so. Then the angel of Yahweh stretched out the end of the staff that was in his hand, and touched the meat and the unleavened cakes; and fire went up out of the rock, and consumed the meat and the unleavened cakes; and the angel of Yahweh departed out of his sight. Gideon saw that he was the angel of Yahweh; and Gideon said, "Alas, Lord Yahweh! Because I have seen the angel of Yahweh face to face!"

Week 3 Day 7   29-Aug

Acts 9:32-42 It happened, as Peter went throughout all those parts, he came down also to the saints who lived at Lydda. There he found a certain man named Aeneas, who had been bedridden for eight years, because he was paralyzed. Peter said to him, "Aeneas, Jesus Christ heals you. Get up and make your bed!" Immediately he arose. All who lived at Lydda and in Sharon saw him, and they turned to the Lord. Now there was at Joppa a certain disciple named Tabitha, which when translated, means Dorcas. This woman was full of good works and acts of mercy which she did. It happened in those days that she fell sick, and died. When they had washed her, they laid her in an upper room. As Lydda was near Joppa, the disciples, hearing that Peter was there, sent two men to him, imploring him not to delay in coming to them. Peter got up and went with them. When he had come, they brought him into the upper room. All the widows stood by him weeping, and showing the coats and garments which Dorcas had made while she was with them. Peter put them all out, and kneeled down and prayed. Turning to the body, he said, "Tabitha, get up!" She opened her eyes, and when she saw Peter, she sat up. He gave her his hand, and raised her up. Calling the saints and widows, he presented her alive. And it became known throughout all Joppa, and many believed in the Lord.

Ex. 14:10-31 When Pharaoh drew near, the children of Israel lifted up their eyes, and behold, the Egyptians were marching after them; and they were very afraid. The children of Israel cried out to Yahweh. They said to Moses, "Because there were no graves in Egypt, have you taken us away to die in the wilderness? Why have you treated us this way, to bring us out of Egypt? Isn't this the word that we spoke to you in Egypt, saying, 'Leave us alone, that we may serve the Egyptians?' For it were better for us to serve the Egyptians, than that we should die in the wilderness." Moses said to the people, "Don't be afraid. Stand still, and see the salvation of Yahweh, which he will work for you today: for the Egyptians whom you have seen today, you shall never see them again. Yahweh will fight for you, and you shall be still." Yahweh said to Moses, "Why do you cry to me? Speak to the children of Israel, that they go forward. Lift up your rod, and stretch out your hand over the sea, and divide it: and the children of Israel shall go into the midst of the sea on dry ground. I, behold, I will harden the hearts of the Egyptians, and they shall go in after them: and I will get myself honor over Pharaoh, and over all his armies, over his chariots, and over his horsemen. The Egyptians shall know that I am Yahweh, when I have gotten myself honor over Pharaoh, over his chariots, and over his horsemen." The angel of God, who went before the camp of Israel, moved and went behind them; and the pillar of cloud moved from before them, and stood behind them. It came between the camp of Egypt and the camp of Israel; and there was the cloud and the darkness, yet gave it light by night: and the one didn't come near the other all the night. Moses stretched out his hand over the sea, and Yahweh caused the sea to go back by a strong east wind all the night, and made the sea dry land, and the waters were divided. The children of Israel went into the midst of the sea on the dry ground, and the waters were a wall to them on their right hand, and on their left. The Egyptians pursued, and went in after them into the midst of the sea: all of Pharaoh's horses, his chariots, and his horsemen. It happened in the morning watch, that Yahweh looked out on the Egyptian army through the pillar of fire and of cloud, and confused the Egyptian army. He took off their chariot wheels, and they drove them heavily; so that the Egyptians said, "Let's flee from the face of Israel, for Yahweh fights for them against the Egyptians!" Yahweh said to Moses, "Stretch out your hand over the sea, that the waters may come again on the Egyptians, on their chariots, and on their horsemen." Moses stretched out his hand over the sea, and the sea returned to its strength when the morning appeared; and the Egyptians fled against it. Yahweh overthrew the Egyptians in the midst of the sea. The waters returned, and covered the chariots and the horsemen, even all Pharaoh's army that went in after them into the sea. There remained not so much as one of them. But the children of Israel walked on dry land in the midst of the sea, and the waters were a wall to them on their right hand, and on their left. Thus Yahweh saved Israel that day out of the hand of the Egyptians; and Israel saw the Egyptians dead on the seashore. Israel saw the great work which Yahweh did to the Egyptians, and the people feared Yahweh; and they believed in Yahweh, and in his servant Moses.

Week 4 Day 1   **31-May**

John 18:33-37 Pilate therefore entered again into the Praetorium, called Jesus, and said to him, "Are you the King of the Jews?" Jesus answered him, "Do you say this by yourself, or did others tell you about me?" Pilate answered, "I'm not a Jew, am I? Your own nation and the chief priests delivered you to me. What have you done?" Jesus answered, "My Kingdom is not of this world. If my Kingdom were of this world, then my servants would fight, that I wouldn't be delivered to the Jews. But now my Kingdom is not from here." Pilate therefore said to him, "Are you a king then?" Jesus answered, "You say that I am a king. For this reason I have been born, and for this reason I have come into the world, that I should testify to the truth. Everyone who is of the truth listens to my voice."

John 19:11 Jesus answered, "You would have no power at all against me, unless it were given to you from above. Therefore he who delivered me to you has greater sin."

Acts 12:1-11 Now about that time, King Herod stretched out his hands to oppress some of the assembly. He killed James, the brother of John, with the sword. When he saw that it pleased the Jews, he proceeded to seize Peter also. This was during the days of unleavened bread. When he had arrested him, he put him in prison, and delivered him to four squads of four soldiers each to guard him, intending to bring him out to the people after the Passover. Peter therefore was kept in the prison, but constant prayer was made by the assembly to God for him. The same night when Herod was about to bring him out, Peter was sleeping between two soldiers, bound with two chains. Guards in front of the door kept the prison. And behold, an angel of the Lord stood by him, and a light shone in the cell. He struck Peter on the side, and woke him up, saying, "Stand up quickly!" His chains fell off from his hands. The angel said to him, "Get dressed and put on your sandals." He did so. He said to him, "Put on your cloak, and follow me." And he went out and followed him. He didn't know that what was being done by the angel was real, but thought he saw a vision. When they were past the first and the second guard, they came to the iron gate that leads into the city, which opened to them by itself. They went out, and went down one street, and immediately the angel departed from him. When Peter had come to himself, he said, "Now I truly know that the Lord has sent out his angel and delivered me out of the hand of Herod, and from everything the Jewish people were expecting."

Dan. 3:13-18 Then Nebuchadnezzar in *his* rage and fury commanded to bring Shadrach, Meshach, and Abednego. Then they brought these men before the king. Nebuchadnezzar answered them, Is it on purpose, Shadrach, Meshach, and Abednego, that you don't serve my god, nor worship the golden image which I have set up? Now if you are ready whenever you hear the sound of the horn, flute, zither, lyre, harp, pipe, and all kinds of music to fall down and worship the image which I have made, *well*: but if you don't worship, you shall be cast the same hour into the midst of a burning fiery furnace; and who is that god that shall deliver you out of my hands? Shadrach, Meshach, and Abednego answered the king, Nebuchadnezzar, we have no need to answer you in this matter. If it be *so*, our God whom we serve is able to deliver us from the burning fiery furnace; and he will deliver us out of your hand, O king. But if not, be it known to you, O king, that we will not serve your gods, nor worship the golden image which you have set up.

Week 4 Day 2   16-Jan

John 10:1-10 "Most certainly, I tell you, one who doesn't enter by the door into the sheep fold, but climbs up some other way, the same is a thief and a robber. But one who enters in by the door is the shepherd of the sheep. The gatekeeper opens the gate for him, and the sheep listen to his voice. He calls his own sheep by name, and leads them out. Whenever he brings out his own sheep, he goes before them, and the sheep follow him, for they know his voice. They will by no means follow a stranger, but will flee from him; for they don't know the voice of strangers." Jesus spoke this parable to them, but they didn't understand what he was telling them. Jesus therefore said to them again, "Most certainly, I tell you, I am the sheep's door. All who came before me are thieves and robbers, but the sheep didn't listen to them. I am the door. If anyone enters in by me, he will be saved, and will go in and go out, and will find pasture. The thief only comes to steal, kill, and destroy. I came that they may have life, and may have it abundantly."

Heb. 13:20-21 Now may the God of peace, who brought again from the dead the great shepherd of the sheep with the blood of an eternal covenant, our Lord Jesus, make you complete in every good work to do his will, working in you that which is well pleasing in his sight, through Jesus Christ, to whom be the glory forever and ever. Amen.

Ps. 23 Yahweh is my shepherd: I shall lack nothing. He makes me lie down in green pastures. He leads me beside still waters. He restores my soul. He guides me in the paths of righteousness for his name's sake. Even though I walk through the valley of the shadow of death, I will fear no evil, for you are with me. Your rod and your staff, they comfort me. You prepare a table before me in the presence of my enemies. You anoint my head with oil. My cup runs over. Surely goodness and loving kindness shall follow me all the days of my life, and I will dwell in Yahweh's house forever.

Week 4 Day 3   11-Nov

John 10:11-18 "I am the good shepherd. The good shepherd lays down his life for the sheep. He who is a hired hand, and not a shepherd, who doesn't own the sheep, sees the wolf coming, leaves the sheep, and flees. The wolf snatches the sheep, and scatters them. The hired hand flees because he is a hired hand, and doesn't care for the sheep. I am the good shepherd. I know my own, and I'm known by my own; even as the Father knows me, and I know the Father. I lay down my life for the sheep. I have other sheep, which are not of this fold. I must bring them also, and they will hear my voice. They will become one flock with one shepherd. Therefore the Father loves me, because I lay down my life, that I may take it again. No one takes it away from me, but I lay it down by myself. I have power to lay it down, and I have power to take it again. I received this commandment from my Father."

I Jo. 5:6-12 This is he who came by water and blood, Jesus Christ; not with the water only, but with the water and the blood. It is the Spirit who testifies, because the Spirit is the truth. For there are three who testify the Spirit, the water, and the blood; and the three agree as one. If we receive the witness of men, the witness of God is greater; for this is God's testimony which he has testified concerning his Son. He who believes in the Son of God has the testimony in himself. He who doesn't believe God has made him a liar, because he has not believed in the testimony that God has given concerning his Son. The testimony is this, that God gave to us eternal life, and this life is in his Son. He who has the Son has the life. He who doesn't have God's Son doesn't have the life.

Job 19:23-27 "Oh that my words were now written! Oh that they were inscribed in a book! That with an iron pen and lead they were engraved in the rock forever! But as for me, I know that my Redeemer lives. In the end, he will stand upon the earth. After my skin is destroyed, then in my flesh shall I see God, Whom I, even I, shall see on my side. My eyes shall see, and not as a stranger. My heart is consumed within me."

Week 4 Day 4   **27-Jul**

John 7:16-18 Jesus therefore answered them, "My teaching is not mine, but his who sent me. If anyone desires to do his will, he will know about the teaching, whether it is from God, or if I am speaking from myself. He who speaks from himself seeks his own glory, but he who seeks the glory of him who sent him is true, and no unrighteousness is in him."

John 7:37-39 Now on the last and greatest day of the feast, Jesus stood and cried out, "If anyone is thirsty, let him come to me and drink! He who believes in me, as the Scripture has said, from within him will flow rivers of living water." But he said this about the Spirit, which those believing in him were to receive. For the Holy Spirit was not yet given, because Jesus wasn't yet glorified.

II Jo. 7-11 For many deceivers have gone out into the world, those who don't confess that Jesus Christ came in the flesh. This is the deceiver and the Antichrist. Watch yourselves, that we don't lose the things which we have accomplished, but that we receive a full reward. Whoever transgresses and doesn't remain in the teaching of Christ, doesn't have God. He who remains in the teaching, the same has both the Father and the Son. If anyone comes to you, and doesn't bring this teaching, don't receive him into your house, and don't welcome him, for he who welcomes him participates in his evil works.

Ez. 47:1-12 He brought me back to the door of the house; and behold, waters issued out from under the threshold of the house eastward; (for the forefront of the house was toward the east;) and the waters came down from under, from the right side of the house, on the south of the altar. Then he brought me out by the way of the gate northward, and led me round by the way outside to the outer gate, by the way of *the gate* that looks toward the east; and behold, there ran out waters on the right side. When the man went forth eastward with the line in his hand, he measured one thousand cubits, and he caused me to pass through the waters, waters that were to the ankles. Again he measured one thousand, and caused me to pass through the waters, waters that were to the knees. Again he measured one thousand, and caused me to pass through *the waters*, waters that were to the waist. Afterward he measured one thousand; *and it was* a river that I could not pass through; for the waters were risen, waters to swim in, a river that could not be passed through. He said to me, Son of man, have you seen *this*? Then he brought me, and caused me to return to the bank of the river. Now when I had returned, behold, on the bank of the river were very many trees on the one side and on the other. Then he said to me, These waters issue forth toward the eastern region, and shall go down into the Arabah; and they shall go toward the sea; into the sea *shall the waters go* which were made to issue forth; and the waters shall be healed. It shall happen, that every living creature which swarms, in every place where the rivers come, shall live; and there shall be a very great multitude of fish; for these waters have come there, and *the waters of the sea* shall be healed, and everything shall live wherever the river comes. It shall happen, that fishermen shall stand by it: from En Gedi even to En Eglaim shall be a place for the spreading of nets;

their fish shall be after their kinds, as the fish of the great sea, exceeding many. But the miry places of it, and its marshes, shall not be healed; they shall be given up to salt. By the river on its bank, on this side and on that side, shall grow every tree for food, whose leaf shall not wither, neither shall its fruit fail: it shall bring forth new fruit every month, because its waters issue out of the sanctuary; and its fruit shall be for food, and its leaf for healing.

Week 4 Day 5 17-Nov

John 8:31-36 Jesus therefore said to those Jews who had believed him, "If you remain in my word, then you are truly my disciples. You will know the truth, and the truth will make you free." They answered him, "We are Abraham's seed, and have never been in bondage to anyone. How do you say, 'You will be made free?'?" Jesus answered them, "Most certainly I tell you, everyone who commits sin is the bondservant of sin. A bondservant doesn't live in the house forever. A son remains forever. If therefore the Son makes you free, you will be free indeed."

John 8:47 "He who is of God hears the words of God. For this cause you don't hear, because you are not of God."

John 8:50-51 "But I don't seek my own glory. There is one who seeks and judges. Most certainly, I tell you, if a person keeps my word, he will never see death."

Rom. 6:15-23 What then? Shall we sin, because we are not under law, but under grace? May it never be! Don't you know that to whom you present yourselves as servants to obedience, his servants you are whom you obey; whether of sin to death, or of obedience to righteousness? But thanks be to God, that, whereas you were bondservants of sin, you became obedient from the heart to that form of teaching to which you were delivered. Being made free from sin, you became bondservants of righteousness. I speak in human terms because of the weakness of your flesh, for as you presented your members as servants to uncleanness and to wickedness upon wickedness, even so now present your members as servants to righteousness for sanctification. For when you were servants of sin, you were free in regard to righteousness. What fruit then did you have at that time in the things of which you are now ashamed? For the end of those things is death. But now, being made free from sin, and having become servants of God, you have your fruit of sanctification, and the result of eternal life. For the wages of sin is death, but the free gift of God is eternal life in Christ Jesus our Lord.

Ge. 21:1-10 Yahweh visited Sarah as he had said, and Yahweh did to Sarah as he had spoken. Sarah conceived, and bore Abraham a son in his old age, at the set time of which God had spoken to him. Abraham called his son who was born to him, whom Sarah bore to him, Isaac. Abraham circumcised his son, Isaac, when he was eight days old, as God had commanded him. Abraham was one hundred years old when his son, Isaac, was born to him. Sarah said, "God has made me laugh. Everyone who hears will laugh with me." She said, "Who would have said to Abraham, that Sarah would nurse children? For I have borne him a son in his old age." The child grew, and was weaned. Abraham made a great feast on the day that Isaac was weaned. Sarah saw the son of Hagar the Egyptian, whom she had borne to Abraham, mocking. Therefore she said to Abraham, "Cast out this handmaid and her son! For the son of this handmaid will not be heir with my son, Isaac."

Week 4 Day 6 6-Apr

Luke 13:1-9 Now there were some present at the same time who told him about the Galileans, whose blood Pilate had mixed with their sacrifices. Jesus answered them, "Do you think that these Galileans were worse sinners than all the other Galileans, because they suffered such things? I tell you, no, but unless you repent, you will all perish in the same way. Or those eighteen, on whom the tower in Siloam fell, and killed them; do you think that they were worse offenders than all the men who dwell in Jerusalem? I tell you, no, but, unless you repent, you will all perish in the same way." He spoke this parable. "A certain man had a fig tree planted in his vineyard, and he came seeking fruit on it, and found none. He said to the vine dresser, 'Behold, these three years I have come looking for fruit on this fig tree, and found none. Cut it down. Why does it waste the soil?' He answered, 'Lord, leave it alone this year also, until I dig around it, and fertilize it. If it bears fruit, fine; but if not, after that, you can cut it down.'"

Acts 2:38-41 Peter said to them, "Repent, and be baptized, every one of you, in the name of Jesus Christ for the forgiveness of sins, and you will receive the gift of the Holy Spirit. For the promise is to you, and to your children, and to all who are far off, even as many as the Lord our God will call to himself." With many other words he testified, and exhorted them, saying, "Save yourselves from this crooked generation!" Then those who gladly received his word were baptized. There were added that day about three thousand souls.

Is. 5:1-7 Let me sing for my well beloved a song of my beloved about his vineyard. My beloved had a vineyard on a very fruitful hill. He dug it up, gathered out its stones, planted it with the choicest vine, built a tower in its midst, and also cut out a winepress therein. He looked for it to yield grapes, but it yielded wild grapes. "Now, inhabitants of Jerusalem and men of Judah, please judge between me and my vineyard. What could have been done more to my vineyard, that I have not done in it? Why, when I looked for it to yield grapes, did it yield wild grapes? Now I will tell you what I will do to my vineyard. I will take away its hedge, and it will be eaten up. I will break down its wall of it, and it will be trampled down. I will lay it a wasteland. It won't be pruned nor hoed, but it will grow briers and thorns. I will also command the clouds that they rain no rain on it." For the vineyard of Yahweh of Armies is the house of Israel, and the men of Judah his pleasant plant: and he looked for justice, but, behold, oppression; for righteousness, but, behold, a cry of distress.

Week 4 Day 7   18-Nov

II Cor. 6:14-7:1 Don't be unequally yoked with unbelievers, for what fellowship have righteousness and iniquity? Or what fellowship has light with darkness? What agreement has Christ with Belial? Or what portion has a believer with an unbeliever? What agreement has a temple of God with idols? For you are a temple of the living God. Even as God said, "I will dwell in them, and walk in them; and I will be their God, and they will be my people." Therefore "'Come out from among them, and be separate,' says the Lord. 'Touch no unclean thing. I will receive you. I will be to you a Father. You will be to me sons and daughters,' says the Lord Almighty." Having therefore these promises, beloved, let us cleanse ourselves from all defilement of flesh and spirit, perfecting holiness in the fear of God.

Is. 52:1-12 Awake, awake, put on your strength, Zion; put on your beautiful garments, Jerusalem, the holy city: for henceforth there shall no more come into you the uncircumcised and the unclean. Shake yourself from the dust! Arise, sit up, Jerusalem! Release yourself from the bonds of your neck, captive daughter of Zion! For thus says Yahweh, "You were sold for nothing; and you shall be redeemed without money." For thus says the Lord Yahweh, "My people went down at the first into Egypt to live there: and the Assyrian has oppressed them without cause. "Now therefore, what do I do here," says Yahweh, "seeing that my people are taken away for nothing? Those who rule over them mock," says Yahweh, "and my name continually all the day is blasphemed. Therefore my people shall know my name. Therefore they shall know in that day that I am he who speaks; behold, it is I." How beautiful on the mountains are the feet of him who brings good news, who publishes peace, who brings good news of good, who publishes salvation, who says to Zion, "Your God reigns!" The voice of your watchmen! they lift up the voice, together do they sing; for they shall see eye to eye, when Yahweh returns to Zion. Break forth into joy, sing together, you waste places of Jerusalem; for Yahweh has comforted his people, he has redeemed Jerusalem. Yahweh has made bare his holy arm in the eyes of all the nations; and all the ends of the earth have seen the salvation of our God. Depart, depart, go out from there, touch no unclean thing! Go out of the midst of her! Cleanse yourselves, you who bear the vessels of Yahweh. For you shall not go out in haste, neither shall you go by flight: for Yahweh will go before you; and the God of Israel will be your rear guard.

Week 5 Day 1   21-Jul

Matt. 5:1-12 Seeing the multitudes, he went up onto the mountain. When he had sat down, his disciples came to him. He opened his mouth and taught them, saying, "Blessed are the poor in spirit, for theirs is the Kingdom of

Heaven. Blessed are those who mourn, for they shall be comforted. Blessed are the gentle, for they shall inherit the earth. Blessed are those who hunger and thirst after righteousness, for they shall be filled. Blessed are the merciful, for they shall obtain mercy. Blessed are the pure in heart, for they shall see God. Blessed are the peacemakers, for they shall be called children of God. Blessed are those who have been persecuted for righteousness' sake, for theirs is the Kingdom of Heaven. Blessed are you when people reproach you, persecute you, and say all kinds of evil against you falsely, for my sake. Rejoice, and be exceedingly glad, for great is your reward in heaven. For that is how they persecuted the prophets who were before you."

Php. 4:8-9 Finally, brothers, whatever things are true, whatever things are honorable, whatever things are just, whatever things are pure, whatever things are lovely, whatever things are of good report; if there is any virtue, and if there is any praise, think about these things. The things which you learned, received, heard, and saw in me: do these things, and the God of peace will be with you.

Ec. 3:1-15 For everything there is a season, and a time for every purpose under heaven: a time to be born, and a time to die; a time to plant, and a time to pluck up that which is planted; a time to kill, and a time to heal; a time to break down, and a time to build up; a time to weep, and a time to laugh; a time to mourn, and a time to dance; a time to cast away stones, and a time to gather stones together; a time to embrace, and a time to refrain from embracing; a time to seek, and a time to lose; a time to keep, and a time to cast away; a time to tear, and a time to sew; a time to keep silence, and a time to speak; a time to love, and a time to hate; a time for war, and a time for peace. What profit has he who works in that in which he labors? I have seen the burden which God has given to the sons of men to be afflicted with. He has made everything beautiful in its time. He has also set eternity in their hearts, yet so that man can't find out the work that God has done from the beginning even to the end. I know that there is nothing better for them than to rejoice, and to do good as long as they live. Also that every man should eat and drink, and enjoy good in all his labor, is the gift of God. I know that whatever God does, it shall be forever. Nothing can be added to it, nor anything taken from it; and God has done it, that men should fear before him. That which is has been long ago, and that which is to be has been long ago: and God seeks again that which is passed away.

Week 5 Day 2   3-Jan

Matt. 5:13-16 "You are the salt of the earth, but if the salt has lost its flavor, with what will it be salted? It is then good for nothing, but to be cast out and trodden under the feet of men. You are the light of the world. A city located on a hill can't be hidden. Neither do you light a lamp, and put it under a measuring basket, but on a stand; and it shines to all who are in the house. Even so, let your light shine before men; that they may see your good works, and glorify your Father who is in heaven."

Php. 2:12-18 So then, my beloved, even as you have always obeyed, not only in my presence, but now much more in my absence, work out your own salvation with fear and trembling. For it is God who works in you both to will and to work, for his good pleasure. Do all things without murmurings and disputes, that you may become blameless and harmless, children of God without blemish in the midst of a crooked and perverse generation, among whom you are seen as lights in the world, holding up the word of life; that I may have something to boast in the day of Christ, that I didn't run in vain nor labor in vain. Yes, and if I am poured out on the sacrifice and service of your faith, I rejoice, and rejoice with you all. In the same way, you also rejoice, and rejoice with me.

Is. 60:1-22 "Arise, shine; for your light has come, and the glory of Yahweh is risen on you. For, behold, darkness shall cover the earth, and gross darkness the peoples; but Yahweh will arise on you, and his glory shall be seen on you. Nations shall come to your light, and kings to the brightness of your rising. Lift up your eyes all around, and see: they all gather themselves together, they come to you; your sons shall come from far, and your daughters shall be carried in the arms. Then you shall see and be radiant, and your heart shall thrill and be enlarged; because the abundance of the sea shall be turned to you, the wealth of the nations shall come to you. The multitude of camels shall cover you, the dromedaries of Midian and Ephah; all they from Sheba shall come; they shall bring gold and frankincense, and shall proclaim the praises of Yahweh. All the flocks of Kedar shall be gathered together to you, the rams of Nebaioth shall minister to you; they shall come up with acceptance on my altar; and I will glorify the house of my glory. Who are these who fly as a cloud, and as the doves to their windows? Surely the islands shall wait for me, and the ships of Tarshish first, to bring your sons from far, their silver and their gold with them, for the name of Yahweh your God, and for the Holy One of Israel, because he has glorified you. Foreigners shall build up your walls, and their kings shall minister to you: for in my wrath I struck you, but in my favor have I had mercy on you. Your gates also shall be open continually; they shall not be shut day nor night; that men may bring to you the wealth of the nations, and their kings led captive. For that nation and kingdom that will not serve you shall perish; yes, those nations shall be utterly wasted. The glory of Lebanon shall come to you, the fir tree, the pine, and the box tree together, to beautify the place of my sanctuary; and I will make the place of my feet glorious. The sons of those who afflicted you shall come bending to you; and all those who despised you shall bow themselves down at the soles of your feet; and they shall call you The city of Yahweh, The Zion of the Holy One of Israel. Whereas you have been forsaken and hated, so that no man passed through you, I will make you an eternal excellency, a joy of many generations. You shall also drink the milk of the nations, and shall nurse from royal breasts; and you shall know that I, Yahweh, am your Savior, and your Redeemer, the Mighty One of Jacob. For brass I will bring gold, and for iron I will bring silver, and for wood brass, and for stones iron. I will also make your officers peace, and righteousness your ruler. Violence shall no more be heard in your land, desolation nor destruction within your borders; but you shall call your walls Salvation, and your gates Praise. The sun shall be no more your light by day; neither for brightness shall the moon give light to you: but Yahweh will be to you an everlasting light, and your God your glory. Your sun shall no more go down, neither shall your moon withdraw itself; for Yahweh will be your everlasting light, and the days of your mourning shall be ended. Your people also shall be all righteous; they shall inherit the land forever, the branch of my planting, the work of my hands, that I may be glorified. The little one shall become a thousand, and the small one a strong nation; I, Yahweh, will hasten it in its time."

Week 5 Day 3   27-Aug

John 12:35-36 Jesus therefore said to them, "Yet a little while the light is with you. Walk while you have the light, that darkness doesn't overtake you. He who walks in the darkness doesn't know where he is going. While you have the light, believe in the light, that you may become children of light." Jesus said these things, and he departed and hid himself from them.

John 12:44-50 Jesus cried out and said, "Whoever believes in me, believes not in me, but in him who sent me. He who sees me sees him who sent me. I have come as a light into the world, that whoever believes in me may not remain in the darkness. If anyone listens to my sayings, and doesn't believe, I don't judge him. For I came not to judge the world, but to save the world. He who rejects me, and doesn't receive my sayings, has one who judges him. The word that I spoke, the same will judge him in the last day. For I spoke not from myself, but the Father who sent me, he gave me a commandment, what I should say, and what I should speak. I know that his commandment is eternal life. The things therefore which I speak, even as the Father has said to me, so I speak."

I Thes. 5:4-11 But you, brothers, aren't in darkness, that the day should overtake you like a thief. You are all children of light, and children of the day. We don't belong to the night, nor to darkness, so then let's not sleep, as the rest do, but let's watch and be sober. For those who sleep, sleep in the night, and those who are drunk are drunk in the night. But let us, since we belong to the day, be sober, putting on the breastplate of faith and love, and, for a helmet, the hope of salvation. For God didn't appoint us to wrath, but to the obtaining of salvation through our Lord Jesus Christ, who died for us, that, whether we wake or sleep, we should live together with him. Therefore exhort one another, and build each other up, even as you also do.

Is. 9:1-7 But there shall be no more gloom for her who was in anguish. In the former time, he brought into contempt the land of Zebulun and the land of Naphtali; but in the latter time he has made it glorious, by the way of the sea, beyond the Jordan, Galilee of the nations. The people who walked in darkness have seen a great light. Those who lived in the land of the shadow of death, on them the light has shined. You have multiplied the nation. You have increased their joy. They rejoice before you according to the joy in harvest, as men rejoice when they divide the spoil. For the yoke of his burden, and the staff of his shoulder, the rod of his oppressor, you have broken as in the day of Midian. For all the armor of the armed man in the noisy battle, and the garments rolled in blood, will be for burning, fuel for the fire. For to us a child is born. To us a son is given; and the government will be on his shoulders. His name will be called Wonderful, Counselor, Mighty God, Everlasting Father, Prince of Peace. Of the increase of his government and of peace there shall be no end, on the throne of David, and on his kingdom, to establish it, and to uphold it with justice and with righteousness from that time on, even forever. The zeal of Yahweh of Armies will perform this.

Week 5 Day 4   **15-Mar**

John 8:12 Again, therefore, Jesus spoke to them, saying, "I am the light of the world He who follows me will not walk in the darkness, but will have the light of life."

John 11:9-10 Jesus answered, "Aren't there twelve hours of daylight? If a man walks in the day, he doesn't stumble, because he sees the light of this world. But if a man walks in the night, he stumbles, because the light isn't in him."

Jas. 1:2-8 Count it all joy, my brothers, when you fall into various temptations, knowing that the testing of your faith produces endurance. Let endurance have its perfect work, that you may be perfect and complete, lacking in nothing. But if any of you lacks wisdom, let him ask of God, who gives to all liberally and without reproach; and it will be given to him. But let him ask in faith, without any doubting, for he who doubts is like a wave of the sea, driven by the wind and tossed. For let that man not think that he will receive anything from the Lord. He is a double-minded man, unstable in all his ways.

Jas. 1:16-18 Don't be deceived, my beloved brothers. Every good gift and every perfect gift is from above, coming down from the Father of lights, with whom can be no variation, nor turning shadow. Of his own will he brought us forth by the word of truth, that we should be a kind of first fruits of his creatures.

Ps. 27 Yahweh is my light and my salvation. Whom shall I fear? Yahweh is the strength of my life. Of whom shall I be afraid? When evildoers came at me to eat up my flesh, even my adversaries and my foes, they stumbled and fell. Though an army should encamp against me, my heart shall not fear. Though war should rise against me, even then I will be confident. One thing I have asked of Yahweh, that I will seek after, that I may dwell in the house of Yahweh all the days of my life, to see Yahweh's beauty, and to inquire in his temple. For in the day of trouble he will keep me secretly in his pavilion. In the covert of his tabernacle he will hide me. He will lift me up on a rock. Now my head will be lifted up above my enemies around me. I will offer sacrifices of joy in his tent. I will sing, yes, I will sing praises to Yahweh. Hear, Yahweh, when I cry with my voice. Have mercy also on me, and answer me. When you said, "Seek my face," my heart said to you, "I will seek your face, Yahweh." Don't hide your face from me. Don't put your servant away in anger. You have been my help. Don't abandon me, neither forsake me, God of my salvation. When my father and my mother forsake me, then Yahweh will take me up. Teach me your way, Yahweh. Lead me in a straight path, because of my enemies. Don't deliver me over to the desire of my adversaries, for false witnesses have risen up against me, such as breathe out cruelty. I am still confident of this: I will see the goodness of Yahweh in the land of the living. Wait for Yahweh. Be strong, and let your heart take courage. Yes, wait for Yahweh.

Week 5 Day 5   **13-Aug**

Luke 8:16-18 "No one, when he has lit a lamp, covers it with a container, or puts it under a bed; but puts it on a stand, that those who enter in may see the light. For nothing is hidden, that will not be revealed; nor anything secret, that will not be known and come to light. Be careful therefore how you hear. For whoever has, to him will be given; and whoever doesn't have, from him will be taken away even that which he thinks he has."

Luke 11:33-36 "No one, when he has lit a lamp, puts it in a cellar or under a basket, but on a stand, that those who come in may see the light. The lamp of the body is the eye. Therefore when your eye is good, your whole body is also full of light; but when it is evil, your body also is full of darkness. Therefore see whether the light that is in you isn't darkness. If therefore your whole body is full of light, having no part dark, it will be wholly full of light, as when the lamp with its bright shining gives you light."

Jas. 1:19-27 So, then, my beloved brothers, let every man be swift to hear, slow to speak, and slow to anger; for the anger of man doesn't produce the righteousness of God. Therefore, putting away all filthiness and overflowing of wickedness, receive with humility the implanted word, which is able to save your souls. But be doers of the word, and not only hearers, deluding your own selves. For if anyone is a hearer of the word and not a doer, he is like a man looking at his natural face in a mirror; for he sees himself, and goes away, and immediately forgets what kind of man he was. But he who looks into the perfect law of freedom, and continues, not being a hearer who forgets, but a doer of the work, this man will be blessed in what he does. If anyone among you thinks himself to be religious while he doesn't bridle his tongue, but deceives his heart, this man's religion is worthless. Pure religion and undefiled before our God and Father is this: to visit the fatherless and widows in their affliction, and to keep oneself unstained by the world.

Ps. 119:105-112 Your word is a lamp to my feet, and a light for my path. I have sworn, and have confirmed it, that I will obey your righteous ordinances. I am afflicted very much. Revive me, Yahweh, according to your word. Accept, I beg you, the willing offerings of my mouth. Yahweh, teach me your ordinances. My soul is continually in my hand, yet I won't forget your law. The wicked have laid a snare for me, yet I haven't gone astray from your precepts. I have taken your testimonies as a heritage forever, for they are the joy of my heart. I have set my heart to perform your statutes forever, even to the end.

Week 5 Day 6   29-Mar

Luke 12:35-48 "Let your waist be dressed and your lamps burning. Be like men watching for their lord, when he returns from the marriage feast; that, when he comes and knocks, they may immediately open to him. Blessed are those servants, whom the lord will find watching when he comes. Most certainly I tell you, that he will dress himself, and make them recline, and will come and serve them. They will be blessed if he comes in the second or third watch, and finds them so. But know this, that if the master of the house had known in what hour the thief was coming, he would have watched, and not allowed his house to be broken into. Therefore be ready also, for the Son of Man is coming in an hour that you don't expect him." Peter said to him, "Lord, are you telling this parable to us, or to everybody?" The Lord said, "Who then is the faithful and wise steward, whom his lord will set over his household, to give them their portion of food at the right times? Blessed is that servant whom his lord will find doing so when he comes. Truly I tell you, that he will set him over all that he has. But if that servant says in his heart, 'My lord delays his coming,' and begins to beat the menservants and the maidservants, and to eat and drink, and to be drunken, then the lord of that servant will come in a day when he isn't expecting him, and in an hour that he doesn't know, and will cut him in two, and place his portion with the unfaithful. That servant, who knew his lord's will, and didn't prepare, nor do what he wanted, will be beaten with many stripes, but he who didn't know, and did things worthy of stripes, will be beaten with few stripes. To whomever much is given, of him will much be required; and to whom much was entrusted, of him more will be asked."

II Pet. 3:1-10 This is now, beloved, the second letter that I have written to you; and in both of them I stir up your sincere mind by reminding you; that you should remember the words which were spoken before by the holy prophets, and the commandments of us, the apostles of the Lord and Savior: knowing this first, that in the last days mockers will come, walking after their own lusts, and saying, "Where is the promise of his coming? For, from the day that the fathers fell asleep, all things continue as they were from the beginning of the creation." For this they willfully forget, that there were heavens from of old, and an earth formed out of water and amid water, by the word of God; by which means the world that then was, being overflowed with water, perished. But the heavens that now are, and the earth, by the same word have been stored up for fire, being reserved against the day of judgment and destruction of ungodly men. But don't forget this one thing, beloved, that one day is with the

Lord as a thousand years, and a thousand years as one day. The Lord is not slow concerning his promise, as some count slowness; but is patient with us, not wishing that any should perish, but that all should come to repentance. But the day of the Lord will come as a thief in the night; in which the heavens will pass away with a great noise, and the elements will be dissolved with fervent heat, and the earth and the works that are in it will be burned up.

Is. 1:2-20 Hear, heavens, and listen, earth; for Yahweh has spoken: "I have nourished and brought up children, and they have rebelled against me. The ox knows his owner, and the donkey his master's crib; but Israel doesn't know, my people don't consider." Ah sinful nation, a people loaded with iniquity, a seed of evildoers, children who deal corruptly! They have forsaken Yahweh. They have despised the Holy One of Israel. They are estranged and backward. Why should you be beaten more, that you revolt more and more? The whole head is sick, and the whole heart faint. From the sole of the foot even to the head there is no soundness in it: wounds, welts, and open sores. They haven't been closed, neither bandaged, neither soothed with oil. Your country is desolate. Your cities are burned with fire. Strangers devour your land in your presence, and it is desolate, as overthrown by strangers. The daughter of Zion is left like a shelter in a vineyard, like a hut in a field of melons, like a besieged city. Unless Yahweh of Armies had left to us a very small remnant, we would have been as Sodom; we would have been like Gomorrah. Hear the word of Yahweh, you rulers of Sodom! Listen to the law of our God, you people of Gomorrah! "What are the multitude of your sacrifices to me?," says Yahweh. "I have had enough of the burnt offerings of rams, and the fat of fed animals. I don't delight in the blood of bulls, or of lambs, or of male goats. When you come to appear before me, who has required this at your hand, to trample my courts? Bring no more vain offerings. Incense is an abomination to me; new moons, Sabbaths, and convocations: I can't bear with evil assemblies. My soul hates your New Moons and your appointed feasts. They are a burden to me. I am weary of bearing them. When you spread forth your hands, I will hide my eyes from you. Yes, when you make many prayers, I will not hear. Your hands are full of blood. Wash yourselves, make yourself clean. Put away the evil of your doings from before my eyes. Cease to do evil. Learn to do well. Seek justice. Relieve the oppressed. Judge the fatherless. Plead for the widow." "Come now, and let us reason together," says Yahweh: "Though your sins be as scarlet, they shall be as white as snow. Though they be red like crimson, they shall be as wool. If you are willing and obedient, you shall eat the good of the land; but if you refuse and rebel, you shall be devoured with the sword; for the mouth of Yahweh has spoken it."

Week 5 Day 7   15-Jun

Eph. 1:3-14 Blessed be the God and Father of our Lord Jesus Christ, who has blessed us with every spiritual blessing in the heavenly places in Christ; even as he chose us in him before the foundation of the world, that we would be holy and without blemish before him in love; having predestined us for adoption as children through Jesus Christ to himself, according to the good pleasure of his desire, to the praise of the glory of his grace, by which he freely bestowed favor on us in the Beloved, in whom we have our redemption through his blood, the forgiveness of our trespasses, according to the riches of his grace, which he made to abound toward us in all wisdom and prudence, making known to us the mystery of his will, according to his good pleasure which he purposed in him to an administration of the fullness of the times, to sum up all things in Christ, the things in the heavens, and the things on the earth, in him; in whom also we were assigned an inheritance, having been foreordained according to the purpose of him who works all things after the counsel of his will; to the end that we should be to the praise of his glory, we who had before hoped in Christ: in whom you also, having heard the word of the truth, the Good News of your salvation—in whom, having also believed, you were sealed with the Holy Spirit of promise, who is a pledge of our inheritance, to the redemption of God's own possession, to the praise of his glory.

Is. 62:1-12 For Zion's sake will I not hold my peace, and for Jerusalem's sake I will not rest, until her righteousness go forth as brightness, and her salvation as a lamp that burns. The nations shall see your righteousness, and all kings your glory, and you shall be called by a new name, which the mouth of Yahweh shall name. You shall also be a crown of beauty in the hand of Yahweh, and a royal diadem in the hand of your God. You shall no more be termed Forsaken; neither shall your land any more be termed Desolate: but you shall be called Hephzibah, and your land Beulah; for Yahweh delights in you, and your land shall be married. For as a young man marries a virgin, so your sons shall marry you; and as the bridegroom rejoices over the bride, so your God will rejoice over you. I have set watchmen on your walls, Jerusalem; they shall never hold their peace day nor night: you who call on Yahweh, take no rest, and give him no rest, until he establishes, and until he makes Jerusalem a praise in the earth. Yahweh has sworn by his right hand, and by the arm of his strength, "Surely I will no more give your grain to be food for your enemies; and foreigners shall not drink your new wine, for which you have labored: but those who have garnered it shall eat it, and praise Yahweh; and those who have gathered it shall drink it in the courts of my sanctuary." Go through, go through the gates! Prepare the way of the people! Cast up, cast up the highway! Gather out the stones! Lift up a banner for the peoples. Behold, Yahweh has proclaimed to the end of the earth, "Say to the daughter of Zion, 'Behold, your salvation comes. Behold, his reward is with him, and his recompense before him.'" They shall call them The holy people, The redeemed of Yahweh: and you shall be called Sought out, a city not forsaken.

Week 6 Day 1   24-Jul

Matt. 5:17-20 "Don't think that I came to destroy the law or the prophets. I didn't come to destroy, but to fulfill. For most certainly, I tell you, until heaven and earth pass away, not even one smallest letter or one tiny pen stroke shall in any way pass away from the law, until all things are accomplished. Whoever, therefore, shall break one of these least commandments, and teach others to do so, shall be called least in the Kingdom of Heaven; but whoever shall do and teach them shall be called great in the Kingdom of Heaven. For I tell you that unless your righteousness exceeds that of the scribes and Pharisees, there is no way you will enter into the Kingdom of Heaven."

I Jo. 1:5-2:6 This is the message which we have heard from him and announce to you, that God is light, and in him is no darkness at all. If we say that we have fellowship with him and walk in the darkness, we lie, and don't tell the truth. But if we walk in the light, as he is in the light, we have fellowship with one another, and the blood of Jesus Christ, his Son, cleanses us from all sin. If we say that we have no sin, we deceive ourselves, and the truth is not in us. If we confess our sins, he is faithful and righteous to forgive us the sins, and to cleanse us from all unrighteousness. If we say that we haven't sinned, we make him a liar, and his word is not in us. My little children, I write these things to you so that you may not sin. If anyone sins, we have a Counselor with the Father, Jesus Christ, the righteous. And he is the atoning sacrifice for our sins, and not for ours only, but also for the whole world. This is how we know that we know him: if we keep his commandments. One who says, "I know him," and doesn't keep his commandments, is a liar, and the truth isn't in him. But whoever keeps his word, God's love has most certainly been perfected in him. This is how we know that we are in him: he who says he remains in him ought himself also to walk just like he walked.

Ex. 20:1-21 God spoke all these words, saying, "I am Yahweh your God, who brought you out of the land of Egypt, out of the house of bondage. You shall have no other gods before me. You shall not make for yourselves an idol, nor any image of anything that is in the heavens above, or that is in the earth beneath, or that is in the water under the earth: you shall not bow yourself down to them, nor serve them, for I, Yahweh your God, am a jealous God, visiting the iniquity of the fathers on the children, on the third and on the fourth generation of those who hate me, and showing loving kindness to thousands of those who love me and keep my commandments. You shall not take the name of Yahweh your God in vain, for Yahweh will not hold him guiltless who takes his name in vain. Remember the Sabbath day, to keep it holy. You shall labor six days, and do all your work, but the seventh day is a Sabbath to Yahweh your God. You shall not do any work in it, you, nor your son, nor your daughter, your male servant, nor your female servant, nor your livestock, nor your stranger who is within your gates; for in six days Yahweh made heaven and earth, the sea, and all that is in them, and rested the seventh day; therefore Yahweh blessed the Sabbath day, and made it holy. Honor your father and your mother, that your days may be long in the land which Yahweh your God gives you. You shall not murder. You shall not commit adultery. You shall not steal. You shall not give false testimony against your neighbor. You shall not covet your neighbor's house. You shall not covet your neighbor's wife, nor his male servant, nor his female servant, nor his ox, nor his donkey, nor anything that is your neighbor's." All the people perceived the thunderings, the lightnings, the sound of the trumpet, and the mountain smoking. When the people saw it, they trembled, and stayed at a distance. They said to Moses, "Speak with us yourself, and we will listen; but don't let God speak with us, lest we die." Moses said to the people, "Don't be afraid, for God has come to test you, and that his fear may be before you, that you won't sin." The people stayed at a distance, and Moses drew near to the thick darkness where God was.

Week 6 Day 2   15-Apr

Matt. 18:5-9 "Whoever receives one such little child in my name receives me, but whoever causes one of these little ones who believe in me to stumble, it would be better for him that a huge millstone should be hung around his neck, and that he should be sunk in the depths of the sea. Woe to the world because of occasions of stumbling! For it must be that the occasions come, but woe to that person through whom the occasion comes! If your hand or your foot causes you to stumble, cut it off, and cast it from you. It is better for you to enter into life maimed or crippled, rather than having two hands or two feet to be cast into the eternal fire. If your eye causes you to stumble, pluck it out, and cast it from you. It is better for you to enter into life with one eye, rather than having two eyes to be cast into the Gehenna of fire."

II Pet. 3:11-18 Therefore since all these things will be destroyed like this, what kind of people ought you to be in holy living and godliness, looking for and earnestly desiring the coming of the day of God, which will cause the burning heavens to be dissolved, and the elements will melt with fervent heat? But, according to his promise, we look for new heavens and a new earth, in which righteousness dwells. Therefore, beloved, seeing that you look for these things, be diligent to be found in peace, without blemish and blameless in his sight. Regard the patience of our Lord as salvation; even as our beloved brother Paul also, according to the wisdom given to him, wrote to you; as also in all of his letters, speaking in them of these things. In those, there are some things that are hard to understand, which the ignorant and unsettled twist, as they also do to the other Scriptures, to their own destruction. You therefore, beloved, knowing these things beforehand, beware, lest being carried away with the error of the wicked, you fall from your own steadfastness. But grow in the grace and knowledge of our Lord and Savior Jesus Christ. To him be the glory both now and forever. Amen.

De. 11:18-28 Therefore you shall lay up these my words in your heart and in your soul; and you shall bind them for a sign on your hand, and they shall be for symbols between your eyes. You shall teach them your children, talking of them, when you sit in your house, and when you walk by the way, and when you lie down, and when you rise up. You shall write them on the door posts of your house, and on your gates; that your days may be multiplied, and the days of your children, in the land which Yahweh swore to your fathers to give them, as the days of the heavens above the earth. For if you shall diligently keep all this commandment which I command you, to do it, to love Yahweh your God, to walk in all his ways, and to cling to him; then will Yahweh drive out all these nations from before you, and you shall dispossess nations greater and mightier than yourselves. Every place whereon the sole of your foot shall tread shall be yours: from the wilderness, and Lebanon, from the river, the river Euphrates, even to the hinder sea shall be your border. No man shall be able to stand before you: Yahweh your God shall lay the fear of you and the dread of you on all the land that you shall tread on, as he has spoken to you. Behold, I set before you this day a blessing and a curse: the blessing, if you shall listen to the commandments of Yahweh your God, which I command you this day; and the curse, if you shall not listen to the commandments of Yahweh your God, but turn aside out of the way which I command you this day, to go after other gods, which you have not known.

Week 6 Day 3   7-Aug

Luke 18:15-17 They were also bringing their babies to him, that he might touch them. But when the disciples saw it, they rebuked them. Jesus summoned them, saying, "Allow the little children to come to me, and don't hinder them, for the Kingdom of God belongs to such as these. Most certainly, I tell you, whoever doesn't receive the Kingdom of God like a little child, he will in no way enter into it."

I Jo. 2:28-3:3 Now, little children, remain in him, that when he appears, we may have boldness, and not be ashamed before him at his coming. If you know that he is righteous, you know that everyone who practices righteousness is born of him. Behold, how great a love the Father has bestowed on us, that we should be called children of God! For this cause the world doesn't know us, because it didn't know him. Beloved, now we are children of God, and it is not yet revealed what we will be. But we know that, when he is revealed, we will be like him; for we will see him just as he is. Everyone who has this hope set on him purifies himself, even as he is pure.

De. 4:9-14 Only take heed to yourself, and keep your soul diligently, lest you forget the things which your eyes saw, and lest they depart from your heart all the days of your life; but make them known to your children and your children's children; the day that you stood before Yahweh your God in Horeb, when Yahweh said to me, "Assemble me the people, and I will make them hear my words, that they may learn to fear me all the days that they live on the earth, and that they may teach their children." You came near and stood under the mountain; and the mountain burned with fire to the heart of the sky, with darkness, cloud, and thick darkness. Yahweh spoke to you out of the midst of the fire: you heard the voice of words, but you saw no form; you only heard a voice. He declared to you his covenant, which he commanded you to perform, even the ten commandments; and he wrote them on two tables of stone. Yahweh commanded me at that time to teach you statutes and ordinances, that you might do them in the land where you go over to possess it.

Week 6 Day 4   17-Jul

Matt. 5:33-37 "Again you have heard that it was said to them of old time, 'You shall not make false vows, but shall perform to the Lord your vows,' but I tell you, don't swear at all: neither by heaven, for it is the throne of God; nor by the earth, for it is the footstool of his feet; nor by Jerusalem, for it is the city of the great King. Neither shall you swear by your head, for you can't make one hair white or black. But let your 'Yes' be 'Yes' and your 'No' be 'No.' Whatever is more than these is of the evil one."

Matt. 12:33-37 "Either make the tree good, and its fruit good, or make the tree corrupt, and its fruit corrupt; for the tree is known by its fruit. You offspring of vipers, how can you, being evil, speak good things? For out of the abundance of the heart, the mouth speaks. The good man out of his good treasure brings out good things, and the evil man out of his evil treasure brings out evil things. I tell you that every idle word that men speak, they will give account of it in the day of judgment. For by your words you will be justified, and by your words you will be condemned."

Jas. 4:13-17 Come now, you who say, "Today or tomorrow let's go into this city, and spend a year there, trade, and make a profit." Whereas you don't know what your life will be like tomorrow. For what is your life? For you are a vapor, that appears for a little time, and then vanishes away. For you ought to say, "If the Lord wills, we will both live, and do this or that." But now you glory in your boasting. All such boasting is evil. To him therefore who knows to do good, and doesn't do it, to him it is sin.

Num. 30:1-16 Moses spoke to the heads of the tribes of the children of Israel, saying, "This is the thing which Yahweh has commanded. When a man vows a vow to Yahweh, or swears an oath to bind his soul with a bond, he shall not break his word; he shall do according to all that proceeds out of his mouth. Also when a woman vows a vow to Yahweh, and binds herself by a bond, being in her father's house, in her youth, and her father hears her vow, and her bond with which she has bound her soul, and her father holds his peace at her; then all her vows shall stand, and every bond with which she has bound her soul shall stand. But if her father disallow her in the day that he hears, none of her vows, or of her bonds with which she has bound her soul, shall stand: and Yahweh will forgive her, because her father disallowed her. If she has a husband, while her vows are on her, or the rash utterance of her lips, with which she has bound her soul, and her husband hears it, and hold his peace at her in the day that he hears it; then her vows shall stand, and her bonds with which she has bound her soul shall stand. But if her husband forbids her in the day that he hears it, then he shall make void her vow which is on her, and the rash utterance of her lips, with which she has bound her soul: and Yahweh will forgive her. But the vow of a widow, or of her who is divorced, everything with which she has bound her soul, shall stand against her. If she vowed in her husband's house, or bound her soul by a bond with an oath, and her husband heard it, and held his peace at her, and didn't disallow her; then all her vows shall stand, and every bond with which she bound her soul shall stand. But if her husband made them null and void in the day that he heard them, then whatever proceeded out of her lips concerning her vows, or concerning the bond of her soul, shall not stand: her husband has made them void; and Yahweh will forgive her. Every vow, and every binding oath to afflict the soul, her husband may establish it, or her husband may make it void. But if her husband altogether hold his peace at her from day to day, then he establishes all her vows, or all her bonds, which are on her: he has established them, because he held his peace at her in the day that he heard them. But if he shall make them null and void after that he has heard them, then he shall bear her iniquity." These are the statutes, which Yahweh commanded Moses, between a man and his wife, between a father and his daughter, being in her youth, in her father's house.

Week 6 Day 5   15-Sep

Luke 11:24-28 "The unclean spirit, when he has gone out of the man, passes through dry places, seeking rest, and finding none, he says, 'I will turn back to my house from which I came out.' When he returns, he finds it swept and put in order. Then he goes, and takes seven other spirits more evil than himself, and they enter in and dwell there. The last state of that man becomes worse than the first." It came to pass, as he said these things, a certain woman out of the multitude lifted up her voice, and said to him, "Blessed is the womb that bore you, and the breasts which nursed you!" But he said, "On the contrary, blessed are those who hear the word of God, and keep it."

Rev. 2:18-29 "To the angel of the assembly in Thyatira write: "The Son of God, who has his eyes like a flame of fire, and his feet are like burnished brass, says these things: "I know your works, your love, faith, service, patient endurance, and that your last works are more than the first. But I have this against you, that you tolerate your woman, Jezebel, who calls herself a prophetess. She teaches and seduces my servants to commit sexual immorality, and to eat things sacrificed to idols. I gave her time to repent, but she refuses to repent of her sexual immorality. Behold, I will throw her into a bed, and those who commit adultery with her into great oppression, unless they repent of her works. I will kill her children with Death, and all the assemblies will know that I am he who searches the minds and hearts. I will give to each one of you according to your deeds. But to you I say, to the rest who are in Thyatira, as many as don't have this teaching, who don't know what some call 'the deep things of Satan,' to you I say, I am not putting any other burden on you. Nevertheless, hold that which you have firmly until I come. He who overcomes, and he who keeps my works to the end, to him I will give authority over the nations. He will rule them with a rod of iron, shattering them like clay pots; as I also have received of my Father and I will give him the morning star. He who has an ear, let him hear what the Spirit says to the assemblies.""

Pr. 1:20-33 Wisdom calls aloud in the street. She utters her voice in the public squares. She calls at the head of noisy places. At the entrance of the city gates, she utters her words: "How long, you simple ones, will you love simplicity? How long will mockers delight themselves in mockery, and fools hate knowledge? Turn at my reproof. Behold, I will pour out my spirit on you. I will make known my words to you. Because I have called, and you have refused; I have stretched out my hand, and no one has paid attention; but you have ignored all my counsel, and wanted none of my reproof; I also will laugh at your disaster. I will mock when calamity overtakes you; when calamity overtakes you like a storm, when your disaster comes on like a whirlwind; when distress and anguish come on you. Then will they call on me, but I will not answer. They will seek me diligently, but they will not find me; because they hated knowledge, and didn't choose the fear of Yahweh. They wanted none of my counsel. They despised all my reproof. Therefore they will eat of the fruit of their own way, and be filled with their own schemes. For the backsliding of the simple will kill them. The careless ease of fools will destroy them. But whoever listens to me will dwell securely, and will be at ease, without fear of harm."

Week 6 Day 6   26-Jul

Matt. 15:10-20 He summoned the multitude, and said to them, "Hear, and understand. That which enters into the mouth doesn't defile the man; but that which proceeds out of the mouth, this defiles the man." Then the disciples came, and said to him, "Do you know that the Pharisees were offended, when they heard this saying?" But he answered, "Every plant which my heavenly Father didn't plant will be uprooted. Leave them alone. They are blind guides of the blind. If the blind guide the blind, both will fall into a pit." Peter answered him, "Explain the parable to us." So Jesus said, "Do you also still not understand? Don't you understand that whatever goes into the mouth passes into the belly, and then out of the body? But the things which proceed out of the mouth come out of the heart, and they defile the man. For out of the heart come forth evil thoughts, murders, adulteries, sexual sins, thefts, false testimony, and blasphemies. These are the things which defile the man; but to eat with unwashed hands doesn't defile the man."

I Cor. 10:23-11:1 "All things are lawful for me," but not all things are profitable. "All things are lawful for me," but not all things build up. Let no one seek his own, but each one his neighbor's good. Whatever is sold in the butcher shop, eat, asking no question for the sake of conscience, for "the earth is the Lord's, and its fullness." But if one of those who don't believe invites you to a meal, and you are inclined to go, eat whatever is set before you, asking no questions for the sake of conscience. But if anyone says to you, "This was offered to idols," don't eat it for the sake of the one who told you, and for the sake of conscience. For "the earth is the Lord's, and all its fullness." Conscience, I say, not your own, but the other's conscience. For why is my liberty judged by another conscience? If I partake with thankfulness, why am I denounced for that for which I give thanks? Whether therefore you eat, or drink, or whatever you do, do all to the glory of God. Give no occasions for stumbling, either to Jews, or to Greeks, or to the assembly of God; even as I also please all men in all things, not seeking my own profit, but the profit of the many, that they may be saved. Be imitators of me, even as I also am of Christ.

Mal. 2:1-9 "Now, you priests, this commandment is for you. If you will not listen, and if you will not lay it to heart, to give glory to my name," says Yahweh of Armies, "then will I send the curse on you, and I will curse your blessings. Indeed, I have cursed them already, because you do not lay it to heart. Behold, I will rebuke your seed, and will spread dung on your faces, even the dung of your feasts; and you will be taken away with it. You will know that I have sent this commandment to you, that my covenant may be with Levi," says Yahweh of Armies. "My covenant was with him of life and peace; and I gave them to him that he might be reverent toward me; and he was reverent toward me, and stood in awe of my name. The law of truth was in his mouth, and unrighteousness was not found in his lips. He walked with me in peace and uprightness, and turned many away from iniquity. For the priest's lips should keep knowledge, and they should seek the law at his mouth; for he is the messenger of Yahweh of Armies. But you have turned aside out of the way. You have caused many to stumble in the law. You have corrupted the covenant of Levi," says Yahweh of Armies. "Therefore I have also made you contemptible and base before all the people, according to the way you have not kept my ways, but have had respect for persons in the law."

Week 6 Day 7   1-Dec

Rom. 7:1-6 Or don't you know, brothers (for I speak to men who know the law), that the law has dominion over a man for as long as he lives? 2 For the woman that has a husband is bound by law to the husband while he lives, but if the husband dies, she is discharged from the law of the husband. So then if, while the husband lives, she is joined to another man, she would be called an adulteress. But if the husband dies, she is free from the law, so that she is no adulteress, though she is joined to another man. Therefore, my brothers, you also were made dead to the law through the body of Christ, that you would be joined to another, to him who was raised from the dead, that we might bring forth fruit to God. For when we were in the flesh, the sinful passions which were through the law, worked in our members to bring forth fruit to death. But now we have been discharged from the law, having died to that in which we were held; so that we serve in newness of the spirit, and not in oldness of the letter.

Ps. 119:129-136 Your testimonies are wonderful, therefore my soul keeps them. The entrance of your words gives light. It gives understanding to the simple. I opened my mouth wide and panted, for I longed for your commandments. Turn to me, and have mercy on me, as you always do to those who love your name. Establish my footsteps in your word. Don't let any iniquity have dominion over me. Redeem me from the oppression of man, so I will observe your precepts. Make your face shine on your servant. Teach me your statutes. Streams of tears run down my eyes, because they don't observe your law.

Week 7 Day 1   29-Jun

Matt. 5:27-32 "You have heard that it was said, 'You shall not commit adultery;' but I tell you that everyone who gazes at a woman to lust after her has committed adultery with her already in his heart. If your right eye causes you to stumble, pluck it out and throw it away from you. For it is more profitable for you that one of your members should perish, than for your whole body to be cast into Gehenna. If your right hand causes you to stumble, cut it off, and throw it away from you. For it is more profitable for you that one of your members should perish, than for your whole body to be cast into Gehenna. "It was also said, 'Whoever shall put away his wife, let him give her a writing of divorce,' but I tell you that whoever puts away his wife, except for the cause of sexual immorality, makes her an adulteress; and whoever marries her when she is put away commits adultery."

Gal 5:16-21 But I say, walk by the Spirit, and you won't fulfill the lust of the flesh. For the flesh lusts against the Spirit, and the Spirit against the flesh; and these are contrary to one another, that you may not do the things that you desire. But if you are led by the Spirit, you are not under the law. Now the works of the flesh are obvious, which are: adultery, sexual immorality, uncleanness, lustfulness, idolatry, sorcery, hatred, strife, jealousies, outbursts of anger, rivalries, divisions, heresies, envyings, murders, drunkenness, orgies, and things like these; of which I forewarn you, even as I also forewarned you, that those who practice such things will not inherit the Kingdom of God.

Jer. 5:7-11 "How can I pardon you? Your children have forsaken me, and sworn by what are no gods. When I had fed them to the full, they committed adultery, and assembled themselves in troops at the prostitutes' houses. They were as fed horses roaming at large: everyone neighed after his neighbor's wife. Shouldn't I punish them for these things?" says Yahweh; "and shouldn't my soul be avenged on such a nation as this? Go up on her walls, and destroy; but don't make a full end. Take away her branches; for they are not Yahweh's. For the house of Israel and the house of Judah have dealt very treacherously against me," says Yahweh.

Week 7 Day 2   **17-Jun**

Matt. 7:1-6 "Don't judge, so that you won't be judged. For with whatever judgment you judge, you will be judged; and with whatever measure you measure, it will be measured to you. Why do you see the speck that is in your brother's eye, but don't consider the beam that is in your own eye? Or how will you tell your brother, 'Let me remove the speck from your eye;' and behold, the beam is in your own eye? You hypocrite! First remove the beam out of your own eye, and then you can see clearly to remove the speck out of your brother's eye. Don't give that which is holy to the dogs, neither throw your pearls before the pigs, lest perhaps they trample them under their feet, and turn and tear you to pieces."

Luke 6:37-38 "Don't judge, and you won't be judged. Don't condemn, and you won't be condemned. Set free, and you will be set free. "Give, and it will be given to you: good measure, pressed down, shaken together, and running over, will be given to you. For with the same measure you measure it will be measured back to you."

Rom. 2:1-16 Therefore you are without excuse, O man, whoever you are who judge. For in that which you judge another, you condemn yourself. For you who judge practice the same things. We know that the judgment of God is according to truth against those who practice such things. Do you think this, O man who judges those who practice such things, and do the same, that you will escape the judgment of God? Or do you despise the riches of his goodness, forbearance, and patience, not knowing that the goodness of God leads you to repentance? But according to your hardness and unrepentant heart you are treasuring up for yourself wrath in the day of wrath, revelation, and of the righteous judgment of God; who "will pay back to everyone according to their works:" to those who by patience in well-doing seek for glory, honor, and incorruptibility, eternal life; but to those who are self-seeking, and don't obey the truth, but obey unrighteousness, will be wrath and indignation, oppression and anguish, on every soul of man who works evil, to the Jew first, and also to the Greek. But glory, honor, and peace go to every man who works good, to the Jew first, and also to the Greek. For there is no partiality with God. For as many as have sinned without law will also perish without the law. As many as have sinned under the law will be judged by the law. For it isn't the hearers of the law who are righteous before God, but the doers of the law will be justified (for when Gentiles who don't have the law do by nature the things of the law, these, not having the law, are a law to themselves, in that they show the work of the law written in their hearts, their conscience testifying with them, and their thoughts among themselves accusing or else excusing them) in the day when God will judge the secrets of men, according to my Good News, by Jesus Christ.

I Sa. 26:2-25 Then Saul arose, and went down to the wilderness of Ziph, having three thousand chosen men of Israel with him, to seek David in the wilderness of Ziph. Saul encamped in the hill of Hachilah, which is before the desert, by the way. But David stayed in the wilderness, and he saw that Saul came after him into the wilderness. David therefore sent out spies, and understood that Saul had certainly come. David arose, and came to the place where Saul had encamped; and David saw the place where Saul lay, and Abner the son of Ner, the captain of his army: and Saul lay within the place of the wagons, and the people were encamped around him. Then answered David and said to Ahimelech the Hittite, and to Abishai the son of Zeruiah, brother to Joab, saying, "Who will go down with me to Saul to the camp?" Abishai said, "I will go down with you." So David and Abishai came to the people by night: and, behold, Saul lay sleeping within the place of the wagons, with his spear stuck in the ground at his head; and Abner and the people lay around him. Then Abishai said to David, "God has delivered up your enemy into your hand this day. Now therefore please let me strike him with the spear to the earth at one stroke, and I will not strike him the second time." David said to Abishai, "Don't destroy him; for who can put forth his hand against Yahweh's anointed, and be guiltless?" David said, "As Yahweh lives, Yahweh will strike him; or his day shall come to die; or he shall go down into battle and perish. Yahweh forbid that I should put forth my hand against Yahweh's anointed; but now please take the spear that is at his head, and the jar of water, and let us go." So David took the spear and the jar of water from Saul's head; and they went away: and no man saw it, nor knew it, neither did any awake; for they were all asleep, because a deep sleep from Yahweh was fallen on them. Then David went over to the other side, and stood on the top of the mountain afar off; a great space being between them; and David cried to the people, and to Abner the son of Ner, saying, "Don't you answer, Abner?" Then Abner answered, "Who are you who cries to the king?" David said to Abner, "Aren't you a man? Who is like you in Israel? Why then have you not kept watch over your lord, the king? For one of the people came in to destroy the king your lord. This thing isn't good that you have done. As Yahweh lives, you are worthy to die, because you have not kept watch over your lord, Yahweh's anointed. Now see where the king's spear is, and the jar of water that was at his head." Saul knew David's voice, and said, "Is this your voice, my son David?" David said, "It is my voice, my lord, O king." He said, "Why does my lord pursue after his servant? For what have I done? Or what evil is in my hand? Now therefore, please let my lord the king hear the words of his servant. If it is so that Yahweh has stirred you up against me, let him accept an offering. But if it is the children of men, they are cursed before Yahweh; for they have driven me out this day that I shouldn't cling to Yahweh's inheritance, saying, 'Go, serve other gods!' Now therefore, don't let my blood fall to the earth away from the presence of Yahweh; for the king of Israel has come out to seek a flea, as when one hunts a partridge in the mountains." Then Saul said, "I have sinned. Return, my son David; for I will no more do you harm, because my life was precious in your eyes this day. Behold, I have played the fool, and have erred exceedingly." David answered, "Behold the spear, O king! Then let one of the young men come over and get it. Yahweh will render to every man his righteousness and his faithfulness; because Yahweh delivered you into my hand today, and I wouldn't put forth my hand against Yahweh's anointed. prevail." So David went his way, and Saul returned to his place.

Week 7 Day 3   **23-Jun**

John 8:1-11 Jesus went to the Mount of Olives. Now very early in the morning, he came again into the temple, and all the people came to him. He sat down, and taught them. The scribes and the Pharisees brought a woman taken in adultery. Having set her in the midst, they told him, "Teacher, we found this woman in adultery, in the very act. Now in our law, Moses commanded us to stone such. What then do you say about her?" They said this testing him, that they might have something to accuse him of. But Jesus stooped down, and wrote on the ground with his finger. But when they continued asking him, he looked up and said to them, "He who is without sin among you, let him throw the first stone at her." Again he stooped down, and with his finger wrote on the ground. They, when they heard it, being convicted by their conscience, went out one by one, beginning from the oldest, even to the last. Jesus was left alone with the woman where she was, in the middle. Jesus, standing up, saw her and said, "Woman, where are your accusers? Did no one condemn you?" She said, "No one, Lord." Jesus said, "Neither do I condemn you. Go your way. From now on, sin no more."

Rom. 2:17-29 Indeed you bear the name of a Jew, and rest on the law, and glory in God, and know his will, and approve the things that are excellent, being instructed out of the law, and are confident that you yourself are a guide of the blind, a light to those who are in darkness, a corrector of the foolish, a teacher of babies, having in the law the form of knowledge and of the truth. You therefore who teach another, don't you teach yourself? You who preach that a man shouldn't steal, do you steal? You who say a man shouldn't commit adultery. Do you commit adultery? You who abhor idols, do you rob temples? You who glory in the law, through your disobedience of the law do you dishonor God? For "the name of God is blasphemed among the Gentiles because of you," just as it is written. For circumcision indeed profits, if you are a doer of the law, but if you are a transgressor of the law, your circumcision has become uncircumcision. If therefore the uncircumcised keep the ordinances of the law, won't his uncircumcision be accounted as circumcision? Won't the uncircumcision which is by nature, if it fulfills the law, judge you, who with the letter and circumcision are a transgressor of the law? For he is not a Jew who is one outwardly, neither is that circumcision which is outward in the flesh; but he is a Jew who is one inwardly, and circumcision is that of the heart, in the spirit not in the letter; whose praise is not from men, but from God.

De. 17:2-7 If there is found in the midst of you, within any of your gates which Yahweh your God gives you, man or woman, who does that which is evil in the sight of Yahweh your God, in transgressing his covenant, and has gone and served other gods, and worshiped them, or the sun, or the moon, or any of the army of the sky, which I have not commanded; and it be told you, and you have heard of it, then you shall inquire diligently; and behold, if it be true, and the thing certain, that such abomination is done in Israel, then you shall bring forth that man or that woman, who has done this evil thing, to your gates, even the man or the woman; and you shall stone them to death with stones. At the mouth of two witnesses, or three witnesses, shall he who is to die be put to death; at the mouth of one witness he shall not be put to death. The hand of the witnesses shall be first on him to put him to death, and afterward the hand of all the people. So you shall put away the evil from the midst of you.

Week 7 Day 4   **15-Nov**

Mark 9:38-41 John said to him, "Teacher, we saw someone who doesn't follow us casting out demons in your name; and we forbade him, because he doesn't follow us." But Jesus said, "Don't forbid him, for there is no one who will do a mighty work in my name, and be able quickly to speak evil of me. For whoever is not against us is on our side. For whoever will give you a cup of water to drink in my name, because you are Christ's, most certainly I tell you, he will in no way lose his reward."

I Cor. 1:10-17 Now I beg you, brothers, through the name of our Lord, Jesus Christ, that you all speak the same thing and that there be no divisions among you, but that you be perfected together in the same mind and in the same judgment. For it has been reported to me concerning you, my brothers, by those who are from Chloe's household, that there are contentions among you. Now I mean this, that each one of you says, "I follow Paul," "I follow Apollos," "I follow Cephas," and, "I follow Christ." Is Christ divided? Was Paul crucified for you? Or were you baptized into the name of Paul? I thank God that I baptized none of you, except Crispus and Gaius, so that no one should say that I had baptized you into my own name. (I also baptized the household of Stephanas; besides them, I don't know whether I baptized any other.) For Christ sent me not to baptize, but to preach the Good News—not in wisdom of words, so that the cross of Christ wouldn't be made void.

Num. 11:27-30 A young man ran, and told Moses, and said, "Eldad and Medad are prophesying in the camp!" Joshua the son of Nun, the servant of Moses, one of his chosen men, answered, "My lord Moses, forbid them!" Moses said to him, "Are you jealous for my sake? I wish that all Yahweh's people were prophets, that Yahweh would put his Spirit on them!" Moses went into the camp, he and the elders of Israel.

Week 7 Day 5   **22-May**

John 17:20-26 "Not for these only do I pray, but for those also who believe in me through their word, that they may all be one; even as you, Father, are in me, and I in you, that they also may be one in us; that the world may believe that you sent me. The glory which you have given me, I have given to them; that they may be one, even as we are one; I in them, and you in me, that they may be perfected into one; that the world may know that you sent me, and loved them, even as you loved me. Father, I desire that they also whom you have given me be with me where

I am, that they may see my glory, which you have given me, for you loved me before the foundation of the world. Righteous Father, the world hasn't known you, but I knew you; and these knew that you sent me. I made known to them your name, and will make it known; that the love with which you loved me may be in them, and I in them."

Eph. 2:11-22 Therefore remember that once you, the Gentiles in the flesh, who are called "uncircumcision" by that which is called "circumcision," (in the flesh, made by hands); that you were at that time separate from Christ, alienated from the commonwealth of Israel, and strangers from the covenants of the promise, having no hope and without God in the world. But now in Christ Jesus you who once were far off are made near in the blood of Christ. For he is our peace, who made both one, and broke down the middle wall of partition, having abolished in the flesh the hostility, the law of commandments contained in ordinances, that he might create in himself one new man of the two, making peace; and might reconcile them both in one body to God through the cross, having killed the hostility thereby. He came and preached peace to you who were far off and to those who were near. For through him we both have our access in one Spirit to the Father. So then you are no longer strangers and foreigners, but you are fellow citizens with the saints, and of the household of God, being built on the foundation of the apostles and prophets, Christ Jesus himself being the chief cornerstone; in whom the whole building, fitted together, grows into a holy temple in the Lord; in whom you also are built together for a habitation of God in the Spirit.

De. 33:1-5 This is the blessing, with which Moses the man of God blessed the children of Israel before his death. He said, "Yahweh came from Sinai, And rose from Seir to them. He shone forth from Mount Paran. He came from the ten thousands of holy ones. At his right hand was a fiery law for them. Yes, he loves the people. All his saints are in your hand. They sat down at your feet; each receives your words. Moses commanded us a law, an inheritance for the assembly of Jacob. He was king in Jeshurun, when the heads of the people were gathered, all the tribes of Israel together."

De. 33: 26-29 "There is none like God, Jeshurun, who rides on the heavens for your help, In his excellency on the skies. The eternal God is your dwelling place. Underneath are the everlasting arms. He thrust out the enemy from before you, and said, 'Destroy!' Israel dwells in safety; the fountain of Jacob alone, In a land of grain and new wine. Yes, his heavens drop down dew. You are happy, Israel. Who is like you, a people saved by Yahweh, the shield of your help, the sword of your excellency! Your enemies shall submit themselves to you. You shall tread on their high places."

Week 7 Day 6   **25-Apr**

Matt. 24:36-44 "But no one knows of that day and hour, not even the angels of heaven, but my Father only. As the days of Noah were, so will be the coming of the Son of Man. For as in those days which were before the flood they were eating and drinking, marrying and giving in marriage, until the day that Noah entered into the ship, and they didn't know until the flood came, and took them all away, so will be the coming of the Son of Man. Then two men will be in the field: one will be taken and one will be left; two women grinding at the mill, one will be taken and one will be left. Watch therefore, for you don't know in what hour your Lord comes. But know this, that if the master of the house had known in what watch of the night the thief was coming, he would have watched, and would not have allowed his house to be broken into. Therefore also be ready, for in an hour that you don't expect, the Son of Man will come."

I Tim. 4:1-16 But the Spirit says expressly that in later times some will fall away from the faith, paying attention to seducing spirits and doctrines of demons, through the hypocrisy of men who speak lies, branded in their own conscience as with a hot iron; forbidding marriage and commanding to abstain from foods which God created to be received with thanksgiving by those who believe and know the truth. For every creature of God is good, and nothing is to be rejected, if it is received with thanksgiving. For it is sanctified through the word of God and prayer. If you instruct the brothers of these things, you will be a good servant of Christ Jesus, nourished in the words of the faith, and of the good doctrine which you have followed. But refuse profane and old wives' fables. Exercise yourself toward godliness. For bodily exercise has some value, but godliness has value in all things, having the promise of the life which is now, and of that which is to come. This saying is faithful and worthy of all acceptance. For to this end we both labor and suffer reproach, because we have set our trust in the living God, who is the Savior of all men, especially of those who believe. Command and teach these things. Let no man despise your youth; but be an example to those who believe, in word, in your way of life, in love, in spirit, in faith, and in purity. Until I come, pay attention to reading, to exhortation, and to teaching. Don't neglect the gift that is in you, which was given to you by prophecy, with the laying on of the hands of the elders. Be diligent in these things. Give yourself wholly to them, that your progress may be revealed to all. Pay attention to yourself, and to your teaching. Continue in these things, for in doing this you will save both yourself and those who hear you.

Is. 2:1-5 This is what Isaiah the son of Amoz saw concerning Judah and Jerusalem. It shall happen in the latter days, that the mountain of Yahweh's house shall be established on the top of the mountains, and shall be raised above the hills; and all nations shall flow to it. Many peoples shall go and say, "Come, let's go up to the mountain of Yahweh, to the house of the God of Jacob; and he will teach us of his ways, and we will walk in his paths." For out of Zion the law shall go forth, and the word of Yahweh from Jerusalem. He will judge between the nations, and will decide concerning many peoples; and they shall beat their swords into plowshares, and their spears into pruning hooks. Nation shall not lift up sword against nation, neither shall they learn war any more. House of Jacob, come, and let us walk in the light of Yahweh.

Week 7 Day 7   **12-Dec**

Rom. 14:1-23 Now accept one who is weak in faith, but not for disputes over opinions. One man has faith to eat all things, but he who is weak eats only vegetables. Don't let him who eats despise him who doesn't eat. Don't let him who doesn't eat judge him who eats, for God has accepted him. Who are you who judge another's servant? To his own lord he stands or falls. Yes, he will be made to stand, for God has power to make him stand. One man esteems one day as more important. Another esteems every day alike. Let each man be fully assured in his own mind. He who observes the day, observes it to the Lord; and he who does not observe the day, to the Lord he does not observe it. He who eats, eats to the Lord, for he gives God thanks. He who doesn't eat, to the Lord he doesn't eat, and gives God thanks. For none of us lives to himself, and none dies to himself. For if we live, we live to the Lord. Or if we die, we die to the Lord. If therefore we live or die, we are the Lord's. For to this end Christ died, rose, and lived again, that he might be Lord of both the dead and the living. But you, why do you judge your brother? Or you again, why do you despise your brother? For we will all stand before the judgment seat of Christ. For it is written, "'As I live,' says the Lord, 'to me every knee will bow. Every tongue will confess to God.'" So then each one of us will give account of himself to God. Therefore let's not judge one another any more, but judge this rather, that no man put a stumbling block in his brother's way, or an occasion for falling. I know, and am persuaded in the Lord Jesus, that nothing is unclean of itself; except that to him who considers anything to be unclean, to him it is unclean. Yet if because of food your brother is grieved, you walk no longer in love. Don't destroy with your food him for whom Christ died. Then don't let your good be slandered, for the Kingdom of God is not eating and drinking, but righteousness, peace, and joy in the Holy Spirit. For he who serves Christ in these things is acceptable to God and approved by men. So then, let us follow after things which make for peace, and things by which we may build one another up. Don't overthrow God's work for food's sake. All things indeed are clean, however it is evil for that man who creates a stumbling block by eating. It is good to not eat meat, drink wine, nor do anything by which your brother stumbles, is offended, or is made weak. Do you have faith? Have it to yourself before God. Happy is he who doesn't judge himself in that which he approves. But he who doubts is condemned if he eats, because it isn't of faith; and whatever is not of faith is sin.

Ps. 133 See how good and how pleasant it is for brothers to live together in unity! It is like the precious oil on the head, that ran down on the beard, even Aaron's beard; that came down on the edge of his robes; like the dew of Hermon, that comes down on the hills of Zion: for there Yahweh gives the blessing, even life forevermore.

Week 8 Day 1   **1-Jul**

Matt. 5:21-26 "You have heard that it was said to the ancient ones, 'You shall not murder;' and 'Whoever shall murder shall be in danger of the judgment.' But I tell you, that everyone who is angry with his brother without a cause shall be in danger of the judgment; and whoever shall say to his brother, 'Raca!' shall be in danger of the council; and whoever shall say, 'You fool!' shall be in danger of the fire of Gehenna. If therefore you are offering your gift at the altar, and there remember that your brother has anything against you, leave your gift there before the altar, and go your way. First be reconciled to your brother, and then come and offer your gift. Agree with your adversary quickly, while you are with him in the way; lest perhaps the prosecutor deliver you to the judge, and the judge deliver you to the officer, and you be cast into prison. Most certainly I tell you, you shall by no means get out of there, until you have paid the last penny."

Matt. 5:38-42 "You have heard that it was said, 'An eye for an eye, and a tooth for a tooth.' But I tell you, don't resist him who is evil; but whoever strikes you on your right cheek, turn to him the other also. If anyone sues you to take away your coat, let him have your cloak also. Whoever compels you to go one mile, go with him two. Give to him who asks you, and don't turn away him who desires to borrow from you."

I Jo. 3:11-15 For this is the message which you heard from the beginning, that we should love one another; unlike Cain, who was of the evil one, and killed his brother. Why did he kill him? Because his works were evil, and his brother's righteous. Don't be surprised, my brothers, if the world hates you. We know that we have passed out of death into life, because we love the brothers. He who doesn't love his brother remains in death. Whoever hates his brother is a murderer, and you know that no murderer has eternal life remaining in him.

Pr. 25:21-22 If your enemy is hungry, give him food to eat. If he is thirsty, give him water to drink: for you will heap coals of fire on his head, and Yahweh will reward you.

Week 8 Day 2   **30-Jun**

Luke 12:54-59 He said to the multitudes also, "When you see a cloud rising from the west, immediately you say, 'A shower is coming,' and so it happens. When a south wind blows, you say, 'There will be a scorching heat,' and it happens. You hypocrites! You know how to interpret the appearance of the earth and the sky, but how is it that you don't interpret this time? Why don't you judge for yourselves what is right? For when you are going with your adversary before the magistrate, try diligently on the way to be released from him, lest perhaps he drag you to the judge, and the judge deliver you to the officer, and the officer throw you into prison. I tell you, you will by no means get out of there, until you have paid the very last penny."

Luke 17:3-4 "Be careful. If your brother sins against you, rebuke him. If he repents, forgive him. If he sins against you seven times in the day, and seven times returns, saying, 'I repent,' you shall forgive him."

I Cor. 6:1-11 Dare any of you, having a matter against his neighbor, go to law before the unrighteous, and not before the saints? Don't you know that the saints will judge the world? And if the world is judged by you, are you unworthy to judge the smallest matters? Don't you know that we will judge angels? How much more, things that pertain to this life? If then, you have to judge things pertaining to this life, do you set them to judge who are of no account in the assembly? I say this to move you to shame. Isn't there even one wise man among you who would be able to decide between his brothers? But brother goes to law with brother, and that before unbelievers! Therefore it is already altogether a defect in you, that you have lawsuits one with another. Why not rather be wronged? Why not rather be defrauded? No, but you yourselves do wrong, and defraud, and that against your brothers. Or don't you know that the unrighteous will not inherit the Kingdom of God? Don't be deceived. Neither the sexually immoral, nor idolaters, nor adulterers, nor male prostitutes, nor homosexuals, nor thieves, nor covetous, nor drunkards, nor slanderers, nor extortioners, will inherit the Kingdom of God. Such were some of you, but you were washed. But you were sanctified. But you were justified in the name of the Lord Jesus, and in the Spirit of our God

Pr. 6:1-5 My son, if you have become collateral for your neighbor, if you have struck your hands in pledge for a stranger; you are trapped by the words of your mouth. You are ensnared with the words of your mouth. Do this now, my son, and deliver yourself, since you have come into the hand of your neighbor. Go, humble yourself. Press your plea with your neighbor. Give no sleep to your eyes, nor slumber to your eyelids. Free yourself, like a gazelle from the hand of the hunter, like a bird from the snare of the fowler.

Week 8 Day 3   28-Jan

Matt. 18:15-20 "If your brother sins against you, go, show him his fault between you and him alone. If he listens to you, you have gained back your brother. But if he doesn't listen, take one or two more with you, that at the mouth of two or three witnesses every word may be established. If he refuses to listen to them, tell it to the assembly. If he refuses to hear the assembly also, let him be to you as a Gentile or a tax collector. Most certainly I tell you, whatever things you bind on earth will have been bound in heaven, and whatever things you release on earth will have been released in heaven. Again, assuredly I tell you, that if two of you will agree on earth concerning anything that they will ask, it will be done for them by my Father who is in heaven. For where two or three are gathered together in my name, there I am in their midst."

II Cor. 13:1-4 This is the third time I am coming to you. "At the mouth of two or three witnesses shall every word be established." I have said beforehand, and I do say beforehand, as when I was present the second time, so now, being absent, I write to those who have sinned before now, and to all the rest, that, if I come again, I will not spare; seeing that you seek a proof of Christ who speaks in me; who toward you is not weak, but is powerful in you. For he was crucified through weakness, yet he lives through the power of God. For we also are weak in him, but we will live with him through the power of God toward you.

Ez. 33:1-11 The word of Yahweh came to me, saying, Son of man, speak to the children of your people, and tell them, When I bring the sword on a land, and the people of the land take a man from among them, and set him for their watchman; if, when he sees the sword come on the land, he blow the trumpet, and warn the people; then whoever hears the sound of the trumpet, and doesn't take warning, if the sword come, and take him away, his blood shall be on his own head. He heard the sound of the trumpet, and didn't take warning; his blood shall be on him; whereas if he had taken warning, he would have delivered his soul. But if the watchman sees the sword come, and doesn't blow the trumpet, and the people aren't warned, and the sword comes, and take any person from among them; he is taken away in his iniquity, but his blood will I require at the watchman's hand. So you, son of man, I have set you a watchman to the house of Israel; therefore hear the word at my mouth, and give them warning from me. When I tell the wicked, O wicked man, you shall surely die, and you don't speak to warn the wicked from his way; that wicked man shall die in his iniquity, but his blood will I require at your hand. Nevertheless, if you warn the wicked of his way to turn from it, and he doesn't turn from his way; he shall die in his iniquity, but you have delivered your soul. You, son of man, tell the house of Israel: Thus you speak, saying, Our transgressions and our sins are on us, and we pine away in them; how then can we live? Tell them, As I live, says the Lord Yahweh, I have no pleasure in the death of the wicked; but that the wicked turn from his way and live: turn, turn from your evil ways; for why will you die, house of Israel?

Week 8 Day 4   12-Apr

Matt. 18:21-35 Then Peter came and said to him, "Lord, how often shall my brother sin against me, and I forgive him? Until seven times?" Jesus said to him, "I don't tell you until seven times, but, until seventy times seven. Therefore the Kingdom of Heaven is like a certain king, who wanted to reconcile accounts with his servants. When he had begun to reconcile, one was brought to him who owed him ten thousand talents. But because he couldn't pay, his lord commanded him to be sold, with his wife, his children, and all that he had, and payment to be made. The servant therefore fell down and kneeled before him, saying, 'Lord, have patience with me, and I will repay you all!' The lord of that servant, being moved with compassion, released him, and forgave him the debt. But that servant went out, and found one of his fellow servants, who owed him one hundred denarii, and he grabbed him, and took him by the throat, saying, 'Pay me what you owe!' So his fellow servant fell down at his feet and begged him, saying, 'Have patience with me, and I will repay you!' He would not, but went and cast him into prison, until he should pay back that which was due. So when his fellow servants saw what was done, they were exceedingly sorry, and came and told to their lord all that was done. Then his lord called him in, and said to him,

'You wicked servant! I forgave you all that debt, because you begged me. Shouldn't you also have had mercy on your fellow servant, even as I had mercy on you?' His lord was angry, and delivered him to the tormentors, until he should pay all that was due to him. So my heavenly Father will also do to you, if you don't each forgive your brother from your hearts for his misdeeds."

II Cor. 2:5-11 But if any has caused sorrow, he has caused sorrow, not to me, but in part (that I not press too heavily) to you all. Sufficient to such a one is this punishment which was inflicted by the many; so that on the contrary you should rather forgive him and comfort him, lest by any means such a one should be swallowed up with his excessive sorrow. Therefore I beg you to confirm your love toward him. For to this end I also wrote, that I might know the proof of you, whether you are obedient in all things. Now I also forgive whomever you forgive anything. For if indeed I have forgiven anything, I have forgiven that one for your sakes in the presence of Christ, that no advantage may be gained over us by Satan; for we are not ignorant of his schemes.

I Sa. 25:2-39 There was a man in Maon, whose possessions were in Carmel; and the man was very great, and he had three thousand sheep, and a thousand goats: and he was shearing his sheep in Carmel. Now the name of the man was Nabal; and the name of his wife Abigail; and the woman was of good understanding, and of a beautiful face: but the man was churlish and evil in his doings; and he was of the house of Caleb. David heard in the wilderness that Nabal was shearing his sheep. David sent ten young men, and David said to the young men, "Go up to Carmel, and go to Nabal, and greet him in my name. You shall tell him, 'Long life to you! Peace be to you, and peace be to your house, and peace be to all that you have. Now I have heard that you have shearers. Your shepherds have now been with us, and we didn't hurt them, neither was there anything missing from them, all the while they were in Carmel. Ask your young men, and they will tell you. Therefore let the young men find favor in your eyes; for we come in a good day. Please give whatever comes to your hand, to your servants, and to your son David.'" When David's young men came, they spoke to Nabal according to all those words in the name of David, and ceased. Nabal answered David's servants, and said, "Who is David? Who is the son of Jesse? There are many servants who break away from their masters these days. Shall I then take my bread, and my water, and my meat that I have killed for my shearers, and give it to men who I don't know where they come from?" So David's young men turned on their way, and went back, and came and told him according to all these words. David said to his men, "Every man put on his sword!" Every man put on his sword. David also put on his sword. About four hundred men followed David; and two hundred stayed by the baggage. But one of the young men told Abigail, Nabal's wife, saying, "Behold, David sent messengers out of the wilderness to greet our master; and he railed at them. But the men were very good to us, and we were not hurt, neither missed we anything, as long as we went with them, when we were in the fields. They were a wall to us both by night and by day, all the while we were with them keeping the sheep. Now therefore know and consider what you will do; for evil is determined against our master, and against all his house; for he is such a worthless fellow that one can't speak to him." Then Abigail hurried and took two hundred loaves of bread, two bottles of wine, five sheep ready dressed, five measures of parched grain, one hundred clusters of raisins, and two hundred cakes of figs, and laid them on donkeys. She said to her young men, "Go on before me. Behold, I come after you." But she didn't tell her husband, Nabal. It was so, as she rode on her donkey, and came down by the covert of the mountain, that behold, David and his men came down toward her; and she met them. Now David had said, "Surely in vain have I kept all that this fellow has in the wilderness, so that nothing was missed of all that pertained to him. He has returned me evil for good. God do so to the enemies of David, and more also, if I leave of all that belongs to him by the morning light so much as one who urinates on a wall." When Abigail saw David, she hurried, and alighted from her donkey, and fell before David on her face, and bowed herself to the ground. She fell at his feet, and said, "On me, my lord, on me be the iniquity; and please let your handmaid speak in your ears. Hear the words of your handmaid. Please don't let my lord regard this worthless fellow, even Nabal; for as his name is, so is he. Nabal is his name, and folly is with him; but I, your handmaid, didn't see the young men of my lord, whom you sent. Now therefore, my lord, as Yahweh lives, and as your soul lives, since Yahweh has withheld you from blood guiltiness, and from avenging yourself with your own hand, now therefore let your enemies, and those who seek evil to my lord, be as Nabal. Now this present which your servant has brought to my lord, let it be given to the young men who follow my lord. Please forgive the trespass of your handmaid. For Yahweh will certainly make my lord a sure house, because my lord fights the battles of Yahweh; and evil shall not be found in you all your days. Though men may rise up to pursue you, and to seek your soul, yet the soul of my lord shall be bound in the bundle of life with Yahweh your God. He will sling out the souls of your enemies, as from the hollow of a sling. It shall come to pass, when Yahweh has done to my lord according to all the good that he has spoken concerning you, and shall have appointed you prince over Israel, that this shall be no grief to you, nor offense of heart to my lord, either that you have shed blood without cause, or that my lord has avenged himself. When Yahweh has dealt well with my lord, then remember your handmaid." David said to Abigail, "Blessed is Yahweh, the God of Israel, who sent you this day to meet me! Blessed is your discretion, and blessed are you, that have kept me this day from blood guiltiness, and from avenging myself with my own hand. For indeed, as Yahweh, the God of Israel, lives, who has withheld me from hurting you, unless you had hurried and come to meet me, surely there wouldn't have been left to Nabal by the morning light so much as one who urinates on a wall." So David received of her hand that which she had brought him: and he said to her, "Go up in peace to your house. Behold, I have listened to your voice, and have granted your request." Abigail came to Nabal; and behold, he held a feast in his house, like the feast of a king. Nabal's heart was merry within him, for he was very drunken. Therefore she told him nothing, less or more, until the morning light. It happened in the morning, when the wine was gone out of Nabal, that his wife told him these things, and his heart died within him, and he became as a stone. It happened about ten days after, that Yahweh struck Nabal, so that he died. When David heard that Nabal was dead, he said, "Blessed is Yahweh, who has pleaded the cause of my reproach from the hand of Nabal, and has kept back his servant from evil. Yahweh has returned the evildoing of Nabal on his own head." David sent and spoke concerning Abigail, to take her to him as wife.

Week 8 Day 5   **16-Mar**

Luke 7:36-50 One of the Pharisees invited him to eat with him. He entered into the Pharisee's house, and sat at the table. Behold, a woman in the city who was a sinner, when she knew that he was reclining in the Pharisee's house, she brought an alabaster jar of ointment. Standing behind at his feet weeping, she began to wet his feet with her tears, and she wiped them with the hair of her head, kissed his feet, and anointed them with the ointment. Now when the Pharisee who had invited him saw it, he said to himself, "This man, if he were a prophet, would have perceived who and what kind of woman this is who touches him, that she is a sinner." Jesus answered him, "Simon, I have something to tell you." He said, "Teacher, say on." "A certain lender had two debtors. The one owed five hundred denarii, and the other fifty. When they couldn't pay, he forgave them both. Which of them therefore will love him most?" Simon answered, "He, I suppose, to whom he forgave the most." He said to him, "You have judged correctly." Turning to the woman, he said to Simon, "Do you see this woman? I entered into your house, and you gave me no water for my feet, but she has wet my feet with her tears, and wiped them with the hair of her head. You gave me no kiss, but she, since the time I came in, has not ceased to kiss my feet. You didn't anoint my head with oil, but she has anointed my feet with ointment. Therefore I tell you, her sins, which are many, are forgiven, for she loved much. But to whom little is forgiven, the same loves little." He said to her, "Your sins are forgiven." Those who sat at the table with him began to say to themselves, "Who is this who even forgives sins?" He said to the woman, "Your faith has saved you. Go in peace."

Eph. 5:1-21 Be therefore imitators of God, as beloved children. Walk in love, even as Christ also loved you, and gave himself up for us, an offering and a sacrifice to God for a sweet-smelling fragrance. But sexual immorality, and all uncleanness, or covetousness, let it not even be mentioned among you, as becomes saints; nor filthiness, nor foolish talking, nor jesting, which are not appropriate; but rather giving of thanks. Know this for sure, that no sexually immoral person, nor unclean person, nor covetous man, who is an idolater, has any inheritance in the Kingdom of Christ and God. Let no one deceive you with empty words. For because of these things, the wrath of God comes on the children of disobedience. Therefore don't be partakers with them. For you were once darkness, but are now light in the Lord. Walk as children of light, for the fruit of the Spirit is in all goodness and righteous-ness and truth, proving what is well pleasing to the Lord. Have no fellowship with the unfruitful works of dark-ness, but rather even reprove them. For the things which are done by them in secret, it is a shame even to speak of. But all things, when they are reproved, are revealed by the light, for everything that reveals is light. Therefore he says, "Awake, you who sleep, and arise from the dead, and Christ will shine on you." Therefore watch carefully how you walk, not as unwise, but as wise; redeeming the time, because the days are evil. Therefore don't be fool-ish, but understand what the will of the Lord is. Don't be drunken with wine, in which is dissipation, but be filled with the Spirit, speaking to one another in psalms, hymns, and spiritual songs; singing, and making melody in your heart to the Lord; giving thanks always concerning all things in the name of our Lord Jesus Christ, to God, even the Father; subjecting yourselves one to another in the fear of Christ.

Hos. 14:1-9 Israel, return to Yahweh your God; for you have fallen because of your sin. Take words with you, and return to Yahweh. Tell him, "Forgive all our sins, and accept that which is good: so we offer our lips like bulls. Assyria can't save us. We won't ride on horses; neither will we say any more to the work of our hands, 'Our gods!' for in you the fatherless finds mercy." "I will heal their waywardness. I will love them freely; for my anger is turned away from him. I will be like the dew to Israel. He will blossom like the lily, and send down his roots like Lebanon. His branches will spread, and his beauty will be like the olive tree, and his fragrance like Lebanon. Men will dwell in his shade. They will revive like the grain, and blossom like the vine. Their fragrance will be like the wine of Lebanon. Ephraim, what have I to do any more with idols? I answer, and will take care of him. I am like a green fir tree; from me your fruit is found." Who is wise, that he may understand these things? Who is prudent, that he may know them? For the ways of Yahweh are right, and the righteous walk in them; but the rebellious stumble in them.

Week 8 Day 6   7-Jun

Matt. 16:13-20 Now when Jesus came into the parts of Caesarea Philippi, he asked his disciples, saying, "Who do men say that I, the Son of Man, am?" They said, "Some say John the Baptizer, some, Elijah, and others, Jeremiah, or one of the prophets." He said to them, "But who do you say that I am?" Simon Peter answered, "You are the Christ, the Son of the living God." Jesus answered him, "Blessed are you, Simon Bar Jonah, for flesh and blood has not revealed this to you, but my Father who is in heaven. I also tell you that you are Peter, and on this rock I will build my assembly, and the gates of Hades will not prevail against it. I will give to you the keys of the Kingdom of Heaven, and whatever you bind on earth will have been bound in heaven; and whatever you release on earth will have been released in heaven." Then he commanded the disciples that they should tell no one that he was Jesus the Christ.

Acts 15:1-29 Some men came down from Judea and taught the brothers, "Unless you are circumcised after the custom of Moses, you can't be saved." Therefore when Paul and Barnabas had no small discord and discussion with them, they appointed Paul and Barnabas, and some others of them, to go up to Jerusalem to the apostles and elders about this question. They, being sent on their way by the assembly, passed through both Phoenicia and Samaria, declaring the conversion of the Gentiles. They caused great joy to all the brothers. When they had come to Jerusalem, they were received by the assembly and the apostles and the elders, and they reported all things that God had done with them. But some of the sect of the Pharisees who believed rose up, saying, "It is necessary to circumcise them, and to command them to keep the law of Moses." The apostles and the elders were gathered together to see about this matter. When there had been much discussion, Peter rose up and said to them, "Brothers, you know that a good while ago God made a choice among you, that by my mouth the nations should hear the word of the Good News, and believe. God, who knows the heart, testified about them, giving them the Holy Spirit, just like he did to us. He made no distinction between us and them, cleansing their hearts by faith. Now therefore why do you tempt God, that you should put a yoke on the neck of the disciples which neither our fathers nor we were able to bear? But we believe that we are saved through the grace of the Lord Jesus, just as they are." All the multitude kept silence, and they listened to Barnabas and Paul reporting what signs and wonders God had done among the nations through them. After they were silent, James answered, "Brothers, listen to me. Simeon has reported how God first visited the nations, to take out of them a people for his name. This agrees with the words of the prophets. As it is written, 'After these things I will return. I will again build the tabernacle of David, which has fallen. I will again build its ruins. I will set it up, That the rest of men may seek after the Lord; All the Gentiles who are called by my name, Says the Lord, who does all these things. All his works are known to God from eternity.' "Therefore my judgment is that we don't trouble those from among the Gentiles who turn to God, but that we write to them that they abstain from the pollution of idols, from sexual immorality, from what is strangled, and from blood. For Moses from generations of old has in every city those who preach him, being read in the synagogues every Sabbath." Then it seemed good to the apostles and the elders, with the whole assembly, to choose men out of their company, and send them to Antioch with Paul and Barnabas: Judas called Barsabbas, and Silas, chief men among the brothers. They wrote these things by their hand: "The apostles, the elders, and the brothers, to the brothers who are of the Gentiles in Antioch, Syria, and Cilicia: greetings. Because we have heard that some who went out from us have troubled you with words, unsettling your souls, saying, 'You must be circumcised and keep the law,' to whom we gave no commandment; it seemed good to us, having come to one accord, to choose out men and send them to you with our beloved Barnabas and Paul, men who have risked their lives for the name of our Lord Jesus Christ. We have sent therefore Judas and Silas, who themselves will also tell you the same things by word of mouth. For it seemed good to the Holy Spirit, and to us, to lay no greater burden on you than these necessary things: that you abstain from things sacrificed to idols, from blood, from things strangled, and from sexual immorality, from which if you keep yourselves, it will be well with you. Farewell."

Dan. 7:13-14 I saw in the night visions, and behold, there came with the clouds of the sky one like a son of man, and he came even to the ancient of days, and they brought him near before him. There was given him dominion, and glory, and a kingdom, that all the peoples, nations, and languages should serve him: his dominion is an everlasting dominion, which shall not pass away, and his kingdom that which shall not be destroyed.

Week 8 Day 7   **24-Sep**

Acts 7:54-60 Now when they heard these things, they were cut to the heart, and they gnashed at him with their teeth. But he, being full of the Holy Spirit, looked up steadfastly into heaven, and saw the glory of God, and Jesus standing on the right hand of God, and said, "Behold, I see the heavens opened, and the Son of Man standing at the right hand of God!" But they cried out with a loud voice, and stopped their ears, and rushed at him with one accord. They threw him out of the city, and stoned him. The witnesses placed their garments at the feet of a young man named Saul. They stoned Stephen as he called out, saying, "Lord Jesus, receive my spirit!" He kneeled down, and cried with a loud voice, "Lord, don't hold this sin against them!" When he had said this, he fell asleep.

Ps. 51 Have mercy on me, God, according to your loving kindness. According to the multitude of your tender mercies, blot out my transgressions. Wash me thoroughly from my iniquity. Cleanse me from my sin. For I know my transgressions. My sin is constantly before me. Against you, and you only, have I sinned, and done that which is evil in your sight; that you may be proved right when you speak, and justified when you judge. Behold, I was brought forth in iniquity. In sin my mother conceived me. Behold, you desire truth in the inward parts. You teach me wisdom in the inmost place. Purify me with hyssop, and I will be clean. Wash me, and I will be whiter than snow. Let me hear joy and gladness, that the bones which you have broken may rejoice. Hide your face from my sins, and blot out all of my iniquities. Create in me a clean heart, O God. Renew a right spirit within me. Don't throw me from your presence, and don't take your holy Spirit from me. Restore to me the joy of your salvation. Uphold me with a willing spirit. Then I will teach transgressors your ways. Sinners shall be converted to you. Deliver me from bloodguiltiness, O God, the God of my salvation. My tongue shall sing aloud of your righteousness. Lord, open my lips. My mouth shall declare your praise. For you don't delight in sacrifice, or else I would give it. You have no pleasure in burnt offering. The sacrifices of God are a broken spirit. A broken and contrite heart, O God, you will not despise. Do well in your good pleasure to Zion. Build the walls of Jerusalem. Then you will delight in the sacrifices of righteousness, in burnt offerings and in whole burnt offerings. Then they will offer bulls on your altar.

Week 9 Day 1   **20-Sep**

Matt. 5:43-48 "You have heard that it was said, 'You shall love your neighbor, and hate your enemy. But I tell you, love your enemies, bless those who curse you, do good to those who hate you, and pray for those who mistreat you and persecute you, that you may be children of your Father who is in heaven. For he makes his sun to rise on the evil and the good, and sends rain on the just and the unjust. For if you love those who love you, what reward do you have? Don't even the tax collectors do the same? If you only greet your friends, what more do you do than others? Don't even the tax collectors do the same? Therefore you shall be perfect, just as your Father in heaven is perfect."

Rom. 12:9-21 Let love be without hypocrisy. Abhor that which is evil. Cling to that which is good. In love of the brothers be tenderly affectionate one to another; in honor preferring one another; not lagging in diligence; fervent in spirit; serving the Lord; rejoicing in hope; enduring in troubles; continuing steadfastly in prayer; contributing to the needs of the saints; given to hospitality. Bless those who persecute you; bless, and don't curse. Rejoice with those who rejoice. Weep with those who weep. Be of the same mind one toward another. Don't set your mind on high things, but associate with the humble. Don't be wise in your own conceits. Repay no one evil for evil. Respect what is honorable in the sight of all men. If it is possible, as much as it is up to you, be at peace with all men. Don't seek revenge yourselves, beloved, but give place to God's wrath. For it is written, "Vengeance belongs to me; I will repay, says the Lord." "If your enemy is hungry, feed him. If he is thirsty, give him a drink; for in doing so, you will heap coals of fire on his head." Don't be overcome by evil, but overcome evil with good.

II Sam. 16:5-12 When king David came to Bahurim, behold, a man of the family of the house of Saul came out, whose name was Shimei, the son of Gera. He came out, and cursed still as he came. He cast stones at David, and at all the servants of king David, and all the people and all the mighty men were on his right hand and on his left. Shimei said when he cursed, "Be gone, be gone, you man of blood, and base fellow! Yahweh has returned on you all the blood of the house of Saul, in whose place you have reigned! Yahweh has delivered the kingdom into the hand of Absalom your son! Behold, you are caught by your own mischief, because you are a man of blood!" Then Abishai the son of Zeruiah said to the king, "Why should this dead dog curse my lord the king? Please let me go over and take off his head." The king said, "What have I to do with you, you sons of Zeruiah? Because he curses, and because Yahweh has said to him, 'Curse David;' who then shall say, 'Why have you done so?'" David said to Abishai, and to all his servants, "Behold, my son, who came forth from my bowels, seeks my life. How much more this Benjamite, now? Leave him alone, and let him curse; for Yahweh has invited him. It may be that Yahweh will look on the wrong done to me, and that Yahweh will repay me good for the cursing of me today."

Week 9 Day 2   21-Sep

Luke 10:25-37 Behold, a certain lawyer stood up and tested him, saying, "Teacher, what shall I do to inherit eternal life?" He said to him, "What is written in the law? How do you read it?" He answered, "You shall love the Lord your God with all your heart, with all your soul, with all your strength, and with all your mind; and your neighbor as yourself." He said to him, "You have answered correctly. Do this, and you will live." But he, desiring to justify himself, asked Jesus, "Who is my neighbor?" Jesus answered, "A certain man was going down from Jerusalem to Jericho, and he fell among robbers, who both stripped him and beat him, and departed, leaving him half dead. By chance a certain priest was going down that way. When he saw him, he passed by on the other side. In the same way a Levite also, when he came to the place, and saw him, passed by on the other side. But a certain Samaritan, as he traveled, came where he was. When he saw him, he was moved with compassion, came to him, and bound up his wounds, pouring on oil and wine. He set him on his own animal, and brought him to an inn, and took care of him. On the next day, when he departed, he took out two denarii, and gave them to the host, and said to him, 'Take care of him. Whatever you spend beyond that, I will repay you when I return.' Now which of these three do you think seemed to be a neighbor to him who fell among the robbers?" He said, "He who showed mercy on him." Then Jesus said to him, "Go and do likewise."

I Jo. 3:16-24 By this we know love, because he laid down his life for us. And we ought to lay down our lives for the brothers. But whoever has the world's goods, and sees his brother in need, and closes his heart of compassion against him, how does the love of God remain in him? My little children, let's not love in word only, neither with the tongue only, but in deed and truth. And by this we know that we are of the truth, and persuade our hearts before him, because if our heart condemns us, God is greater than our heart, and knows all things. Beloved, if our hearts don't condemn us, we have boldness toward God; and whatever we ask, we receive from him, because we keep his commandments and do the things that are pleasing in his sight. This is his commandment, that we should believe in the name of his Son, Jesus Christ, and love one another, even as he commanded. He who keeps his commandments remains in him, and he in him. By this we know that he remains in us, by the Spirit which he gave us.

De. 30:11-16 For this commandment which I command you this day, it is not too hard for you, neither is it far off. It is not in heaven, that you should say, "Who shall go up for us to heaven, and bring it to us, and make us to hear it, that we may do it?" Neither is it beyond the sea, that you should say, "Who shall go over the sea for us, and bring it to us, and make us to hear it, that we may do it?" But the word is very near to you, in your mouth, and in your heart, that you may do it. Behold, I have set before you this day life and good, and death and evil; in that I command you this day to love Yahweh your God, to walk in his ways, and to keep his commandments and his statutes and his ordinances, that you may live and multiply, and that Yahweh your God may bless you in the land where you go in to possess it.

Week 9 Day 3   27-Jun

Luke 16:19-31 "Now there was a certain rich man, and he was clothed in purple and fine linen, living in luxury every day. A certain beggar, named Lazarus, was laid at his gate, full of sores, and desiring to be fed with the crumbs that fell from the rich man's table. Yes, even the dogs came and licked his sores. It happened that the beggar died, and that he was carried away by the angels to Abraham's bosom. The rich man also died, and was buried. In Hades, he lifted up his eyes, being in torment, and saw Abraham far off, and Lazarus at his bosom. He cried and said, 'Father Abraham, have mercy on me, and send Lazarus, that he may dip the tip of his finger in water, and cool my tongue! For I am in anguish in this flame.' "But Abraham said, 'Son, remember that you, in your lifetime, received your good things, and Lazarus, in the same way, bad things. But now here he is comforted and you are in anguish. Besides all this, between us and you there is a great gulf fixed, that those who want to pass from here to you are not able, and that none may cross over from there to us.' "He said, 'I ask you therefore, father, that you would send him to my father's house; for I have five brothers, that he may testify to them, so they won't also come into this place of torment.' "But Abraham said to him, 'They have Moses and the prophets. Let them listen to them.' "He said, 'No, father Abraham, but if one goes to them from the dead, they will repent.' "He said to him, 'If they don't listen to Moses and the prophets, neither will they be persuaded if one rises from the dead.'"

Acts 4:32-37 The multitude of those who believed were of one heart and soul. Not one of them claimed that anything of the things which he possessed was his own, but they had all things in common. With great power, the apostles gave their testimony of the resurrection of the Lord Jesus. Great grace was on them all. For neither was there among them any who lacked, for as many as were owners of lands or houses sold them, and brought the proceeds of the things that were sold, and laid them at the apostles' feet, and distribution was made to each, according as anyone had need. Joses, who by the apostles was surnamed Barnabas (which is, being interpreted, Son of Encouragement), a Levite, a man of Cyprus by race, having a field, sold it, and brought the money and laid it at the apostles' feet.

Am. 6:1-7 Woe to those who are at ease in Zion, and to those who are secure on the mountain of Samaria, the notable men of the chief of the nations, to whom the house of Israel come! Go to Calneh, and see; and from there go to Hamath the great; then go down to Gath of the Philistines. are they better than these kingdoms? or is their border greater than your border? Those who put far away the evil day, and cause the seat of violence to come near; who lie on beds of ivory, and stretch themselves on their couches, and eat the lambs out of the flock, and the calves out of the midst of the stall; who strum on the strings of a harp; who invent for themselves instruments of music, like David; who drink wine in bowls, and anoint themselves with the best oils; but they are not grieved for the affliction of Joseph. Therefore they will now go captive with the first who go captive; and the feasting and lounging will end.

Week 9 Day 4   21-Jan

Matt. 25:31-46 "But when the Son of Man comes in his glory, and all the holy angels with him, then he will sit on the throne of his glory. Before him all the nations will be gathered, and he will separate them one from another, as a shepherd separates the sheep from the goats. He will set the sheep on his right hand, but the goats on the left. Then the King will tell those on his right hand, 'Come, blessed of my Father, inherit the Kingdom prepared for you from the foundation of the world; for I was hungry, and you gave me food to eat. I was thirsty, and you gave me drink. I was a stranger, and you took me in. I was naked, and you clothed me. I was sick, and you visited me. I was in prison, and you came to me.' Then the righteous will answer him, saying, 'Lord, when did we see you hungry, and feed you; or thirsty, and give you a drink? When did we see you as a stranger, and take you in; or naked, and clothe you? When did we see you sick, or in prison, and come to you?' The King will answer them, 'Most certainly I tell you, inasmuch as you did it to one of the least of these my brothers, you did it to me.' Then he will say also to those on the left hand, 'Depart from me, you cursed, into the eternal fire which is prepared for the devil and his angels; for I was hungry, and you didn't give me food to eat; I was thirsty, and you gave me no drink; I was a stranger, and you didn't take me in; naked, and you didn't clothe me; sick, and in prison, and you didn't visit me.' Then they will also answer, saying, 'Lord, when did we see you hungry, or thirsty, or a stranger, or naked, or sick, or in prison, and didn't help you?' Then he will answer them, saying, 'Most certainly I tell you, inasmuch as you didn't do it to one of the least of these, you didn't do it to me.' These will go away into eternal punishment, but the righteous into eternal life."

II Cor. 5:1-10 For we know that if the earthly house of our tent is dissolved, we have a building from God, a house not made with hands, eternal, in the heavens. For most certainly in this we groan, longing to be clothed with our habitation which is from heaven; if so be that being clothed we will not be found naked. For indeed we who are in this tent do groan, being burdened; not that we desire to be unclothed, but that we desire to be clothed, that what is mortal may be swallowed up by life. Now he who made us for this very thing is God, who also gave to us the down payment of the Spirit. Therefore we are always confident and know that while we are at home in the body, we are absent from the Lord; for we walk by faith, not by sight. We are courageous, I say, and are willing rather to be absent from the body, and to be at home with the Lord. Therefore also we make it our aim, whether at home or absent, to be well pleasing to him. For we must all be revealed before the judgment seat of Christ; that each one may receive the things in the body, according to what he has done, whether good or bad.

Ez. 34:17-24 As for you, O my flock, thus says the Lord Yahweh: Behold, I judge between sheep and sheep, the rams and the male goats. Does it seem a small thing to you to have fed on the good pasture, but you must tread down with your feet the residue of your pasture? And to have drunk of the clear waters, but you must foul the residue with your feet? As for my sheep, they eat that which you have trodden with your feet, and they drink that which you have fouled with your feet. Therefore thus says the Lord Yahweh to them: Behold, I, even I, will judge between the fat sheep and the lean sheep. Because you thrust with side and with shoulder, and push all the diseased with your horns, until you have scattered them abroad; therefore will I save my flock, and they shall no more be a prey; and I will judge between sheep and sheep. I will set up one shepherd over them, and he shall feed them, even my servant David; he shall feed them, and he shall be their shepherd. I, Yahweh, will be their God, and my servant David prince among them; I, Yahweh, have spoken it.

Week 9 Day 5   28-Apr

Luke 12:13-21 One of the multitude said to him, "Teacher, tell my brother to divide the inheritance with me." But he said to him, "Man, who made me a judge or an arbitrator over you?" He said to them, "Beware! Keep yourselves from covetousness, for a man's life doesn't consist of the abundance of the things which he possesses." He spoke a parable to them, saying, "The ground of a certain rich man brought forth abundantly. He reasoned within himself, saying, 'What will I do, because I don't have room to store my crops?' He said, 'This is what I will do. I will pull down my barns, and build bigger ones, and there I will store all my grain and my goods. I will tell my soul, "Soul, you have many goods laid up for many years. Take your ease, eat, drink, be merry."' "But God said to him, 'You foolish one, tonight your soul is required of you. The things which you have prepared—whose will they be?' So is he who lays up treasure for himself, and is not rich toward God."

Jas. 1:9-11 But let the brother in humble circumstances glory in his high position; and the rich, in that he is made humble, because like the flower in the grass, he will pass away. For the sun arises with the scorching wind, and withers the grass, and the flower in it falls, and the beauty of its appearance perishes. So also will the rich man fade away in his pursuits.

Ec. 1:2-14 "Vanity of vanities," says the Preacher; "Vanity of vanities, all is vanity." What does man gain from all his labor in which he labors under the sun? One generation goes, and another generation comes; but the earth remains forever. The sun also rises, and the sun goes down, and hurries to its place where it rises. The wind goes toward the south, and turns around to the north. It turns around continually as it goes, and the wind returns again to its courses. All the rivers run into the sea, yet the sea is not full. To the place where the rivers flow, there they flow again. All things are full of weariness beyond uttering. The eye is not satisfied with seeing, nor the ear filled with hearing. That which has been is that which shall be; and that which has been done is that which shall be done: and there is no new thing under the sun. Is there a thing of which it may be said, "Behold, this is new?" It has been long ago, in the ages which were before us. There is no memory of the former; neither shall there be any memory of the latter that are to come, among those that shall come after. I, the Preacher, was king over Israel in Jerusalem. I applied my heart to seek and to search out by wisdom concerning all that is done under the sky. It is a heavy burden that God has given to the sons of men to be afflicted with. I have seen all the works that are done under the sun; and behold, all is vanity and a chasing after wind.

Ec. 2:18-23 I hated all my labor in which I labored under the sun, because I must leave it to the man who comes after me. Who knows whether he will be a wise man or a fool? Yet he will have rule over all of my labor in which I have labored, and in which I have shown myself wise under the sun. This also is vanity. Therefore I began to cause my heart to despair concerning all the labor in which I had labored under the sun. For there is a man whose labor is with wisdom, with knowledge, and with skillfulness; yet he shall leave it for his portion to a man who has not labored for it. This also is vanity and a great evil. For what has a man of all his labor, and of the striving of his heart, in which he labors under the sun? For all his days are sorrows, and his travail is grief; yes, even in the night his heart takes no rest. This also is vanity.

Week 9 Day 6   24-Nov

Luke 6:20-26 He lifted up his eyes to his disciples, and said, "Blessed are you who are poor, for yours is the Kingdom of God. Blessed are you who hunger now, for you will be filled. Blessed are you who weep now, for you will laugh. Blessed are you when men shall hate you, and when they shall exclude and mock you, and throw out your name as evil, for the Son of Man's sake. Rejoice in that day, and leap for joy, for behold, your reward is great in heaven, for their fathers did the same thing to the prophets. But woe to you who are rich! For you have received your consolation. Woe to you, you who are full now, for you will be hungry. Woe to you who laugh now, for you will mourn and weep. Woe, when men speak well of you, for their fathers did the same thing to the false prophets."

Jas. 5:1-6 Come now, you rich, weep and howl for your miseries that are coming on you. Your riches are corrupted and your garments are moth-eaten. Your gold and your silver are corroded, and their corrosion will be for a testimony against you, and will eat your flesh like fire. You have laid up your treasure in the last days. Behold, the wages of the laborers who mowed your fields, which you have kept back by fraud, cry out, and the cries of those who reaped have entered into the ears of the Lord of Armies. You have lived delicately on the earth, and taken your pleasure. You have nourished your hearts as in a day of slaughter. You have condemned, you have murdered the righteous one. He doesn't resist you.

Is. 49:8-13 Thus says Yahweh, "In an acceptable time have I answered you, and in a day of salvation have I helped you; and I will preserve you, and give you for a covenant of the people, to raise up the land, to make them inherit the desolate heritage: saying to those who are bound, 'Come out!'; to those who are in darkness, 'Show yourselves!' "They shall feed in the ways, and on all bare heights shall be their pasture. They shall not hunger nor thirst; neither shall the heat nor sun strike them: for he who has mercy on them will lead them, even by springs of water he will guide them. I will make all my mountains a way, and my highways shall be exalted. Behold, these shall come from far; and behold, these from the north and from the west; and these from the land of Sinim." Sing, heavens; and be joyful, earth; and break forth into singing, mountains: for Yahweh has comforted his people, and will have compassion on his afflicted.

Php. 4:10-20 But I rejoice in the Lord greatly, that now at length you have revived your thought for me; in which you did indeed take thought, but you lacked opportunity. Not that I speak in respect to lack, for I have learned in whatever state I am, to be content in it. I know how to be humbled, and I know also how to abound. In everything and in all things I have learned the secret both to be filled and to be hungry, both to abound and to be in need. I can do all things through Christ, who strengthens me. However you did well that you shared in my affliction. You yourselves also know, you Philippians, that in the beginning of the Good News, when I departed from Macedonia, no assembly shared with me in the matter of giving and receiving but you only. For even in Thessalonica you sent once and again to my need. Not that I seek for the gift, but I seek for the fruit that increases to your account. But I have all things, and abound. I am filled, having received from Epaphroditus the things that came from you, a sweet-smelling fragrance, an acceptable and well-pleasing sacrifice to God. My God will supply every need of yours according to his riches in glory in Christ Jesus. Now to our God and Father be the glory forever and ever! Amen.

Hag. 1:2-11 "This is what Yahweh of Armies says: These people say, 'The time hasn't yet come, the time for Yahweh's house to be built.'" Then the Word of Yahweh came by Haggai, the prophet, saying, "Is it a time for you yourselves to dwell in your paneled houses, while this house lies waste? Now therefore this is what Yahweh of Armies says: Consider your ways. You have sown much, and bring in little. You eat, but you don't have enough. You drink, but you aren't filled with drink. You clothe yourselves, but no one is warm, and he who earns wages earns wages to put them into a bag with holes in it." This is what Yahweh of Armies says: "Consider your ways. Go up to the mountain, bring wood, and build the house. I will take pleasure in it, and I will be glorified," says Yahweh. "You looked for much, and, behold, it came to little; and when you brought it home, I blew it away. Why?" says Yahweh of Armies, "Because of my house that lies waste, while each of you is busy with his own house. Therefore for your sake the heavens withhold the dew, and the earth withholds its fruit. I called for a drought on the land, on the mountains, on the grain, on the new wine, on the oil, on that which the ground brings forth, on men, on livestock, and on all the labor of the hands."

Luke 20:20-26 They watched him, and sent out spies, who pretended to be righteous, that they might trap him in something he said, so as to deliver him up to the power and authority of the governor. They asked him, "Teacher, we know that you say and teach what is right, and aren't partial to anyone, but truly teach the way of God. Is it lawful for us to pay taxes to Caesar, or not?" But he perceived their craftiness, and said to them, "Why do you test me? Show me a denarius. Whose image and inscription are on it?" They answered, "Caesar's." He said to them, "Then give to Caesar the things that are Caesar's, and to God the things that are God's." They weren't able to trap him in his words before the people. They marveled at his answer, and were silent.

Rom. 13:1-7 Let every soul be in subjection to the higher authorities, for there is no authority except from God, and those who exist are ordained by God. Therefore he who resists the authority, withstands the ordinance of God; and those who withstand will receive to themselves judgment. For rulers are not a terror to the good work, but to the evil. Do you desire to have no fear of the authority? Do that which is good, and you will have praise from the same, for he is a servant of God to you for good. But if you do that which is evil, be afraid, for he doesn't bear the sword in vain; for he is a servant of God, an avenger for wrath to him who does evil. Therefore you need to be in subjection, not only because of the wrath, but also for conscience' sake. For this reason you also pay taxes, for they are servants of God's service, attending continually on this very thing. Give therefore to everyone what you owe: taxes to whom taxes are due; customs to whom customs; respect to whom respect; honor to whom honor.

Pr. 9:1-12 Wisdom has built her house. She has carved out her seven pillars. She has prepared her meat. She has mixed her wine. She has also set her table. She has sent out her maidens. She cries from the highest places of the city: "Whoever is simple, let him turn in here!" As for him who is void of understanding, she says to him, "Come, eat some of my bread, Drink some of the wine which I have mixed! Leave your simple ways, and live. Walk in the way of understanding." He who corrects a mocker invites insult. He who reproves a wicked man invites abuse.

Don't reprove a scoffer, lest he hate you. Reprove a wise man, and he will love you. Instruct a wise man, and he will be still wiser. Teach a righteous man, and he will increase in learning. The fear of Yahweh is the beginning of wisdom. The knowledge of the Holy One is understanding. For by me your days will be multiplied. The years of your life will be increased. If you are wise, you are wise for yourself. If you mock, you alone will bear it.

Week 10 Day 2   25-May

Matt. 17:24-27 When they had come to Capernaum, those who collected the didrachma coins came to Peter, and said, "Doesn't your teacher pay the didrachma?" He said, "Yes." When he came into the house, Jesus anticipated him, saying, "What do you think, Simon? From whom do the kings of the earth receive toll or tribute? From their children, or from strangers?" Peter said to him, "From strangers." Jesus said to him, "Therefore the children are exempt. But, lest we cause them to stumble, go to the sea, cast a hook, and take up the first fish that comes up. When you have opened its mouth, you will find a stater coin. Take that, and give it to them for me and you."

Tit. 3:1-11 Remind them to be in subjection to rulers and to authorities, to be obedient, to be ready for every good work, to speak evil of no one, not to be contentious, to be gentle, showing all humility toward all men. For we were also once foolish, disobedient, deceived, serving various lusts and pleasures, living in malice and envy, hateful, and hating one another. But when the kindness of God our Savior and his love toward mankind appeared, not by works of righteousness, which we did ourselves, but according to his mercy, he saved us, through the washing of regeneration and renewing by the Holy Spirit, whom he poured out on us richly, through Jesus Christ our Savior; that, being justified by his grace, we might be made heirs according to the hope of eternal life. This saying is faithful, and concerning these things I desire that you affirm confidently, so that those who have believed God may be careful to maintain good works. These things are good and profitable to men; but shun foolish questionings, genealogies, strife, and disputes about the law; for they are unprofitable and vain. Avoid a factious man after a first and second warning; knowing that such a one is perverted, and sins, being self-condemned.

Ex. 30:11-16 Yahweh spoke to Moses, saying, "When you take a census of the children of Israel, according to those who are numbered among them, then each man shall give a ransom for his soul to Yahweh, when you number them; that there be no plague among them when you number them. They shall give this, everyone who passes over to those who are numbered, half a shekel after the shekel of the sanctuary; (the shekel is twenty gerahs;) half a shekel for an offering to Yahweh. Everyone who passes over to those who are numbered, from twenty years old and upward, shall give the offering to Yahweh. The rich shall not give more, and the poor shall not give less, than the half shekel, when they give the offering of Yahweh, to make atonement for your souls. You shall take the atonement money from the children of Israel, and shall appoint it for the service of the Tent of Meeting; that it may be a memorial for the children of Israel before Yahweh, to make atonement for your souls."

Week 10 Day 3   13-Sep

Luke 14:25-35 Now great multitudes were going with him. He turned and said to them, "If anyone comes to me, and doesn't disregard his own father, mother, wife, children, brothers, and sisters, yes, and his own life also, he can't be my disciple. Whoever doesn't bear his own cross, and come after me, can't be my disciple. For which of you, desiring to build a tower, doesn't first sit down and count the cost, to see if he has enough to complete it? Or perhaps, when he has laid a foundation, and is not able to finish, everyone who sees begins to mock him, saying, 'This man began to build, and wasn't able to finish.' Or what king, as he goes to encounter another king in war, will not sit down first and consider whether he is able with ten thousand to meet him who comes against him with twenty thousand? Or else, while the other is yet a great way off, he sends an envoy, and asks for conditions of peace. So therefore whoever of you who doesn't renounce all that he has, he can't be my disciple. Salt is good, but if the salt becomes flat and tasteless, with what do you season it? It is fit neither for the soil nor for the manure pile. It is thrown out. He who has ears to hear, let him hear."

Rom. 12:1-2 Therefore I urge you, brothers, by the mercies of God, to present your bodies a living sacrifice, holy, acceptable to God, which is your spiritual service. Don't be conformed to this world, but be transformed by the renewing of your mind, so that you may prove what is the good, well-pleasing, and perfect will of God.

Jos. 9:24-27 They answered Joshua, and said, "Because your servants were certainly told how Yahweh your God commanded his servant Moses to give you all the land, and to destroy all the inhabitants of the land from before you. Therefore we were very afraid for our lives because of you, and have done this thing. Now, behold, we are in your hand. Do to us as it seems good and right to you to do." He did so to them, and delivered them out of the hand of the children of Israel, so that they didn't kill them. That day Joshua made them wood cutters and drawers of water for the congregation and for the altar of Yahweh, to this day, in the place which he should choose.

Week 10 Day 4   **26-Apr**

Matt. 13:44-46 "Again, the Kingdom of Heaven is like a treasure hidden in the field, which a man found, and hid. In his joy, he goes and sells all that he has, and buys that field. Again, the Kingdom of Heaven is like a man who is a merchant seeking fine pearls, who having found one pearl of great price, he went and sold all that he had, and bought it."

Php. 3:7-11 However, what things were gain to me, these have I counted loss for Christ. Yes most certainly, and I count all things to be loss for the excellency of the knowledge of Christ Jesus, my Lord, for whom I suffered the loss of all things, and count them nothing but refuse, that I may gain Christ and be found in him, not having a righteousness of my own, that which is of the law, but that which is through faith in Christ, the righteousness which is from God by faith; that I may know him, and the power of his resurrection, and the fellowship of his sufferings, becoming conformed to his death; if by any means I may attain to the resurrection from the dead.

Ruth 1:1-18 It happened in the days when the judges judged, that there was a famine in the land. A certain man of Bethlehem Judah went to live in the country of Moab, he, and his wife, and his two sons. The name of the man was Elimelech, and the name of his wife Naomi, and the name of his two sons Mahlon and Chilion, Ephrathites of Bethlehem Judah. They came into the country of Moab, and continued there. Elimelech, Naomi's husband, died; and she was left, and her two sons. They took them wives of the women of Moab; the name of the one was Orpah, and the name of the other Ruth: and they lived there about ten years. Mahlon and Chilion both died, and the woman was bereaved of her two children and of her husband. Then she arose with her daughters-in-law, that she might return from the country of Moab: for she had heard in the country of Moab how that Yahweh had visited his people in giving them bread. She went forth out of the place where she was, and her two daughters-in-law with her; and they went on the way to return to the land of Judah. Naomi said to her two daughters-in-law, "Go, return each of you to her mother's house: Yahweh deal kindly with you, as you have dealt with the dead, and with me. Yahweh grant you that you may find rest, each of you in the house of her husband." Then she kissed them, and they lifted up their voice, and wept. They said to her, "No, but we will return with you to your people." Naomi said, "Go back, my daughters. Why do you want to go with me? Do I still have sons in my womb, that they may be your husbands? Go back, my daughters, go your way; for I am too old to have a husband. If I should say, 'I have hope,' if I should even have a husband tonight, and should also bear sons; would you then wait until they were grown? Would you then refrain from having husbands? No, my daughters, for it grieves me much for your sakes, for the hand of Yahweh has gone out against me." They lifted up their voice, and wept again: and Orpah kissed her mother-in-law, but Ruth joined with her. She said, "Behold, your sister-in-law has gone back to her people, and to her god. Follow your sister-in-law." Ruth said, "Don't entreat me to leave you, and to return from following after you, for where you go, I will go; and where you lodge, I will lodge; your people shall be my people, and your God my God; where you die, will I die, and there will I be buried. Yahweh do so to me, and more also, if anything but death part you and me." When she saw that she was steadfastly minded to go with her, she left off speaking to her.

Week 10 Day 5   **28-Sep**

Luke 21:1-4 He looked up, and saw the rich people who were putting their gifts into the treasury. He saw a certain poor widow casting in two small brass coins. He said, "Truly I tell you, this poor widow put in more than all of them, for all these put in gifts for God from their abundance, but she, out of her poverty, put in all that she had to live on."

2 Cor. 8:1-15 "Moreover, brothers, we make known to you the grace of God which has been given in the assemblies of Macedonia; how that in much proof of affliction the abundance of their joy and their deep poverty abounded to the riches of their liberality. For according to their power, I testify, yes and beyond their power, they gave of their own accord, begging us with much entreaty to receive this grace and the fellowship in the service to the saints. This was not as we had hoped, but first they gave their own selves to the Lord, and to us through the will of God. So we urged Titus, that as he made a beginning before, so he would also complete in you this grace. But as you abound in everything, in faith, utterance, knowledge, all earnestness, and in your love to us, see that you also abound in this grace. I speak not by way of commandment, but as proving through the earnestness of others the sincerity also of your love. For you know the grace of our Lord Jesus Christ, that, though he was rich, yet for your sakes he became poor, that you through his poverty might become rich. I give a judgment in this: for this is expedient for you, who were the first to start a year ago, not only to do, but also to be willing. But now complete the doing also, that as there was the readiness to be willing, so there may be the completion also out of your ability. For if the readiness is there, it is acceptable according to what you have, not according to what you don't have. For this is not that others may be eased and you distressed, but for equality. Your abundance at this present time supplies their lack, that their abundance also may become a supply for your lack; that there may be equality. As it is written, "He who gathered much had nothing left over, and he who gathered little had no lack."

1 Sam. 1:1-22 Now there was a certain man of Ramathaim Zophim, of the hill country of Ephraim, and his name was Elkanah, the son of Jeroham, the son of Elihu, the son of Tohu, the son of Zuph, an Ephraimite: and he had two wives; the name of the one was Hannah, and the name of other Peninnah: and Peninnah had children, but Hannah had no children. This man went up out of his city from year to year to worship and to sacrifice to Yahweh of Armies in Shiloh. The two sons of Eli, Hophni and Phinehas, priests to Yahweh, were there. When the day came that Elkanah sacrificed, he gave to Peninnah his wife, and to all her sons and her daughters, portions: but to Hannah he gave a double portion; for he loved Hannah, but Yahweh had shut up her womb. Her rival provoked her severely, to make her fret, because Yahweh had shut up her womb. As he did so year by year, when she went up to the house of Yahweh, so she provoked her; therefore she wept, and didn't eat. Elkanah her husband said to her, "Hannah, why do you weep? Why don't you eat? Why is your heart grieved? Am I not better to you than ten sons?" So Hannah rose up after they had eaten in Shiloh, and after they had drunk. Now Eli the priest was sitting on his seat by the doorpost of Yahweh's temple. She was in bitterness of soul, and prayed to Yahweh, and wept bitterly. She vowed a vow, and said, "Yahweh of Armies, if you will indeed look on the affliction of your handmaid, and remember me, and not forget your handmaid, but will give to your handmaid a boy, then I will give him to Yahweh all the days of his life, and no razor shall come on his head." It happened, as she continued praying before Yahweh, that Eli saw her mouth. Now Hannah spoke in her heart. Only her lips moved, but her voice was not heard. Therefore Eli thought she had been drunken. Eli said to her, "How long will you be drunken? Put away your wine from you." Hannah answered, "No, my lord, I am a woman of a sorrowful spirit. I have drunk neither wine nor strong drink, but I poured out my soul before Yahweh. Don't count your handmaid for a wicked woman; for I have been speaking out of the abundance of my complaint and my provocation." Then Eli answered, "Go in peace; and may the God of Israel grant your petition that you have asked of him." She said, "Let your handmaid find favor in your sight." So the woman went her way, and ate; and her facial expression wasn't sad any more. They rose up in the morning early, and worshiped before Yahweh, and returned, and came to their house to Ramah: and Elkanah knew Hannah his wife; and Yahweh remembered her. It happened, when the time had come, that Hannah conceived, and bore a son; and she named him Samuel, saying, "Because I have asked him of Yahweh." The man Elkanah, and all his house, went up to offer to Yahweh the yearly sacrifice, and his vow. But Hannah didn't go up; for she said to her husband, "Not until the child is weaned; then I will bring him, that he may appear before Yahweh, and stay there forever."

Week 10 Day 6   17-Aug

Mark 10:17-31 As he was going out into the way, one ran to him, knelt before him, and asked him, "Good Teacher, what shall I do that I may inherit eternal life?" Jesus said to him, "Why do you call me good? No one is good except one—God. You know the commandments: 'Do not murder,' 'Do not commit adultery,' 'Do not steal,' 'Do not give false testimony,' 'Do not defraud,' 'Honor your father and mother.'" He said to him, "Teacher, I have observed all these things from my youth." Jesus looking at him loved him, and said to him, "One thing you lack. Go, sell whatever you have, and give to the poor, and you will have treasure in heaven; and come, follow me, taking up the cross." But his face fell at that saying, and he went away sorrowful, for he was one who had great possessions. Jesus looked around, and said to his disciples, "How difficult it is for those who have riches to enter into the Kingdom of God!" The disciples were amazed at his words. But Jesus answered again, "Children, how hard is it for those who trust in riches to enter into the Kingdom of God! It is easier for a camel to go through a needle's eye than for a rich man to enter into the Kingdom of God." They were exceedingly astonished, saying to him, "Then who can be saved?" Jesus, looking at them, said, "With men it is impossible, but not with God, for all things are possible with God." Peter began to tell him, "Behold, we have left all, and have followed you." Jesus said, "Most certainly I tell you, there is no one who has left house, or brothers, or sisters, or father, or mother, or wife, or children, or land, for my sake, and for the sake of the Good News, but he will receive one hundred times more now in this time, houses, brothers, sisters, mothers, children, and land, with persecutions; and in the age to come eternal life. But many who are first will be last; and the last first."

1 Tim. 6:3-12 If anyone teaches a different doctrine, and doesn't consent to sound words, the words of our Lord Jesus Christ, and to the doctrine which is according to godliness, he is conceited, knowing nothing, but obsessed with arguments, disputes, and word battles, from which come envy, strife, insulting, evil suspicions, constant friction of people of corrupt minds and destitute of the truth, who suppose that godliness is a means of gain. Withdraw yourself from such. But godliness with contentment is great gain. For we brought nothing into the world, and we certainly can't carry anything out. But having food and clothing, we will be content with that. But those who are determined to be rich fall into a temptation and a snare and many foolish and harmful lusts, such as drown men in ruin and destruction. For the love of money is a root of all kinds of evil. Some have been led astray from the faith in their greed, and have pierced themselves through with many sorrows. But you, man of God, flee these things, and follow after righteousness, godliness, faith, love, patience, and gentleness. Fight the good fight of faith. Lay hold of the eternal life to which you were called, and you confessed the good confession in the sight of many witnesses.

Ps. 39:4-6 "Yahweh, show me my end, what is the measure of my days. Let me know how frail I am. Behold, you have made my days handbreadths. My lifetime is as nothing before you. Surely every man stands as a breath." Selah. "Surely every man walks like a shadow. Surely they busy themselves in vain. He heaps up, and doesn't know who shall gather."

Week 10 Day 7   11-Jan

Eph. 6:5-9 Servants, be obedient to those who according to the flesh are your masters, with fear and trembling, in singleness of your heart, as to Christ; not in the way of service only when eyes are on you, as men pleasers; but as servants of Christ, doing the will of God from the heart; with good will doing service, as to the Lord, and not to men; knowing that whatever good thing each one does, he will receive the same again from the Lord, whether he is bound or free. You masters, do the same things to them, and give up threatening, knowing that he who is both their Master and yours is in heaven, and there is no partiality with him.

Ps. 19:7-14 Yahweh's law is perfect, restoring the soul. Yahweh's testimony is sure, making wise the simple. Yahweh's precepts are right, rejoicing the heart. Yahweh's commandment is pure, enlightening the eyes. The fear of Yahweh is clean, enduring forever. Yahweh's ordinances are true, and righteous altogether. More to be desired are they than gold, yes, than much fine gold; sweeter also than honey and the extract of the honeycomb. Moreover by them is your servant warned. In keeping them there is great reward. Who can discern his errors? Forgive me from hidden errors. Keep back your servant also from presumptuous sins. Let them not have dominion over me. Then I will be upright. I will be blameless and innocent of great transgression. Let the words of my mouth and the meditation of my heart be acceptable in your sight, Yahweh, my rock, and my redeemer.

Matt. 6:1-4 "Be careful that you don't do your charitable giving before men, to be seen by them, or else you have no reward from your Father who is in heaven. Therefore when you do merciful deeds, don't sound a trumpet before yourself, as the hypocrites do in the synagogues and in the streets, that they may get glory from men. Most certainly I tell you, they have received their reward. But when you do merciful deeds, don't let your left hand know what your right hand does, so that your merciful deeds may be in secret, then your Father who sees in secret will reward you openly."

II Tim. 3:1-9 But know this, that in the last days, grievous times will come. For men will be lovers of self, lovers of money, boastful, arrogant, blasphemers, disobedient to parents, unthankful, unholy, without natural affection, unforgiving, slanderers, without self-control, fierce, no lovers of good, traitors, headstrong, conceited, lovers of pleasure rather than lovers of God; holding a form of godliness, but having denied its power. Turn away from these, also. For some of these are people who creep into houses, and take captive gullible women loaded down with sins, led away by various lusts, always learning, and never able to come to the knowledge of the truth. Even as Jannes and Jambres opposed Moses, so do these also oppose the truth; men corrupted in mind, who concerning the faith, are rejected. But they will proceed no further. For their folly will be evident to all men, as theirs also came to be.

De. 10:12-22 Now, Israel, what does Yahweh your God require of you, but to fear Yahweh your God, to walk in all his ways, and to love him, and to serve Yahweh your God with all your heart and with all your soul, to keep the commandments of Yahweh, and his statutes, which I command you this day for your good? Behold, to Yahweh your God belongs heaven and the heaven of heavens, the earth, with all that is therein. Only Yahweh had a delight in your fathers to love them, and he chose their seed after them, even you above all peoples, as at this day. Circumcise therefore the foreskin of your heart, and be no more stiff-necked. For Yahweh your God, he is God of gods, and Lord of lords, the great God, the mighty, and the awesome, who doesn't respect persons, nor takes reward. He does execute justice for the fatherless and widow, and loves the foreigner, in giving him food and clothing. Therefore love the foreigner; for you were foreigners in the land of Egypt. You shall fear Yahweh your God; you shall serve him; and you shall cling to him, and you shall swear by his name. He is your praise, and he is your God, who has done for you these great and awesome things, which your eyes have seen. Your fathers went down into Egypt with seventy persons; and now Yahweh your God has made you as the stars of the sky for multitude.

Matt. 6:19-24 "Don't lay up treasures for yourselves on the earth, where moth and rust consume, and where thieves break through and steal; but lay up for yourselves treasures in heaven, where neither moth nor rust consume, and where thieves don't break through and steal; for where your treasure is, there your heart will be also. The lamp of the body is the eye. If therefore your eye is sound, your whole body will be full of light. But if your eye is evil, your whole body will be full of darkness. If therefore the light that is in you is darkness, how great is the darkness! No one can serve two masters, for either he will hate the one and love the other; or else he will be devoted to one and despise the other. You can't serve both God and Mammon."

Acts 5:1-11 But a certain man named Ananias, with Sapphira, his wife, sold a possession, and kept back part of the price, his wife also being aware of it, and brought a certain part, and laid it at the apostles' feet. But Peter said, "Ananias, why has Satan filled your heart to lie to the Holy Spirit, and to keep back part of the price of the land? While you kept it, didn't it remain your own? After it was sold, wasn't it in your power? How is it that you have conceived this thing in your heart? You haven't lied to men, but to God." Ananias, hearing these words, fell down and died. Great fear came on all who heard these things. The young men arose and wrapped him up, and they carried him out and buried him. About three hours later, his wife, not knowing what had happened, came in. Peter answered her, "Tell me whether you sold the land for so much." She said, "Yes, for so much." But Peter asked her, "How is it that you have agreed together to tempt the Spirit of the Lord? Behold, the feet of those who have buried your husband are at the door, and they will carry you out." She fell down immediately at his feet, and died. The young men came in and found her dead, and they carried her out and buried her by her husband. Great fear came on the whole assembly, and on all who heard these things.

De. 8:1-20 You shall observe to do all the commandment which I command you this day, that you may live, and multiply, and go in and possess the land which Yahweh swore to your fathers. You shall remember all the way which Yahweh your God has led you these forty years in the wilderness, that he might humble you, to prove you, to know what was in your heart, whether you would keep his commandments, or not. He humbled you, and allowed you to be hungry, and fed you with manna, which you didn't know, neither did your fathers know; that he might make you know that man does not live by bread only, but man lives by everything that proceeds out of the mouth of Yahweh. Your clothing didn't grow old on you, neither did your foot swell, these forty years. You shall consider in your heart that as a man chastens his son, so Yahweh your God chastens you. You shall keep the commandments of Yahweh your God, to walk in his ways, and to fear him. For Yahweh your God brings you into a good land, a land of brooks of water, of springs, and underground water flowing into valleys and hills; a land of wheat and barley, and vines and fig trees and pomegranates; a land of olive trees and honey; a land in which you shall eat bread without scarceness, you shall not lack anything in it; a land whose stones are iron, and out of whose hills you may dig copper. You shall eat and be full, and you shall bless Yahweh your God for the good land which he has given you. Beware lest you forget Yahweh your God, in not keeping his commandments, and his ordinances, and his statutes, which I command you this day: lest, when you have eaten and are full, and have built goodly houses, and lived therein; and when your herds and your flocks multiply, and your silver and your gold is multiplied, and all that you have is multiplied; then your heart be lifted up, and you forget Yahweh your God, who brought you forth out of the land of Egypt, out of the house of bondage; who led you through the great and terrible wilderness, with fiery serpents and scorpions, and thirsty ground where there was no water; who brought you forth water out of the rock of flint; who fed you in the wilderness with manna, which your fathers didn't know; that he might humble you, and that he might prove you, to do you good at your latter end: and lest you say in your heart, "My power and the might of my hand has gotten me this wealth." But you shall remember Yahweh your God, for it is he who gives you power to get wealth; that he may establish his covenant which he swore to your fathers, as at this day. It shall be, if you shall forget Yahweh your God, and walk after other gods, and serve them, and worship them, I testify against you this day that you shall surely perish. As the nations that Yahweh makes to perish before you, so you shall perish; because you wouldn't listen to the voice of Yahweh your God.

Week 11 Day 3   20-Mar

Luke 14:12-14 He also said to the one who had invited him, "When you make a dinner or a supper, don't call your friends, nor your brothers, nor your kinsmen, or rich neighbors, or perhaps they might also return the favor, and pay you back. But when you make a feast, ask the poor, the maimed, the lame, or the blind; and you will be blessed, because they don't have the resources to repay you. For you will be repaid in the resurrection of the righteous."

Gal. 2:10 They only asked us to remember the poor—which very thing I was also zealous to do.

II Sa. 9:1-13 David said, "Is there yet any who is left of the house of Saul, that I may show him kindness for Jonathan's sake?" There was of the house of Saul a servant whose name was Ziba, and they called him to David; and the king said to him, "Are you Ziba?" He said, "Your servant is he." The king said, "Is there not yet any of the house of Saul, that I may show the kindness of God to him?" Ziba said to the king, "Jonathan has yet a son, who is lame of his feet." The king said to him, "Where is he?" Ziba said to the king, "Behold, he is in the house of Machir the son of Ammiel, in Lo Debar." Then king David sent, and fetched him out of the house of Machir the son of Ammiel, from Lo Debar. Mephibosheth, the son of Jonathan, the son of Saul, came to David, and fell on his face, and showed respect. David said, "Mephibosheth." He answered, "Behold, your servant!" David said to him, "Don't be afraid of him; for I will surely show you kindness for Jonathan your father's sake, and will restore to you all the land of Saul your father. You shall eat bread at my table continually." He bowed down, and said, "What is your servant, that you should look on such a dead dog as I am?" Then the king called to Ziba, Saul's servant, and said to him, "All that pertained to Saul and to all his house have I given to your master's son. You shall till the land for him, you, and your sons, and your servants; and you shall bring in the harvest, that your master's son may have bread to eat: but Mephibosheth your master's son shall eat bread always at my table." Now Ziba had fifteen sons and twenty servants. Then Ziba said to the king, "According to all that my lord the king commands his servant, so your shall servant do." So Mephibosheth ate at the king's table, like one of the king's sons. Mephibosheth had a young son, whose name was Mica. All that lived in the house of Ziba were servants to Mephibosheth. So Mephibosheth lived in Jerusalem; for he ate continually at the king's table. He was lame in both his feet.

Week 11 Day 4   2-Sep

Luke 16:1-13 He also said to his disciples, "There was a certain rich man who had a manager. An accusation was made to him that this man was wasting his possessions. He called him, and said to him, 'What is this that I hear about you? Give an accounting of your management, for you can no longer be manager.' "The manager said within himself, 'What will I do, seeing that my lord is taking away the management position from me? I don't have strength to dig. I am ashamed to beg. I know what I will do, so that when I am removed from management, they may receive me into their houses.' Calling each one of his lord's debtors to him, he said to the first, 'How much do you owe to my lord?' He said, 'A hundred batos of oil.' He said to him, 'Take your bill, and sit down quickly and write fifty.' Then he said to another, 'How much do you owe?' He said, 'A hundred cors of wheat.' He said to him, 'Take your bill, and write eighty.' "His lord commended the dishonest manager because he had done wisely, for the children of this world are, in their own generation, wiser than the children of the light. I tell you, make for yourselves friends by means of unrighteous mammon, so that when you fail, they may receive you into the eternal tents. He who is faithful in a very little is faithful also in much. He who is dishonest in a very little is also dishonest in much. If therefore you have not been faithful in the unrighteous mammon, who will commit to your trust the true riches? If you have not been faithful in that which is another's, who will give you that which is your own? No servant can serve two masters, for either he will hate the one, and love the other; or else he will hold to one, and despise the other. You aren't able to serve God and mammon."

I Tim. 6:17-21 Charge those who are rich in this present world that they not be haughty, nor have their hope set on the uncertainty of riches, but on the living God, who richly provides us with everything to enjoy; that they do good, that they be rich in good works, that they be ready to distribute, willing to communicate; laying up in store for themselves a good foundation against the time to come, that they may lay hold of eternal life. Timothy, guard that which is committed to you, turning away from the empty chatter and oppositions of the knowledge which is falsely so called; which some professing have erred concerning the faith. Grace be with you. Amen.

Am. 8:1-14 Thus the Lord Yahweh showed me: behold, a basket of summer fruit. He said, "Amos, what do you see?" I said, "A basket of summer fruit." Then Yahweh said to me, "The end has come on my people Israel. I will not again pass by them any more. The songs of the temple will be wailings in that day," says the Lord Yahweh. "The dead bodies will be many. In every place they will throw them out with silence. Hear this, you who desire to swallow up the needy, and cause the poor of the land to fail, Saying, 'When will the new moon be gone, that we may sell grain? And the Sabbath, that we may market wheat, making the ephah small, and the shekel large, and dealing falsely with balances of deceit; that we may buy the poor for silver, and the needy for a pair of shoes, and sell the sweepings with the wheat?'" Yahweh has sworn by the pride of Jacob, "Surely I will never forget any of their works. Won't the land tremble for this, and everyone mourn who dwells in it? Yes, it will rise up wholly like the River; and it will be stirred up and sink again, like the River of Egypt. It will happen in that day," says the Lord Yahweh, "that I will cause the sun to go down at noon, and I will darken the earth in the clear day. I will turn your feasts into mourning, and all your songs into lamentation; and I will make you wear sackcloth on all your bodies, and baldness on every head. I will make it like the mourning for an only son, and its end like a bitter day. Behold, the days come," says the Lord Yahweh, "that I will send a famine in the land, not a famine of bread, nor a thirst for water, but of hearing the words of Yahweh. They will wander from sea to sea, and from the north even to the east; they will run back and forth to seek the word of Yahweh, and will not find it. In that day the beautiful virgins and the young men will faint for thirst. Those who swear by the sin of Samaria, and say, 'As your god, Dan, lives;' and, 'As the way of Beersheba lives;' they will fall, and never rise up again."

Luke 12:22-34 He said to his disciples, "Therefore I tell you, don't be anxious for your life, what you will eat, nor yet for your body, what you will wear. Life is more than food, and the body is more than clothing. Consider the ravens: they don't sow, they don't reap, they have no warehouse or barn, and God feeds them. How much more valuable are you than birds! Which of you by being anxious can add a cubit to his height? If then you aren't able to do even the least things, why are you anxious about the rest? Consider the lilies, how they grow. They don't toil, neither do they spin; yet I tell you, even Solomon in all his glory was not arrayed like one of these. But if this is how God clothes the grass in the field, which today exists, and tomorrow is cast into the oven, how much more will he clothe you, O you of little faith? Don't seek what you will eat or what you will drink; neither be anxious. For the nations of the world seek after all of these things, but your Father knows that you need these things. But seek God's Kingdom, and all these things will be added to you. Don't be afraid, little flock, for it is your Father's good pleasure to give you the Kingdom. Sell that which you have, and give gifts to the needy. Make for yourselves purses which don't grow old, a treasure in the heavens that doesn't fail, where no thief approaches, neither moth destroys. For where your treasure is, there will your heart be also."

Heb. 9:11-28 But Christ having come as a high priest of the coming good things, through the greater and more perfect tabernacle, not made with hands, that is to say, not of this creation, nor yet through the blood of goats and calves, but through his own blood, entered in once for all into the Holy Place, having obtained eternal redemption. For if the blood of goats and bulls, and the ashes of a heifer sprinkling those who have been defiled, sanctify to the cleanness of the flesh: how much more will the blood of Christ, who through the eternal Spirit offered himself without blemish to God, cleanse your conscience from dead works to serve the living God? For this reason he is the mediator of a new covenant, since a death has occurred for the redemption of the transgressions that were under the first covenant, that those who have been called may receive the promise of the eternal inheritance. For where a last will and testament is, there must of necessity be the death of him who made it. For a will is in force where there has been death, for it is never in force while he who made it lives. Therefore even the first covenant has not been dedicated without blood. For when every commandment had been spoken by Moses to all the people according to the law, he took the blood of the calves and the goats, with water and scarlet wool and hyssop, and sprinkled both the book itself and all the people, saying, "This is the blood of the covenant which God has commanded you." Moreover he sprinkled the tabernacle and all the vessels of the ministry in the same way with the blood. According to the law, nearly everything is cleansed with blood, and apart from shedding of blood there is no remission. It was necessary therefore that the copies of the things in the heavens should be cleansed with these; but the heavenly things themselves with better sacrifices than these. For Christ hasn't entered into holy places made with hands, which are representations of the true, but into heaven itself, now to appear in the presence of God for us; nor yet that he should offer himself often, as the high priest enters into the holy place year by year with blood not his own, or else he must have suffered often since the foundation of the world. But now once at the end of the ages, he has been revealed to put away sin by the sacrifice of himself. Inasmuch as it is appointed for men to die once, and after this, judgment, so Christ also, having been offered once to bear the sins of many, will appear a second time, without sin, to those who are eagerly waiting for him for salvation.

Ps. 37:16-40 Better is a little that the righteous has, than the abundance of many wicked. For the arms of the wicked shall be broken, but Yahweh upholds the righteous. Yahweh knows the days of the upright. Their inheritance shall be forever. They shall not be disappointed in the time of evil. In the days of famine they shall be satisfied. But the wicked shall perish. The enemies of Yahweh shall be like the beauty of the fields. They will vanish—vanish like smoke. The wicked borrow, and don't pay back, but the righteous give generously. For such as are blessed by him shall inherit the land. Those who are cursed by him shall be cut off. A man's goings are established by Yahweh. He delights in his way. Though he stumble, he shall not fall, for Yahweh holds him up with his hand. I have been young, and now am old, yet I have not seen the righteous forsaken, nor his children begging for bread. All day long he deals graciously, and lends. His seed is blessed. Depart from evil, and do good. Live securely forever. For Yahweh loves justice, and doesn't forsake his saints. They are preserved forever, but the children of the wicked shall be cut off. The righteous shall inherit the land, and live in it forever. The mouth of the righteous talks of wisdom. His tongue speaks justice. The law of his God is in his heart. None of his steps shall slide. The wicked watches the righteous, and seeks to kill him. Yahweh will not leave him in his hand, nor condemn him when he is judged. Wait for Yahweh, and keep his way, and he will exalt you to inherit the land. When the wicked are cut off, you shall see it. I have seen the wicked in great power, spreading himself like a green tree in its native soil. But he passed away, and behold, he was not. Yes, I sought him, but he could not be found. Mark the blameless man, and see the upright, for there is a future for the man of peace. As for transgressors, they shall be destroyed together. The future of the wicked shall be cut off. But the salvation of the righteous is from Yahweh. He is their stronghold in the time of trouble. Yahweh helps them, and rescues them. He rescues them from the wicked, and saves them, because they have taken refuge in him.

Week 11 Day 6   21-May

Luke 16:14-18 The Pharisees, who were lovers of money, also heard all these things, and they scoffed at him. He said to them, "You are those who justify yourselves in the sight of men, but God knows your hearts. For that which is exalted among men is an abomination in the sight of God. The law and the prophets were until John. From that time the Good News of the Kingdom of God is preached, and everyone is forcing his way into it. But it is easier for heaven and earth to pass away, than for one tiny stroke of a pen in the law to fall. Everyone who divorces his wife, and marries another, commits adultery. He who marries one who is divorced from a husband commits adultery."

I Tim. 1:3-11 As I urged you when I was going into Macedonia, stay at Ephesus that you might command certain men not to teach a different doctrine, neither to pay attention to myths and endless genealogies, which cause disputes, rather than God's stewardship, which is in faith—but the goal of this command is love, out of a pure heart and a good conscience and sincere faith; from which things some, having missed the mark, have turned aside to vain talking; desiring to be teachers of the law, though they understand neither what they say, nor about what they strongly affirm. But we know that the law is good, if a man uses it lawfully, as knowing this, that law is not made for a righteous man, but for the lawless and insubordinate, for the ungodly and sinners, for the unholy and profane, for murderers of fathers and murderers of mothers, for manslayers, for the sexually immoral, for homosexuals, for slave-traders, for liars, for perjurers, and for any other thing contrary to the sound doctrine; according to the Good News of the glory of the blessed God, which was committed to my trust.

Ps. 119:33-48 Teach me, Yahweh, the way of your statutes. I will keep them to the end. Give me understanding, and I will keep your law. Yes, I will obey it with my whole heart. Direct me in the path of your commandments, for I delight in them. Turn my heart toward your statutes, not toward selfish gain. Turn my eyes away from looking at worthless things. Revive me in your ways. Fulfill your promise to your servant, that you may be feared. Take away my disgrace that I dread, for your ordinances are good. Behold, I long for your precepts! Revive me in your righteousness. Let your loving kindness also come to me, Yahweh, your salvation, according to your word. So I will have an answer for him who reproaches me, for I trust in your word. Don't snatch the word of truth out of my mouth, for I put my hope in your ordinances. So I will obey your law continually, forever and ever. I will walk in liberty, for I have sought your precepts. I will also speak of your statutes before kings, and will not be disappointed. I will delight myself in your commandments, because I love them. I reach out my hands for your commandments, which I love. I will meditate on your statutes.

Week 11 Day 7   7-Sep

II Cor. 9:6-15 Remember this: he who sows sparingly will also reap sparingly. He who sows bountifully will also reap bountifully. Let each man give according as he has determined in his heart; not grudgingly, or under compulsion; for God loves a cheerful giver. And God is able to make all grace abound to you, that you, always having all sufficiency in everything, may abound to every good work. As it is written, "He has scattered abroad, he has given to the poor. His righteousness remains forever." Now may he who supplies seed to the sower and bread for food, supply and multiply your seed for sowing, and increase the fruits of your righteousness; you being enriched in everything to all liberality, which works through us thanksgiving to God. For this service of giving that you perform not only makes up for lack among the saints, but abounds also through many givings of thanks to God;

seeing that through the proof given by this service, they glorify God for the obedience of your confession to the Good News of Christ, and for the liberality of your contribution to them and to all; while they themselves also, with supplication on your behalf, yearn for you by reason of the exceeding grace of God in you. Now thanks be to God for his unspeakable gift!

Ps. 34:1-10 I will bless Yahweh at all times. His praise will always be in my mouth. My soul shall boast in Yahweh. The humble shall hear of it, and be glad. Oh magnify Yahweh with me. Let us exalt his name together. I sought Yahweh, and he answered me, and delivered me from all my fears. They looked to him, and were radiant. Their faces shall never be covered with shame. This poor man cried, and Yahweh heard him, and saved him out of all his troubles. The angel of Yahweh encamps around those who fear him, and delivers them. Oh taste and see that Yahweh is good. Blessed is the man who takes refuge in him. Oh fear Yahweh, you his saints, for there is no lack with those who fear him. The young lions do lack, and suffer hunger, but those who seek Yahweh shall not lack any good thing.

Week 12 Day 1   23-Aug

Matt. 6:5-15 "When you pray, you shall not be as the hypocrites, for they love to stand and pray in the synagogues and in the corners of the streets, that they may be seen by men. Most certainly, I tell you, they have received their reward. But you, when you pray, enter into your inner room, and having shut your door, pray to your Father who is in secret, and your Father who sees in secret will reward you openly. In praying, don't use vain repetitions, as the Gentiles do; for they think that they will be heard for their much speaking. Therefore don't be like them, for your Father knows what things you need, before you ask him. Pray like this: 'Our Father in heaven, may your name be kept holy. Let your Kingdom come. Let your will be done, as in heaven, so on earth. Give us today our daily bread. Forgive us our debts, as we also forgive our debtors. Bring us not into temptation, but deliver us from the evil one. For yours is the Kingdom, the power, and the glory forever. Amen.' "For if you forgive men their trespasses, your heavenly Father will also forgive you. But if you don't forgive men their trespasses, neither will your Father forgive your trespasses."

1 Thes. 5:16-24 Rejoice always. Pray without ceasing. In everything give thanks, for this is the will of God in Christ Jesus toward you. Don't quench the Spirit. Don't despise prophesies. Test all things, and hold firmly that which is good. Abstain from every form of evil. May the God of peace himself sanctify you completely. May your whole spirit, soul, and body be preserved blameless at the coming of our Lord Jesus Christ. He who calls you is faithful, who will also do it.

1 Chr. 29:10-13 Therefore David blessed Yahweh before all the assembly; and David said, "You are blessed, Yahweh, the God of Israel our father, forever and ever. Yours, Yahweh, is the greatness, the power, the glory, the victory, and the majesty! For all that is in the heavens and in the earth is yours. Yours is the kingdom, Yahweh, and you are exalted as head above all. Both riches and honor come from you, and you rule over all; and in your hand is power and might; and it is in your hand to make great, and to give strength to all. Now therefore, our God, we thank you, and praise your glorious name."

Week 12 Day 2   19-Oct

Luke 4:42 When it was day, he departed and went into an uninhabited place, and the multitudes looked for him, and came to him, and held on to him, so that he wouldn't go away from them.

Luke 5:15-16 But the report concerning him spread much more, and great multitudes came together to hear, and to be healed by him of their infirmities. But he withdrew himself into the desert, and prayed.

Luke 6:12-13 It happened in these days, that he went out to the mountain to pray, and he continued all night in prayer to God. When it was day, he called his disciples, and from them he chose twelve, whom he also named apostles.

Acts 10:9-23 Now on the next day as they were on their journey, and got close to the city, Peter went up on the housetop to pray at about noon. He became hungry and desired to eat, but while they were preparing, he fell into a trance. He saw heaven opened and a certain container descending to him, like a great sheet let down by four corners on the earth, in which were all kinds of four-footed animals of the earth, wild animals, reptiles, and birds of the sky. A voice came to him, "Rise, Peter, kill and eat!" But Peter said, "Not so, Lord; for I have never eaten anything that is common or unclean." A voice came to him again the second time, "What God has cleansed, you must not call unclean." This was done three times, and immediately the vessel was received up into heaven. Now while Peter was very perplexed in himself what the vision which he had seen might mean, behold, the men who were sent by Cornelius, having made inquiry for Simon's house, stood before the gate, and called and asked whether Simon, who was surnamed Peter, was lodging there. While Peter was pondering the vision, the Spirit said to him, "Behold, three men seek you. But arise, get down, and go with them, doubting nothing; for I have sent them." Peter went down to the men, and said, "Behold, I am he whom you seek. Why have you come?" They said, "Cornelius, a centurion, a righteous man and one who fears God, and well spoken of by all the nation of the Jews, was directed by a holy angel to invite you to his house, and to listen to what you say." So he called them in and lodged them. On the next day Peter arose and went out with them, and some of the brothers from Joppa accompanied him.

Ps. 5:1-12 Give ear to my words, Yahweh. Consider my meditation. Listen to the voice of my cry, my King and my God; for to you do I pray. Yahweh, in the morning you shall hear my voice. In the morning I will lay my requests before you, and will watch expectantly. For you are not a God who has pleasure in wickedness. Evil can't live with you. The arrogant shall not stand in your sight. You hate all workers of iniquity. You will destroy those who speak lies. Yahweh abhors the bloodthirsty and deceitful man. But as for me, in the abundance of your loving kindness I will come into your house. I will bow toward your holy temple in reverence of you. Lead me, Yahweh, in your righteousness because of my enemies. Make your way straight before my face. For there is no faithfulness in their mouth. Their heart is destruction. Their throat is an open tomb. They flatter with their tongue. Hold them guilty, God. Let them fall by their own counsels; thrust them out in the multitude of their transgressions, for they have rebelled against you. But let all those who take refuge in you rejoice; let them always shout for joy, because you defend them. Let them also who love your name be joyful in you. For you will bless the righteous. Yahweh, you will surround him with favor as with a shield.

Week 12 Day 3   5-Jul

John 10:27-30 "My sheep hear my voice, and I know them, and they follow me. I give eternal life to them. They will never perish, and no one will snatch them out of my hand. My Father, who has given them to me, is greater than all. No one is able to snatch them out of my Father's hand. I and the Father are one."

Heb. 8:7-13 For if that first covenant had been faultless, then no place would have been sought for a second. For finding fault with them, he said, "Behold, the days come," says the Lord, "that I will make a new covenant with the house of Israel and with the house of Judah; according to the covenant that I made with their fathers, in the day that I took them by the hand to lead them out of the land of Egypt; for they didn't continue in my covenant, and I disregarded them," says the Lord. "For this is the covenant that I will make with the house of Israel. After those days," says the Lord; "I will put my laws into their mind, I will also write them on their heart. I will be their God, and they will be my people. They will not teach every man his fellow citizen, and every man his brother, saying, 'Know the Lord,' for all will know me, from their least to their greatest. For I will be merciful to their unrighteousness. I will remember their sins and lawless deeds no more." In that he says, "A new covenant," he has made the first old. But that which is becoming old and grows aged is near to vanishing away.

Num. 27:12-23 Yahweh said to Moses, "Go up into this mountain of Abarim, and see the land which I have given to the children of Israel. When you have seen it, you also shall be gathered to your people, as Aaron your brother was gathered; because you rebelled against my word in the wilderness of Zin, in the strife of the congregation, to sanctify me at the waters before their eyes." (These are the waters of Meribah of Kadesh in the wilderness of Zin.) Moses spoke to Yahweh, saying, "Let Yahweh, the God of the spirits of all flesh, appoint a man over the congregation, who may go out before them, and who may come in before them, and who may lead them out, and who may bring them in; that the congregation of Yahweh not be as sheep which have no shepherd." Yahweh said to Moses, "Take Joshua the son of Nun, a man in whom is the Spirit, and lay your hand on him; and set him before Eleazar the priest, and before all the congregation; and commission him in their sight. You shall put of your honor on him, that all the congregation of the children of Israel may obey. He shall stand before Eleazar the priest, who shall inquire for him by the judgment of the Urim before Yahweh: at his word shall they go out, and at his word they shall come in, both he, and all the children of Israel with him, even all the congregation." Moses did as Yahweh commanded him; and he took Joshua, and set him before Eleazar the priest, and before all the congregation: and he laid his hands on him, and commissioned him, as Yahweh spoke by Moses.

Week 12 Day 4   23-Apr

Luke 10:38-42 It happened as they went on their way, he entered into a certain village, and a certain woman named Martha received him into her house. She had a sister called Mary, who also sat at Jesus' feet, and heard his word. But Martha was distracted with much serving, and she came up to him, and said, "Lord, don't you care that my sister left me to serve alone? Ask her therefore to help me." Jesus answered her, "Martha, Martha, you are anxious and troubled about many things, but one thing is needed. Mary has chosen the good part, which will not be taken away from her."

Heb. 4:1-13 Let us fear therefore, lest perhaps anyone of you should seem to have come short of a promise of entering into his rest. For indeed we have had good news preached to us, even as they also did, but the word they heard didn't profit them, because it wasn't mixed with faith by those who heard. For we who have believed do enter into that rest, even as he has said, "As I swore in my wrath, they will not enter into my rest"; although the works were finished from the foundation of the world. For he has said this somewhere about the seventh day, "God rested on the seventh day from all his works"; and in this place again, "They will not enter into my rest." Seeing therefore it remains that some should enter therein, and they to whom the good news was before preached failed to enter in because of disobedience, he again defines a certain day, today, saying through David so long a time afterward (just as has been said), "Today if you will hear his voice, don't harden your hearts." For if Joshua had given them rest, he would not have spoken afterward of another day. There remains therefore a Sabbath rest for the people of God. For he who has entered into his rest has himself also rested from his works, as God did from his. Let us therefore give diligence to enter into that rest, lest anyone fall after the same example of disobedience. For the word of God is living, and active, and sharper than any two-edged sword, and piercing even to the dividing of soul and spirit, of both joints and marrow, and is able to discern the thoughts and intentions of the heart. There is no creature that is hidden from his sight, but all things are naked and laid open before the eyes of him with whom we have to do.

Ps. 46 God is our refuge and strength, a very present help in trouble. Therefore we won't be afraid, though the earth changes, though the mountains are shaken into the heart of the seas; though its waters roar and are troubled, though the mountains tremble with their swelling. Selah. There is a river, the streams of which make the city of God glad, the holy place of the tents of the Most High. God is in her midst. She shall not be moved. God will help her at dawn. The nations raged. The kingdoms were moved. He lifted his voice, and the earth melted. Yahweh of Armies is with us. The God of Jacob is our refuge. Selah. Come, see Yahweh's works, what desolations he has made in the earth. He makes wars cease to the end of the earth. He breaks the bow, and shatters the spear. He burns the chariots in the fire. "Be still, and know that I am God. I will be exalted among the nations. I will be exalted in the earth." Yahweh of Armies is with us. The God of Jacob is our refuge. Selah.

Week 12 Day 5   10-Jun

Luke 11:5-13 He said to them, "Which of you, if you go to a friend at midnight, and tell him, 'Friend, lend me three loaves of bread, for a friend of mine has come to me from a journey, and I have nothing to set before him,' and he from within will answer and say, 'Don't bother me. The door is now shut, and my children are with me in bed. I can't get up and give it to you'? I tell you, although he will not rise and give it to him because he is his friend, yet because of his persistence, he will get up and give him as many as he needs. I tell you, keep asking, and it will be given you. Keep seeking, and you will find. Keep knocking, and it will be opened to you. For everyone who asks receives. He who seeks finds. To him who knocks it will be opened. Which of you fathers, if your son asks for bread, will give him a stone? Or if he asks for a fish, he won't give him a snake instead of a fish, will he? Or if he asks for an egg, he won't give him a scorpion, will he? If you then, being evil, know how to give good gifts to your children, how much more will your heavenly Father give the Holy Spirit to those who ask him?"

Eph. 1:15-23 For this cause I also, having heard of the faith in the Lord Jesus which is among you, and the love which you have toward all the saints, don't cease to give thanks for you, making mention of you in my prayers, that the God of our Lord Jesus Christ, the Father of glory, may give to you a spirit of wisdom and revelation in the knowledge of him; having the eyes of your hearts enlightened, that you may know what is the hope of his calling, and what are the riches of the glory of his inheritance in the saints, and what is the exceeding greatness of his power toward us who believe, according to that working of the strength of his might which he worked in Christ, when he raised him from the dead, and made him to sit at his right hand in the heavenly places, far above all rule, and authority, and power, and dominion, and every name that is named, not only in this age, but also in that which is to come. He put all things in subjection under his feet, and gave him to be head over all things for the assembly, which is his body, the fullness of him who fills all in all.

Ge. 18:20-33 Yahweh said, "Because the cry of Sodom and Gomorrah is great, and because their sin is very grievous, I will go down now, and see whether their deeds are as bad as the reports which have come to me. If not, I will know." The men turned from there, and went toward Sodom, but Abraham stood yet before Yahweh. Abraham drew near, and said, "Will you consume the righteous with the wicked? What if there are fifty righteous within the city? Will you consume and not spare the place for the fifty righteous who are in it? Be it far from you to do things like that, to kill the righteous with the wicked, so that the righteous should be like the wicked. May that be far from you. Shouldn't the Judge of all the earth do right?" Yahweh said, "If I find in Sodom fifty righteous within the city, then I will spare all the place for their sake." Abraham answered, "See now, I have taken it on myself to speak to the Lord, who am but dust and ashes. What if there will lack five of the fifty righteous? Will you destroy all the city for lack of five?" He said, "I will not destroy it, if I find forty-five there." He spoke to him yet again, and said, "What if there are forty found there?" He said, "I will not do it for the forty's sake." He said, "Oh don't let the Lord be angry, and I will speak. What if there are thirty found there?" He said, "I will not do it, if I find thirty there." He said, "See now, I have taken it on myself to speak to the Lord. What if there are twenty found there?" He said, "I will not destroy it for the twenty's sake." He said, "Oh don't let the Lord be angry, and I will speak just once more. What if ten are found there?" He said, "I will not destroy it for the ten's sake." Yahweh went his way, as soon as he had finished communing with Abraham, and Abraham returned to his place.

Week 12 Day 6   **9-Jul**

Luke 18:1-8 He also spoke a parable to them that they must always pray, and not give up, saying, "There was a judge in a certain city who didn't fear God, and didn't respect man. A widow was in that city, and she often came to him, saying, 'Defend me from my adversary!' He wouldn't for a while, but afterward he said to himself, 'Though I neither fear God, nor respect man, yet because this widow bothers me, I will defend her, or else she will wear me out by her continual coming.'" The Lord said, "Listen to what the unrighteous judge says. Won't God avenge his chosen ones, who are crying out to him day and night, and yet he exercises patience with them? I tell you that he will avenge them quickly. Nevertheless, when the Son of Man comes, will he find faith on the earth?"

II Cor. 12:7-10 By reason of the exceeding greatness of the revelations, that I should not be exalted excessively, there was given to me a thorn in the flesh, a messenger of Satan to torment me, that I should not be exalted excessively. Concerning this thing, I begged the Lord three times that it might depart from me. He has said to me, "My grace is sufficient for you, for my power is made perfect in weakness." Most gladly therefore I will rather glory in my weaknesses, that the power of Christ may rest on me. Therefore I take pleasure in weaknesses, in injuries, in necessities, in persecutions, in distresses, for Christ's sake. For when I am weak, then am I strong.

Ps. 121 I will lift up my eyes to the hills. Where does my help come from? My help comes from Yahweh, who made heaven and earth. He will not allow your foot to be moved. He who keeps you will not slumber. Behold, he who keeps Israel will neither slumber nor sleep. Yahweh is your keeper. Yahweh is your shade on your right hand. The sun will not harm you by day, nor the moon by night. Yahweh will keep you from all evil. He will keep your soul. Yahweh will keep your going out and your coming in, from this time forth, and forevermore.

Week 12 Day 7   6-Aug

Php. 1:3-11 I thank my God whenever I remember you, always in every request of mine on behalf of you all making my requests with joy, for your partnership in furtherance of the Good News from the first day until now; being confident of this very thing, that he who began a good work in you will complete it until the day of Jesus Christ. It is even right for me to think this way on behalf of all of you, because I have you in my heart, because, both in my bonds and in the defense and confirmation of the Good News, you all are partakers with me of grace. For God is my witness, how I long after all of you in the tender mercies of Christ Jesus. This I pray, that your love may abound yet more and more in knowledge and all discernment; so that you may approve the things that are excellent; that you may be sincere and without offense to the day of Christ; being filled with the fruits of righteousness, which are through Jesus Christ, to the glory and praise of God.

Ps. 122 I was glad when they said to me, "Let's go to Yahweh's house!" Our feet are standing within your gates, Jerusalem; Jerusalem, that is built as a city that is compact together; where the tribes go up, even Yah's tribes, according to an ordinance for Israel, to give thanks to the name of Yahweh. For there are set thrones for judgment, the thrones of David's house. Pray for the peace of Jerusalem. Those who love you will prosper. Peace be within your walls, and prosperity within your palaces. For my brothers' and companions' sakes, I will now say, "Peace be within you." For the sake of the house of Yahweh our God, I will seek your good.

Week 13 Day 1   17-Mar

Matt. 6:16-18 "Moreover when you fast, don't be like the hypocrites, with sad faces. For they disfigure their faces, that they may be seen by men to be fasting. Most certainly I tell you, they have received their reward. But you, when you fast, anoint your head, and wash your face; so that you are not seen by men to be fasting, but by your Father who is in secret, and your Father, who sees in secret, will reward you."

Acts 13:1-3 Now in the assembly that was at Antioch there were some prophets and teachers: Barnabas, Simeon who was called Niger, Lucius of Cyrene, Manaen the foster brother of Herod the tetrarch, and Saul. As they served the Lord and fasted, the Holy Spirit said, "Separate Barnabas and Saul for me, for the work to which I have called them." Then, when they had fasted and prayed and laid their hands on them, they sent them away.

Is. 58:1-12 "Cry aloud, don't spare, lift up your voice like a trumpet, and declare to my people their disobedience, and to the house of Jacob their sins. Yet they seek me daily, and delight to know my ways: as a nation that did righteousness, and didn't forsake the ordinance of their God, they ask of me righteous judgments; they delight to draw near to God. 'Why have we fasted,' say they, 'and you don't see? Why have we afflicted our soul, and you take no knowledge?' Behold, in the day of your fast you find pleasure, and exact all your labors. Behold, you fast for strife and contention, and to strike with the fist of wickedness: you don't fast this day so as to make your voice to be heard on high. Is such the fast that I have chosen? the day for a man to afflict his soul? Is it to bow down his head as a rush, and to spread sackcloth and ashes under him? Will you call this a fast, and an acceptable day to Yahweh? Isn't this the fast that I have chosen: to release the bonds of wickedness, to undo the bands of the yoke, and to let the oppressed go free, and that you break every yoke? Isn't it to distribute your bread to the hungry, and that you bring the poor who are cast out to your house? When you see the naked, that you cover him; and that you not hide yourself from your own flesh? Then your light shall break forth as the morning, and your healing shall spring forth speedily; and your righteousness shall go before you; the glory of Yahweh shall be your rear guard. Then you shall call, and Yahweh will answer; you shall cry, and he will say, 'Here I am.' If you take away from the midst of you the yoke, the putting forth of the finger, and speaking wickedly; and if you draw out your soul to the hungry, and satisfy the afflicted soul: then your light shall rise in darkness, and your obscurity be as the noonday; and Yahweh will guide you continually, and satisfy your soul in dry places, and make strong your bones; and you shall be like a watered garden, and like a spring of water, whose waters don't fail. Those who shall be of you shall build the old waste places; you shall raise up the foundations of many generations; and you shall be called the repairer of the breach, the restorer of paths to dwell in."

Week 13 Day 2   23-Jan

Luke 5:33-39 They said to him, "Why do John's disciples often fast and pray, likewise also the disciples of the Pharisees, but yours eat and drink?" He said to them, "Can you make the friends of the bridegroom fast, while the bridegroom is with them? But the days will come when the bridegroom will be taken away from them. Then they will fast in those days." He also told a parable to them. "No one puts a piece from a new garment on an old garment, or else he will tear the new, and also the piece from the new will not match the old. No one puts new wine into old wineskins, or else the new wine will burst the skins, and it will be spilled, and the skins will be destroyed. But new wine must be put into fresh wineskins, and both are preserved. No man having drunk old wine immediately desires new, for he says, 'The old is better.'"

II Pet. 1:3-11 His divine power has granted to us all things that pertain to life and godliness, through the knowledge of him who called us by his own glory and virtue; by which he has granted to us his precious and exceedingly great promises; that through these you may become partakers of the divine nature, having escaped from the corruption that is in the world by lust. Yes, and for this very cause adding on your part all diligence, in your faith supply moral excellence; and in moral excellence, knowledge; and in knowledge, self-control; and in self-control patience; and in patience godliness; and in godliness brotherly affection; and in brotherly affection, love. For if these things are yours and abound, they make you to be not idle nor unfruitful to the knowledge of our Lord Jesus Christ. For he who lacks these things is blind, seeing only what is near, having forgotten the cleansing from his old sins. Therefore, brothers, be more diligent to make your calling and election sure. For if you do these things, you will never stumble. For thus you will be richly supplied with the entrance into the eternal Kingdom of our Lord and Savior, Jesus Christ.

Is. 54:1-8 "Sing, barren, you who didn't bear; break forth into singing, and cry aloud, you who did not travail with child: for more are the children of the desolate than the children of the married wife," says Yahweh. "Enlarge the place of your tent, and let them stretch forth the curtains of your habitations; don't spare: lengthen your cords, and strengthen your stakes. For you shall spread out on the right hand and on the left; and your seed shall possess the nations, and make the desolate cities to be inhabited. Don't be afraid; for you shall not be ashamed: neither be confounded; for you shall not be disappointed: for you shall forget the shame of your youth; and the reproach of your widowhood you shall remember no more. For your Maker is your husband; Yahweh of Armies is his name: and the Holy One of Israel is your Redeemer; the God of the whole earth shall he be called. For Yahweh has called you as a wife forsaken and grieved in spirit, even a wife of youth, when she is cast off," says your God. For a small moment have I forsaken you; but with great mercies will I gather you. In overflowing wrath I hid my face from you for a moment; but with everlasting loving kindness will I have mercy on you," says Yahweh your Redeemer.

Week 13 Day 3   27-Nov

Luke 14:7-11 He spoke a parable to those who were invited, when he noticed how they chose the best seats, and said to them, "When you are invited by anyone to a marriage feast, don't sit in the best seat, since perhaps someone more honorable than you might be invited by him, and he who invited both of you would come and tell you, 'Make room for this person.' Then you would begin, with shame, to take the lowest place. But when you are invited, go and sit in the lowest place, so that when he who invited you comes, he may tell you, 'Friend, move up higher.' Then you will be honored in the presence of all who sit at the table with you. For everyone who exalts himself will be humbled, and whoever humbles himself will be exalted."

I Thes. 4:1-12 Finally then, brothers, we beg and exhort you in the Lord Jesus, that as you received from us how you ought to walk and to please God, that you abound more and more. For you know what instructions we gave you through the Lord Jesus. For this is the will of God: your sanctification, that you abstain from sexual immorality, that each one of you know how to possess himself of his own vessel in sanctification and honor, not in the passion of lust, even as the Gentiles who don't know God; that no one should take advantage of and wrong a brother or sister in this matter; because the Lord is an avenger in all these things, as also we forewarned you and testified. For God called us not for uncleanness, but in sanctification. Therefore he who rejects this doesn't reject man, but God, who has also given his Holy Spirit to you. But concerning brotherly love, you have no need that one write to you. For you yourselves are taught by God to love one another, for indeed you do it toward all the brothers who are in all Macedonia. But we exhort you, brothers, that you abound more and more; and that you make it your ambition to lead a quiet life, and to do your own business, and to work with your own hands, even as we instructed you; that you may walk properly toward those who are outside, and may have need of nothing.

Dan. 5:18-21 You, king, the Most High God gave Nebuchadnezzar your father the kingdom, and greatness, and glory, and majesty: and because of the greatness that he gave him, all the peoples, nations, and languages trembled and feared before him: whom he would he killed, and whom he would he kept alive; and whom he would he raised up, and whom he would he put down. But when his heart was lifted up, and his spirit was hardened so that he dealt proudly, he was deposed from his kingly throne, and they took his glory from him: and he was driven from the sons of men, and his heart was made like the animals', and his dwelling was with the wild donkeys; he was fed with grass like oxen, and his body was wet with the dew of the sky; until he knew that the Most High God rules in the kingdom of men, and that he sets up over it whomever he will.

Week 13 Day 4   30-Nov

Luke 18:9-14 He spoke also this parable to certain people who were convinced of their own righteousness, and who despised all others. "Two men went up into the temple to pray; one was a Pharisee, and the other was a tax collector. The Pharisee stood and prayed to himself like this: 'God, I thank you, that I am not like the rest of men, extortioners, unrighteous, adulterers, or even like this tax collector. I fast twice a week. I give tithes of all that I get.' But the tax collector, standing far away, wouldn't even lift up his eyes to heaven, but beat his breast, saying, 'God, be merciful to me, a sinner!' I tell you, this man went down to his house justified rather than the other; for everyone who exalts himself will be humbled, but he who humbles himself will be exalted."

Jas. 2:1-13 My brothers, don't hold the faith of our Lord Jesus Christ of glory with partiality. For if a man with a gold ring, in fine clothing, comes into your synagogue, and a poor man in filthy clothing also comes in; and you pay special attention to him who wears the fine clothing, and say, "Sit here in a good place"; and you tell the poor man, "Stand there," or "Sit by my footstool"; haven't you shown partiality among yourselves, and become judges with evil thoughts? Listen, my beloved brothers. Didn't God choose those who are poor in this world to be rich in faith, and heirs of the Kingdom which he promised to those who love him? But you have dishonored the poor man. Don't the rich oppress you, and personally drag you before the courts? Don't they blaspheme the honorable name by which you are called? However, if you fulfill the royal law, according to the Scripture, "You shall love your neighbor as yourself," you do well. But if you show partiality, you commit sin, being convicted by the law as transgressors. For whoever keeps the whole law, and yet stumbles in one point, he has become guilty of all. For he who said, "Do not commit adultery," also said, "Do not commit murder." Now if you do not commit adultery, but murder, you have become a transgressor of the law. So speak, and so do, as men who are to be judged by a law of freedom. For judgment is without mercy to him who has shown no mercy. Mercy triumphs over judgment.

Jer. 7:1-8 The word that came to Jeremiah from Yahweh, saying, "Stand in the gate of Yahweh's house, and proclaim there this word, and say, 'Hear the word of Yahweh, all you of Judah, who enter in at these gates to worship Yahweh. Thus says Yahweh of Armies, the God of Israel, Amend your ways and your doings, and I will cause you to dwell in this place. Don't trust in lying words, saying, Yahweh's temple, Yahweh's temple, Yahweh's temple, are these. For if you thoroughly amend your ways and your doings; if you thoroughly execute justice between a man and his neighbor; if you don't oppress the foreigner, the fatherless, and the widow, and don't shed innocent blood in this place, neither walk after other gods to your own hurt: then will I cause you to dwell in this place, in the land that I gave to your fathers, from of old even forevermore. Behold, you trust in lying words, that can't profit.

Week 13 Day 5   19-Sep

Luke 22:24-30 There arose also a contention among them, which of them was considered to be greatest. He said to them, "The kings of the nations lord it over them, and those who have authority over them are called 'benefactors.' But not so with you. But one who is the greater among you, let him become as the younger, and one who is governing, as one who serves. For who is greater, one who sits at the table, or one who serves? Isn't it he who sits at the table? But I am in the midst of you as one who serves. But you are those who have continued with me in my trials. I confer on you a kingdom, even as my Father conferred on me, that you may eat and drink at my table in my Kingdom. You will sit on thrones, judging the twelve tribes of Israel."

I Pet. 2:4-12 You have come to him, the living stone, rejected indeed by men, but chosen by God, precious. You also, as living stones, are built up as a spiritual house, to be a holy priesthood, to offer up spiritual sacrifices, acceptable to God through Jesus Christ. Because it is contained in Scripture, "Behold, I lay in Zion a chief cornerstone, chosen, and precious: He who believes in him will not be disappointed." For you who believe therefore is the honor, but for those who are disobedient, "The stone which the builders rejected, has become the chief cornerstone," and, "a stone of stumbling, and a rock of offense." For they stumble at the word, being disobedient, to which also they were appointed. But you are a chosen race, a royal priesthood, a holy nation, a people for God's own possession, that you may proclaim the excellence of him who called you out of darkness into his marvelous light: who in time past were no people, but now are God's people, who had not obtained mercy, but now have obtained mercy. Beloved, I beg you as foreigners and pilgrims, to abstain from fleshly lusts, which war against the soul; having good behavior among the nations, so in that of which they speak against you as evildoers, they may by your good works, which they see, glorify God in the day of visitation.

I Sa. 16:1-7 Yahweh said to Samuel, "How long will you mourn for Saul, since I have rejected him from being king over Israel? Fill your horn with oil, and go. I will send you to Jesse the Bethlehemite; for I have provided a king for myself among his sons." Samuel said, "How can I go? If Saul hears it, he will kill me." Yahweh said, "Take a heifer with you, and say, I have come to sacrifice to Yahweh. Call Jesse to the sacrifice, and I will show you what you shall do. You shall anoint to me him whom I name to you." Samuel did that which Yahweh spoke, and came to Bethlehem. The elders of the city came to meet him trembling, and said, "Do you come peaceably?" He said, "Peaceably; I have come to sacrifice to Yahweh. Sanctify yourselves, and come with me to the sacrifice." He sanctified Jesse and his sons, and called them to the sacrifice. It happened, when they had come, that he looked at Eliab, and said, "Surely Yahweh's anointed is before him." But Yahweh said to Samuel, "Don't look on his face, or on the height of his stature; because I have rejected him: for I see not as man sees; for man looks at the outward appearance, but Yahweh looks at the heart."

Week 13 Day 6   28-Jun

Luke 19:11-27 As they heard these things, he went on and told a parable, because he was near Jerusalem, and they supposed that the Kingdom of God would be revealed immediately. He said therefore, "A certain nobleman went into a far country to receive for himself a kingdom, and to return. He called ten servants of his, and gave them ten mina coins, and told them, 'Conduct business until I come.' But his citizens hated him, and sent an envoy after him, saying, 'We don't want this man to reign over us.' "It happened when he had come back again, having received the kingdom, that he commanded these servants, to whom he had given the money, to be called to him, that he might know what they had gained by conducting business. The first came before him, saying, 'Lord, your mina has made ten more minas.' "He said to him, 'Well done, you good servant! Because you were found faithful with very little, you shall have authority over ten cities.' "The second came, saying, 'Your mina, Lord, has made five minas.' "So he said to him, 'And you are to be over five cities.' Another came, saying, 'Lord, behold, your mina, which I kept laid away in a handkerchief, for I feared you, because you are an exacting man. You take up that which you didn't lay down, and reap that which you didn't sow.' "He said to him, 'Out of your own mouth will I judge you, you wicked servant! You knew that I am an exacting man, taking up that which I didn't lay down, and reaping that which I didn't sow. Then why didn't you deposit my money in the bank, and at my coming, I might have earned interest on it?' He said to those who stood by, 'Take the mina away from him, and give it to him who has the ten minas.' "They said to him, 'Lord, he has ten minas!' 'For I tell you that to everyone who has, will more be given; but from him who doesn't have, even that which he has will be taken away from him. But bring those enemies of mine who didn't want me to reign over them here, and kill them before me.'"

Rom. 12:3-8 For I say, through the grace that was given me, to every man who is among you, not to think of himself more highly than he ought to think; but to think reasonably, as God has apportioned to each person a measure of faith. For even as we have many members in one body, and all the members don't have the same function, so we, who are many, are one body in Christ, and individually members one of another. Having gifts differing according to the grace that was given to us, if prophecy, let us prophesy according to the proportion of our faith; or service, let us give ourselves to service; or he who teaches, to his teaching; or he who exhorts, to his exhorting: he who gives, let him do it with liberality; he who rules, with diligence; he who shows mercy, with cheerfulness.

Pr. 6:6-11 Go to the ant, you sluggard. Consider her ways, and be wise; which having no chief, overseer, or ruler, provides her bread in the summer, and gathers her food in the harvest. How long will you sleep, sluggard? When will you arise out of your sleep? A little sleep, a little slumber, a little folding of the hands to sleep: so your poverty will come as a robber, and your scarcity as an armed man.

Week 13 Day 7   12-Jan

Rom. 15:1-13 Now we who are strong ought to bear the weaknesses of the weak, and not to please ourselves. Let each one of us please his neighbor for that which is good, to be building him up. For even Christ didn't please himself. But, as it is written, "The reproaches of those who reproached you fell on me." For whatever things were written before were written for our learning, that through patience and through encouragement of the Scriptures we might have hope. Now the God of patience and of encouragement grant you to be of the same mind one with another according to Christ Jesus, that with one accord you may with one mouth glorify the God and Father of our Lord Jesus Christ. Therefore accept one another, even as Christ also accepted you, to the glory of God. Now I say that Christ has been made a servant of the circumcision for the truth of God, that he might confirm the promises given to the fathers, and that the Gentiles might glorify God for his mercy. As it is written, "Therefore will I give praise to you among the Gentiles, and sing to your name." Again he says, "Rejoice, you Gentiles, with his people." Again, "Praise the Lord, all you Gentiles! Let all the peoples praise him." Again, Isaiah says, "There will be the root of Jesse, he who arises to rule over the Gentiles; in him the Gentiles will hope." Now may the God of hope fill you with all joy and peace in believing, that you may abound in hope, in the power of the Holy Spirit.

Ps. 16 Preserve me, God, for in you do I take refuge. My soul, you have said to Yahweh, "You are my Lord. Apart from you I have no good thing." As for the saints who are in the earth, they are the excellent ones in whom is all my delight. Their sorrows shall be multiplied who give gifts to another god. Their drink offerings of blood I will not offer, nor take their names on my lips. Yahweh assigned my portion and my cup. You made my lot secure. The lines have fallen to me in pleasant places. Yes, I have a good inheritance. I will bless Yahweh, who has given me counsel. Yes, my heart instructs me in the night seasons. I have set Yahweh always before me. Because he is at my right hand, I shall not be moved. Therefore my heart is glad, and my tongue rejoices. My body shall also dwell in safety. For you will not leave my soul in Sheol, neither will you allow your holy one to see corruption. You will show me the path of life. In your presence is fullness of joy. In your right hand there are pleasures forevermore.

Week 14 Day 1   5-Jun

Matt. 10:5-20 Jesus sent these twelve out, and commanded them, saying, "Don't go among the Gentiles, and don't enter into any city of the Samaritans. Rather, go to the lost sheep of the house of Israel. As you go, preach, saying, 'The Kingdom of Heaven is at hand!' Heal the sick, cleanse the lepers, and cast out demons. Freely you received, so freely give. Don't take any gold, nor silver, nor brass in your money belts. Take no bag for your journey, neither two coats, nor shoes, nor staff: for the laborer is worthy of his food. Into whatever city or village you enter, find out who in it is worthy; and stay there until you go on. As you enter into the household, greet it. If the household is worthy, let your peace come on it, but if it isn't worthy, let your peace return to you. Whoever doesn't receive you, nor hear your words, as you go out of that house or that city, shake off the dust from your feet. Most certainly I tell you, it will be more tolerable for the land of Sodom and Gomorrah in the day of judgment than for that city. Behold, I send you out as sheep in the midst of wolves. Therefore be wise as serpents, and harmless as doves. But beware of men: for they will deliver you up to councils, and in their synagogues they will scourge you. Yes, and you will be brought before governors and kings for my sake, for a testimony to them and to the nations. But when they deliver you up, don't be anxious how or what you will say, for it will be given you in that hour what you will say. For it is not you who speak, but the Spirit of your Father who speaks in you."

Acts 14:1-7 It happened in Iconium that they entered together into the synagogue of the Jews, and so spoke that a great multitude both of Jews and of Greeks believed. But the disbelieving Jews stirred up and embittered the souls of the Gentiles against the brothers. Therefore they stayed there a long time, speaking boldly in the Lord, who testified to the word of his grace, granting signs and wonders to be done by their hands. But the multitude of the city was divided. Part sided with the Jews, and part with the apostles. When some of both the Gentiles and the Jews, with their rulers, made a violent attempt to mistreat and stone them, they became aware of it, and fled to the cities of Lycaonia, Lystra, Derbe, and the surrounding region. There they preached the Good News.

Ge. 19:1-14 The two angels came to Sodom at evening. Lot sat in the gate of Sodom. Lot saw them, and rose up to meet them. He bowed himself with his face to the earth, and he said, "See now, my lords, please turn aside into your servant's house, stay all night, wash your feet, and you can rise up early, and go on your way." They said, "No, but we will stay in the street all night." He urged them greatly, and they came in with him, and entered into his house. He made them a feast, and baked unleavened bread, and they ate. But before they lay down, the men of the city, the men of Sodom, surrounded the house, both young and old, all the people from every quarter. They called to Lot, and said to him, "Where are the men who came in to you this night? Bring them out to us, that we may have sex with them." Lot went out to them to the door, and shut the door after him. He said, "Please, my brothers, don't act so wickedly. See now, I have two virgin daughters. Please let me bring them out to you, and you may do to them what seems good to you. Only don't do anything to these men, because they have come under the shadow of my roof." They said, "Stand back!" Then they said, "This one fellow came in to live as a foreigner, and he appoints himself a judge. Now will we deal worse with you, than with them!" They pressed hard on the man Lot, and drew near to break the door. But the men reached out their hand, and brought Lot into the house to them, and shut the door. They struck the men who were at the door of the house with blindness, both small and great, so that they wearied themselves to find the door. The men said to Lot, "Do you have anybody else here? Sons-in-law, your sons, your daughters, and whoever you have in the city, bring them out of the place: for we will destroy this place, because the outcry against them has grown great before Yahweh that Yahweh has sent us to destroy it." Lot went out, and spoke to his sons-in-law, who were pledged to marry his daughters, and said, "Get up! Get out of this place, for Yahweh will destroy the city."

Week 14 Day 2   **16-Oct**

Luke 15:1-10 Now all the tax collectors and sinners were coming close to him to hear him. The Pharisees and the scribes murmured, saying, "This man welcomes sinners, and eats with them." He told them this parable. "Which of you men, if you had one hundred sheep, and lost one of them, wouldn't leave the ninety-nine in the wilderness, and go after the one that was lost, until he found it? When he has found it, he carries it on his shoulders, rejoicing. When he comes home, he calls together his friends and his neighbors, saying to them, 'Rejoice with me, for I have found my sheep which was lost!' I tell you that even so there will be more joy in heaven over one sinner who repents, than over ninety-nine righteous people who need no repentance. Or what woman, if she had ten drachma coins, if she lost one drachma coin, wouldn't light a lamp, sweep the house, and seek diligently until she found it? When she has found it, she calls together her friends and neighbors, saying, 'Rejoice with me, for I have found the drachma which I had lost.' Even so, I tell you, there is joy in the presence of the angels of God over one sinner repenting."

Col. 1:3-14 We give thanks to God the Father of our Lord Jesus Christ, praying always for you, having heard of your faith in Christ Jesus, and of the love which you have toward all the saints, because of the hope which is laid up for you in the heavens, of which you heard before in the word of the truth of the Good News, which has come to you; even as it is in all the world and is bearing fruit and growing, as it does in you also, since the day you heard and knew the grace of God in truth; even as you learned of Epaphras our beloved fellow servant, who is a faithful servant of Christ on our behalf, who also declared to us your love in the Spirit. For this cause, we also, since the day we heard this, don't cease praying and making requests for you, that you may be filled with the knowledge of his will in all spiritual wisdom and understanding, that you may walk worthily of the Lord, to please him in all respects, bearing fruit in every good work, and increasing in the knowledge of God; strengthened with all power, according to the might of his glory, for all endurance and perseverance with joy; giving thanks to the Father, who made us fit to be partakers of the inheritance of the saints in light; who delivered us out of the power of darkness, and translated us into the Kingdom of the Son of his love; in whom we have our redemption, the forgiveness of our sins.

I Sa. 9:1-17 Now there was a man of Benjamin, whose name was Kish, the son of Abiel, the son of Zeror, the son of Becorath, the son of Aphiah, the son of a Benjamite, a mighty man of valor. He had a son, whose name was Saul, an impressive young man; and there was not among the children of Israel a better person than he. From his shoulders and upward he was higher than any of the people. The donkeys of Kish, Saul's father, were lost. Kish said to Saul his son, "Take now one of the servants with you, and arise, go seek the donkeys." He passed through the hill country of Ephraim, and passed through the land of Shalishah, but they didn't find them: then they passed through the land of Shaalim, and there they weren't there: and he passed through the land of the Benjamites, but they didn't find them. When they had come to the land of Zuph, Saul said to his servant who was with him, "Come, and let us return, lest my father stop caring about the donkeys, and be anxious for us." He said to him, "See now, there is in this city a man of God, and he is a man who is held in honor. All that he says comes surely to pass. Now let us go there. Perhaps he can tell us concerning our journey whereon we go." Then Saul said to his servant, "But, behold, if we go, what shall we bring the man? For the bread is spent in our vessels, and there is not a present to bring to the man of God. What do we have?" The servant answered Saul again, and said, "Behold, I have in my hand the fourth part of a shekel of silver. I will give that to the man of God, to tell us our way." (In earlier times in Israel, when a man went to inquire of God, thus he said, "Come, and let us go to the seer"; for he who is now called a prophet was before called a Seer.) Then Saul said to his servant, "Well said. Come, let us go." So they went to the city where the man of God was. As they went up the ascent to the city, they found young maidens going out to draw water, and said to them, "Is the seer here?" They answered them, and said, "He is. Behold, he is before you. Hurry now, for he has come today into the city; for the people have a sacrifice today in the high place. As soon as you have come into the city, you shall immediately find him, before he goes up to the high place to eat; for the people will not eat until he come, because he blesses the sacrifice. Afterwards those who are invited eat. Now therefore go up; for at this time you shall find him." They went up to the city. As they came within the city, behold, Samuel came out toward them, to go up to the high place. Now Yahweh had revealed to Samuel a day before Saul came, saying, "Tomorrow about this time I will send you a man out of the land of Benjamin, and you shall anoint him to be prince over my people Israel; and he shall save my people out of the hand of the Philistines: for I have looked on my people, because their cry has come to me." When Samuel saw Saul, Yahweh said to him, "Behold, the man of whom I spoke to you! this same shall have authority over my people."

Week 14 Day 3   20-Oct

Luke 19:1-10 He entered and was passing through Jericho. There was a man named Zacchaeus. He was a chief tax collector, and he was rich. He was trying to see who Jesus was, and couldn't because of the crowd, because he was short. He ran on ahead, and climbed up into a sycamore tree to see him, for he was to pass that way. When Jesus came to the place, he looked up and saw him, and said to him, "Zacchaeus, hurry and come down, for today I must stay at your house." He hurried, came down, and received him joyfully. When they saw it, they all murmured, saying, "He has gone in to lodge with a man who is a sinner." Zacchaeus stood and said to the Lord, "Behold, Lord, half of my goods I give to the poor. If I have wrongfully exacted anything of anyone, I restore four times as much." Jesus said to him, "Today, salvation has come to this house, because he also is a son of Abraham. For the Son of Man came to seek and to save that which was lost."

Acts 19:13-20 Some of the itinerant Jews, exorcists, took on themselves to invoke over those who had the evil spirits the name of the Lord Jesus, saying, "We adjure you by Jesus whom Paul preaches." There were seven sons of one Sceva, a Jewish chief priest, who did this. The evil spirit answered, "Jesus I know, and Paul I know, but who are you?" The man in whom the evil spirit was leaped on them, and overpowered them, and prevailed against them, so that they fled out of that house naked and wounded. This became known to all, both Jews and Greeks, who lived at Ephesus. Fear fell on them all, and the name of the Lord Jesus was magnified. Many also of those who had believed came, confessing, and declaring their deeds. Many of those who practiced magical arts brought their books together and burned them in the sight of all. They counted their price, and found it to be fifty thousand pieces of silver. So the word of the Lord was growing and becoming mighty.

Ex. 22:1-4 If a man steals an ox or a sheep, and kills it, or sells it; he shall pay five oxen for an ox, and four sheep for a sheep. If the thief is found breaking in, and is struck so that he dies, there shall be no guilt of bloodshed for him. If the sun has risen on him, guilt of bloodshed shall be for him; he shall make restitution. If he has nothing, then he shall be sold for his theft. If the stolen property is found in his hand alive, whether it is ox, donkey, or sheep, he shall pay double.

Week 14 Day 4   10-Sep

Matt. 13:1-23 On that day Jesus went out of the house, and sat by the seaside. Great multitudes gathered to him, so that he entered into a boat, and sat, and all the multitude stood on the beach. He spoke to them many things in parables, saying, "Behold, a farmer went out to sow. As he sowed, some seeds fell by the roadside, and the birds came and devoured them. Others fell on rocky ground, where they didn't have much soil, and immediately they sprang up, because they had no depth of earth. When the sun had risen, they were scorched. Because they had no root, they withered away. Others fell among thorns. The thorns grew up and choked them. Others fell on good soil, and yielded fruit: some one hundred times as much, some sixty, and some thirty. He who has ears to hear, let him hear." The disciples came, and said to him, "Why do you speak to them in parables?" He answered them, "To you it is given to know the mysteries of the Kingdom of Heaven, but it is not given to them. For whoever has, to him will be given, and he will have abundance, but whoever doesn't have, from him will be taken away even that which he has. Therefore I speak to them in parables, because seeing they don't see, and hearing, they don't hear, neither do they understand. In them the prophecy of Isaiah is fulfilled, which says, 'By hearing you will hear, and will in no way understand; Seeing you will see, and will in no way perceive: for this people's heart has grown callous, their ears are dull of hearing, they have closed their eyes; or else perhaps they might perceive with their eyes, hear with their ears, understand with their heart, and should turn again; and I would heal them.' But blessed are your eyes, for they see; and your ears, for they hear. For most certainly I tell you that many prophets and righteous men desired to see the things which you see, and didn't see them; and to hear the things which you hear, and didn't hear them. Hear, then, the parable of the farmer. When anyone hears the word of the Kingdom, and doesn't understand it, the evil one comes, and snatches away that which has been sown in his heart. This is what was sown by the roadside. What was sown on the rocky places, this is he who hears the word, and immediately with joy receives it; yet he has no root in himself, but endures for a while. When oppression or persecution arises because of the word, immediately he stumbles. What was sown among the thorns, this is he who hears the word, but the cares of this age and the deceitfulness of riches choke the word, and he becomes unfruitful. What was sown on the good ground, this is he who hears the word, and understands it, who most certainly bears fruit, and brings forth, some one hundred times as much, some sixty, and some thirty."

I Cor. 1:18-31 The word of the cross is foolishness to those who are dying, but to us who are saved it is the power of God. For it is written, "I will destroy the wisdom of the wise, I will bring the discernment of the discerning to nothing." Where is the wise? Where is the scribe? Where is the lawyer of this world? Hasn't God made foolish the wisdom of this world? For seeing that in the wisdom of God, the world through its wisdom didn't know God, it was God's good pleasure through the foolishness of the preaching to save those who believe. For Jews ask for signs, Greeks seek after wisdom, but we preach Christ crucified; a stumbling block to Jews, and foolishness to Greeks, but to those who are called, both Jews and Greeks, Christ is the power of God and the wisdom of God. Because the foolishness of God is wiser than men, and the weakness of God is stronger than men. For you see your calling, brothers, that not many are wise according to the flesh, not many mighty, and not many noble; but God chose the foolish things of the world that he might put to shame those who are wise. God chose the weak things of the world, that he might put to shame the things that are strong; and God chose the lowly things of the world, and the things that are despised, and the things that are not, that he might bring to nothing the things that are: that no flesh should boast before God. But of him, you are in Christ Jesus, who was made to us wisdom from God, and righteousness and sanctification, and redemption: that, according as it is written, "He who boasts, let him boast in the Lord."

Is. 6:9-13 He said, "Go, and tell this people, 'You hear indeed, but don't understand; and you see indeed, but don't perceive.' Make the heart of this people fat. Make their ears heavy, and shut their eyes; lest they see with their eyes, and hear with their ears, and understand with their heart, and turn again, and be healed." Then I said, "Lord, how long?" He answered, "Until cities are waste without inhabitant, and houses without man, and the land becomes utterly waste, And Yahweh has removed men far away, and the forsaken places are many in the midst of the land. If there is a tenth left in it, that also will in turn be consumed: as a terebinth, and as an oak, whose stock remains when they are felled; so the holy seed is its stock."

Week 14 Day 5   **27-Feb**

John 4:1-26 Therefore when the Lord knew that the Pharisees had heard that Jesus was making and baptizing more disciples than John (although Jesus himself didn't baptize, but his disciples), he left Judea, and departed into Galilee. He needed to pass through Samaria. So he came to a city of Samaria, called Sychar, near the parcel of ground that Jacob gave to his son, Joseph. Jacob's well was there. Jesus therefore, being tired from his journey, sat down by the well. It was about the sixth hour. A woman of Samaria came to draw water. Jesus said to her, "Give me a drink." For his disciples had gone away into the city to buy food. The Samaritan woman therefore said to him, "How is it that you, being a Jew, ask for a drink from me, a Samaritan woman?" (For Jews have no dealings with Samaritans.) Jesus answered her, "If you knew the gift of God, and who it is who says to you, 'Give me a drink,' you would have asked him, and he would have given you living water." The woman said to him, "Sir, you have nothing to draw with, and the well is deep. From where then have you that living water? Are you greater than our father, Jacob, who gave us the well, and drank of it himself, as did his children, and his livestock?" Jesus answered her, "Everyone who drinks of this water will thirst again, but whoever drinks of the water that I will give him will never thirst again; but the water that I will give him will become in him a well of water springing up to eternal life." The woman said to him, "Sir, give me this water, so that I don't get thirsty, neither come all the way here to draw." Jesus said to her, "Go, call your husband, and come here." The woman answered, "I have no husband." Jesus said to her, "You said well, 'I have no husband,' for you have had five husbands; and he whom you now have is not your husband. This you have said truly." The woman said to him, "Sir, I perceive that you are a prophet. Our fathers worshiped in this mountain, and you Jews say that in Jerusalem is the place where people ought to worship." Jesus said to her, "Woman, believe me, the hour comes, when neither in this mountain, nor in Jerusalem, will you worship the Father. You worship that which you don't know. We worship that which we know; for salvation is from the Jews. But the hour comes, and now is, when the true worshippers will worship the Father in spirit and truth, for the Father seeks such to be his worshippers. God is spirit, and those who worship him must worship in spirit and truth." The woman said to him, "I know that Messiah comes," (he who is called Christ). "When he has come, he will declare to us all things." Jesus said to her, "I am he, the one who speaks to you."

Heb. 12:18-29 For you have not come to a mountain that might be touched, and that burned with fire, and to blackness, darkness, storm, the sound of a trumpet, and the voice of words; which those who heard it begged that not one more word should be spoken to them, for they could not stand that which was commanded, "If even an animal touches the mountain, it shall be stoned"; and so fearful was the appearance, that Moses said, "I am terrified and trembling." But you have come to Mount Zion, and to the city of the living God, the heavenly Jerusalem, and to innumerable multitudes of angels, to the general assembly and assembly of the firstborn who are enrolled in heaven, to God the Judge of all, to the spirits of just men made perfect, to Jesus, the mediator of a new covenant, and to the blood of sprinkling that speaks better than that of Abel. See that you don't refuse him who speaks. For if they didn't escape when they refused him who warned on the earth, how much more will we not escape who turn away from him who warns from heaven, whose voice shook the earth then, but now he has promised, saying, "Yet once more I will shake not only the earth, but also the heavens." This phrase, "Yet once more," signifies the removing of those things that are shaken, as of things that have been made, that those things which are not shaken may remain. Therefore, receiving a Kingdom that can't be shaken, let us have grace, through which we serve God acceptably, with reverence and awe, for our God is a consuming fire.

Ex. 17:1-7 All the congregation of the children of Israel traveled from the wilderness of Sin, by their journeys, according to Yahweh's commandment, and encamped in Rephidim; but there was no water for the people to drink. Therefore the people quarreled with Moses, and said, "Give us water to drink." Moses said to them, "Why do you quarrel with me? Why do you test Yahweh?" The people were thirsty for water there; and the people murmured against Moses, and said, "Why have you brought us up out of Egypt, to kill us, our children, and our livestock with thirst?" Moses cried to Yahweh, saying, "What shall I do with these people? They are almost ready to stone me." Yahweh said to Moses, "Walk on before the people, and take the elders of Israel with you, and take the rod in your hand with which you struck the Nile, and go. Behold, I will stand before you there on the rock in Horeb. You shall strike the rock, and water will come out of it, that the people may drink." Moses did so in the sight of the elders of Israel. He called the name of the place Massah, and Meribah, because the children of Israel quarreled, and because they tested Yahweh, saying, "Is Yahweh among us, or not?"

Week 14 Day 6   12-Oct

John 4:27-38 At this, his disciples came. They marveled that he was speaking with a woman; yet no one said, "What are you looking for?" or, "Why do you speak with her?" So the woman left her water pot, and went away into the city, and said to the people, "Come, see a man who told me everything that I did. Can this be the Christ?" They went out of the city, and were coming to him. In the meanwhile, the disciples urged him, saying, "Rabbi, eat." But he said to them, "I have food to eat that you don't know about." The disciples therefore said one to another, "Has anyone brought him something to eat?" Jesus said to them, "My food is to do the will of him who sent me, and to accomplish his work. Don't you say, 'There are yet four months until the harvest?' Behold, I tell you, lift up your eyes, and look at the fields, that they are white for harvest already. He who reaps receives wages, and gathers fruit to eternal life; that both he who sows and he who reaps may rejoice together. For in this the saying is true, 'One sows, and another reaps.' I sent you to reap that for which you haven't labored. Others have labored, and you have entered into their labor."

I Cor. 3:5-9 Who then is Apollos, and who is Paul, but servants through whom you believed; and each as the Lord gave to him? I planted. Apollos watered. But God gave the increase. So then neither he who plants is anything, nor he who waters, but God who gives the increase. Now he who plants and he who waters are the same, but each will receive his own reward according to his own labor. For we are God's fellow workers. You are God's farming, God's building.

Ps. 126 When Yahweh brought back those who returned to Zion, we were like those who dream. Then our mouth was filled with laughter, and our tongue with singing. Then they said among the nations, "Yahweh has done great things for them." Yahweh has done great things for us, and we are glad. Restore our fortunes again, Yahweh, like the streams in the Negev. Those who sow in tears will reap in joy. He who goes out weeping, carrying seed for sowing, will certainly come again with joy, carrying his sheaves.

Week 14 Day 7   4-Feb

Col. 4:2-6 Continue steadfastly in prayer, watching therein with thanksgiving; praying together for us also, that God may open to us a door for the word, to speak the mystery of Christ, for which I am also in bonds; that I may reveal it as I ought to speak. Walk in wisdom toward those who are outside, redeeming the time. Let your speech always be with grace, seasoned with salt, that you may know how you ought to answer each one.

Jon. 3:1-10 The word of Yahweh came to Jonah the second time, saying, "Arise, go to Nineveh, that great city, and preach to it the message that I give you." So Jonah arose, and went to Nineveh, according to the word of Yahweh. Now Nineveh was an exceedingly great city, three days' journey across. Jonah began to enter into the city a day's journey, and he cried out, and said, "In forty days, Nineveh will be overthrown!" The people of Nineveh believed God; and they proclaimed a fast, and put on sackcloth, from their greatest even to their least. The news reached the king of Nineveh, and he arose from his throne, and took off his royal robe, covered himself with sackcloth, and sat in ashes. He made a proclamation and published through Nineveh by the decree of the king and his nobles, saying, "Let neither man nor animal, herd nor flock, taste anything; let them not feed, nor drink water; but let them be covered with sackcloth, both man and animal, and let them cry mightily to God. Yes, let them turn everyone from his evil way, and from the violence that is in his hands. Who knows whether God will not turn and relent, and turn away from his fierce anger, so that we might not perish?" God saw their works, that they turned from their evil way. God relented of the disaster which he said he would do to them, and he didn't do it.

Week 15 Day 1   18-Oct

Matt. 18:10-14 "See that you don't despise one of these little ones, for I tell you that in heaven their angels always see the face of my Father who is in heaven. For the Son of Man came to save that which was lost. What do you think? If a man has one hundred sheep, and one of them goes astray, doesn't he leave the ninety-nine, go to the mountains, and seek that which has gone astray? If he finds it, most certainly I tell you, he rejoices over it more than over the ninety-nine which have not gone astray. Even so it is not the will of your Father who is in heaven that one of these little ones should perish."

1 Cor. 5:1-5 It is actually reported that there is sexual immorality among you, and such sexual immorality as is not even named among the Gentiles, that one has his father's wife. You are puffed up, and didn't rather mourn, that he who had done this deed might be removed from among you. For I most certainly, as being absent in body but present in spirit, have already, as though I were present, judged him who has done this thing. In the name of our Lord Jesus Christ, you being gathered together, and my spirit, with the power of our Lord Jesus Christ, are to deliver such a one to Satan for the destruction of the flesh, that the spirit may be saved in the day of the Lord Jesus.

Ez. 34:11-16 For thus says the Lord Yahweh: Behold, I myself, even I, will search for my sheep, and will seek them out. As a shepherd seeks out his flock in the day that he is among his sheep that are scattered abroad, so will I seek out my sheep; and I will deliver them out of all places where they have been scattered in the cloudy and dark day. I will bring them out from the peoples, and gather them from the countries, and will bring them into their own land; and I will feed them on the mountains of Israel, by the watercourses, and in all the inhabited places of the country. I will feed them with good pasture; and on the mountains of the height of Israel shall their fold be: there shall they lie down in a good fold; and on fat pasture shall they feed on the mountains of Israel. I myself will be the shepherd of my sheep, and I will cause them to lie down, says the Lord Yahweh. I will seek that which was lost, and will bring back that which was driven away, and will bind up that which was broken, and will strengthen that which was sick: but the fat and the strong I will destroy; I will feed them in justice.

Week 15 Day 2   10-Dec

Luke 15:11-24 He said, "A certain man had two sons. The younger of them said to his father, 'Father, give me my share of your property.' He divided his livelihood between them. Not many days after, the younger son gathered all of this together and traveled into a far country. There he wasted his property with riotous living. When he had spent all of it, there arose a severe famine in that country, and he began to be in need. He went and joined himself to one of the citizens of that country, and he sent him into his fields to feed pigs. He wanted to fill his belly with the husks that the pigs ate, but no one gave him any. But when he came to himself he said, 'How many hired servants of my father's have bread enough to spare, and I'm dying with hunger! I will get up and go to my father, and will tell him, "Father, I have sinned against heaven, and in your sight. I am no more worthy to be called your son. Make me as one of your hired servants."' He arose, and came to his father. But while he was still far off, his father saw him, and was moved with compassion, and ran, and fell on his neck, and kissed him. The son said to him, 'Father, I have sinned against heaven, and in your sight. I am no longer worthy to be called your son.' But the father said to his servants, 'Bring out the best robe, and put it on him. Put a ring on his hand, and shoes on his feet. Bring the fattened calf, kill it, and let us eat, and celebrate; for this, my son, was dead, and is alive again. He was lost, and is found.' They began to celebrate."

Phm. 8-21 Therefore though I have all boldness in Christ to command you that which is appropriate, yet for love's sake I rather beg, being such a one as Paul, the aged, but also a prisoner of Jesus Christ. I beg you for my child, whom I have become the father of in my chains, Onesimus, who once was useless to you, but now is useful to you and to me. I am sending him back. Therefore receive him, that is, my own heart, whom I desired to keep with me, that on your behalf he might serve me in my chains for the Good News. But I was willing to do nothing without your consent, that your goodness would not be as of necessity, but of free will. For perhaps he was therefore separated from you for a while, that you would have him forever, no longer as a slave, but more than a slave, a beloved brother, especially to me, but how much rather to you, both in the flesh and in the Lord. If then you count me a partner, receive him as you would receive me. But if he has wronged you at all, or owes you anything, put that to my account. I, Paul, write this with my own hand: I will repay it (not to mention to you that you owe to me even your own self besides). Yes, brother, let me have joy from you in the Lord. Refresh my heart in the Lord. Having confidence in your obedience, I write to you, knowing that you will do even beyond what I say.

Gen. 46:28-34 He sent Judah before him to Joseph, to show the way before him to Goshen, and they came into the land of Goshen. Joseph prepared his chariot, and went up to meet Israel, his father, in Goshen. He presented himself to him, and fell on his neck, and wept on his neck a good while. Israel said to Joseph, "Now let me die, since I have seen your face, that you are still alive." Joseph said to his brothers, and to his father's house, "I will go up, and speak with Pharaoh, and will tell him, 'My brothers, and my father's house, who were in the land of Canaan, have come to me. These men are shepherds, for they have been keepers of livestock, and they have brought their flocks, and their herds, and all that they have.' It will happen, when Pharaoh summons you, and will say, 'What is your occupation?' that you shall say, 'Your servants have been keepers of livestock from our youth even until now, both we, and our fathers:' that you may dwell in the land of Goshen; for every shepherd is an abomination to the Egyptians."

Week 15 Day 3   2-Aug

Luke 10:1-16 Now after these things, the Lord also appointed seventy others, and sent them two by two ahead of him into every city and place, where he was about to come. Then he said to them, "The harvest is indeed plentiful, but the laborers are few. Pray therefore to the Lord of the harvest, that he may send out laborers into his harvest. Go your ways. Behold, I send you out as lambs among wolves. Carry no purse, nor wallet, nor sandals. Greet no one on the way. Into whatever house you enter, first say, 'Peace be to this house.' If a son of peace is there, your peace will rest on him; but if not, it will return to you. Remain in that same house, eating and drinking the things they give, for the laborer is worthy of his wages. Don't go from house to house. Into whatever city you enter, and they receive you, eat the things that are set before you. Heal the sick who are therein, and tell them, 'The Kingdom of God has come near to you.' But into whatever city you enter, and they don't receive you, go out into its streets and say, 'Even the dust from your city that clings to us, we wipe off against you. Nevertheless know this, that the Kingdom of God has come near to you.' I tell you, it will be more tolerable in that day for Sodom than for that city. Woe to you, Chorazin! Woe to you, Bethsaida! For if the mighty works had been done in Tyre and Sidon which were done in you, they would have repented long ago, sitting in sackcloth and ashes. But it will be more tolerable for Tyre and Sidon in the judgment than for you. You, Capernaum, who are exalted to heaven, will be brought down to Hades. Whoever listens to you listens to me, and whoever rejects you rejects me. Whoever rejects me rejects him who sent me."

Phm 4-7 I thank my God always, making mention of you in my prayers, hearing of your love, and of the faith which you have toward the Lord Jesus, and toward all the saints; that the fellowship of your faith may become effective, in the knowledge of every good thing which is in us in Christ Jesus. For we have much joy and comfort in your love, because the hearts of the saints have been refreshed through you, brother.

Is. 23:1-18 The burden of Tyre. Howl, you ships of Tarshish! For it is laid waste, so that there is no house, no entering in. From the land of Kittim it is revealed to them. Be still, you inhabitants of the coast, you whom the merchants of Sidon, that pass over the sea, have replenished. On great waters, the seed of the Shihor, the harvest of the Nile, was her revenue. She was the market of nations. Be ashamed, Sidon; for the sea has spoken, the stronghold of the sea, saying, "I have not travailed, nor brought forth, neither have I nourished young men, nor brought up virgins." When the report comes to Egypt, they will be in anguish at the report of Tyre. Pass over to Tarshish! Wail, you inhabitants of the coast! Is this your joyous city, whose antiquity is of ancient days, whose feet carried her far away to travel? Who has planned this against Tyre, the giver of crowns, whose merchants are princes, whose traffickers are the honorable of the earth? Yahweh of Armies has planned it, to stain the pride of all glory, to bring into contempt all the honorable of the earth. Pass through your land like the Nile, daughter of Tarshish. There is no restraint any more. He has stretched out his hand over the sea. He has shaken the kingdoms. Yahweh has ordered the destruction of Canaan's strongholds. He said, "You shall rejoice no more, you oppressed virgin daughter of Sidon. Arise, pass over to Kittim. Even there you will have no rest." Behold, the land of the Chaldeans. This people was not. The Assyrians founded it for those who dwell in the wilderness. They set up their towers. They overthrew its palaces. They made it a ruin. Howl, you ships of Tarshish, for your stronghold is laid waste! It will come to pass in that day that Tyre will be forgotten seventy years, according to the days of one king. After the end of seventy years it will be to Tyre like in the song of the prostitute. Take a harp; go about the city, you prostitute that has been forgotten. Make sweet melody. Sing many songs, that you may be remembered. It will happen after the end of seventy years that Yahweh will visit Tyre, and she shall return to her wages, and will play the prostitute with all the kingdoms of the world on the surface of the earth. Her merchandise and her wages will be holiness to Yahweh. It will not be treasured nor laid up; for her merchandise will be for those who dwell before Yahweh, to eat sufficiently, and for durable clothing.

Week 15 Day 4   24-Apr

Luke 10:17-24 The seventy returned with joy, saying, "Lord, even the demons are subject to us in your name!" He said to them, "I saw Satan having fallen like lightning from heaven. Behold, I give you authority to tread on serpents and scorpions, and over all the power of the enemy. Nothing will in any way hurt you. Nevertheless, don't rejoice in this, that the spirits are subject to you, but rejoice that your names are written in heaven." In that same hour Jesus rejoiced in the Holy Spirit, and said, "I thank you, O Father, Lord of heaven and earth, that you have hidden these things from the wise and understanding, and revealed them to little children. Yes, Father, for so it was well-pleasing in your sight." Turning to the disciples, he said, "All things have been delivered to me by my Father. No one knows who the Son is, except the Father, and who the Father is, except the Son, and he to whomever the Son desires to reveal him." Turning to the disciples, he said privately, "Blessed are the eyes which see the things that you see, for I tell you that many prophets and kings desired to see the things which you see, and didn't see them, and to hear the things which you hear, and didn't hear them."

Rev. 20:1-10 I saw an angel coming down out of heaven, having the key of the abyss and a great chain in his hand. He seized the dragon, the old serpent, which is the devil and Satan, who deceives the whole inhabited earth, and bound him for a thousand years, and cast him into the abyss, and shut it, and sealed it over him, that he should deceive the nations no more, until the thousand years were finished. After this, he must be freed for a short time. I saw thrones, and they sat on them, and judgment was given to them. I saw the souls of those who had been beheaded for the testimony of Jesus, and for the word of God, and such as didn't worship the beast nor his image, and didn't receive the mark on their forehead and on their hand. They lived, and reigned with Christ for a thousand years. The rest of the dead didn't live until the thousand years were finished. This is the first resurrection. Blessed and holy is he who has part in the first resurrection. Over these, the second death has no power, but they will be priests of God and of Christ, and will reign with him one thousand years. And after the thousand years, Satan will be released from his prison, and he will come out to deceive the nations which are in the four corners of the earth, Gog and Magog, to gather them together to the war; the number of whom is as the sand of the sea. They went up over the breadth of the earth, and surrounded the camp of the saints, and the beloved city. Fire came down out of heaven from God, and devoured them. The devil who deceived them was thrown into the lake of fire and sulfur, where the beast and the false prophet are also. They will be tormented day and night forever and ever.

Is. 66:10-16 "Rejoice with Jerusalem, and be glad for her, all you who love her: rejoice for joy with her, all you who mourn over her; that you may nurse and be satisfied at the comforting breasts; that you may drink deeply, and be delighted with the abundance of her glory." For thus says Yahweh, "Behold, I will extend peace to her like a river, and the glory of the nations like an overflowing stream: and you will nurse. You will be carried on her side, and will be dandled on her knees. As one whom his mother comforts, so will I comfort you; and you will be comforted in Jerusalem." You will see it, and your heart shall rejoice, and your bones shall flourish like the tender grass: and the hand of Yahweh shall be known toward his servants; and he will have indignation against his enemies. For, behold, Yahweh will come with fire, and his chariots shall be like the whirlwind; to render his anger with fierceness, and his rebuke with flames of fire. For by fire will Yahweh execute judgment, and by his sword, on all flesh; and the slain of Yahweh shall be many.

Week 15 Day 5   27-Jan

Luke 22:35-38 He said to them, "When I sent you out without purse, and wallet, and shoes, did you lack anything?" They said, "Nothing." Then he said to them, "But now, whoever has a purse, let him take it, and likewise a wallet. Whoever has none, let him sell his cloak, and buy a sword. For I tell you that this which is written must still be fulfilled in me: 'He was counted with transgressors.' For that which concerns me has an end." They said, "Lord, behold, here are two swords." He said to them, "That is enough."

1 Cor. 9:7-27 What soldier ever serves at his own expense? Who plants a vineyard, and doesn't eat of its fruit? Or who feeds a flock, and doesn't drink from the flock's milk? Do I speak these things according to the ways of men? Or doesn't the law also say the same thing? For it is written in the law of Moses, "You shall not muzzle an ox while it treads out the grain." Is it for the oxen that God cares, or does he say it assuredly for our sake? Yes, it was written for our sake, because he who plows ought to plow in hope, and he who threshes in hope should partake of his hope. If we sowed to you spiritual things, is it a great thing if we reap your fleshly things? If others partake of this right over you, don't we yet more? Nevertheless we did not use this right, but we bear all things, that we may cause no hindrance to the Good News of Christ. Don't you know that those who serve around sacred things eat from the things of the temple, and those who wait on the altar have their portion with the altar? Even so the Lord ordained that those who proclaim the Good News should live from the Good News. But I have used none of these things, and I don't write these things that it may be done so in my case; for I would rather die, than that anyone should make my boasting void. For if I preach the Good News, I have nothing to boast about; for necessity is laid on me; but woe is to me, if I don't preach the Good News. For if I do this of my own will, I have a reward. But if not of my own will, I have a stewardship entrusted to me. What then is my reward? That, when I preach the Good News, I may present the Good News of Christ without charge, so as not to abuse my authority in the Good News. For though I was free from all, I brought myself under bondage to all, that I might gain the more. To the Jews I became as a Jew, that I might gain Jews; to those who are under the law, as under the law, that I might gain those who are under the law; to those who are without law, as without law (not being without law toward God, but under law toward Christ), that I might win those who are without law. To the weak I became as weak, that I might gain the weak. I have become all things to all men, that I may by all means save some. Now I do this for the sake of the Good News, that I may be a joint partaker of it. Don't you know that those who run in a race all run, but one receives the prize? Run like that, that you may win. Every man who strives in the games exercises self-control in all things. Now they do it to receive a corruptible crown, but we an incorruptible. I therefore run like that, as not uncertainly. I fight like that, as not beating the air, but I beat my body and bring it into submission, lest by any means, after I have preached to others, I myself should be rejected.

Ex. 4:1-17 Moses answered, "But, behold, they will not believe me, nor listen to my voice; for they will say, 'Yahweh has not appeared to you.'" Yahweh said to him, "What is that in your hand?" He said, "A rod." He said, "Throw it on the ground." He threw it on the ground, and it became a snake; and Moses ran away from it. Yahweh said to Moses, "Stretch out your hand, and take it by the tail." He stretched out his hand, and took hold of it, and it became a rod in his hand. "That they may believe that Yahweh, the God of their fathers, the God of Abraham, the God of Isaac, and the God of Jacob, has appeared to you." Yahweh said furthermore to him, "Now put your hand inside your cloak." He put his hand inside his cloak, and when he took it out, behold, his hand was leprous, as white as snow. He said, "Put your hand inside your cloak again." He put his hand inside his cloak again, and when he took it out of his cloak, behold, it had turned again as his other flesh. "It will happen, if they will neither believe you nor listen to the voice of the first sign, that they will believe the voice of the latter sign. It will happen, if they will not believe even these two signs, neither listen to your voice, that you shall take of the water of the river, and pour it on the dry land. The water which you take out of the river will become blood on the dry land." Moses said to Yahweh, "O Lord, I am not eloquent, neither before now, nor since you have spoken to your servant; for I am slow of speech, and of a slow tongue." Yahweh said to him, "Who made man's mouth? Or who makes one mute, or deaf, or seeing, or blind? Isn't it I, Yahweh? Now therefore go, and I will be with your mouth, and teach you what you shall speak." He said, "Oh, Lord, please send someone else." The anger of Yahweh was kindled against Moses, and he said, "What about Aaron, your brother, the Levite? I know that he can speak well. Also, behold, he comes out to meet you. When he sees you, he will be glad in his heart. You shall speak to him, and put the words in his mouth. I will be with your mouth, and with his mouth, and will teach you what you shall do. He will be your spokesman to the people; and it will happen, that he will be to you a mouth, and you will be to him as God. You shall take this rod in your hand, with which you shall do the signs."

Week 15 Day 6   **20-Apr**

Matt. 25:14-30 "For it is like a man, going into another country, who called his own servants, and entrusted his goods to them. To one he gave five talents, to another two, to another one; to each according to his own ability. Then he went on his journey. Immediately he who received the five talents went and traded with them, and made another five talents. In the same way, he also who got the two gained another two. But he who received the one went away and dug in the earth, and hid his lord's money. Now after a long time the lord of those servants came, and reconciled accounts with them. He who received the five talents came and brought another five talents, saying, 'Lord, you delivered to me five talents. Behold, I have gained another five talents besides them.' His lord said to him, 'Well done, good and faithful servant. You have been faithful over a few things, I will set you over many things. Enter into the joy of your lord.' He also who got the two talents came and said, 'Lord, you delivered to me two talents. Behold, I have gained another two talents besides them.' His lord said to him, 'Well done, good and faithful servant. You have been faithful over a few things, I will set you over many things. Enter into the joy of your lord.' He also who had received the one talent came and said, 'Lord, I knew you that you are a hard man, reaping where you did not sow, and gathering where you did not scatter. I was afraid, and went away and hid your talent in the earth. Behold, you have what is yours.' But his lord answered him, 'You wicked and slothful servant. You knew that I reap where I didn't sow, and gather where I didn't scatter. You ought therefore to have deposited my money with the bankers, and at my coming I should have received back my own with interest. Take away therefore the talent from him, and give it to him who has the ten talents. For to everyone who has will be given, and he will have abundance, but from him who doesn't have, even that which he has will be taken away. Throw out the unprofitable servant into the outer darkness, where there will be weeping and gnashing of teeth.'"

1 Cor. 12:1-11 Now concerning spiritual things, brothers, I don't want you to be ignorant. You know that when you were heathen, you were led away to those mute idols, however you might be led. Therefore I make known to you that no man speaking by God's Spirit says, "Jesus is accursed." No one can say, "Jesus is Lord," but by the Holy Spirit. Now there are various kinds of gifts, but the same Spirit. There are various kinds of service, and the same Lord. There are various kinds of workings, but the same God, who works all things in all. But to each one is given the manifestation of the Spirit for the profit of all. For to one is given through the Spirit the word of wisdom, and to another the word of knowledge, according to the same Spirit; to another faith, by the same Spirit; and to another gifts of healings, by the same Spirit; and to another workings of miracles; and to another prophecy; and to another discerning of spirits; to another different kinds of languages; and to another the interpretation of languages. But the one and the same Spirit works all of these, distributing to each one separately as he desires.

Zeph. 1:7-18 Be silent at the presence of the Lord Yahweh, for the day of Yahweh is at hand. For Yahweh has prepared a sacrifice. He has consecrated his guests. It will happen in the day of Yahweh's sacrifice, that I will punish the princes, the king's sons, and all those who are clothed with foreign clothing. In that day, I will punish all those who leap over the threshold, who fill their master's house with violence and deceit. In that day, says Yahweh, there will be the noise of a cry from the fish gate, a wailing from the second quarter, and a great crashing from the hills. Wail, you inhabitants of Maktesh, for all the people of Canaan are undone! All those who were loaded with silver are cut off. It will happen at that time, that I will search Jerusalem with lamps, and I will punish the men who are settled on their dregs, who say in their heart, "Yahweh will not do good, neither will he do evil." Their wealth will become a spoil, and their houses a desolation. Yes, they will build houses, but won't inhabit them. They will plant vineyards, but won't drink their wine. The great day of Yahweh is near. It is near, and hurries greatly, the voice of the day of Yahweh. The mighty man cries there bitterly. That day is a day of wrath, a day of distress and anguish, a day of trouble and ruin, a day of darkness and gloom, a day of clouds and blackness, a day of the trumpet and alarm, against the fortified cities, and against the high battlements. I will bring distress on men, that they will walk like blind men, because they have sinned against Yahweh, and their blood will be poured out like dust, and their flesh like dung. Neither their silver nor their gold will be able to deliver them in the day of Yahweh's wrath, but the whole land will be devoured by the fire of his jealousy; for he will make an end, yes, a terrible end, of all those who dwell in the land.

Week 15 Day 7   16-May

2 Cor. 6:3-10 We give no occasion of stumbling in anything, that our service may not be blamed, but in everything commending ourselves, as servants of God, in great endurance, in afflictions, in hardships, in distresses, in beatings, in imprisonments, in riots, in labors, in watchings, in fastings; in pureness, in knowledge, in patience, in kindness, in the Holy Spirit, in sincere love, in the word of truth, in the power of God; by the armor of righteousness on the right hand and on the left, by glory and dishonor, by evil report and good report; as deceivers, and yet true; as unknown, and yet well known; as dying, and behold, we live; as punished, and not killed; as sorrowful, yet always rejoicing; as poor, yet making many rich; as having nothing, and yet possessing all things.

Ps. 18 I love you, Yahweh, my strength. Yahweh is my rock, my fortress, and my deliverer; my God, my rock, in whom I take refuge; my shield, and the horn of my salvation, my high tower. I call on Yahweh, who is worthy to be praised; and I am saved from my enemies. The cords of death surrounded me. The floods of ungodliness made me afraid. The cords of Sheol were around me. The snares of death came on me. In my distress I called on Yahweh, and cried to my God. He heard my voice out of his temple. My cry before him came into his ears. Then the earth shook and trembled. The foundations also of the mountains quaked and were shaken, because he was angry. Smoke went out of his nostrils. Consuming fire came out of his mouth. Coals were kindled by it. He bowed the heavens also, and came down. Thick darkness was under his feet. He rode on a cherub, and flew. Yes, he soared on the wings of the wind. He made darkness his hiding place, his pavilion around him, darkness of waters, thick clouds of the skies. At the brightness before him his thick clouds passed, hailstones and coals of fire. Yahweh also thundered in the sky. The Most High uttered his voice: hailstones and coals of fire. He sent out his arrows, and scattered them; Yes, great lightning bolts, and routed them. Then the channels of waters appeared. The foundations of the world were laid bare at your rebuke, Yahweh, at the blast of the breath of your nostrils. He sent from on high. He took me. He drew me out of many waters. He delivered me from my strong enemy, from those who hated me; for they were too mighty for me. They came on me in the day of my calamity, but Yahweh was my support. He brought me forth also into a large place. He delivered me, because he delighted in me. Yahweh has rewarded me according to my righteousness. According to the cleanness of my hands has he recompensed me. For I have kept the ways of Yahweh, and have not wickedly departed from my God. For all his ordinances were before me. I didn't put away his statutes from me. I was also blameless with him. I kept myself from my iniquity. Therefore Yahweh has rewarded me according to my righteousness, according to the cleanness of my hands in his eyesight. With the merciful you will show yourself merciful. With the upright man, you will show yourself upright. With the pure, you will show yourself pure. With the crooked you will show yourself shrewd. For you will save the afflicted people, but the haughty eyes you will bring down. For you will light my lamp, Yahweh. My God will light up my darkness. For by you, I advance through a troop. By my God, I leap over a wall. As for God, his way is perfect. The word of Yahweh is tried. He is a shield to all those who take refuge in him. For who is God, except Yahweh? Who is a rock, besides our God, the God who arms me with strength, and makes my way perfect? He makes my feet like deer's feet, and sets me on my high places. He teaches my hands to war, so that my arms bend a bow of bronze. You have also given me the shield of your salvation. Your right hand sustains me.

Your gentleness has made me great. You have enlarged my steps under me, my feet have not slipped. I will pursue my enemies, and overtake them. Neither will I turn again until they are consumed. I will strike them through, so that they will not be able to rise. They shall fall under my feet. For you have armed me with strength to the battle. You have subdued under me those who rose up against me. You have also made my enemies turn their backs to me, that I might cut off those who hate me. They cried, but there was none to save; even to Yahweh, but he didn't answer them. Then I beat them small as the dust before the wind. I cast them out as the mire of the streets. You have delivered me from the strivings of the people. You have made me the head of the nations. A people whom I have not known shall serve me. As soon as they hear of me they shall obey me. The foreigners shall submit themselves to me. The foreigners shall fade away, and shall come trembling out of their close places. Yahweh lives; and blessed be my rock. Exalted be the God of my salvation, even the God who executes vengeance for me, and subdues peoples under me. He rescues me from my enemies. Yes, you lift me up above those who rise up against me. You deliver me from the violent man. Therefore I will give thanks to you, Yahweh, among the nations, and will sing praises to your name. He gives great deliverance to his king, and shows loving kindness to his anointed, to David and to his seed, forevermore.

Week 16 Day 1   14-Feb

Matt. 10:21-31 "Brother will deliver up brother to death, and the father his child. Children will rise up against parents, and cause them to be put to death. You will be hated by all men for my name's sake, but he who endures to the end will be saved. But when they persecute you in this city, flee into the next, for most certainly I tell you, you will not have gone through the cities of Israel, until the Son of Man has come. A disciple is not above his teacher, nor a servant above his lord. It is enough for the disciple that he be like his teacher, and the servant like his lord. If they have called the master of the house Beelzebul, how much more those of his household! Therefore don't be afraid of them, for there is nothing covered that will not be revealed; and hidden that will not be known. What I tell you in the darkness, speak in the light; and what you hear whispered in the ear, proclaim on the housetops. Don't be afraid of those who kill the body, but are not able to kill the soul. Rather, fear him who is able to destroy both soul and body in Gehenna. Aren't two sparrows sold for a small coin? Not one of them falls on the ground apart from your Father's will, but the very hairs of your head are all numbered. Therefore don't be afraid. You are of more value than many sparrows."

I Pet. 3:8-22 Finally, be all like-minded, compassionate, loving as brothers, tenderhearted, courteous, not rendering evil for evil, or insult for insult; but instead blessing; knowing that to this were you called, that you may inherit a blessing. For, "He who would love life, and see good days, let him keep his tongue from evil, and his lips from speaking deceit. Let him turn away from evil, and do good. Let him seek peace, and pursue it. For the eyes of the Lord are on the righteous, and his ears open to their prayer; but the face of the Lord is against those who do evil." Now who is he who will harm you, if you become imitators of that which is good? But even if you should suffer for righteousness' sake, you are blessed. "Don't fear what they fear, neither be troubled." But sanctify the Lord God in your hearts; and always be ready to give an answer to everyone who asks you a reason concerning the hope that is in you, with humility and fear: having a good conscience; that, while you are spoken against as evildoers, they may be disappointed who curse your good way of life in Christ. For it is better, if it is God's will, that you suffer for doing well than for doing evil. Because Christ also suffered for sins once, the righteous for the unrighteous, that he might bring you to God; being put to death in the flesh, but made alive in the spirit; in which he also went and preached to the spirits in prison, who before were disobedient, when God waited patiently in the days of Noah, while the ship was being built. In it, few, that is, eight souls, were saved through water. This is a symbol of baptism, which now saves you—not the putting away of the filth of the flesh, but the answer of a good conscience toward God, through the resurrection of Jesus Christ, who is at the right hand of God, having gone into heaven, angels and authorities and powers being made subject to him.

Ps. 107 Give thanks to Yahweh, for he is good, for his loving kindness endures forever. Let the redeemed by Yahweh say so, whom he has redeemed from the hand of the adversary, And gathered out of the lands, from the east and from the west, from the north and from the south. They wandered in the wilderness in a desert way. They found no city to live in. Hungry and thirsty, their soul fainted in them. Then they cried to Yahweh in their trouble, and he delivered them out of their distresses, he led them also by a straight way, that they might go to a city to live in. Let them praise Yahweh for his loving kindness, for his wonderful works to the children of men! For he satisfies the longing soul. He fills the hungry soul with good. Some sat in darkness and in the shadow of death, being bound in affliction and iron, because they rebelled against the words of God, and condemned the counsel of the Most High. Therefore he brought down their heart with labor. They fell down, and there was none to help. Then they cried to Yahweh in their trouble, and he saved them out of their distresses. He brought them out of darkness and the shadow of death, and broke their bonds in sunder. Let them praise Yahweh for his loving kindness, for his wonderful works to the children of men! For he has broken the gates of brass, and cut through bars of iron. Fools are afflicted because of their disobedience, and because of their iniquities. Their soul abhors all kinds of food. They draw near to the gates of death. Then they cry to Yahweh in their trouble, he saves them out of their distresses. He sends his word, and heals them, and delivers them from their graves. Let them praise Yahweh for his loving kindness, for his wonderful works to the children of men! Let them offer the sacrifices of thanksgiving, and declare his works with singing. Those who go down to the sea in ships, who do business in great waters; these see Yahweh's works, and his wonders in the deep. For he commands, and raises the stormy wind, which lifts up its waves. They mount up to the sky; they go down again to the depths. Their soul melts away because of trouble. They reel back and forth, and stagger like a drunken man, and are at their wits' end. Then they cry to Yahweh in their trouble, and he brings them out of their distress. He makes the storm a calm, so that its waves are still. Then they are glad because it is calm, so he brings them to their desired haven. Let them praise Yahweh for his loving kindness, for his wonderful works for the children of men! Let them exalt him also in the assembly of the people, and praise him in the seat of the elders. He turns rivers into a desert, water springs into a thirsty ground, and a fruitful land into a salt waste, for the wickedness of those who dwell in it. He turns a desert into a pool of water, and a dry land into water springs. There he makes the hungry live, that they may prepare a city to live in, sow fields, plant vineyards, and reap the fruits of increase. He blesses them also, so that they are multiplied greatly. He doesn't allow their livestock to decrease. Again, they are diminished and bowed down through oppression, trouble, and sorrow. He pours contempt on princes, and causes them to wander in a trackless waste. Yet he lifts the needy out of their affliction, and increases their families like a flock. The upright will see it, and be glad. All the wicked will shut their mouths. Whoever is wise will pay attention to these things. They will consider the loving kindnesses of Yahweh.

Week 16 Day 2   **19-Dec**

Matt. 10:32-42 Everyone therefore who confesses me before men, him I will also confess before my Father who is in heaven. But whoever denies me before men, him I will also deny before my Father who is in heaven. Don't think that I came to send peace on the earth. I didn't come to send peace, but a sword. For I came to set a man at odds against his father, and a daughter against her mother, and a daughter-in-law against her mother-in-law. A man's foes will be those of his own household. He who loves father or mother more than me is not worthy of me; and he who loves son or daughter more than me isn't worthy of me. He who doesn't take his cross and follow after me, isn't worthy of me. He who seeks his life will lose it; and he who loses his life for my sake will find it. He who receives you receives me, and he who receives me receives him who sent me. He who receives a prophet in the name of a prophet will receive a prophet's reward. He who receives a righteous man in the name of a righteous man will receive a righteous man's reward. Whoever gives one of these little ones just a cup of cold water to drink in the name of a disciple, most certainly I tell you he will in no way lose his reward."

Matt. 23:33-39 "You serpents, you offspring of vipers, how will you escape the judgment of Gehenna? Therefore behold, I send to you prophets, wise men, and scribes. Some of them you will kill and crucify; and some of them you will scourge in your synagogues, and persecute from city to city; that on you may come all the righteous blood shed on the earth, from the blood of righteous Abel to the blood of Zachariah son of Barachiah, whom you killed between the sanctuary and the altar. Most certainly I tell you, all these things will come upon this generation. Jerusalem, Jerusalem, who kills the prophets, and stones those who are sent to her! How often I would have gathered your children together, even as a hen gathers her chicks under her wings, and you would not! Behold, your house is left to you desolate. For I tell you, you will not see me from now on, until you say, 'Blessed is he who comes in the name of the Lord!'"

II Tim. 2:1-13 You therefore, my child, be strengthened in the grace that is in Christ Jesus. The things which you have heard from me among many witnesses, commit the same to faithful men, who will be able to teach others also. You therefore must endure hardship, as a good soldier of Christ Jesus. No soldier on duty entangles himself in the affairs of life, that he may please him who enrolled him as a soldier. Also, if anyone competes in athletics, he isn't crowned unless he has competed by the rules. The farmers who labor must be the first to get a share of the crops. Consider what I say, and may the Lord give you understanding in all things. Remember Jesus Christ, risen from the dead, of the seed of David, according to my Good News, in which I suffer hardship to the point of chains as a criminal. But God's word isn't chained. Therefore I endure all things for the chosen ones' sake, that they also may obtain the salvation which is in Christ Jesus with eternal glory. This saying is faithful: "For if we died with him, we will also live with him. If we endure, we will also reign with him. If we deny him, he also will deny us. If we are faithless, he remains faithful. He can't deny himself."

Mic. 7:5-10 Don't trust in a neighbor. Don't put confidence in a friend. With the woman lying in your embrace, be careful of the words of your mouth! For the son dishonors the father, the daughter rises up against her mother, the daughter-in-law against her mother-in-law; a man's enemies are the men of his own house. But as for me, I will look to Yahweh. I will wait for the God of my salvation. My God will hear me. Don't rejoice against me, my enemy. When I fall, I will arise. When I sit in darkness, Yahweh will be a light to me. I will bear the indignation of Yahweh, because I have sinned against him, until he pleads my case, and executes judgment for me. He will bring me forth to the light. I will see his righteousness. Then my enemy will see it, and shame will cover her who said to me, where is Yahweh your God? Then my enemy will see me and will cover her shame. Now she will be trodden down like the mire of the streets.

Week 16 Day 3   14-Aug

Matt. 12:22-32 Then one possessed by a demon, blind and mute, was brought to him and he healed him, so that the blind and mute man both spoke and saw. All the multitudes were amazed, and said, "Can this be the son of David?" But when the Pharisees heard it, they said, "This man does not cast out demons, except by Beelzebul, the prince of the demons." Knowing their thoughts, Jesus said to them, "Every kingdom divided against itself is brought to desolation, and every city or house divided against itself will not stand. If Satan casts out Satan, he is divided against himself. How then will his kingdom stand? If I by Beelzebul cast out demons, by whom do your children cast them out? Therefore they will be your judges. But if I by the Spirit of God cast out demons, then the Kingdom of God has come upon you. Or how can one enter into the house of the strong man, and plunder his goods, unless he first bind the strong man? Then he will plunder his house. He who is not with me is against me, and he who doesn't gather with me, scatters. Therefore I tell you, every sin and blasphemy will be forgiven men, but the blasphemy against the Spirit will not be forgiven men. Whoever speaks a word against the Son of Man, it will be forgiven him; but whoever speaks against the Holy Spirit, it will not be forgiven him, neither in this age, nor in that which is to come."

Eph. 4:1-32 I therefore, the prisoner in the Lord, beg you to walk worthily of the calling with which you were called, with all lowliness and humility, with patience, bearing with one another in love; being eager to keep the unity of the Spirit in the bond of peace. There is one body, and one Spirit, even as you also were called in one hope of your calling; one Lord, one faith, one baptism, one God and Father of all, who is over all, and through all, and in us all. But to each one of us was the grace given according to the measure of the gift of Christ. Therefore he says, "When he ascended on high, he led captivity captive, and gave gifts to men." Now this, "He ascended," what is it but that he also first descended into the lower parts of the earth? He who descended is the one who also ascended far above all the heavens, that he might fill all things. He gave some to be apostles; and some, prophets; and some, evangelists; and some, shepherds and teachers; for the perfecting of the saints, to the work of serving, to the building up of the body of Christ; until we all attain to the unity of the faith, and of the knowledge of the Son of God, to a full grown man, to the measure of the stature of the fullness of Christ; that we may no longer be children, tossed back and forth and carried about with every wind of doctrine, by the trickery of men, in craftiness, after the wiles of error; but speaking truth in love, we may grow up in all things into him, who is the head, Christ; from whom all the body, being fitted and knit together through that which every joint supplies, according to the working in measure of each individual part, makes the body increase to the building up of itself in love. This I say therefore, and testify in the Lord, that you no longer walk as the rest of the Gentiles also walk, in the futility of their mind, being darkened in their understanding, alienated from the life of God, because of the ignorance that is in them, because of the hardening of their hearts; who having become callous gave themselves up to lust, to work all uncleanness with greediness. But you did not learn Christ that way; if indeed you heard him, and were taught in him, even as truth is in Jesus: that you put away, as concerning your former way of life, the old man, that grows corrupt after the lusts of deceit; and that you be renewed in the spirit of your mind, and put on the new man, who in the likeness of God has been created in righteousness and holiness of truth. Therefore putting away falsehood, speak truth each one with his neighbor. For we are members of one another. "Be angry, and don't sin." Don't let the sun go down on your wrath, neither give place to the devil. Let him who stole steal no more; but rather let him labor, working with his hands the thing that is good, that he may have something to give to him who has need. Let no corrupt speech proceed out of your mouth, but such as is good for building up as the need may be, that it may give grace to those who hear. Don't grieve the Holy Spirit of God, in whom you were sealed for the day of redemption. Let all bitterness, wrath, anger, outcry, and slander, be put away from you, with all malice. And be kind to one another, tenderhearted, forgiving each other, just as God also in Christ forgave you.

I Ki. 12:1-19 Rehoboam went to Shechem: for all Israel had come to Shechem to make him king. It happened, when Jeroboam the son of Nebat heard of it (for he was yet in Egypt, where he had fled from the presence of king Solomon, and Jeroboam lived in Egypt, and they sent and called him), that Jeroboam and all the assembly of Israel came, and spoke to Rehoboam, saying, "Your father made our yoke grievous: now therefore make you the grievous service of your father, and his heavy yoke which he put on us, lighter, and we will serve you." He said to them, "Depart for three days, then come back to me." The people departed. King Rehoboam took counsel with the old men, who had stood before Solomon his father while he yet lived, saying, "What counsel do you give me to return answer to this people?" They spoke to him, saying, "If you will be a servant to this people this day, and will serve them, and answer them, and speak good words to them, then they will be your servants forever." But he forsook the counsel of the old men which they had given him, and took counsel with the young men who had grown up with him, who stood before him. He said to them, "What counsel do you give, that we may return answer to this people, who have spoken to me, saying, 'Make the yoke that your father put on us lighter?'" The young men who had grown up with him spoke to him, saying, "Thus you shall tell this people who spoke to you, saying, 'Your father made our yoke heavy, but make it lighter to us;' you shall say to them, 'My little finger is thicker than my father's waist. Now whereas my father burdened you with a heavy yoke, I will add to your yoke: my father chastised you with whips, but I will chastise you with scorpions.'" So Jeroboam and all the people came to Rehoboam the third day, as the king asked, saying, "Come to me again the third day." The king answered the people roughly, and forsook the counsel of the old men which they had given him, and spoke to them according to the counsel of the young men, saying, "My father made your yoke heavy, but I will add to your yoke. My father chastised you with whips, but I will chastise you with scorpions." So the king didn't listen to the people; for it was a thing brought about of Yahweh, that he might establish his word, which Yahweh spoke by Ahijah the Shilonite to Jeroboam the son of Nebat. When all Israel saw that the king didn't listen to them, the people answered the king, saying, "What portion have we in David? Neither do we have an inheritance in the son of Jesse. To your tents, Israel! Now see to your own house, David." So Israel departed to their tents. But as for the children of Israel who lived in the cities of Judah, Rehoboam reigned over them. Then king Rehoboam sent Adoram, who was over the men subject to forced labor; and all Israel stoned him to death with stones. King Rehoboam made speed to get him up to his chariot, to flee to Jerusalem. So Israel rebelled against the house of David to this day.

Week 16 Day 4   29-Jan

Matt. 13:24-30 He set another parable before them, saying, "The Kingdom of Heaven is like a man who sowed good seed in his field, but while people slept, his enemy came and sowed darnel weeds also among the wheat, and went away. But when the blade sprang up and brought forth fruit, then the darnel weeds appeared also. The servants of the householder came and said to him, 'Sir, didn't you sow good seed in your field? Where did this darnel come from?' He said to them, 'An enemy has done this.' "The servants asked him, 'Do you want us to go and gather them up?' But he said, 'No, lest perhaps while you gather up the darnel weeds, you root up the wheat with them. Let both grow together until the harvest, and in the harvest time I will tell the reapers, "First, gather up the darnel weeds, and bind them in bundles to burn them; but gather the wheat into my barn."""

Matt. 13:36-43 Then Jesus sent the multitudes away, and went into the house. His disciples came to him, saying, "Explain to us the parable of the darnel weeds of the field." He answered them, "He who sows the good seed is the Son of Man, the field is the world; and the good seed, these are the children of the Kingdom; and the darnel weeds are the children of the evil one. The enemy who sowed them is the devil. The harvest is the end of the age, and the reapers are angels. As therefore the darnel weeds are gathered up and burned with fire; so will it be at the end of this age. The Son of Man will send out his angels, and they will gather out of his Kingdom all things that cause stumbling, and those who do iniquity, and will cast them into the furnace of fire. There will be weeping and the gnashing of teeth. Then the righteous will shine forth like the sun in the Kingdom of their Father. He who has ears to hear, let him hear."

Rev. 20:11-15 I saw a great white throne, and him who sat on it, from whose face the earth and the heaven fled away. There was found no place for them. I saw the dead, the great and the small, standing before the throne, and they opened books. Another book was opened, which is the book of life. The dead were judged out of the things which were written in the books, according to their works. The sea gave up the dead who were in it. Death and Hades gave up the dead who were in them. They were judged, each one according to his works. Death and Hades were thrown into the lake of fire. This is the second death, the lake of fire. If anyone was not found written in the book of life, he was cast into the lake of fire.

Ps. 86 Hear, Yahweh, and answer me, for I am poor and needy. Preserve my soul, for I am godly. You, my God, save your servant who trusts in you. Be merciful to me, Lord, for I call to you all day long. Bring joy to the soul of your servant, for to you, Lord, do I lift up my soul. For you, Lord, are good, and ready to forgive; abundant in loving kindness to all those who call on you. Hear, Yahweh, my prayer. Listen to the voice of my petitions. In the day of my trouble I will call on you, for you will answer me. There is no one like you among the gods, Lord, nor any deeds like your deeds. All nations you have made will come and worship before you, Lord. They shall glorify your name. For you are great, and do wondrous things. You are God alone. Teach me your way, Yahweh. I will walk in your truth. Make my heart undivided to fear your name. I will praise you, Lord my God, with my whole heart. I will glorify your name forevermore. For your loving kindness is great toward me. You have delivered my soul from the lowest Sheol. God, the proud have risen up against me. A company of violent men have sought after my soul, and they don't hold regard for you before them. But you, Lord, are a merciful and gracious God, slow to anger, and abundant in loving kindness and truth. Turn to me, and have mercy on me! Give your strength to your servant. Save the son of your handmaid. Show me a sign of your goodness, that those who hate me may see it, and be shamed, because you, Yahweh, have helped me, and comforted me.

Week 16 Day 5   4-Mar

Matt. 13:47-52 "Again, the Kingdom of Heaven is like a dragnet, that was cast into the sea, and gathered some fish of every kind, which, when it was filled, they drew up on the beach. They sat down, and gathered the good into containers, but the bad they threw away. So will it be in the end of the world. The angels will come forth, and separate the wicked from among the righteous, and will cast them into the furnace of fire. There will be the weeping and the gnashing of teeth." Jesus said to them, "Have you understood all these things?" They answered him, "Yes, Lord." He said to them, "Therefore every scribe who has been made a disciple in the Kingdom of Heaven is like a man who is a householder, who brings out of his treasure new and old things."

II Thes. 1:3-12 We are bound to always give thanks to God for you, brothers, even as it is appropriate, because your faith grows exceedingly, and the love of each and every one of you towards one another abounds; so that we ourselves boast about you in the assemblies of God for your patience and faith in all your persecutions and in the afflictions which you endure. This is an obvious sign of the righteous judgment of God, to the end that you may be counted worthy of the Kingdom of God, for which you also suffer. Since it is a righteous thing with God to repay affliction to those who afflict you, and to give relief to you who are afflicted with us, when the Lord Jesus is revealed from heaven with his mighty angels in flaming fire, giving vengeance to those who don't know God, and to those who don't obey the Good News of our Lord Jesus, who will pay the penalty: eternal destruction from the face of the Lord and from the glory of his might, when he comes to be glorified in his saints, and to be admired among all those who have believed (because our testimony to you was believed) in that day. To this end we also pray always for you, that our God may count you worthy of your calling, and fulfill every desire of goodness and work of faith, with power; that the name of our Lord Jesus may be glorified in you, and you in him, according to the grace of our God and the Lord Jesus Christ.

Num. 16:1-35 Now Korah, the son of Izhar, the son of Kohath, the son of Levi, with Dathan and Abiram, the sons of Eliab, and On, the son of Peleth, sons of Reuben, took men: and they rose up before Moses, with certain of the children of Israel, two hundred fifty princes of the congregation, called to the assembly, men of renown; and they assembled themselves together against Moses and against Aaron, and said to them, "You take too much on yourself, since all the congregation are holy, everyone of them, and Yahweh is among them: why then lift yourselves up above the assembly of Yahweh?" When Moses heard it, he fell on his face: and he spoke to Korah and to all his company, saying, "In the morning Yahweh will show who are his, and who is holy, and will cause him to come near to him: even him whom he shall choose he will cause to come near to him. Do this: take censers, Korah, and all his company; and put fire in them, and put incense on them before Yahweh tomorrow: and it shall be that the man whom Yahweh chooses, he shall be holy. You have gone too far, you sons of Levi!" Moses said to Korah, "Hear now, you sons of Levi! Is it a small thing to you, that the God of Israel has separated you from the congregation of Israel, to bring you near to himself, to do the service of the tabernacle of Yahweh, and to stand before the congregation to minister to them; and that he has brought you near, and all your brothers the sons of Levi with you? and do you seek the priesthood also? Therefore you and all your company are gathered together against Yahweh: and Aaron, what is he that you murmur against him?" Moses sent to call Dathan and Abiram, the sons of Eliab; and they said, "We won't come up: is it a small thing that you have brought us up out of a land flowing with milk and honey, to kill us in the wilderness, but you must also make yourself a prince over us? Moreover you haven't brought us into a land flowing with milk and honey, nor given us inheritance of fields and vineyards: will you put out the eyes of these men? We won't come up." Moses was very angry, and said to Yahweh, "Don't respect their offering: I have not taken one donkey from them, neither have I hurt one of them." Moses said to Korah, "You and all your company go before Yahweh, you, and they, and Aaron, tomorrow: and each man take his censer, and put incense on them, and each man bring before Yahweh his censer, two hundred fifty censers; you also, and Aaron, each his censer." They each took his censer, and put fire in them, and laid incense thereon, and stood at the door of the Tent of Meeting with Moses and Aaron. Korah assembled all the congregation against them to the door of the Tent of Meeting: and the glory of Yahweh appeared to all the congregation. Yahweh spoke to Moses and to Aaron, saying, "Separate yourselves from among this congregation, that I may consume them in a moment!" They fell on their faces, and said, "God, the God of the spirits of all flesh, shall one man sin, and will you be angry with all the congregation?" Yahweh spoke to Moses, saying, "Speak to the congregation, saying, 'Get away from around the tent of Korah, Dathan, and Abiram!'" Moses rose up and went to Dathan and Abiram; and the elders of Israel followed him. He spoke to the congregation, saying, "Depart, please, from the tents of these wicked men, and touch nothing of theirs, lest you be consumed in all their sins!" So they went away from the tent of Korah, Dathan, and Abiram, on every side: and Dathan and Abiram came out, and stood at the door of their tents, and their wives, and their sons, and their little ones. Moses said, "Hereby you shall know that Yahweh has sent me to do all these works; for they are not from my own mind. If these men die the common death of all men, or if they be visited after the visitation of all men; then Yahweh hasn't sent me. But if Yahweh make a new thing, and the ground open its mouth, and swallow them up, with all that appertain to them, and they go down alive into Sheol; then you shall understand that these men have despised Yahweh." It happened, as he made an end of speaking all these words, that the ground split apart that was under them; and the earth opened its mouth, and swallowed them up, and their households, and all the men who appertained to Korah, and all their goods. So they, and all that appertained to them, went down alive into Sheol: and the earth closed on them, and they perished from among the assembly. All Israel that were around them fled at their cry; for they said, "Lest the earth swallow us up!" Fire came forth from Yahweh, and devoured the two hundred fifty men who offered the incense.

John 15:18-27 "If the world hates you, you know that it has hated me before it hated you. If you were of the world, the world would love its own. But because you are not of the world, since I chose you out of the world, therefore the world hates you. Remember the word that I said to you: 'A servant is not greater than his lord.' If they persecuted me, they will also persecute you. If they kept my word, they will keep yours also. But all these things will they do to you for my name's sake, because they don't know him who sent me. If I had not come and spoken to them, they would not have had sin; but now they have no excuse for their sin. He who hates me, hates my Father also. If I hadn't done among them the works which no one else did, they wouldn't have had sin. But now have they seen and also hated both me and my Father. But this happened so that the word may be fulfilled which was written in their law, 'They hated me without a cause.' When the Counselor has come, whom I will send to you from the Father, the Spirit of truth, who proceeds from the Father, he will testify about me. You will also testify, because you have been with me from the beginning."

II Tim. 3:10-17 But you did follow my teaching, conduct, purpose, faith, patience, love, steadfastness, persecutions, and sufferings: those things that happened to me at Antioch, Iconium, and Lystra. I endured those persecutions. Out of them all the Lord delivered me. Yes, and all who desire to live godly in Christ Jesus will suffer persecution. But evil men and impostors will grow worse and worse, deceiving and being deceived. But you remain in the things which you have learned and have been assured of, knowing from whom you have learned them. From infancy, you have known the holy Scriptures which are able to make you wise for salvation through faith, which is in Christ Jesus. Every Scripture is God-breathed and profitable for teaching, for reproof, for correction, and for instruction in righteousness, that the man of God may be complete, thoroughly equipped for every good work.

Jer. 1:4-19 Now the word of Yahweh came to me, saying, "Before I formed you in the belly, I knew you. Before you came forth out of the womb, I sanctified you. I have appointed you a prophet to the nations." Then I said, "Ah, Lord Yahweh! Behold, I don't know how to speak; for I am a child." But Yahweh said to me, "Don't say, 'I am a child;' for to whoever I shall send you, you shall go, and whatever I shall command you, you shall speak. Don't be afraid because of them; for I am with you to deliver you," says Yahweh. Then Yahweh put forth his hand, and touched my mouth; and Yahweh said to me, "Behold, I have put my words in your mouth. Behold, I have this day set you over the nations and over the kingdoms, to pluck up and to break down and to destroy and to overthrow, to build and to plant." Moreover the word of Yahweh came to me, saying, "Jeremiah, what do you see?" I said, "I see a branch of an almond tree." Then Yahweh said to me, "You have seen well; for I watch over my word to perform it." The word of Yahweh came to me the second time, saying, "What do you see?" I said, "I see a boiling caldron; and it is tipping away from the north." Then Yahweh said to me, "Out of the north evil will break out on all the inhabitants of the land. For, behold, I will call all the families of the kingdoms of the north," says Yahweh; "and they shall come, and they shall each set his throne at the entrance of the gates of Jerusalem, and against all its walls all around, and against all the cities of Judah. I will utter my judgments against them touching all their wickedness, in that they have forsaken me, and have burned incense to other gods, and worshiped the works of their own hands. "You therefore put your belt on your waist, arise, and speak to them all that I command you. Don't be dismayed at them, lest I dismay you before them. For, behold, I have made you this day a fortified city, and an iron pillar, and bronze walls, against the whole land, against the kings of Judah, against its princes, against its priests, and against the people of the land. They will fight against you; but they will not prevail against you; for I am with you," says Yahweh, "to deliver you."

Week 16 Day 7   19-Mar

Heb. 11:1-40 Now faith is assurance of things hoped for, proof of things not seen. For by this, the elders obtained testimony. By faith, we understand that the universe has been framed by the word of God, so that what is seen has not been made out of things which are visible. By faith, Abel offered to God a more excellent sacrifice than Cain, through which he had testimony given to him that he was righteous, God testifying with respect to his gifts; and through it he, being dead, still speaks. By faith, Enoch was taken away, so that he wouldn't see death, and he was not found, because God translated him. For he has had testimony given to him that before his translation he had been well pleasing to God. Without faith it is impossible to be well pleasing to him, for he who comes to God must believe that he exists, and that he is a rewarder of those who seek him. By faith, Noah, being warned about things not yet seen, moved with godly fear, prepared a ship for the saving of his house, through which he condemned the world, and became heir of the righteousness which is according to faith. By faith, Abraham, when he was called, obeyed to go out to the place which he was to receive for an inheritance. He went out, not knowing where he went. By faith, he lived as an alien in the land of promise, as in a land not his own, dwelling in tents, with Isaac and Jacob, the heirs with him of the same promise. For he looked for the city which has the foundations, whose builder and maker is God. By faith, even Sarah herself received power to conceive, and she bore a child when she was past age, since she counted him faithful who had promised. Therefore as many as the stars of the sky in multitude, and as innumerable as the sand which is by the sea shore, were fathered by one man, and him as good as dead. These all died in faith, not having received the promises, but having seen them and embraced them from afar, and having confessed that they were strangers and pilgrims on the earth. For those who say such things make it clear that they are seeking a country of their own. If indeed they had been thinking of that country from which they went out, they would have had enough time to return. But now they desire a better country, that is, a heavenly one. Therefore God is not ashamed of them, to be called their God, for he has prepared a city for them. By faith, Abraham, being tested, offered up Isaac. Yes, he who had gladly received the promises was offering up his one and only son; even he to whom it was said, "In Isaac will your seed be called"; concluding that God is able to raise up even from the dead. Figuratively speaking, he also did receive him back from the dead. By faith, Isaac blessed Jacob and Esau, even concerning things to come. By faith, Jacob, when he was dying, blessed each of the sons of Joseph, and worshiped, leaning on the top of his staff. By faith, Joseph, when his end was near, made mention of the departure of the children of Israel; and gave instructions concerning his bones. By faith, Moses, when he was born, was hidden for three months by his parents, because they saw that he was a beautiful child, and they were not afraid of the king's commandment. By faith, Moses, when he had grown up, refused to be called the son of Pharaoh's daughter, choosing rather to share ill treatment with God's people, than to enjoy the pleasures of sin for a time; accounting reproach for the sake of Christ greater riches than the treasures of Egypt; for he looked to the reward. By faith, he left Egypt, not fearing the wrath of the king; for he endured, as seeing him who is invisible. By faith, he kept the Passover, and the sprinkling of the blood, that the destroyer of the firstborn should not touch them. By faith, they passed through the Red Sea as on dry land. When the Egyptians tried to do so, they were swallowed up. By faith, the walls of Jericho fell down, after they had been encircled for seven days. By faith, Rahab the prostitute, didn't perish with those who were disobedient, having received the spies in peace. What more shall I say? I don't have time to tell of Gideon, Barak, Samson, Jephthah, David, Samuel, and the prophets; who, through faith subdued kingdoms, worked out righteousness, obtained promises, stopped the mouths of lions, quenched the power of fire, escaped the edge of the sword, from weakness were made strong, grew mighty in war, and caused foreign armies to flee. Women received their dead by resurrection. Others were tortured, not accepting their deliverance, that they might obtain a better resurrection. Others were tried by mocking and scourging, yes, moreover by bonds and imprisonment. They were stoned. They were sawn apart. They were tempted. They were slain with the sword. They went around in sheep skins and in goat skins; being destitute, afflicted, ill-treated (of whom the world was not worthy), wandering in deserts, mountains, caves, and the holes of the earth. These all, having had testimony given to them through their faith, didn't receive the promise, God having provided some better thing concerning us, so that apart from us they should not be made perfect.

Ps. 17 Hear, Yahweh, my righteous plea; give ear to my prayer, that doesn't go out of deceitful lips. Let my sentence come forth from your presence. Let your eyes look on equity. You have proved my heart. You have visited me in the night. You have tried me, and found nothing. I have resolved that my mouth shall not disobey. As for the works of men, by the word of your lips, I have kept myself from the ways of the violent. My steps have held fast to your paths. My feet have not slipped. I have called on you, for you will answer me, God. Turn your ear to me. Hear my speech. Show your marvelous loving kindness, you who save those who take refuge by your right hand from their enemies. Keep me as the apple of your eye. Hide me under the shadow of your wings, from the wicked who oppress me, my deadly enemies, who surround me. They close up their callous hearts. With their mouth they speak proudly. They have now surrounded us in our steps. They set their eyes to cast us down to the earth. He is like a lion that is greedy of his prey, as it were a young lion lurking in secret places. Arise, Yahweh, confront him. Cast him down. Deliver my soul from the wicked by your sword; from men by your hand, Yahweh, from men of the world, whose portion is in this life. You fill the belly of your cherished ones. Your sons have plenty, and they store up wealth for their children. As for me, I shall see your face in righteousness. I shall be satisfied, when I awake, with seeing your form.

Week 17 Day 1   11-Jul

Matt. 12:1-14 At that time, Jesus went on the Sabbath day through the grain fields. His disciples were hungry and began to pluck heads of grain and to eat. But the Pharisees, when they saw it, said to him, "Behold, your disciples do what is not lawful to do on the Sabbath." But he said to them, "Haven't you read what David did, when he was hungry, and those who were with him; how he entered into God's house, and ate the show bread, which was not lawful for him to eat, neither for those who were with him, but only for the priests? Or have you not read in the law, that on the Sabbath day, the priests in the temple profane the Sabbath, and are guiltless? But I tell you that one greater than the temple is here. But if you had known what this means, 'I desire mercy, and not sacrifice,' you would not have condemned the guiltless. For the Son of Man is Lord of the Sabbath." He departed there, and went into their synagogue. And behold there was a man with a withered hand. They asked him, "Is it lawful to heal on the Sabbath day?" that they might accuse him. He said to them, "What man is there among you, who has one sheep, and if this one falls into a pit on the Sabbath day, won't he grab on to it, and lift it out? Of how much more value then is a man than a sheep! Therefore it is lawful to do good on the Sabbath day." Then he told the man, "Stretch out your hand." He stretched it out; and it was restored whole, just like the other. But the Pharisees went out, and conspired against him, how they might destroy him.

Acts 4:13-20 Now when they saw the boldness of Peter and John, and had perceived that they were unlearned and ignorant men, they marveled. They recognized that they had been with Jesus. Seeing the man who was healed standing with them, they could say nothing against it. But when they had commanded them to go aside out of the council, they conferred among themselves, saying, "What shall we do to these men? Because indeed a notable miracle has been done through them, as can be plainly seen by all who dwell in Jerusalem, and we can't deny it. But so that this spreads no further among the people, let's threaten them, that from now on they don't speak to anyone in this name." They called them, and commanded them not to speak at all nor teach in the name of Jesus. But Peter and John answered them, "Whether it is right in the sight of God to listen to you rather than to God, judge for yourselves, for we can't help telling the things which we saw and heard."

1 Sam. 21:1-6 Then came David to Nob to Ahimelech the priest. Ahimelech came to meet David trembling, and said to him, "Why are you alone, and no man with you?" David said to Ahimelech the priest, "The king has commanded me a business, and has said to me, 'Let no man know anything of the business about which I send you, and what I have commanded you; and I have appointed the young men to such and such a place.' Now therefore what is under your hand? Give me five loaves of bread in my hand, or whatever there is present." The priest answered David, and said, "There is no common bread under my hand, but there is holy bread; if only the young men have kept themselves from women." David answered the priest, and said to him, "Truly, women have been kept from us about these three days. When I came out, the vessels of the young men were holy, though it was but a common journey. How much more then today shall their vessels be holy?" So the priest gave him holy bread; for there was no bread there but the show bread, that was taken from before Yahweh, to put hot bread in the day when it was taken away.

Week 17 Day 2   12-May

Matt. 15:1-9 Then Pharisees and scribes came to Jesus from Jerusalem, saying, "Why do your disciples disobey the tradition of the elders? For they don't wash their hands when they eat bread." He answered them, "Why do you also disobey the commandment of God because of your tradition? For God commanded, 'Honor your father and your mother,' and, 'He who speaks evil of father or mother, let him be put to death.' But you say, 'Whoever may tell his father or his mother, "Whatever help you might otherwise have gotten from me is a gift devoted to God," he shall not honor his father or mother.' You have made the commandment of God void because of your tradition.

You hypocrites! Well did Isaiah prophesy of you, saying, 'These people draw near to me with their mouth, and honor me with their lips; but their heart is far from me. And in vain do they worship me, teaching as doctrine rules made by men.'"

Col. 2:6-23 As therefore you received Christ Jesus, the Lord, walk in him, rooted and built up in him, and established in the faith, even as you were taught, abounding in it in thanksgiving. Be careful that you don't let anyone rob you through his philosophy and vain deceit, after the tradition of men, after the elements of the world, and not after Christ. For in him all the fullness of the Godhead dwells bodily, and in him you are made full, who is the head of all principality and power; in whom you were also circumcised with a circumcision not made with hands, in the putting off of the body of the sins of the flesh, in the circumcision of Christ; having been buried with him in baptism, in which you were also raised with him through faith in the working of God, who raised him from the dead. You were dead through your trespasses and the uncircumcision of your flesh. He made you alive together with him, having forgiven us all our trespasses, wiping out the handwriting in ordinances which was against us; and he has taken it out of the way, nailing it to the cross; having stripped the principalities and the powers, he made a show of them openly, triumphing over them in it. Let no one therefore judge you in eating, or in drinking, or with respect to a feast day or a new moon or a Sabbath day, which are a shadow of the things to come; but the body is Christ's. Let no one rob you of your prize by a voluntary humility and worshipping of the angels, dwelling in the things which he has not seen, vainly puffed up by his fleshly mind, and not holding firmly to the Head, from whom all the body, being supplied and knit together through the joints and ligaments, grows with God's growth. If you died with Christ from the elements of the world, why, as though living in the world, do you subject yourselves to ordinances, "Don't handle, nor taste, nor touch" (all of which perish with use), according to the precepts and doctrines of men? Which things indeed appear like wisdom in self-imposed worship, and humility, and severity to the body; but aren't of any value against the indulgence of the flesh.

Hos. 6:1-11 Come, and let us return to Yahweh; for he has torn us to pieces, and he will heal us; he has injured us, and he will bind up our wounds. After two days he will revive us. On the third day he will raise us up, and we will live before him. Let us acknowledge Yahweh. Let us press on to know Yahweh. As surely as the sun rises, Yahweh will appear. He will come to us like the rain, like the spring rain that waters the earth. Ephraim, what shall I do to you? Judah, what shall I do to you? For your love is like a morning cloud, and like the dew that disappears early. Therefore I have cut them to pieces with the prophets; I killed them with the words of my mouth. Your judgments are like a flash of lightning. For I desire mercy, and not sacrifice; and the knowledge of God more than burnt offerings. But they, like Adam, have broken the covenant. They were unfaithful to me, there. Gilead is a city of those who work iniquity; it is stained with blood. As gangs of robbers wait to ambush a man, so the company of priests murder in the way toward Shechem, committing shameful crimes. In the house of Israel I have seen a horrible thing. There is prostitution in Ephraim. Israel is defiled. Also, Judah, there is a harvest appointed for you, when I restore the fortunes of my people.

Week 17 Day 3   7-Dec

Matt. 23:1-12 Then Jesus spoke to the multitudes and to his disciples, saying, "The scribes and the Pharisees sat on Moses' seat. All things therefore whatever they tell you to observe, observe and do, but don't do their works; for they say, and don't do. For they bind heavy burdens that are grievous to be borne, and lay them on men's shoulders; but they themselves will not lift a finger to help them. But all their works they do to be seen by men. They make their phylacteries broad, enlarge the fringes of their garments, and love the place of honor at feasts, the best seats in the synagogues, the salutations in the marketplaces, and to be called 'Rabbi, Rabbi' by men. But don't you be called 'Rabbi,' for one is your teacher, the Christ, and all of you are brothers. Call no man on the earth your father, for one is your Father, he who is in heaven. Neither be called masters, for one is your master, the Christ. But he who is greatest among you will be your servant. Whoever exalts himself will be humbled, and whoever humbles himself will be exalted."

1 Pet. 2:13-25 Therefore subject yourselves to every ordinance of man for the Lord's sake: whether to the king, as supreme; or to governors, as sent by him for vengeance on evildoers and for praise to those who do well. For this is the will of God, that by well-doing you should put to silence the ignorance of foolish men: as free, and not using your freedom for a cloak of wickedness, but as bondservants of God. Honor all men. Love the brotherhood. Fear God. Honor the king. Servants, be in subjection to your masters with all fear; not only to the good and gentle, but also to the wicked. For it is commendable if someone endures pain, suffering unjustly, because of conscience toward God. For what glory is it if, when you sin, you patiently endure beating? But if, when you do well, you patiently endure suffering, this is commendable with God. For to this you were called, because Christ also suffered for us, leaving you an example, that you should follow his steps, who did not sin, "neither was deceit found in his mouth." Who, when he was cursed, didn't curse back. When he suffered, didn't threaten, but committed himself to him who judges righteously; who his own self bore our sins in his body on the tree, that we, having died to sins, might live to righteousness; by whose stripes you were healed. For you were going astray like sheep; but now have returned to the Shepherd and Overseer of your souls.

Mic. 3:1-12 I said, "Please listen, you heads of Jacob, and rulers of the house of Israel: Isn't it for you to know justice? You who hate the good, and love the evil; who tear off their skin, and their flesh from off their bones; who also eat the flesh of my people, and flay their skin from off them, and break their bones, and chop them in pieces, as for the pot, and as flesh within the caldron. Then they will cry to Yahweh, but he will not answer them. Yes, he will hide his face from them at that time, because they made their deeds evil." Thus says Yahweh concerning the prophets who lead my people astray; for those who feed their teeth, they proclaim, "Peace!" and whoever doesn't provide for their mouths, they prepare war against him: "Therefore night is over you, with no vision, and it is dark to you, that you may not divine; and the sun will go down on the prophets, and the day will be black over them. The seers shall be disappointed, and the diviners confounded. Yes, they shall all cover their lips; for there is no answer from God." But as for me, I am full of power by the Spirit of Yahweh, and of judgment, and of might, to declare to Jacob his disobedience, and to Israel his sin. Please listen to this, you heads of the house of Jacob, and rulers of the house of Israel, who abhor justice, and pervert all equity. They build up Zion with blood, and Jerusalem with iniquity. Her leaders judge for bribes, and her priests teach for a price, and her prophets of it tell fortunes for money: yet they lean on Yahweh, and say, "Isn't Yahweh in the midst of us? No disaster will come on us." Therefore Zion for your sake will be plowed like a field, and Jerusalem will become heaps of rubble, and the mountain of the temple like the high places of a forest.

Week 17 Day 4   1-Nov

Matthew 23:13-32 "Woe to you, scribes and Pharisees, hypocrites! For you devour widows' houses, and as a pretense you make long prayers. Therefore you will receive greater condemnation. But woe to you, scribes and Pharisees, hypocrites! Because you shut up the Kingdom of Heaven against men; for you don't enter in yourselves, neither do you allow those who are entering in to enter. Woe to you, scribes and Pharisees, hypocrites! For you travel around by sea and land to make one proselyte; and when he becomes one, you make him twice as much of a son of Gehenna as yourselves. Woe to you, you blind guides, who say, 'Whoever swears by the temple, it is nothing; but whoever swears by the gold of the temple, he is obligated.' You blind fools! For which is greater, the gold, or the temple that sanctifies the gold? 'Whoever swears by the altar, it is nothing; but whoever swears by the gift that is on it, he is obligated?' You blind fools! For which is greater, the gift, or the altar that sanctifies the gift? He therefore who swears by the altar, swears by it, and by everything on it. He who swears by the temple, swears by it, and by him who was living in it. He who swears by heaven, swears by the throne of God, and by him who sits on it. Woe to you, scribes and Pharisees, hypocrites! For you tithe mint, dill, and cumin, and have left undone the weightier matters of the law: justice, mercy, and faith. But you ought to have done these, and not to have left the other undone. You blind guides, who strain out a gnat, and swallow a camel!" "Woe to you, scribes and Pharisees, hypocrites! For you clean the outside of the cup and of the platter, but within they are full of extortion and unrighteousness. You blind Pharisee, first clean the inside of the cup and of the platter, that its outside may become clean also. "Woe to you, scribes and Pharisees, hypocrites! For you are like whitened tombs, which outwardly appear beautiful, but inwardly are full of dead men's bones, and of all uncleanness. Even so you also outwardly appear righteous to men, but inwardly you are full of hypocrisy and iniquity. "Woe to you, scribes and Pharisees, hypocrites! For you build the tombs of the prophets, and decorate the tombs of the righteous, and say, 'If we had lived in the days of our fathers, we wouldn't have been partakers with them in the blood of the prophets.' Therefore you testify to yourselves that you are children of those who killed the prophets. Fill up, then, the measure of your fathers.

Jude 3-16 Beloved, while I was very eager to write to you about our common salvation, I was constrained to write to you exhorting you to contend earnestly for the faith which was once for all delivered to the saints. For there are certain men who crept in secretly, even those who were long ago written about for this condemnation: ungodly men, turning the grace of our God into indecency, and denying our only Master, God, and Lord, Jesus Christ. Now I desire to remind you, though you already know this, that the Lord, having saved a people out of the land of Egypt, afterward destroyed those who didn't believe. Angels who didn't keep their first domain, but deserted their own dwelling place, he has kept in everlasting bonds under darkness for the judgment of the great day. Even as Sodom and Gomorrah, and the cities around them, having, in the same way as these, given themselves over to sexual immorality and gone after strange flesh, are set forth as an example, suffering the punishment of eternal fire. Yet in the same way, these also in their dreaming defile the flesh, despise authority, and slander celestial beings. But Michael, the archangel, when contending with the devil and arguing about the body of Moses, dared not bring against him an abusive condemnation, but said, "May the Lord rebuke you!" But these speak evil of whatever things they don't know. What they understand naturally, like the creatures without reason, they are destroyed in these things. Woe to them! For they went in the way of Cain, and ran riotously in the error of Balaam for hire, and perished in Korah's rebellion. These are hidden rocky reefs in your love feasts when they feast with you, shepherds who without fear feed themselves; clouds without water, carried along by winds; autumn leaves without fruit, twice dead, plucked up by the roots; wild waves of the sea, foaming out their own shame; wandering stars, for whom the blackness of darkness has been reserved forever. About these also Enoch, the seventh from Adam, prophesied, saying, "Behold, the Lord came with ten thousands of his holy ones, to execute judgment on all, and to convict all the ungodly of all their works of ungodliness which they have done in an ungodly way, and of all the hard things which ungodly sinners have spoken against him." These are murmurers and complainers, walking after their lusts (and their mouth speaks proud things), showing respect of persons to gain advantage.

Zech. 7:4-14 Then the word of Yahweh of Armies came to me, saying, "Speak to all the people of the land, and to the priests, saying, 'When you fasted and mourned in the fifth and in the seventh month for these seventy years, did you at all fast to me, really to me? When you eat, and when you drink, don't you eat for yourselves, and drink for yourselves? Aren't these the words which Yahweh proclaimed by the former prophets, when Jerusalem was inhabited and in prosperity, and its cities around her, and the South and the lowland were inhabited?'" The word of Yahweh came to Zechariah, saying, "Thus has Yahweh of Armies spoken, saying, 'Execute true judgment, and show kindness and compassion every man to his brother. Don't oppress the widow, nor the fatherless, the foreigner, nor the poor; and let none of you devise evil against his brother in your heart.' But they refused to listen, and turned their backs, and stopped their ears, that they might not hear. Yes, they made their hearts as hard as flint, lest they might hear the law, and the words which Yahweh of Armies had sent by his Spirit by the former prophets. Therefore great wrath came from Yahweh of Armies. It has come to pass that, as he called, and they refused to listen, so they will call, and I will not listen," said Yahweh of Armies; "but I will scatter them with a whirlwind among all the nations which they have not known. Thus the land was desolate after them, so that no man passed through nor returned: for they made the pleasant land desolate."

Week 17 Day 5   23-Sep

Luke 13:22-30 He went on his way through cities and villages, teaching, and traveling on to Jerusalem. One said to him, "Lord, are they few who are saved?" He said to them, "Strive to enter in by the narrow door, for many, I tell you, will seek to enter in, and will not be able. When once the master of the house has risen up, and has shut the door, and you begin to stand outside, and to knock at the door, saying, 'Lord, Lord, open to us!' then he will answer and tell you, 'I don't know you or where you come from.' Then you will begin to say, 'We ate and drank in your presence, and you taught in our streets.' He will say, 'I tell you, I don't know where you come from. Depart from me, all you workers of iniquity.' There will be weeping and gnashing of teeth, when you see Abraham, Isaac, Jacob, and all the prophets, in the Kingdom of God, and yourselves being thrown outside. They will come from the east, west, north, and south, and will sit down in the Kingdom of God. Behold, there are some who are last who will be first, and there are some who are first who will be last."

1 Jo. 2:18-27 Little children, these are the end times, and as you heard that the Antichrist is coming, even now many antichrists have arisen. By this we know that it is the final hour. They went out from us, but they didn't belong to us; for if they had belonged to us, they would have continued with us. But they left, that they might be revealed that none of them belong to us. You have an anointing from the Holy One, and you all have knowledge. I have not written to you because you don't know the truth, but because you know it, and because no lie is of the truth. Who is the liar but he who denies that Jesus is the Christ? This is the Antichrist, he who denies the Father and the Son. Whoever denies the Son, the same doesn't have the Father. He who confesses the Son has the Father also. Therefore, as for you, let that remain in you which you heard from the beginning. If that which you heard from the beginning remains in you, you also will remain in the Son, and in the Father. This is the promise which he promised us, the eternal life. These things I have written to you concerning those who would lead you astray. As for you, the anointing which you received from him remains in you, and you don't need for anyone to teach you. But as his anointing teaches you concerning all things, and is true, and is no lie, and even as it taught you, you will remain in him.

Is. 65:17-25 "For, behold, I create new heavens and a new earth; and the former things shall not be remembered, nor come into mind. But be you glad and rejoice forever in that which I create; for, behold, I create Jerusalem a rejoicing, and her people a joy. I will rejoice in Jerusalem, and joy in my people; and there shall be heard in her no more the voice of weeping and the voice of crying. There shall be no more there an infant of days, nor an old man who has not filled his days; for the child shall die one hundred years old, and the sinner being one hundred years old shall be accursed. They shall build houses, and inhabit them; and they shall plant vineyards, and eat their fruit. They shall not build, and another inhabit; they shall not plant, and another eat: for as the days of a tree shall be the days of my people, and my chosen shall long enjoy the work of their hands. They shall not labor in vain, nor bring forth for calamity; for they are the seed of the blessed of Yahweh, and their offspring with them. It shall happen that, before they call, I will answer; and while they are yet speaking, I will hear. The wolf and the lamb shall feed together, and the lion shall eat straw like the ox; and dust shall be the serpent's food. They shall not hurt nor destroy in all my holy mountain," says Yahweh.

Week 17 Day 6   7-Jul

Matt. 7:13-23 "Enter in by the narrow gate; for wide is the gate and broad is the way that leads to destruction, and many are those who enter in by it. How narrow is the gate, and restricted is the way that leads to life! Few are those who find it. Beware of false prophets, who come to you in sheep's clothing, but inwardly are ravening wolves. By their fruits you will know them. Do you gather grapes from thorns, or figs from thistles? Even so, every good tree produces good fruit; but the corrupt tree produces evil fruit. A good tree can't produce evil fruit, neither can a corrupt tree produce good fruit. Every tree that doesn't grow good fruit is cut down, and thrown into the fire. Therefore by their fruits you will know them. Not everyone who says to me, 'Lord, Lord,' will enter into the Kingdom of Heaven; but he who does the will of my Father who is in heaven. Many will tell me in that day, 'Lord, Lord, didn't we prophesy in your name, in your name cast out demons, and in your name do many mighty works?' Then I will tell them, 'I never knew you. Depart from me, you who work iniquity.'"

1 Jo. 4:1-6 Beloved, don't believe every spirit, but test the spirits, whether they are of God, because many false prophets have gone out into the world. By this you know the Spirit of God: every spirit who confesses that Jesus Christ has come in the flesh is of God, and every spirit who doesn't confess that Jesus Christ has come in the flesh is not of God, and this is the spirit of the Antichrist, of whom you have heard that it comes. Now it is in the world already. You are of God, little children, and have overcome them; because greater is he who is in you than he who is in the world. They are of the world. Therefore they speak of the world, and the world hears them. We are of God. He who knows God listens to us. He who is not of God doesn't listen to us. By this we know the spirit of truth, and the spirit of error.

Is. 55:1-13 "Come, everyone who thirsts, to the waters! Come, he who has no money, buy, and eat! Yes, come, buy wine and milk without money and without price. Why do you spend money for that which is not bread? and your labor for that which doesn't satisfy? listen diligently to me, and eat you that which is good, and let your soul delight itself in fatness. Turn your ear, and come to me; hear, and your soul shall live: and I will make an everlasting covenant with you, even the sure mercies of David. Behold, I have given him for a witness to the peoples, a leader and commander to the peoples. Behold, you shall call a nation that you don't know; and a nation that didn't know you shall run to you, because of Yahweh your God, and for the Holy One of Israel; for he has glorified you." Seek Yahweh while he may be found; call you on him while he is near: let the wicked forsake his way, and the unrighteous man his thoughts; and let him return to Yahweh, and he will have mercy on him; and to our God, for he will abundantly pardon. "For my thoughts are not your thoughts, neither are your ways my ways," says Yahweh. "For as the heavens are higher than the earth, so are my ways higher than your ways, and my thoughts than your thoughts. For as the rain comes down and the snow from the sky, and doesn't return there, but waters the earth, and makes it bring forth and bud, and gives seed to the sower and bread to the eater; so shall my word be that goes forth out of my mouth: it shall not return to me void, but it shall accomplish that which I please, and it shall prosper in the thing I sent it to do. For you shall go out with joy, and be led forth with peace: the mountains and the hills shall break forth before you into singing; and all the trees of the fields shall clap their hands. Instead of the thorn shall come up the fir tree; and instead of the brier shall come up the myrtle tree: and it shall be to Yahweh for a name, for an everlasting sign that shall not be cut off."

Week 17 Day 7   1-Aug

1 Cor. 3:10-23 According to the grace of God which was given to me, as a wise master builder I laid a foundation, and another builds on it. But let each man be careful how he builds on it. For no one can lay any other foundation than that which has been laid, which is Jesus Christ. But if anyone builds on the foundation with gold, silver, costly stones, wood, hay, or stubble; each man's work will be revealed. For the Day will declare it, because it is revealed in fire; and the fire itself will test what sort of work each man's work is. If any man's work remains which he built on it, he will receive a reward. If any man's work is burned, he will suffer loss, but he himself will be saved, but as through fire. Don't you know that you are a temple of God, and that God's Spirit lives in you? If anyone destroys the temple of God, God will destroy him; for God's temple is holy, which you are. Let no one deceive himself. If anyone thinks that he is wise among you in this world, let him become a fool, that he may become wise. For the wisdom of this world is foolishness with God. For it is written, "He has taken the wise in their craftiness." And again, "The Lord knows the reasoning of the wise, that it is worthless." Therefore let no one boast in men. For all things are yours, whether Paul, or Apollos, or Cephas, or the world, or life, or death, or things present, or things to come. All are yours, and you are Christ's, and Christ is God's.

Is. 5:8-30 Woe to those who join house to house, who lay field to field, until there is no room, and you are made to dwell alone in the midst of the land! In my ears, Yahweh of Armies says: "Surely many houses will be desolate, even great and beautiful, unoccupied. For ten acres of vineyard shall yield one bath, and a homer of seed shall yield an ephah." Woe to those who rise up early in the morning, that they may follow strong drink; who stay late into the night, until wine inflames them! The harp, lyre, tambourine, and flute, with wine, are at their feasts; but they don't respect the work of Yahweh, neither have they considered the operation of his hands. Therefore my people go into captivity for lack of knowledge. Their honorable men are famished, and their multitudes are parched with thirst. Therefore Sheol has enlarged its desire, and opened its mouth without measure; and their glory, their multitude, their pomp, and he who rejoices among them, descend into it. So man is brought low, mankind is humbled, and the eyes of the arrogant ones are humbled; but Yahweh of Armies is exalted in justice, and God the Holy One is sanctified in righteousness. Then the lambs will graze as in their pasture, and strangers will eat the ruins of the rich. Woe to those who draw iniquity with cords of falsehood, and wickedness as with cart rope; who say, "Let him make speed, let him hasten his work, that we may see it; and let the counsel of the Holy One of Israel draw near and come, that we may know it!" Woe to those who call evil good, and good evil; who put darkness for light, and light for darkness; who put bitter for sweet, and sweet for bitter! Woe to those who are wise in their own eyes, and prudent in their own sight! Woe to those who are mighty to drink wine, and champions at mixing strong drink; who acquit the guilty for a bribe, but deny justice for the innocent! Therefore as the tongue of fire devours the stubble, and as the dry grass sinks down in the flame, so their root shall be as rottenness, and their blossom shall go up as dust; because they have rejected the law of Yahweh of Armies, and despised the word of the Holy One of Israel. Therefore Yahweh's anger burns against his people, and he has stretched out his hand against them, and has struck them. The mountains tremble, and their dead bodies are as refuse in the midst of the streets. For all this, his anger is not turned away, but his hand is still stretched out. He will lift up a banner to the nations from far, and he will whistle for them from the end of the earth. Behold, they will come speedily and swiftly. None shall be weary nor stumble among them; none shall slumber nor sleep; neither shall the belt of their waist be untied, nor the latchet of their shoes be broken: whose arrows are sharp, and all their bows bent. Their horses' hoofs will be like flint, and their wheels like a whirlwind. Their roaring will be like a lioness. They will roar like young lions. Yes, they shall roar, and seize their prey and carry it off, and there will be no one to deliver. They will roar against them in that day like the roaring of the sea. If one looks to the land behold, darkness and distress. The light is darkened in its clouds.

Week 18 Day 1   **6-Dec**

Matt. 20:1-16 "For the Kingdom of Heaven is like a man who was the master of a household, who went out early in the morning to hire laborers for his vineyard. When he had agreed with the laborers for a denarius a day, he sent them into his vineyard. He went out about the third hour, and saw others standing idle in the marketplace. To them he said, 'You also go into the vineyard, and whatever is right I will give you.' So they went their way. Again he went out about the sixth and the ninth hour, and did likewise. About the eleventh hour he went out, and found others standing idle. He said to them, 'Why do you stand here all day idle?' They said to him, 'Because no one has hired us.' He said to them, 'You also go into the vineyard, and you will receive whatever is right.' When evening had come, the lord of the vineyard said to his manager, 'Call the laborers and pay them their wages, beginning from the last to the first.' When those who were hired at about the eleventh hour came, they each received a denarius. When the first came, they supposed that they would receive more; and they likewise each received a denarius. When they received it, they murmured against the master of the household, saying, 'These last have spent one hour, and you have made them equal to us, who have borne the burden of the day and the scorching heat!' But he answered one of them, 'Friend, I am doing you no wrong. Didn't you agree with me for a denarius? Take that which is yours, and go your way. It is my desire to give to this last just as much as to you. Isn't it lawful for me to do what I want to with what I own? Or is your eye evil, because I am good?' So the last will be first, and the first last. For many are called, but few are chosen."

Rom. 9:1-29 I tell the truth in Christ. I am not lying, my conscience testifying with me in the Holy Spirit, that I have great sorrow and unceasing pain in my heart. For I could wish that I myself were accursed from Christ for my brothers' sake, my relatives according to the flesh, who are Israelites; whose is the adoption, the glory, the covenants, the giving of the law, the service, and the promises; of whom are the fathers, and from whom is Christ as concerning the flesh, who is over all, God, blessed forever. Amen. But it is not as though the word of God has come to nothing. For they are not all Israel, that are of Israel. Neither, because they are Abraham's seed, are they all children. But, "In Isaac will your seed be called." That is, it is not the children of the flesh who are children of God, but the children of the promise are counted as a seed. For this is a word of promise, "At the appointed time I will come, and Sarah will have a son." Not only so, but Rebecca also conceived by one, by our father Isaac. For being not yet born, neither having done anything good or bad, that the purpose of God according to election might stand, not of works, but of him who calls, it was said to her, "The elder will serve the younger." Even as it is written, "Jacob I loved, but Esau I hated." What shall we say then? Is there unrighteousness with God? May it never be! For he said to Moses, "I will have mercy on whom I have mercy, and I will have compassion on whom I have compassion." So then it is not of him who wills, nor of him who runs, but of God who has mercy. For the Scripture says to Pharaoh, "For this very purpose I caused you to be raised up, that I might show in you my power, and that my name might be proclaimed in all the earth." So then, he has mercy on whom he desires, and he hardens whom he desires. You will say then to me, "Why does he still find fault? For who withstands his will?" But indeed, O man, who are you to reply against God? Will the thing formed ask him who formed it, "Why did you make me like this?" Or hasn't the potter a right over the clay, from the same lump to make one part a vessel for honor, and another for dishonor? What if God, willing to show his wrath, and to make his power known, endured with much patience vessels of wrath made for destruction, and that he might make known the riches of his glory on vessels of mercy, which he prepared beforehand for glory, us, whom he also called, not from the Jews only, but also from the Gentiles? As he says also in Hosea, "I will call them 'my people,' which were not my people; and her 'beloved,' who was not beloved." "It will be that in the place where it was said to them, 'You are not my people, There they will be called 'children of the living God.'" Isaiah cries concerning Israel, "If the number of the children of Israel are as the sand of the sea, it is the remnant who will be saved; for He will finish the work and cut it short in righteousness, because the LORD will make a short work upon the earth." As Isaiah has said before, "Unless the Lord of Armies had left us a seed, we would have become like Sodom, and would have been made like Gomorrah."

Jon. 3:10-4:11 God saw their works, that they turned from their evil way. God relented of the disaster which he said he would do to them, and he didn't do it. But it displeased Jonah exceedingly, and he was angry. He prayed to Yahweh, and said, "Please, Yahweh, wasn't this what I said when I was still in my own country? Therefore I hurried to flee to Tarshish, for I knew that you are a gracious God, and merciful, slow to anger, and abundant in loving kindness, and you relent of doing harm. Therefore now, Yahweh, take, I beg you, my life from me; for it is better for me to die than to live." Yahweh said, "Is it right for you to be angry?" Then Jonah went out of the city, and sat on the east side of the city, and there made himself a booth, and sat under it in the shade, until he might see what would become of the city. Yahweh God prepared a vine, and made it to come up over Jonah, that it might be a shade over his head, to deliver him from his discomfort. So Jonah was exceedingly glad because of the vine. But God prepared a worm at dawn the next day, and it chewed on the vine, so that it withered. It happened, when the sun arose, that God prepared a sultry east wind; and the sun beat on Jonah's head, so that he fainted, and requested for himself that he might die, and said, "It is better for me to die than to live." God said to Jonah, "Is it right for you to be angry about the vine?" He said, "I am right to be angry, even to death." Yahweh said, "You have been concerned for the vine, for which you have not labored, neither made it grow; which came up in a night, and perished in a night. Shouldn't I be concerned for Nineveh, that great city, in which are more than one hundred twenty thousand persons who can't discern between their right hand and their left hand; and also much livestock?"

Week 18 Day 2   4-Aug

Luke 15:25-32 "Now his elder son was in the field. As he came near to the house, he heard music and dancing. He called one of the servants to him, and asked what was going on. He said to him, 'Your brother has come, and your father has killed the fattened calf, because he has received him back safe and healthy.' But he was angry, and would not go in. Therefore his father came out, and begged him. But he answered his father, 'Behold, these many years I have served you, and I never disobeyed a commandment of yours, but you never gave me a goat, that I might celebrate with my friends. But when this, your son, came, who has devoured your living with prostitutes, you killed the fattened calf for him.' He said to him, 'Son, you are always with me, and all that is mine is yours. But it was appropriate to celebrate and be glad, for this, your brother, was dead, and is alive again. He was lost, and is found.'"

Heb. 12:4-17 You have not yet resisted to blood, striving against sin; and you have forgotten the exhortation which reasons with you as with children, "My son, don't take lightly the chastening of the Lord, nor faint when you are reproved by him; For whom the Lord loves, he chastens, and scourges every son whom he receives." It is for discipline that you endure. God deals with you as with children, for what son is there whom his father doesn't discipline? But if you are without discipline, of which all have been made partakers, then are you illegitimate, and not children. Furthermore, we had the fathers of our flesh to chasten us, and we paid them respect. Shall we not much rather be in subjection to the Father of spirits, and live? For they indeed, for a few days, punished us as seemed good to them; but he for our profit, that we may be partakers of his holiness. All chastening seems for the present to be not joyous but grievous; yet afterward it yields the peaceful fruit of righteousness to those who have been exercised thereby. Therefore lift up the hands that hang down and the feeble knees, and make straight paths for your feet, so that which is lame may not be dislocated, but rather be healed. Follow after peace with all men, and the sanctification without which no man will see the Lord, looking carefully lest there be any man who falls short of the grace of God; lest any root of bitterness springing up trouble you, and many be defiled by it; lest there be any sexually immoral person, or profane person, like Esau, who sold his birthright for one meal. For you know that even when he afterward desired to inherit the blessing, he was rejected, for he found no place for a change of mind though he sought it diligently with tears.

Ge. 4:1-7 The man knew Eve his wife. She conceived, and gave birth to Cain, and said, "I have gotten a man with Yahweh's help." Again she gave birth, to Cain's brother Abel. Abel was a keeper of sheep, but Cain was a tiller of the ground. As time passed, it happened that Cain brought an offering to Yahweh from the fruit of the ground. Abel also brought some of the firstborn of his flock and of its fat. Yahweh respected Abel and his offering, but he didn't respect Cain and his offering. Cain was very angry, and the expression on his face fell. Yahweh said to Cain, "Why are you angry? Why has the expression of your face fallen? If you do well, will it not be lifted up? If you don't do well, sin crouches at the door. Its desire is for you, but you are to rule over it."

Week 18 Day 3   5-Feb

Luke 17:7-10 "But who is there among you, having a servant plowing or keeping sheep, that will say, when he comes in from the field, 'Come immediately and sit down at the table,' and will not rather tell him, 'Prepare my supper, clothe yourself properly, and serve me, while I eat and drink. Afterward you shall eat and drink'? Does he thank that servant because he did the things that were commanded? I think not. Even so you also, when you have done all the things that are commanded you, say, 'We are unworthy servants. We have done our duty.'"

I Pet. 4:1-11 Forasmuch then as Christ suffered for us in the flesh, arm yourselves also with the same mind; for he who has suffered in the flesh has ceased from sin; that you no longer should live the rest of your time in the flesh for the lusts of men, but for the will of God. For we have spent enough of our past time doing the desire of the Gentiles, and having walked in lewdness, lusts, drunken binges, orgies, carousings, and abominable idolatries. They think it is strange that you don't run with them into the same excess of riot, blaspheming: who will give account to him who is ready to judge the living and the dead. For to this end the Good News was preached even to the dead, that they might be judged indeed as men in the flesh, but live as to God in the spirit. But the end of all things is near. Therefore be of sound mind, self-controlled, and sober in prayer. And above all things be earnest in your love among yourselves, for love covers a multitude of sins. Be hospitable to one another without grumbling. As each has received a gift, employ it in serving one another, as good managers of the grace of God in its various forms. If anyone speaks, let it be as it were the very words of God. If anyone serves, let it be as of the strength which God supplies, that in all things God may be glorified through Jesus Christ, to whom belong the glory and the dominion forever and ever. Amen.

Ps. 37:1-15 Don't fret because of evildoers, neither be envious against those who work unrighteousness. For they shall soon be cut down like the grass, and wither like the green herb. Trust in Yahweh, and do good. Dwell in the land, and enjoy safe pasture. Also delight yourself in Yahweh, and he will give you the desires of your heart. Commit your way to Yahweh. Trust also in him, and he will do this: he will make your righteousness go forth as the light, and your justice as the noon day sun. Rest in Yahweh, and wait patiently for him. Don't fret because of him who prospers in his way, because of the man who makes wicked plots happen. Cease from anger, and forsake wrath. Don't fret, it leads only to evildoing. For evildoers shall be cut off, but those who wait for Yahweh shall inherit the land. For yet a little while, and the wicked will be no more. Yes, though you look for his place, he isn't there. But the humble shall inherit the land, and shall delight themselves in the abundance of peace. The wicked plots against the just, and gnashes at him with his teeth. The Lord will laugh at him, for he sees that his day is coming. The wicked have drawn out the sword, and have bent their bow, to cast down the poor and needy, to kill those who are upright in the way. Their sword shall enter into their own heart. Their bows shall be broken.

Week 18 Day 4   4-Nov

Matt. 21:28-32 "But what do you think? A man had two sons, and he came to the first, and said, 'Son, go work today in my vineyard.' He answered, 'I will not,' but afterward he changed his mind, and went. He came to the second, and said the same thing. He answered, 'I go, sir,' but he didn't go. Which of the two did the will of his father?" They said to him, "The first." Jesus said to them, "Most certainly I tell you that the tax collectors and the prostitutes are entering into the Kingdom of God before you. For John came to you in the way of righteousness, and you didn't believe him, but the tax collectors and the prostitutes believed him. When you saw it, you didn't even repent afterward, that you might believe him."

Jas. 2:14-26 What good is it, my brothers, if a man says he has faith, but has no works? Can faith save him? And if a brother or sister is naked and in lack of daily food, and one of you tells them, "Go in peace, be warmed and filled"; and yet you didn't give them the things the body needs, what good is it? Even so faith, if it has no works, is dead in itself. Yes, a man will say, "You have faith, and I have works." Show me your faith without works, and I by my works will show you my faith. You believe that God is one. You do well. The demons also believe, and shudder. But do you want to know, vain man, that faith apart from works is dead? Wasn't Abraham our father justified by works, in that he offered up Isaac his son on the altar? You see that faith worked with his works, and by works faith was perfected; and the Scripture was fulfilled which says, "Abraham believed God, and it was accounted to him as righteousness"; and he was called the friend of God. You see then that by works, a man is justified, and not only by faith. In the same way, wasn't Rahab the prostitute also justified by works, in that she received the messengers, and sent them out another way? For as the body apart from the spirit is dead, even so faith apart from works is dead.

Ez. 18:1-32 The word of Yahweh came to me again, saying, What do you mean, that you use this proverb concerning the land of Israel, saying, The fathers have eaten sour grapes, and the children's teeth are set on edge? As I live, says the Lord Yahweh, you shall not have *occasion* any more to use this proverb in Israel. Behold, all souls are mine; as the soul of the father, so also the soul of the son is mine: the soul who sins, he shall die. But if a man is just, and does that which is lawful and right, and has not eaten on the mountains, neither has lifted up his eyes to the idols of the house of Israel, neither has defiled his neighbor's wife, neither has come near to a woman in her impurity, and has not wronged any, but has restored to the debtor his pledge, has taken nothing by robbery, has given his bread to the hungry, and has covered the naked with a garment; he who has not given forth on interest, neither has taken any increase, who has withdrawn his hand from iniquity, has executed true justice between man and man, has walked in my statutes, and has kept my ordinances, to deal truly; he is just, he shall surely live, says the Lord Yahweh. If he fathers a son who is a robber, a shedder of blood, and who does any one of these things, and who does not any of those *duties*, but even has eaten on the mountains, and defiled his neighbor's wife, has wronged the poor and needy, has taken by robbery, has not restored the pledge, and has lifted up his eyes to the idols, has committed abomination, has given forth on interest, and has taken increase; shall he then live? he shall not live: he has done all these abominations; he shall surely die; his blood shall be on him. Now, behold, if he fathers a son, who sees all his father's sins, which he has done, and fears, and does not such like; who has not eaten on the mountains, neither has lifted up his eyes to the idols of the house of Israel, has not defiled his neighbor's wife, neither has wronged any, has not taken anything to pledge, neither has taken by robbery, but has given his bread to the hungry, and has covered the naked with a garment; who has withdrawn his hand from the poor, who has not received interest nor increase, has executed my ordinances, has walked in my statutes; he shall not die for the iniquity of his father, he shall surely live. As for his father, because he cruelly oppressed, robbed his brother, and did that which is not good among his people, behold, he shall die in his iniquity. Yet you say, Why doesn't the son bear the iniquity of the father? When the son has done that which is lawful and right, and has kept all my statutes, and has done them, he shall surely live. The soul who sins, he shall die: the son shall not bear the iniquity of the father, neither shall the father bear the iniquity of the son; the righteousness of the righteous shall be on him, and the wickedness of the wicked shall be on him. But if the wicked turn from all his sins that he has committed, and keep all my statutes, and do that which is lawful and right, he shall surely live, he shall not die. None of his transgressions that he has committed shall be remembered against him: in his righteousness that he has done he shall live. Have I any pleasure in the death of the wicked? says the Lord Yahweh; and not rather that he should return from his way, and live? But when the righteous turns away from his righteousness, and commits iniquity, and does according to all the abominations that the wicked man does, shall he live? None of his righteous deeds that he has done shall be remembered: in his trespass that he has trespassed, and in his sin that he has sinned, in them shall he die. Yet you say, The way of the Lord is not equal. Hear now, house of Israel: Is my way not equal? Aren't your ways unequal? When the righteous man turns away from his righteousness, and commits iniquity, and dies therein; in his iniquity that he has done shall he die. Again, when the wicked man turns away from his wickedness that he has committed, and does that which is lawful and right, he shall save his soul alive. Because he considers, and turns away from all his transgressions that he has committed, he shall surely live, he shall not die. Yet the house of Israel says, "The way of the Lord is not fair." House of Israel, aren't my ways fair? Aren't your ways unfair? Therefore I will judge you, house of Israel, everyone according to his ways, says the Lord Yahweh. Return, and turn yourselves from all your transgressions; so iniquity shall not be your ruin. Cast away from you all your transgressions, in which you have transgressed; and make yourself a new heart and a new spirit: for why will you die, house of Israel? For I have no pleasure in the death of him who dies, says the Lord Yahweh: therefore turn yourselves, and live.

Week 18 Day 5   **14-May**

Matt. 12:46-50 While he was yet speaking to the multitudes, behold, his mother and his brothers stood outside, seeking to speak to him. One said to him, "Behold, your mother and your brothers stand outside, seeking to speak to you." But he answered him who spoke to him, "Who is my mother? Who are my brothers?" He stretched out his hand towards his disciples, and said, "Behold, my mother and my brothers! For whoever does the will of my Father who is in heaven, he is my brother, and sister, and mother."

Tit. 2:1-15 But say the things which fit sound doctrine, that older men should be temperate, sensible, sober minded, sound in faith, in love, and in patience: and that older women likewise be reverent in behavior, not slanderers nor enslaved to much wine, teachers of that which is good; that they may train the young women to love their husbands, to love their children, to be sober minded, chaste, workers at home, kind, being in subjection to their own husbands, that God's word may not be blasphemed. Likewise, exhort the younger men to be sober minded; in all things showing yourself an example of good works; in your teaching showing integrity, seriousness, incorruptibility, and soundness of speech that can't be condemned; that he who opposes you may be ashamed, having no evil thing to say about us. Exhort servants to be in subjection to their own masters, and to be well-pleasing in all things; not contradicting; not stealing, but showing all good fidelity; that they may adorn the doctrine of God, our Savior, in all things. For the grace of God has appeared, bringing salvation to all men, instructing us to the intent that, denying ungodliness and worldly lusts, we would live soberly, righteously, and godly in this present world; looking for the blessed hope and appearing of the glory of our great God and Savior, Jesus Christ; who gave himself for us, that he might redeem us from all iniquity, and purify for himself a people for his own possession, zealous for good works. Say these things and exhort and reprove with all authority. Let no man despise you.

Ge. 45:1-15 Then Joseph couldn't control himself before all those who stood before him, and he cried, "Cause everyone to go out from me!" No one else stood with him, while Joseph made himself known to his brothers. He wept aloud. The Egyptians heard, and the house of Pharaoh heard. Joseph said to his brothers, "I am Joseph! Does my father still live?" His brothers couldn't answer him; for they were terrified at his presence. Joseph said to his brothers, "Come near to me, please." They came near. "He said, I am Joseph, your brother, whom you sold into Egypt. Now don't be grieved, nor angry with yourselves, that you sold me here, for God sent me before you to preserve life. For these two years the famine has been in the land, and there are yet five years, in which there will be neither plowing nor harvest. God sent me before you to preserve for you a remnant in the earth, and to save you alive by a great deliverance. So now it wasn't you who sent me here, but God, and he has made me a father to Pharaoh, lord of all his house, and ruler over all the land of Egypt. Hurry, and go up to my father, and tell him, 'This is what your son Joseph says, "God has made me lord of all Egypt. Come down to me. Don't wait. You shall dwell in the land of Goshen, and you will be near to me, you, your children, your children's children, your flocks, your herds, and all that you have. There I will nourish you; for there are yet five years of famine; lest you come to poverty, you, and your household, and all that you have."' Behold, your eyes see, and the eyes of my brother Benjamin, that it is my mouth that speaks to you. You shall tell my father of all my glory in Egypt, and of all that you have seen. You shall hurry and bring my father down here." He fell on his brother Benjamin's neck, and wept, and Benjamin wept on his neck. He kissed all his brothers, and wept on them. After that his brothers talked with him.

Luke 9:23-26 He said to all, "If anyone desires to come after me, let him deny himself, take up his cross, and follow me. For whoever desires to save his life will lose it, but whoever will lose his life for my sake, the same will save it. For what does it profit a man if he gains the whole world, and loses or forfeits his own self? For whoever will be ashamed of me and of my words, of him will the Son of Man be ashamed, when he comes in his glory, and the glory of the Father, and of the holy angels."

II Tim. 1:3-14 I thank God, whom I serve as my forefathers did, with a pure conscience. How unceasing is my memory of you in my petitions, night and day longing to see you, remembering your tears, that I may be filled with joy; having been reminded of the sincere faith that is in you; which lived first in your grandmother Lois, and your mother Eunice, and, I am persuaded, in you also. For this cause, I remind you that you should stir up the gift of God which is in you through the laying on of my hands. For God didn't give us a spirit of fear, but of power, love, and self-control. Therefore don't be ashamed of the testimony of our Lord, nor of me his prisoner; but endure hardship for the Good News according to the power of God, who saved us and called us with a holy calling, not according to our works, but according to his own purpose and grace, which was given to us in Christ Jesus before times eternal, but has now been revealed by the appearing of our Savior, Christ Jesus, who abolished death, and brought life and immortality to light through the Good News. For this, I was appointed as a preacher, an apostle, and a teacher of the Gentiles. For this cause I also suffer these things. Yet I am not ashamed, for I know him whom I have believed, and I am persuaded that he is able to guard that which I have committed to him against that day. Hold the pattern of sound words which you have heard from me, in faith and love which is in Christ Jesus. That good thing which was committed to you, guard through the Holy Spirit who dwells in us.

De. 4:1-8 Now, Israel, listen to the statutes and to the ordinances, which I teach you, to do them; that you may live, and go in and possess the land which Yahweh, the God of your fathers, gives you. You shall not add to the word which I command you, neither shall you diminish from it, that you may keep the commandments of Yahweh your God which I command you. Your eyes have seen what Yahweh did because of Baal Peor; for all the men who followed Baal Peor, Yahweh your God has destroyed them from the midst of you. But you who were faithful to Yahweh your God are all alive this day. Behold, I have taught you statutes and ordinances, even as Yahweh my God commanded me, that you should do so in the midst of the land where you go in to possess it. Keep therefore and do them; for this is your wisdom and your understanding in the sight of the peoples, who shall hear all these statutes, and say, "Surely this great nation is a wise and understanding people." For what great nation is there, that has a god so near to them, as Yahweh our God is whenever we call on him? What great nation is there, that has statutes and ordinances so righteous as all this law, which I set before you this day?

Gal. 5:22-6:10 But the fruit of the Spirit is love, joy, peace, patience, kindness, goodness, faith, gentleness, and self-control. Against such things there is no law. Those who belong to Christ have crucified the flesh with its passions and lusts. If we live by the Spirit, let's also walk by the Spirit. Let's not become conceited, provoking one another, and envying one another. Brothers, even if a man is caught in some fault, you who are spiritual must restore such a one in a spirit of gentleness; looking to yourself so that you also aren't tempted. Bear one another's burdens, and so fulfill the law of Christ. For if a man thinks himself to be something when he is nothing, he deceives himself. But let each man test his own work, and then he will take pride in himself and not in his neighbor. For each man will bear his own burden. But let him who is taught in the word share all good things with him who teaches. Don't be deceived. God is not mocked, for whatever a man sows, that he will also reap. For he who sows to his own flesh will from the flesh reap corruption. But he who sows to the Spirit will from the Spirit reap eternal life. Let us not be weary in doing good, for we will reap in due season, if we don't give up. So then, as we have opportunity, let's do what is good toward all men, and especially toward those who are of the household of the faith.

Joel 2:12-17 "Yet even now," says Yahweh, "turn to me with all your heart, and with fasting, and with weeping, and with mourning." Tear your heart, and not your garments, and turn to Yahweh, your God; for he is gracious and merciful, slow to anger, and abundant in loving kindness, and relents from sending calamity. Who knows? He may turn and relent, and leave a blessing behind him, even a meal offering and a drink offering to Yahweh, your God. Blow the trumpet in Zion! Sanctify a fast. Call a solemn assembly. Gather the people. Sanctify the assembly. Assemble the elders. Gather the children, and those who nurse from breasts. Let the bridegroom go forth from his room, and the bride out of her room. Let the priests, the ministers of Yahweh, weep between the porch and the altar, and let them say, "Spare your people, Yahweh, and don't give your heritage to reproach, that the nations should rule over them. Why should they say among the peoples, 'Where is their God?'"

Week 19 Day 1   **26-May**

Luke 17:5-6 The apostles said to the Lord, "Increase our faith." The Lord said, "If you had faith like a grain of mustard seed, you would tell this sycamore tree, 'Be uprooted, and be planted in the sea,' and it would obey you."

Matt. 17:14-21 When they came to the multitude, a man came to him, kneeling down to him, saying, "Lord, have mercy on my son, for he is epileptic, and suffers grievously; for he often falls into the fire, and often into the water. So I brought him to your disciples, and they could not cure him." Jesus answered, "Faithless and perverse generation! How long will I be with you? How long will I bear with you? Bring him here to me." Jesus rebuked him, the demon went out of him, and the boy was cured from that hour. Then the disciples came to Jesus privately, and said, "Why weren't we able to cast it out?" He said to them, "Because of your unbelief. For most certainly I tell you, if you have faith as a grain of mustard seed, you will tell this mountain, 'Move from here to there,' and it will move; and nothing will be impossible for you. But this kind doesn't go out except by prayer and fasting."

1 Cor. 13:1-13 If I speak with the languages of men and of angels, but don't have love, I have become sounding brass, or a clanging cymbal. If I have the gift of prophecy, and know all mysteries and all knowledge; and if I have all faith, so as to remove mountains, but don't have love, I am nothing. If I dole out all my goods to feed the poor, and if I give my body to be burned, but don't have love, it profits me nothing. Love is patient and is kind; love doesn't envy. Love doesn't brag, is not proud, doesn't behave itself inappropriately, doesn't seek its own way, is not provoked, takes no account of evil; doesn't rejoice in unrighteousness, but rejoices with the truth; bears all things, believes all things, hopes all things, endures all things. Love never fails. But where there are prophecies, they will be done away with. Where there are various languages, they will cease. Where there is knowledge, it will be done away with. For we know in part, and we prophesy in part; but when that which is complete has come, then that which is partial will be done away with. When I was a child, I spoke as a child, I felt as a child, I thought as a child. Now that I have become a man, I have put away childish things. For now we see in a mirror, dimly, but then face to face. Now I know in part, but then I will know fully, even as I was also fully known. But now faith, hope, and love remain—these three. The greatest of these is love.

Hab. 1:1-4 The oracle which Habakkuk the prophet saw. Yahweh, how long will I cry, and you will not hear? I cry out to you "Violence!" and will you not save? Why do you show me iniquity, and look at perversity? For destruction and violence are before me. There is strife, and contention rises up. Therefore the law is paralyzed, and justice never goes forth; for the wicked surround the righteous; therefore justice goes forth perverted.

Hab. 2:1-4 I will stand at my watch, and set myself on the ramparts, and will look out to see what he will say to me, and what I will answer concerning my complaint. Yahweh answered me, "Write the vision, and make it plain on tablets, that he who runs may read it. For the vision is yet for the appointed time, and it hurries toward the end, and won't prove false. Though it takes time, wait for it; because it will surely come. It won't delay. Behold, his soul is puffed up. It is not upright in him, but the righteous will live by his faith."

Week 19 Day 2   **30-Oct**

Luke 7:1-10 After he had finished speaking in the hearing of the people, he entered into Capernaum. A certain centurion's servant, who was dear to him, was sick and at the point of death. When he heard about Jesus, he sent to him elders of the Jews, asking him to come and save his servant. When they came to Jesus, they begged him earnestly, saying, "He is worthy for you to do this for him, for he loves our nation, and he built our synagogue for us." Jesus went with them. When he was now not far from the house, the centurion sent friends to him, saying to him, "Lord, don't trouble yourself, for I am not worthy for you to come under my roof. Therefore I didn't even think myself worthy to come to you; but say the word, and my servant will be healed. For I also am a man placed under authority, having under myself soldiers. I tell this one, 'Go!' and he goes; and to another, 'Come!' and he comes; and to my servant, 'Do this,' and he does it." When Jesus heard these things, he marveled at him, and turned and said to the multitude who followed him, "I tell you, I have not found such great faith, no, not in Israel." Those who were sent, returning to the house, found that the servant who had been sick was well.

Acts 3:1-10 Peter and John were going up into the temple at the hour of prayer, the ninth hour. A certain man who was lame from his mother's womb was being carried, whom they laid daily at the door of the temple which is called Beautiful, to ask gifts for the needy of those who entered into the temple. Seeing Peter and John about to go into the temple, he asked to receive gifts for the needy. Peter, fastening his eyes on him, with John, said, "Look at us." He listened to them, expecting to receive something from them. But Peter said, "Silver and gold have I none, but what I have, that I give you. In the name of Jesus Christ of Nazareth, get up and walk!" He took him by the right hand, and raised him up. Immediately his feet and his ankle bones received strength. Leaping up, he stood, and began to walk. He entered with them into the temple, walking, leaping, and praising God. All the people saw him walking and praising God. They recognized him, that it was he who used to sit begging for gifts for the needy at the Beautiful Gate of the temple. They were filled with wonder and amazement at what had happened to him.

2 Ki. 5:1-19 Now Naaman, captain of the army of the king of Syria, was a great man with his master, and honorable, because by him Yahweh had given victory to Syria: he was also a mighty man of valor, but he was a leper. The Syrians had gone out in bands, and had brought away captive out of the land of Israel a little maiden; and she waited on Naaman's wife. She said to her mistress, "I wish that my lord were with the prophet who is in Samaria! Then he would heal him of his leprosy." Someone went in, and told his lord, saying, "The maiden who is from the land of Israel said this." The king of Syria said, "Go now, and I will send a letter to the king of Israel." He departed, and took with him ten talents of silver, and six thousand pieces of gold, and ten changes of clothing. He brought the letter to the king of Israel, saying, "Now when this letter has come to you, behold, I have sent Naaman my servant to you, that you may heal him of his leprosy." It happened, when the king of Israel had read the letter, that he tore his clothes, and said, "Am I God, to kill and to make alive, that this man sends to me to heal a man of his leprosy? But please consider and see how he seeks a quarrel against me." It was so, when Elisha the man of God heard that the king of Israel had torn his clothes, that he sent to the king, saying, "Why have you torn your clothes? Let him come now to me, and he shall know that there is a prophet in Israel." So Naaman came with his horses and with his chariots, and stood at the door of the house of Elisha. Elisha sent a messenger to him, saying, "Go and wash in the Jordan seven times, and your flesh shall come again to you, and you shall be clean." But Naaman was angry, and went away, and said, "Behold, I thought, 'He will surely come out to me, and stand, and call on the name of Yahweh his God, and wave his hand over the place, and heal the leper.' Aren't Abanah and Pharpar, the rivers of Damascus, better than all the waters of Israel? Couldn't I wash in them, and be clean?" So he turned and went away in a rage. His servants came near, and spoke to him, and said, "My father, if the prophet had asked you do some great thing, wouldn't you have done it? How much rather then, when he says to you, 'Wash, and be clean?'" Then went he down, and dipped himself seven times in the Jordan, according to the saying of the man of God; and his flesh was restored like the flesh of a little child, and he was clean. He returned to the man of God, he and all his company, and came, and stood before him; and he said, "See now, I know that there is no God in all the earth, but in Israel. Now therefore, please take a gift from your servant." But he said, "As Yahweh lives, before whom I stand, I will receive none." He urged him to take it; but he refused. Naaman said, "If not, then, please let two mules' burden of earth be given to your servant; for your servant will from now on offer neither burnt offering nor sacrifice to other gods, but to Yahweh. In this thing may Yahweh pardon your servant: when my master goes into the house of Rimmon to worship there, and he leans on my hand, and I bow myself in the house of Rimmon. When I bow myself in the house of Rimmon, may Yahweh pardon your servant in this thing." He said to him, "Go in peace." So he departed from him a little way.

Week 19 Day 3   **15-Aug**

Mark 11:12-14 The next day, when they had come out from Bethany, he was hungry. Seeing a fig tree afar off having leaves, he came to see if perhaps he might find anything on it. When he came to it, he found nothing but leaves, for it was not the season for figs. Jesus told it, "May no one ever eat fruit from you again!" and his disciples heard it.

Mark 11:20-26 As they passed by in the morning, they saw the fig tree withered away from the roots. Peter, remembering, said to him, "Rabbi, look! The fig tree which you cursed has withered away." Jesus answered them, "Have faith in God. For most certainly I tell you, whoever may tell this mountain, 'Be taken up and cast into the sea,' and doesn't doubt in his heart, but believes that what he says is happening; he shall have whatever he says. Therefore I tell you, all things whatever you pray and ask for, believe that you have received them, and you shall have them. Whenever you stand praying, forgive, if you have anything against anyone; so that your Father, who is in heaven, may also forgive you your transgressions. But if you do not forgive, neither will your Father in heaven forgive your transgressions."

Ja. 5:13-20 Is any among you suffering? Let him pray. Is any cheerful? Let him sing praises. Is any among you sick? Let him call for the elders of the assembly, and let them pray over him, anointing him with oil in the name of the Lord, and the prayer of faith will heal him who is sick, and the Lord will raise him up. If he has committed sins, he will be forgiven. Confess your offenses to one another, and pray for one another, that you may be healed. The insistent prayer of a righteous person is powerfully effective. Elijah was a man with a nature like ours, and he prayed earnestly that it might not rain, and it didn't rain on the earth for three years and six months. He prayed again, and the sky gave rain, and the earth brought forth its fruit. Brothers, if any among you wanders from the truth, and someone turns him back, let him know that he who turns a sinner from the error of his way will save a soul from death, and will cover a multitude of sins.

Mic. 7:1-4 Misery is mine! Indeed, I am like one who gathers the summer fruits, as gleanings of the vineyard: There is no cluster of grapes to eat. My soul desires to eat the early fig. The godly man has perished out of the earth, and there is no one upright among men. They all lie in wait for blood; every man hunts his brother with a net. Their hands are on that which is evil to do it diligently. The ruler and judge ask for a bribe; and the powerful man dictates the evil desire of his soul. Thus they conspire together. The best of them is like a brier. The most upright is worse than a thorn hedge. The day of your watchmen, even your visitation, has come; now is the time of their confusion.

Hos. 9:15-16 All their wickedness is in Gilgal; for there I hated them. Because of the wickedness of their deeds I will drive them out of my house! I will love them no more. All their princes are rebels. Ephraim is struck. Their root has dried up. They will bear no fruit. Even though they bring forth, yet I will kill the beloved ones of their womb.

Week 19 Day 4   **17-Oct**

John 14:12-14 "Most certainly I tell you, he who believes in me, the works that I do, he will do also; and he will do greater works than these, because I am going to my Father. Whatever you will ask in my name, that will I do, that the Father may be glorified in the Son. If you will ask anything in my name, I will do it."

Eph. 3:14-21 For this cause, I bow my knees to the Father of our Lord Jesus Christ, from whom every family in heaven and on earth is named, that he would grant you, according to the riches of his glory, that you may be strengthened with power through his Spirit in the inward man; that Christ may dwell in your hearts through faith; to the end that you, being rooted and grounded in love, may be strengthened to comprehend with all the saints what is the breadth and length and height and depth, and to know Christ's love which surpasses knowledge, that you may be filled with all the fullness of God. Now to him who is able to do exceedingly abundantly above all that we ask or think, according to the power that works in us, to him be the glory in the assembly and in Christ Jesus to all generations forever and ever. Amen.

1 Ki. 3:1-15 Solomon made affinity with Pharaoh king of Egypt, and took Pharaoh's daughter, and brought her into the city of David, until he had made an end of building his own house, and the house of Yahweh, and the wall of Jerusalem all around. Only the people sacrificed in the high places, because there was no house built for the name of Yahweh until those days. Solomon loved Yahweh, walking in the statutes of David his father: only he sacrificed and burnt incense in the high places. The king went to Gibeon to sacrifice there; for that was the great high place. Solomon offered a thousand burnt offerings on that altar. In Gibeon Yahweh appeared to Solomon in a dream by night; and God said, "Ask what I shall give you." Solomon said, "You have shown to your servant David my father great loving kindness, according as he walked before you in truth, and in righteousness, and in uprightness of heart with you. You have kept for him this great loving kindness, that you have given him a son to sit on his throne, as it is this day. Now, Yahweh my God, you have made your servant king instead of David my father. I am but a little child. I don't know how to go out or come in. Your servant is in the midst of your people which you have chosen, a great people, that can't be numbered nor counted for multitude. Give your servant therefore an understanding heart to judge your people, that I may discern between good and evil; for who is able to judge this your great people?" The speech pleased the Lord, that Solomon had asked this thing. God said to him, "Because you have asked this thing, and have not asked for yourself long life, neither have asked riches for yourself, nor have asked the life of your enemies, but have asked for yourself understanding to discern justice; behold, I have done according to your word. Behold, I have given you a wise and an understanding heart; so that there has been none like you before you, neither after you shall any arise like you. I have also given you that which you have not asked, both riches and honor, so that there shall not be any among the kings like you, all your days. If you will walk in my ways, to keep my statutes and my commandments, as your father David walked, then I will lengthen your days." Solomon awoke; and behold, it was a dream. Then he came to Jerusalem, and stood before the ark of the covenant of Yahweh, and offered up burnt offerings, offered peace offerings, and made a feast to all his servants. He returned to Jerusalem, stood before the ark of the Lord's covenant and sacrificed burnt offerings and fellowship offerings. Then he gave a feast for all his court.

Week 19 Day 5   14-Nov

John 15:5-8 "I am the vine. You are the branches. He who remains in me, and I in him, the same bears much fruit, for apart from me you can do nothing. If a man doesn't remain in me, he is thrown out as a branch, and is withered; and they gather them, throw them into the fire, and they are burned. If you remain in me, and my words remain in you, you will ask whatever you desire, and it will be done for you. In this is my Father glorified, that you bear much fruit; and so you will be my disciples."

Heb. 6:7-12 For the land which has drunk the rain that comes often on it, and brings forth a crop suitable for them for whose sake it is also tilled, receives blessing from God; but if it bears thorns and thistles, it is rejected and near being cursed, whose end is to be burned. But, beloved, we are persuaded of better things for you, and things that accompany salvation, even though we speak like this. For God is not unrighteous, so as to forget your work and the labor of love which you showed toward his name, in that you served the saints, and still do serve them. We desire that each one of you may show the same diligence to the fullness of hope even to the end, that you won't be sluggish, but imitators of those who through faith and patience inherited the promises.

Is. 41:17-20 The poor and needy seek water, and there is none. Their tongue fails for thirst. I, Yahweh, will answer them. I, the God of Israel, will not forsake them. I will open rivers on the bare heights, and springs in the midst of the valleys. I will make the wilderness a pool of water, and the dry land springs of water. I will put cedar, acacia, myrtle, and oil trees in the wilderness. I will set fir trees, pine, and box trees together in the desert; that they may see, know, consider, and understand together, that the hand of Yahweh has done this, and the Holy One of Israel has created it.

Week 19 Day 6   29-May

John 16:16-33 "A little while, and you will not see me. Again a little while, and you will see me." Some of his disciples therefore said to one another, "What is this that he says to us, 'A little while, and you won't see me, and again a little while, and you will see me;' and, 'Because I go to the Father?'" They said therefore, "What is this that he says, 'A little while?' We don't know what he is saying." Therefore Jesus perceived that they wanted to ask him, and he said to them, "Do you inquire among yourselves concerning this, that I said, 'A little while, and you won't see me, and again a little while, and you will see me?' Most certainly I tell you, that you will weep and lament, but the world will rejoice. You will be sorrowful, but your sorrow will be turned into joy. A woman, when she gives birth, has sorrow, because her time has come. But when she has delivered the child, she doesn't remember the anguish any more, for the joy that a human being is born into the world. Therefore you now have sorrow, but I will see you again, and your heart will rejoice, and no one will take your joy away from you. In that day you will ask me no questions. Most certainly I tell you, whatever you may ask of the Father in my name, he will give it to you. Until now, you have asked nothing in my name. Ask, and you will receive, that your joy may be made full. I have spoken these things to you in figures of speech. But the time is coming when I will no more speak to you in figures of speech, but will tell you plainly about the Father. In that day you will ask in my name; and I don't say to you, that I will pray to the Father for you, for the Father himself loves you, because you have loved me, and have believed that I came forth from God. I came out from the Father, and have come into the world. Again, I leave the world, and go to the Father." His disciples said to him, "Behold, now you speak plainly, and speak no figures of speech. Now we know that you know all things, and don't need for anyone to question you. By this we believe that you came forth from God." Jesus answered them, "Do you now believe? Behold, the time is coming, yes, and has now come, that you will be scattered, everyone to his own place, and you will leave me alone. Yet I am not alone, because the Father is with me. I have told you these things, that in me you may have peace. In the world you have oppression; but cheer up! I have overcome the world."

Rom. 5:1-11 Being therefore justified by faith, we have peace with God through our Lord Jesus Christ; through whom we also have our access by faith into this grace in which we stand. We rejoice in hope of the glory of God. Not only this, but we also rejoice in our sufferings, knowing that suffering works perseverance; and perseverance, proven character; and proven character, hope: and hope doesn't disappoint us, because God's love has been poured out into our hearts through the Holy Spirit who was given to us. For while we were yet weak, at the right time Christ died for the ungodly. For one will hardly die for a righteous man. Yet perhaps for a righteous person someone would even dare to die. But God commends his own love toward us, in that while we were yet sinners, Christ died for us. Much more then, being now justified by his blood, we will be saved from God's wrath through him. For if, while we were enemies, we were reconciled to God through the death of his Son, much more, being reconciled, we will be saved by his life. Not only so, but we also rejoice in God through our Lord Jesus Christ, through whom we have now received the reconciliation.

2 Chr. 20:27-30 Then they returned, every man of Judah and Jerusalem, and Jehoshaphat in their forefront, to go again to Jerusalem with joy; for Yahweh had made them to rejoice over their enemies. They came to Jerusalem with stringed instruments and harps and trumpets to the house of Yahweh. The fear of God was on all the kingdoms of the countries, when they heard that Yahweh fought against the enemies of Israel. So the realm of Jehoshaphat was quiet; for his God gave him rest all around.

Week 19 Day 7   9-Aug

Heb. 10:19-39 Having therefore, brothers, boldness to enter into the holy place by the blood of Jesus, by the way which he dedicated for us, a new and living way, through the veil, that is to say, his flesh; and having a great priest over God's house, let's draw near with a true heart in fullness of faith, having our hearts sprinkled from an evil conscience, and having our body washed with pure water, let us hold fast the confession of our hope without wavering; for he who promised is faithful. Let us consider how to provoke one another to love and good works, not forsaking our own assembling together, as the custom of some is, but exhorting one another; and so much the more, as you see the Day approaching. For if we sin willfully after we have received the knowledge of the truth, there remains no more a sacrifice for sins, but a certain fearful expectation of judgment, and a fierceness of fire which will devour the adversaries. A man who disregards Moses' law dies without compassion on the word of two or three witnesses. How much worse punishment, do you think, will he be judged worthy of, who has trodden under foot the Son of God, and has counted the blood of the covenant with which he was sanctified an unholy thing, and has insulted the Spirit of grace? For we know him who said, "Vengeance belongs to me," says the Lord, "I will repay." Again, "The Lord will judge his people." It is a fearful thing to fall into the hands of the living God. But remember the former days, in which, after you were enlightened, you endured a great struggle with sufferings; partly, being exposed to both reproaches and oppressions; and partly, becoming partakers with those who were treated so. For you both had compassion on me in my chains, and joyfully accepted the plundering of your possessions, knowing that you have for yourselves a better possession and an enduring one in the heavens. Therefore don't throw away your boldness, which has a great reward. For you need endurance so that, having done the will of God, you may receive the promise. "In a very little while, he who comes will come, and will not wait. But the righteous will live by faith. If he shrinks back, my soul has no pleasure in him." but we are not of those who shrink back to destruction, but of those who have faith to the saving of the soul.

Hab. 2:1-20 I will stand at my watch, and set myself on the ramparts, and will look out to see what he will say to me, and what I will answer concerning my complaint. Yahweh answered me, "Write the vision, and make it plain on tablets, that he who runs may read it. For the vision is yet for the appointed time, and it hurries toward the end, and won't prove false. Though it takes time, wait for it; because it will surely come. It won't delay. Behold, his soul is puffed up. It is not upright in him, but the righteous will live by his faith. Yes, moreover, wine is treacherous. A haughty man who doesn't stay at home, who enlarges his desire as Sheol, and he is like death, and can't be satisfied, but gathers to himself all nations, and heaps to himself all peoples. Won't all these take up a parable against him, and a taunting proverb against him, and say, 'Woe to him who increases that which is not his, and who enriches himself by extortion! How long?' Won't your debtors rise up suddenly, and wake up those who make you tremble, and you will be their victim? Because you have plundered many nations, all the remnant of the peoples will plunder you, because of men's blood, and for the violence done to the land, to the city and to all who dwell in it. Woe to him who gets an evil gain for his house, that he may set his nest on high, that he may be delivered from the hand of evil! You have devised shame to your house, by cutting off many peoples, and have sinned against your soul. For the stone will cry out of the wall, and the beam out of the woodwork will answer it. Woe to him who builds a town with blood, and establishes a city by iniquity! Behold, isn't it of Yahweh of Armies that the peoples labor for the fire, and the nations weary themselves for vanity? For the earth will be filled with the knowledge of the glory of Yahweh, as the waters cover the sea. Woe to him who gives his neighbor drink, pouring your inflaming wine until they are drunk, so that you may gaze at their naked bodies! You are filled with shame, and not glory. You will also drink, and be exposed! The cup of Yahweh's right hand will come around to you, and disgrace will cover your glory. For the violence done to Lebanon will overwhelm you, and the destruction of the animals, which made them afraid; because of men's blood, and for the violence done to the land, to every city and to those who dwell in them. What value does the engraved image have, that its maker has engraved it; the molten image, even the teacher of lies, that he who fashions its form trusts in it, to make mute idols? Woe to him who says to the wood, 'Awake!' or to the mute stone, 'Arise!' Shall this teach? Behold, it is overlaid with gold and silver, and there is no breath at all in its midst. But Yahweh is in his holy temple. Let all the earth be silent before him!"

Week 20 Day 1   **11-Sep**   (READ 'WEEK 20' ON PAGE 99)

John 13:1-17 Now before the feast of the Passover, Jesus, knowing that his time had come that he would depart from this world to the Father, having loved his own who were in the world, he loved them to the end. During supper, the devil having already put into the heart of Judas Iscariot, Simon's son, to betray him, Jesus, knowing that the Father had given all things into his hands, and that he came forth from God, and was going to God, arose from supper, and laid aside his outer garments. He took a towel, and wrapped a towel around his waist. Then he poured water into the basin, and began to wash the disciples' feet, and to wipe them with the towel that was wrapped around him. Then he came to Simon Peter. He said to him, "Lord, do you wash my feet?" Jesus answered him, "You don't know what I am doing now, but you will understand later." Peter said to him, "You will never wash my feet!" Jesus answered him, "If I don't wash you, you have no part with me." Simon Peter said to him, "Lord, not my feet only, but also my hands and my head!" Jesus said to him, "Someone who has bathed only needs to have his feet washed, but is completely clean. You are clean, but not all of you." For he knew him who would betray him, therefore he said, "You are not all clean." So when he had washed their feet, put his outer garment back on, and sat down again, he said to them, "Do you know what I have done to you? You call me, 'Teacher' and 'Lord.' You say so correctly, for so I am. If I then, the Lord and the Teacher, have washed your feet, you also ought to wash one another's feet. For I have given you an example, that you also should do as I have done to you. Most certainly I tell you, a servant is not greater than his lord, neither one who is sent greater than he who sent him. If you know these things, blessed are you if you do them."

Php. 2:1-11 If there is therefore any exhortation in Christ, if any consolation of love, if any fellowship of the Spirit, if any tender mercies and compassion, make my joy full, by being like-minded, having the same love, being of one accord, of one mind; doing nothing through rivalry or through conceit, but in humility, each counting others better than himself; each of you not just looking to his own things, but each of you also to the things of others. Have this in your mind, which was also in Christ Jesus, who, existing in the form of God, didn't consider equality with God a thing to be grasped, but emptied himself, taking the form of a servant, being made in the likeness of men. And being found in human form, he humbled himself, becoming obedient to death, yes, the death of the cross. Therefore God also highly exalted him, and gave to him the name which is above every name; that at the name of Jesus every knee should bow, of those in heaven, those on earth, and those under the earth, and that every tongue should confess that Jesus Christ is Lord, to the glory of God the Father.

Is. 42:1-7 "Behold, my servant, whom I uphold; my chosen, in whom my soul delights—I have put my Spirit on him. He will bring justice to the nations. He will not shout, nor raise his voice, nor cause it to be heard in the street. He won't break a bruised reed. He won't quench a dimly burning wick. He will faithfully bring justice. He will not fail nor be discouraged, until he has set justice in the earth, and the islands will wait for his law." Thus says God Yahweh, he who created the heavens and stretched them out, he who spread out the earth and that which comes out of it, he who gives breath to its people and spirit to those who walk in it. "I, Yahweh, have called you in righteousness, and will hold your hand, and will keep you, and make you a covenant for the people, as a light for the nations; to open the blind eyes, to bring the prisoners out of the dungeon, and those who sit in darkness out of the prison."

Week 20 Day 2   16-Jun

Matt. 22:34-40 But the Pharisees, when they heard that he had silenced the Sadducees, gathered themselves together. One of them, a lawyer, asked him a question, testing him. "Teacher, which is the greatest commandment in the law?" Jesus said to him, "'You shall love the Lord your God with all your heart, with all your soul, and with all your mind.' This is the first and great commandment. A second likewise is this, 'You shall love your neighbor as yourself.' The whole law and the prophets depend on these two commandments."

Matt. 7:12 "Therefore whatever you desire for men to do to you, you shall also do to them; for this is the law and the prophets."

I Jo. 4:7-15 Beloved, let us love one another, for love is of God; and everyone who loves is born of God, and knows God. He who doesn't love doesn't know God, for God is love. By this God's love was revealed in us, that God has sent his one and only Son into the world that we might live through him. In this is love, not that we loved God, but that he loved us, and sent his Son as the atoning sacrifice for our sins. Beloved, if God loved us in this way, we also ought to love one another. No one has seen God at any time. If we love one another, God remains in us, and his love has been perfected in us. By this we know that we remain in him and he in us, because he has given us of his Spirit. We have seen and testify that the Father has sent the Son as the Savior of the world. Whoever confesses that Jesus is the Son of God, God remains in him, and he in God.

De. 6:1-9 Now this is the commandment, the statutes, and the ordinances, which Yahweh your God commanded to teach you, that you might do them in the land where you go over to possess it; that you might fear Yahweh your God, to keep all his statutes and his commandments, which I command you, you, and your son, and your son's son, all the days of your life; and that your days may be prolonged. Hear therefore, Israel, and observe to do it; that it may be well with you, and that you may increase mightily, as Yahweh, the God of your fathers, has promised to you, in a land flowing with milk and honey. Hear, Israel: Yahweh is our God; Yahweh is one: and you shall love Yahweh your God with all your heart, and with all your soul, and with all your might. These words, which I command you this day, shall be on your heart; and you shall teach them diligently to your children, and shall talk of them when you sit in your house, and when you walk by the way, and when you lie down, and when you rise up. You shall bind them for a sign on your hand, and they shall be for symbols between your eyes.

Lev 19:18 You shall not take vengeance, nor bear any grudge against the children of your people; but you shall love your neighbor as yourself. I am Yahweh.

Week 20 Day 3   11-May

John 13:34-35 "A new commandment I give to you, that you love one another, just like I have loved you; that you also love one another. By this everyone will know that you are my disciples, if you have love for one another."

I Jo. 4:16-21 We know and have believed the love which God has for us. God is love, and he who remains in love remains in God, and God remains in him. In this love has been made perfect among us, that we may have boldness in the day of judgment, because as he is, even so are we in this world. There is no fear in love; but perfect love casts out fear, because fear has punishment. He who fears is not made perfect in love. We love him, because he first loved us. If a man says, "I love God," and hates his brother, he is a liar; for he who doesn't love his brother whom he has seen, how can he love God whom he has not seen? This commandment we have from him, that he who loves God should also love his brother.

Lev. 19:1-18 Yahweh spoke to Moses, saying, "Speak to all the congregation of the children of Israel, and tell them, 'You shall be holy; for I Yahweh your God am holy. Each one of you shall respect his mother and his father. You shall keep my Sabbaths. I am Yahweh your God. Don't turn to idols, nor make molten gods for yourselves. I am Yahweh your God. When you offer a sacrifice of peace offerings to Yahweh, you shall offer it so that you may be accepted. It shall be eaten the same day you offer it, and on the next day: and if anything remains until the third day, it shall be burned with fire. If it is eaten at all on the third day, it is an abomination. It will not be accepted; but everyone who eats it shall bear his iniquity, because he has profaned the holy thing of Yahweh, and that soul shall be cut off from his people. When you reap the harvest of your land, you shall not wholly reap the corners of your field, neither shall you gather the gleanings of your harvest. You shall not glean your vineyard, neither shall you gather the fallen grapes of your vineyard; you shall leave them for the poor and for the foreigner. I am Yahweh your God. You shall not steal. You shall not lie. You shall not deceive one another. You shall not swear by my name falsely, and profane the name of your God. I am Yahweh. You shall not oppress your neighbor, nor rob him. The wages of a hired servant shall not remain with you all night until the morning. You shall not curse the deaf, nor put a stumbling block before the blind; but you shall fear your God. I am Yahweh. You shall do no injustice in judgment: you shall not be partial to the poor, nor show favoritism to the great; but you shall judge your neighbor in righteousness. You shall not go up and down as a slanderer among your people. You shall not endanger the life of your neighbor. I am Yahweh. You shall not hate your brother in your heart. You shall surely rebuke your neighbor, and not bear sin because of him. You shall not take vengeance, nor bear any grudge against the children of your people; but you shall love your neighbor as yourself. I am Yahweh.'"

Week 20 Day 4   31-Aug

John 15:9-17 "Even as the Father has loved me, I also have loved you. Remain in my love. If you keep my commandments, you will remain in my love; even as I have kept my Father's commandments, and remain in his love. I have spoken these things to you, that my joy may remain in you, and that your joy may be made full. This is my commandment, that you love one another, even as I have loved you. Greater love has no one than this, that someone lay down his life for his friends. You are my friends, if you do whatever I command you. No longer do I call you servants, for the servant doesn't know what his lord does. But I have called you friends, for everything that I heard from my Father, I have made known to you. You didn't choose me, but I chose you, and appointed you, that you should go and bear fruit, and that your fruit should remain; that whatever you will ask of the Father in my name, he may give it to you. I command these things to you, that you may love one another."

I Jo. 5:1-5 Whoever believes that Jesus is the Christ is born of God. Whoever loves the Father also loves the child who is born of him. By this we know that we love the children of God, when we love God and keep his commandments. For this is the love of God, that we keep his commandments. His commandments are not grievous. For whatever is born of God overcomes the world. This is the victory that has overcome the world: your faith. Who is he who overcomes the world, but he who believes that Jesus is the Son of God?

Es. 4:9-16 Hathach came and told Esther the words of Mordecai. Then Esther spoke to Hathach, and gave him a message to Mordecai. "All the king's servants, and the people of the king's provinces, know, that whoever, whether man or woman, comes to the king into the inner court without being called, there is one law for him, that he be put to death, except those to whom the king might hold out the golden scepter, that he may live. I have not been called to come in to the king these thirty days." They told to Mordecai Esther's words. Then Mordecai asked them return answer to Esther, "Don't think to yourself that you will escape in the king's house any more than all the Jews. For if you remain silent now, then relief and deliverance will come to the Jews from another place, but you and your father's house will perish. Who knows if you haven't come to the kingdom for such a time as this?" Then Esther asked them to answer Mordecai, "Go, gather together all the Jews who are present in Shushan, and fast for me, and neither eat nor drink three days, night or day. I and my maidens will also fast the same way. Then I will go in to the king, which is against the law; and if I perish, I perish."

Week 20 Day 5   5-Nov

Matt. 13:31-35 He set another parable before them, saying, "The Kingdom of Heaven is like a grain of mustard seed, which a man took, and sowed in his field; which indeed is smaller than all seeds. But when it is grown, it is greater than the herbs, and becomes a tree, so that the birds of the air come and lodge in its branches." He spoke another parable to them. "The Kingdom of Heaven is like yeast, which a woman took, and hid in three measures of meal, until it was all leavened." Jesus spoke all these things in parables to the multitudes; and without a parable, he didn't speak to them, that it might be fulfilled which was spoken through the prophet, saying, "I will open my mouth in parables; I will utter things hidden from the foundation of the world."

I Cor. 5:6-8 Your boasting is not good. Don't you know that a little yeast leavens the whole lump? Purge out the old yeast, that you may be a new lump, even as you are unleavened. For indeed Christ, our Passover, has been sacrificed in our place. Therefore let us keep the feast, not with old yeast, neither with the yeast of malice and wickedness, but with the unleavened bread of sincerity and truth.

Ez. 17:22-24 Thus says the Lord Yahweh: I will also take of the lofty top of the cedar, and will set it; I will crop off from the topmost of its young twigs a tender one, and I will plant it on a high and lofty mountain: in the mountain of the height of Israel will I plant it; and it shall bring forth boughs, and bear fruit, and be a goodly cedar: and under it shall dwell all birds of every wing; in the shade of its branches shall they dwell. All the trees of the field shall know that I, Yahweh, have brought down the high tree, have exalted the low tree, have dried up the green tree, and have made the dry tree to flourish; I, Yahweh, have spoken and have done it.

Week 20 Day 6   25-Jun

John 12:23-33 Jesus answered them, "The time has come for the Son of Man to be glorified. Most certainly I tell you, unless a grain of wheat falls into the earth and dies, it remains by itself alone. But if it dies, it bears much fruit. He who loves his life will lose it. He who hates his life in this world will keep it to eternal life. If anyone serves me, let him follow me. Where I am, there will my servant also be. If anyone serves me, the Father will honor him. "Now my soul is troubled. What shall I say? 'Father, save me from this time?' But for this cause I came to this time. Father, glorify your name!" Then there came a voice out of the sky, saying, "I have both glorified it, and will glorify it again." The multitude therefore, who stood by and heard it, said that it had thundered. Others said, "An angel has spoken to him." Jesus answered, "This voice hasn't come for my sake, but for your sakes. Now is the judgment of this world. Now the prince of this world will be cast out. And I, if I am lifted up from the earth, will draw all people to myself." But he said this, signifying by what kind of death he should die.

Eph. 2:1-10 You were made alive when you were dead in transgressions and sins, in which you once walked according to the course of this world, according to the prince of the power of the air, the spirit who now works in the children of disobedience; among whom we also all once lived in the lust of our flesh, doing the desires of the flesh and of the mind, and were by nature children of wrath, even as the rest. But God, being rich in mercy, for his great love with which he loved us, even when we were dead through our trespasses, made us alive together with Christ (by grace you have been saved), and raised us up with him, and made us to sit with him in the heavenly places in Christ Jesus, that in the ages to come he might show the exceeding riches of his grace in kindness toward us in Christ Jesus; for by grace you have been saved through faith, and that not of yourselves; it is the gift of God, not of works, that no one would boast. For we are his workmanship, created in Christ Jesus for good works, which God prepared before that we would walk in them.

Jer. 31:27-34 Behold, the days come, says Yahweh, that I will sow the house of Israel and the house of Judah with the seed of man, and with the seed of animal. It shall happen that, like as I have watched over them to pluck up and to break down and to overthrow and to destroy and to afflict, so will I watch over them to build and to plant, says Yahweh. In those days they shall say no more, The fathers have eaten sour grapes, and the children's teeth are set on edge. But everyone shall die for his own iniquity: every man who eats the sour grapes, his teeth shall be set on edge. Behold, the days come, says Yahweh, that I will make a new covenant with the house of Israel, and with the house of Judah: not according to the covenant that I made with their fathers in the day that I took them by the hand to bring them out of the land of Egypt; which my covenant they broke, although I was a husband to them, says Yahweh. But this is the covenant that I will make with the house of Israel after those days, says Yahweh: I will put my law in their inward parts, and in their heart will I write it; and I will be their God, and they shall be my people: and they shall teach no more every man his neighbor, and every man his brother, saying, Know Yahweh; for they shall all know me, from their least to their greatest, says Yahweh: for I will forgive their iniquity, and their sin will I remember no more.

Week 20 Day 7   25-Aug

Rom. 13:8-14 Owe no one anything, except to love one another; for he who loves his neighbor has fulfilled the law. For the commandments, "You shall not commit adultery," "You shall not murder," "You shall not steal," "You shall not give false testimony," "You shall not covet," and whatever other commandments there are, are all summed up in this saying, namely, "You shall love your neighbor as yourself." Love doesn't harm a neighbor. Love therefore is the fulfillment of the law. Do this, knowing the time, that it is already time for you to awaken out of sleep, for salvation is now nearer to us than when we first believed. The night is far gone, and the day is near. Let's therefore throw off the works of darkness, and let's put on the armor of light. Let us walk properly, as in the day; not in reveling and drunkenness, not in sexual promiscuity and lustful acts, and not in strife and jealousy. But put on the Lord Jesus Christ, and make no provision for the flesh, for its lusts.

Jos. 1:10-18 Then Joshua commanded the officers of the people, saying, "Pass through the midst of the camp, and command the people, saying, 'Prepare food; for within three days you are to pass over this Jordan, to go in to possess the land, which Yahweh your God gives you to possess it.'" Joshua spoke to the Reubenites, and to the Gadites, and to the half-tribe of Manasseh, saying, "Remember the word which Moses the servant of Yahweh commanded you, saying, 'Yahweh your God gives you rest, and will give you this land. Your wives, your little ones, and your livestock, shall live in the land which Moses gave you beyond the Jordan; but you shall pass over before your brothers armed, all the mighty men of valor, and shall help them until Yahweh has given your brothers rest, as he has given you, and they have also possessed the land which Yahweh your God gives them. Then you shall return to the land of your possession, and possess it, which Moses the servant of Yahweh gave you beyond the Jordan toward the sunrise.' They answered Joshua, saying, "All that you have commanded us we will do, and wherever you send us we will go. Just as we listened to Moses in all things, so will we listen to you. Only may Yahweh your God be with you, as he was with Moses. Whoever rebels against your commandment, and doesn't listen to your words in all that you command him, he shall be put to death. Only be strong and courageous."

Week 21 Day 1   4-Jan

John 8:25-29 They said therefore to him, "Who are you?" Jesus said to them, "Just what I have been saying to you from the beginning. I have many things to speak and to judge concerning you. However he who sent me is true; and the things which I heard from him, these I say to the world." They didn't understand that he spoke to them about the Father. Jesus therefore said to them, "When you have lifted up the Son of Man, then you will know that I am he, and I do nothing of myself, but as my Father taught me, I say these things. He who sent me is with me. The Father hasn't left me alone, for I always do the things that are pleasing to him."

I Cor. 15:12-28 Now if Christ is preached, that he has been raised from the dead, how do some among you say that there is no resurrection of the dead? But if there is no resurrection of the dead, neither has Christ been raised. If Christ has not been raised, then our preaching is in vain, and your faith also is in vain. Yes, we are found false witnesses of God, because we testified about God that he raised up Christ, whom he didn't raise up, if it is so that the dead are not raised. For if the dead aren't raised, neither has Christ been raised. If Christ has not been raised, your faith is vain; you are still in your sins. Then they also who are fallen asleep in Christ have perished. If we have only hoped in Christ in this life, we are of all men most pitiable. But now Christ has been raised from the dead. He became the first fruits of those who are asleep. For since death came by man, the resurrection of the dead also came by man. For as in Adam all die, so also in Christ all will be made alive. But each in his own order: Christ the first fruits, then those who are Christ's, at his coming. Then the end comes, when he will deliver up the Kingdom to God, even the Father; when he will have abolished all rule and all authority and power. For he must reign until he has put all his enemies under his feet. The last enemy that will be abolished is death. For, "He put all things in subjection under his feet." But when he says, "All things are put in subjection," it is evident that he is excepted who subjected all things to him. When all things have been subjected to him, then the Son will also himself be subjected to him who subjected all things to him, that God may be all in all.

Is. 52:13-15 Behold, my servant shall deal wisely, he shall be exalted and lifted up, and shall be very high. Like as many were astonished at you (his appearance was marred more than any man, and his form more than the sons of men), so shall he sprinkle many nations; kings shall shut their mouths at him: for that which had not been told them shall they see; and that which they had not heard shall they understand.

Week 21 Day 2   4-Sep

John 17:1-19 Jesus said these things, and lifting up his eyes to heaven, he said, "Father, the time has come. Glorify your Son, that your Son may also glorify you; even as you gave him authority over all flesh, he will give eternal life to all whom you have given him. This is eternal life, that they should know you, the only true God, and him whom you sent, Jesus Christ. I glorified you on the earth. I have accomplished the work which you have given me to do. Now, Father, glorify me with your own self with the glory which I had with you before the world existed. I revealed your name to the people whom you have given me out of the world. They were yours, and you have given them to me. They have kept your word. Now they have known that all things whatever you have given me are from you, for the words which you have given me I have given to them, and they received them, and knew for sure that I came forth from you, and they have believed that you sent me. I pray for them. I don't pray for the world, but for those whom you have given me, for they are yours. All things that are mine are yours, and yours are mine, and I am glorified in them. I am no more in the world, but these are in the world, and I am coming to you. Holy Father, keep them through your name which you have given me, that they may be one, even as we are. While I was with them in the world, I kept them in your name. Those whom you have given me I have kept. None of them is lost, except the son of destruction, that the Scripture might be fulfilled. But now I come to you, and I say these things in the world, that they may have my joy made full in themselves. I have given them your word. The world hated them, because they are not of the world, even as I am not of the world. I pray not that you would take them from the world, but that you would keep them from the evil one. They are not of the world even as I am not of the world. Sanctify them in your truth. Your word is truth. As you sent me into the world, even so I have sent them into the world. For their sakes I sanctify myself, that they themselves also may be sanctified in truth."

I Pet. 4:12-19 Beloved, don't be astonished at the fiery trial which has come upon you, to test you, as though a strange thing happened to you. But because you are partakers of Christ's sufferings, rejoice; that at the revelation of his glory you also may rejoice with exceeding joy. If you are insulted for the name of Christ, you are blessed; because the Spirit of glory and of God rests on you. On their part he is blasphemed, but on your part he is glorified. For let none of you suffer as a murderer, or a thief, or an evil doer, or a meddler in other men's matters. But if one of you suffers for being a Christian, let him not be ashamed; but let him glorify God in this matter. For the time has come for judgment to begin with the household of God. If it begins first with us, what will happen to those who don't obey the Good News of God? "If it is hard for the righteous to be saved, what will happen to the ungodly and the sinner?" Therefore let them also who suffer according to the will of God in doing good entrust their souls to him, as to a faithful Creator.

Ps. 68 Let God arise! Let his enemies be scattered! Let them who hate him also flee before him. As smoke is driven away, so drive them away. As wax melts before the fire, so let the wicked perish at the presence of God. But let the righteous be glad. Let them rejoice before God. Yes, let them rejoice with gladness. Sing to God! Sing praises to his name! Extol him who rides on the clouds: to Yah, his name! Rejoice before him! A father of the fatherless, and a defender of the widows, is God in his holy habitation. God sets the lonely in families. He brings out the prisoners with singing, but the rebellious dwell in a sun-scorched land. God, when you went forth before your people, when you marched through the wilderness. Selah. The earth trembled. The sky also poured down rain at the presence of the God of Sinai—at the presence of God, the God of Israel. You, God, sent a plentiful rain. You confirmed your inheritance, when it was weary. Your congregation lived therein. You, God, prepared your goodness for the poor. The Lord announced the word. The ones who proclaim it are a great company. "Kings of armies flee! They flee!" She who waits at home divides the spoil, while you sleep among the campfires, the wings of a dove sheathed with silver, her feathers with shining gold. When the Almighty scattered kings in her, it snowed on Zalmon. The mountains of Bashan are majestic mountains. The mountains of Bashan are rugged. Why do you look in envy, you rugged mountains, at the mountain where God chooses to reign? Yes, Yahweh will dwell there forever. The chariots of God are tens of thousands and thousands of thousands. The Lord is among them, from Sinai, into the sanctuary. You have ascended on high. You have led away captives. You have received gifts among men, yes, among the rebellious also, that Yah God might dwell there. Blessed be the Lord, who daily bears our burdens, even the God who is our salvation. Selah. God is to us a God of deliverance. To Yahweh, the Lord, belongs escape from death. But God will strike through the head of his enemies, the hairy scalp of such a one as still continues in his guiltiness. The Lord said, "I will bring you again from Bashan, I will bring you again from the depths of the sea; That you may crush them, dipping your foot in blood, that the tongues of your dogs may have their portion from your enemies." They have seen your processions, God, even the processions of my God, my King, into the sanctuary. The singers went before, the minstrels followed after, in the midst of the ladies playing with tambourines, "Bless God in the congregations, even the Lord in the assembly of Israel!" There is little Benjamin, their ruler, the princes of Judah, their council, the princes of Zebulun, and the princes of Naphtali. Your God has commanded your strength. Strengthen, God, that which you have done for us. Because of your temple at Jerusalem, kings shall bring presents to you. Rebuke the wild animal of the reeds, the multitude of the bulls, with the calves of the peoples. Being humbled, may it bring bars of silver. Scatter the nations that delight in war. Princes shall come out of Egypt. Ethiopia shall hurry to stretch out her hands to God. Sing to God, you kingdoms of the earth! Sing praises to the Lord! Selah. To him who rides on the heaven of heavens, which are of old; behold, he utters his voice, a mighty voice. Ascribe strength to God! His excellency is over Israel, his strength is in the skies. You are awesome, God, in your sanctuaries. The God of Israel gives strength and power to his people. Praise be to God!

Week 21 Day 3   7-Nov

Luke 23:26-34 When they led him away, they grabbed one Simon of Cyrene, coming from the country, and laid on him the cross, to carry it after Jesus. A great multitude of the people followed him, including women who also mourned and lamented him. But Jesus, turning to them, said, "Daughters of Jerusalem, don't weep for me, but weep for yourselves and for your children. For behold, the days are coming in which they will say, 'Blessed are the barren, the wombs that never bore, and the breasts that never nursed.' Then they will begin to tell the mountains, 'Fall on us!' and tell the hills, 'Cover us.' For if they do these things in the green tree, what will be done in the dry?" There were also others, two criminals, led with him to be put to death. When they came to the place that is called The Skull, they crucified him there with the criminals, one on the right and the other on the left. Jesus said, "Father, forgive them, for they don't know what they are doing." Dividing his garments among them, they cast lots.

I Jo. 2:7-17 Brothers, I write no new commandment to you, but an old commandment which you had from the beginning. The old commandment is the word which you heard from the beginning. Again, I write a new commandment to you, which is true in him and in you; because the darkness is passing away, and the true light already shines. He who says he is in the light and hates his brother, is in the darkness even until now. He who loves his brother remains in the light, and there is no occasion for stumbling in him. But he who hates his brother is in the darkness, and walks in the darkness, and doesn't know where he is going, because the darkness has blinded his eyes. I write to you, little children, because your sins are forgiven you for his name's sake. I write to you, fathers, because you know him who is from the beginning. I write to you, young men, because you have overcome the evil one. I write to you, little children, because you know the Father. I have written to you, fathers, because you know him who is from the beginning. I have written to you, young men, because you are strong, and the word of God remains in you, and you have overcome the evil one. Don't love the world, neither the things that are in the world. If anyone loves the world, the Father's love isn't in him. For all that is in the world, the lust of the flesh, the lust of the eyes, and the pride of life, isn't the Father's, but is the world's. The world is passing away with its lusts, but he who does God's will remains forever.

Ge. 50:14-21 Joseph returned into Egypt—he, and his brothers, and all that went up with him to bury his father, after he had buried his father. When Joseph's brothers saw that their father was dead, they said, "It may be that Joseph will hate us, and will fully pay us back for all of the evil which we did to him." They sent a message to Joseph, saying, "Your father commanded before he died, saying, 'You shall tell Joseph, "Now please forgive the disobedience of your brothers, and their sin, because they did evil to you."' Now, please forgive the disobedience of the servants of the God of your father." Joseph wept when they spoke to him. His brothers also went and fell down before his face; and they said, "Behold, we are your servants." Joseph said to them, "Don't be afraid, for am I in the place of God? As for you, you meant evil against me, but God meant it for good, to bring to pass, as it is this day, to save many people alive. Now therefore don't be afraid. I will nourish you and your little ones." He comforted them, and spoke kindly to them.

Week 21 Day 4   9-Apr

Luke 24:13-27 Behold, two of them were going that very day to a village named Emmaus, which was sixty stadia from Jerusalem. They talked with each other about all of these things which had happened. It happened, while they talked and questioned together, that Jesus himself came near, and went with them. But their eyes were kept from recognizing him. He said to them, "What are you talking about as you walk, and are sad?" One of them, named Cleopas, answered him, "Are you the only stranger in Jerusalem who doesn't know the things which have happened there in these days?" He said to them, "What things?" They said to him, "The things concerning Jesus, the Nazarene, who was a prophet mighty in deed and word before God and all the people; and how the chief priests and our rulers delivered him up to be condemned to death, and crucified him. But we were hoping that it was he who would redeem Israel. Yes, and besides all this, it is now the third day since these things happened. Also, certain women of our company amazed us, having arrived early at the tomb; and when they didn't find his body, they came saying that they had also seen a vision of angels, who said that he was alive. Some of us went to the tomb, and found it just like the women had said, but they didn't see him." He said to them, "Foolish men, and slow of heart to believe in all that the prophets have spoken! Didn't the Christ have to suffer these things and to enter into his glory?" Beginning from Moses and from all the prophets, he explained to them in all the Scriptures the things concerning himself.

Col. 1:24-29 Now I rejoice in my sufferings for your sake, and fill up on my part that which is lacking of the afflictions of Christ in my flesh for his body's sake, which is the assembly; of which I was made a servant, according to the stewardship of God which was given me toward you, to fulfill the word of God, the mystery which has been hidden for ages and generations. But now it has been revealed to his saints, to whom God was pleased to make known what are the riches of the glory of this mystery among the Gentiles, which is Christ in you, the hope of glory; whom we proclaim, admonishing every man and teaching every man in all wisdom, that we may present every man perfect in Christ Jesus; for which I also labor, striving according to his working, which works in me mightily.

Is. 53:1-12 Who has believed our message? To whom has the arm of Yahweh been revealed? For he grew up before him as a tender plant, and as a root out of dry ground. He has no good looks or majesty. When we see him, there is no beauty that we should desire him. He was despised, and rejected by men; a man of suffering, and acquainted with disease. He was despised as one from whom men hide their face; and we didn't respect him. Surely he has borne our sickness, and carried our suffering; yet we considered him plagued, struck by God, and afflicted. But he was pierced for our transgressions. He was crushed for our iniquities. The punishment that brought our peace was on him; and by his wounds we are healed. All we like sheep have gone astray. Everyone has turned to his own way; and Yahweh has laid on him the iniquity of us all. He was oppressed, yet when he was afflicted he didn't open his mouth. As a lamb that is led to the slaughter, and as a sheep that before its shearers is mute, so he didn't open his mouth. He was taken away by oppression and judgment; and as for his generation, who considered that he was cut off out of the land of the living and stricken for the disobedience of my people? They made his grave with the wicked, and with a rich man in his death; although he had done no violence, neither was any deceit in his mouth. Yet it pleased Yahweh to bruise him. He has caused him to suffer. When you make his soul an offering for sin, he shall see his seed. He shall prolong his days, and the pleasure of Yahweh shall prosper in his hand. After the suffering of his soul, he will see the light and be satisfied. My righteous servant will justify many by the knowledge of himself; and he will bear their iniquities. Therefore will I divide him a portion with the great, and he shall divide the spoil with the strong; because he poured out his soul to death, and was numbered with the transgressors; yet he bore the sin of many, and made intercession for the transgressors.

Week 21 Day 5   7-Mar

John 14:1-4 "Don't let your heart be troubled. Believe in God. Believe also in me. In my Father's house are many homes. If it weren't so, I would have told you. I am going to prepare a place for you. If I go and prepare a place for you, I will come again, and will receive you to myself; that where I am, you may be there also. Where I go, you know, and you know the way."

II Cor. 4:1-18 Therefore seeing we have this ministry, even as we obtained mercy, we don't faint. But we have renounced the hidden things of shame, not walking in craftiness, nor handling the word of God deceitfully; but by the manifestation of the truth commending ourselves to every man's conscience in the sight of God. Even if our Good News is veiled, it is veiled in those who perish; in whom the god of this world has blinded the minds of the unbelieving, that the light of the Good News of the glory of Christ, who is the image of God, should not dawn on them. For we don't preach ourselves, but Christ Jesus as Lord, and ourselves as your servants for Jesus' sake; seeing it is God who said, "Light will shine out of darkness," who has shone in our hearts, to give the light of the knowledge of the glory of God in the face of Jesus Christ. But we have this treasure in clay vessels, that the exceeding greatness of the power may be of God, and not from ourselves. We are pressed on every side, yet not crushed; perplexed, yet not to despair; pursued, yet not forsaken; struck down, yet not destroyed; always carrying in the body the putting to death of the Lord Jesus, that the life of Jesus may also be revealed in our body. For we who live are always delivered to death for Jesus' sake, that the life also of Jesus may be revealed in our mortal flesh. So then death works in us, but life in you. But having the same spirit of faith, according to that which is written, "I believed, and therefore I spoke." We also believe, and therefore also we speak; knowing that he who raised the Lord Jesus will raise us also with Jesus, and will present us with you. For all things are for your sakes, that the grace, being multiplied through the many, may cause the thanksgiving to abound to the glory of God. Therefore we don't faint, but though our outward man is decaying, yet our inward man is renewed day by day. For our light affliction, which is for the moment, works for us more and more exceedingly an eternal weight of glory; while we don't look at the things which are seen, but at the things which are not seen. For the things which are seen are temporal, but the things which are not seen are eternal.

De. 32:48-52 Yahweh spoke to Moses that same day, saying, "Go up into this mountain of Abarim, to Mount Nebo, which is in the land of Moab, that is over against Jericho; and see the land of Canaan, which I give to the children of Israel for a possession; and die on the mountain where you go up, and be gathered to your people, as Aaron your brother died on Mount Hor, and was gathered to his people: because you trespassed against me in the midst of the children of Israel at the waters of Meribah of Kadesh, in the wilderness of Zin; because you didn't sanctify me in the midst of the children of Israel. For you shall see the land before you; but you shall not go there into the land which I give the children of Israel."

Week 21 Day 6   **4-Apr**

Luke 17:20-37 Being asked by the Pharisees when the Kingdom of God would come, he answered them, "The Kingdom of God doesn't come with observation; neither will they say, 'Look, here!' or, 'Look, there!' for behold, the Kingdom of God is within you." He said to the disciples, "The days will come, when you will desire to see one of the days of the Son of Man, and you will not see it. They will tell you, 'Look, here!' or 'Look, there!' Don't go away, nor follow after them, for as the lightning, when it flashes out of the one part under the sky, shines to the other part under the sky; so will the Son of Man be in his day. But first, he must suffer many things and be rejected by this generation. As it happened in the days of Noah, even so will it be also in the days of the Son of Man. They ate, they drank, they married, they were given in marriage, until the day that Noah entered into the ship, and the flood came, and destroyed them all. Likewise, even as it happened in the days of Lot: they ate, they drank, they bought, they sold, they planted, they built; but in the day that Lot went out from Sodom, it rained fire and sulfur from the sky, and destroyed them all. It will be the same way in the day that the Son of Man is revealed. In that day, he who will be on the housetop, and his goods in the house, let him not go down to take them away. Let him who is in the field likewise not turn back. Remember Lot's wife! Whoever seeks to save his life loses it, but whoever loses his life preserves it. I tell you, in that night there will be two people in one bed. The one will be taken, and the other will be left. There will be two grinding grain together. One will be taken, and the other will be left." They, answering, asked him, "Where, Lord?" He said to them, "Where the body is, there will the vultures also be gathered together."

II Thes. 2:1-12 Now, brothers, concerning the coming of our Lord Jesus Christ, and our gathering together to him, we ask you not to be quickly shaken in your mind, nor yet be troubled, either by spirit, or by word, or by letter as from us, saying that the day of Christ had come. Let no one deceive you in any way. For it will not be, unless the departure comes first, and the man of sin is revealed, the son of destruction, he who opposes and exalts himself against all that is called God or that is worshiped; so that he sits as God in the temple of God, setting himself up as God. Don't you remember that, when I was still with you, I told you these things? Now you know what is restraining him, to the end that he may be revealed in his own season. For the mystery of lawlessness already works. Only there is one who restrains now, until he is taken out of the way. Then the lawless one will be revealed, whom the Lord will kill with the breath of his mouth, and destroy by the manifestation of his coming; even he whose coming is according to the working of Satan with all power and signs and lying wonders, and with all deception of wickedness for those who are being lost, because they didn't receive the love of the truth, that they might be saved. Because of this, God sends them a working of error, that they should believe a lie; that they all might be judged who didn't believe the truth, but had pleasure in unrighteousness.

Ge. 19:15-29 When the morning came, then the angels hurried Lot, saying, "Get up! Take your wife, and your two daughters who are here, lest you be consumed in the iniquity of the city." But he lingered; and the men grabbed his hand, his wife's hand, and his two daughters' hands, Yahweh being merciful to him; and they took him out, and set him outside of the city. It came to pass, when they had taken them out, that he said, "Escape for your life! Don't look behind you, and don't stay anywhere in the plain. Escape to the mountains, lest you be consumed!" Lot said to them, "Oh, not so, my lord. See now, your servant has found favor in your sight, and you have magnified your loving kindness, which you have shown to me in saving my life. I can't escape to the mountain, lest evil overtake me, and I die. See now, this city is near to flee to, and it is a little one. Oh let me escape there (isn't it a little one?), and my soul will live." He said to him, "Behold, I have granted your request concerning this thing also, that I will not overthrow the city of which you have spoken. Hurry, escape there, for I can't do anything until you get there." Therefore the name of the city was called Zoar. The sun had risen on the earth when Lot came to Zoar. Then Yahweh rained on Sodom and on Gomorrah sulfur and fire from Yahweh out of the sky. He overthrew those cities, all the plain, all the inhabitants of the cities, and that which grew on the ground. But his wife looked back from behind him, and she became a pillar of salt. Abraham got up early in the morning to the place where he had stood before Yahweh. He looked toward Sodom and Gomorrah, and toward all the land of the plain, and looked, and saw that the smoke of the land went up as the smoke of a furnace. It happened, when God destroyed the cities of the plain, that God remembered Abraham, and sent Lot out of the middle of the overthrow, when he overthrew the cities in which Lot lived.

Week 21 Day 7   20-Jul

I Cor. 15:35-58 But someone will say, "How are the dead raised?" and, "With what kind of body do they come?" You foolish one, that which you yourself sow is not made alive unless it dies. That which you sow, you don't sow the body that will be, but a bare grain, maybe of wheat, or of some other kind. But God gives it a body even as it pleased him, and to each seed a body of its own. All flesh is not the same flesh, but there is one flesh of men, another flesh of animals, another of fish, and another of birds. There are also celestial bodies, and terrestrial bodies; but the glory of the celestial differs from that of the terrestrial. There is one glory of the sun, another glory of the moon, and another glory of the stars; for one star differs from another star in glory. So also is the resurrection of the dead. It is sown in corruption; it is raised in incorruption. It is sown in dishonor; it is raised in glory. It is sown in weakness; it is raised in power. It is sown a natural body; it is raised a spiritual body. There is a natural body and there is also a spiritual body. So also it is written, "The first man, Adam, became a living soul." The last Adam became a life-giving spirit. However that which is spiritual isn't first, but that which is natural, then that which is spiritual. The first man is of the earth, made of dust. The second man is the Lord from heaven. As is the one made of dust, such are those who are also made of dust; and as is the heavenly, such are they also that are heavenly. As we have borne the image of those made of dust, let's also bear the image of the heavenly. Now I say this, brothers, that flesh and blood can't inherit the Kingdom of God; neither does corruption inherit incorruption. Behold, I tell you a mystery. We will not all sleep, but we will all be changed, in a moment, in the twinkling of an eye, at the last trumpet. For the trumpet will sound, and the dead will be raised incorruptible, and we will be changed. For this corruptible must put on incorruption, and this mortal must put on immortality. But when this corruptible will have put on incorruption, and this mortal will have put on immortality, then what is written will happen: "Death is swallowed up in victory." "Death, where is your sting? Hades, where is your victory?" The sting of death is sin, and the power of sin is the law. But thanks be to God, who gives us the victory through our Lord Jesus Christ. Therefore, my beloved brothers, be steadfast, immovable, always abounding in the Lord's work, because you know that your labor is not in vain in the Lord.

Is. 25:1-9 Yahweh, you are my God. I will exalt you! I will praise your name, for you have done wonderful things, things planned long ago, in complete faithfulness and truth. For you have made a city into a heap, a fortified city into a ruin, a palace of strangers to be no city. It will never be built. Therefore a strong people will glorify you. A city of awesome nations will fear you. For you have been a stronghold to the poor, a stronghold to the needy in his distress, a refuge from the storm, a shade from the heat, when the blast of the dreaded ones is like a storm against the wall. As the heat in a dry place will you bring down the noise of strangers; as the heat by the shade of a cloud, the song of the dreaded ones will be brought low. In this mountain, Yahweh of Armies will make all peoples a feast of fat things, a feast of choice wines, of fat things full of marrow, of well refined choice wines. He will destroy in this mountain the surface of the covering that covers all peoples, and the veil that is spread over all nations. He has swallowed up death forever! The Lord Yahweh will wipe away tears from off all faces. He will take the reproach of his people away from off all the earth, for Yahweh has spoken it. It shall be said in that day, "Behold, this is our God! We have waited for him, and he will save us! This is Yahweh! We have waited for him. We will be glad and rejoice in his salvation!"

Matt. 7:24-29 "Everyone therefore who hears these words of mine, and does them, I will liken him to a wise man, who built his house on a rock. The rain came down, the floods came, and the winds blew, and beat on that house; and it didn't fall, for it was founded on the rock. Everyone who hears these words of mine, and doesn't do them will be like a foolish man, who built his house on the sand. The rain came down, the floods came, and the winds blew, and beat on that house; and it fell—and great was its fall." It happened, when Jesus had finished saying these things, that the multitudes were astonished at his teaching, for he taught them with authority, and not like the scribes.

II Thes. 2:13-17 But we are bound to always give thanks to God for you, brothers loved by the Lord, because God chose you from the beginning for salvation through sanctification of the Spirit and belief in the truth; to which he called you through our Good News, for the obtaining of the glory of our Lord Jesus Christ. So then, brothers, stand firm, and hold the traditions which you were taught by us, whether by word, or by letter. Now our Lord Jesus Christ himself, and God our Father, who loved us and gave us eternal comfort and good hope through grace, comfort your hearts and establish you in every good work and word.

Ps. 119:1-16 Blessed are those whose ways are blameless, who walk according to Yahweh's law. Blessed are those who keep his statutes, who seek him with their whole heart. Yes, they do nothing wrong. They walk in his ways. You have commanded your precepts, that we should fully obey them. Oh that my ways were steadfast to obey your statutes! Then I wouldn't be disappointed, when I consider all of your commandments. I will give thanks to you with uprightness of heart, when I learn your righteous judgments. I will observe your statutes. Don't utterly forsake me. How can a young man keep his way pure? By living according to your word. With my whole heart, I have sought you. Don't let me wander from your commandments. I have hidden your word in my heart, that I might not sin against you. Blessed are you, Yahweh. Teach me your statutes. With my lips, I have declared all the ordinances of your mouth. I have rejoiced in the way of your testimonies, as much as in all riches. I will meditate on your precepts, and consider your ways. I will delight myself in your statutes. I will not forget your word.

John 14:15-21 "If you love me, keep my commandments. I will pray to the Father, and he will give you another Counselor, that he may be with you forever,—the Spirit of truth, whom the world can't receive; for it doesn't see him, neither knows him. You know him, for he lives with you, and will be in you. I will not leave you orphans. I will come to you. Yet a little while, and the world will see me no more; but you will see me. Because I live, you will live also. In that day you will know that I am in my Father, and you in me, and I in you. One who has my commandments, and keeps them, that person is one who loves me. One who loves me will be loved by my Father, and I will love him, and will reveal myself to him."

I Jo. 3:4-10 Everyone who sins also commits lawlessness. Sin is lawlessness. You know that he was revealed to take away our sins, and in him is no sin. Whoever remains in him doesn't sin. Whoever sins hasn't seen him, neither knows him. Little children, let no one lead you astray. He who does righteousness is righteous, even as he is righteous. He who sins is of the devil, for the devil has been sinning from the beginning. To this end the Son of God was revealed, that he might destroy the works of the devil. Whoever is born of God doesn't commit sin, because his seed remains in him; and he can't sin, because he is born of God. In this the children of God are revealed, and the children of the devil. Whoever doesn't do righteousness is not of God, neither is he who doesn't love his brother.

De. 4:32-40 For ask now of the days that are past, which were before you, since the day that God created man on the earth, and from the one end of the sky to the other, whether there has been anything as this great thing is, or has been heard like it? Did a people ever hear the voice of God speaking out of the midst of the fire, as you have heard, and live? Or has God tried to go and take a nation for himself from the midst of another nation, by trials, by signs, and by wonders, and by war, and by a mighty hand, and by an outstretched arm, and by great terrors, according to all that Yahweh your God did for you in Egypt before your eyes? It was shown to you so that you might know that Yahweh is God. There is no one else besides him. Out of heaven he made you to hear his voice, that he might instruct you: and on earth he made you to see his great fire; and you heard his words out of the midst of the fire. Because he loved your fathers, therefore he chose their seed after them, and brought you out with his presence, with his great power, out of Egypt; to drive out nations from before you greater and mightier than you, to bring you in, to give you their land for an inheritance, as at this day. Know therefore this day, and lay it to your heart, that Yahweh he is God in heaven above and on the earth beneath; there is none else. You shall keep his statutes, and his commandments, which I command you this day, that it may go well with you, and with your children after you, and that you may prolong your days in the land, which Yahweh your God gives you, forever.

Week 22 Day 3   8-Aug

John 14:22-24 Judas (not Iscariot) said to him, "Lord, what has happened that you are about to reveal yourself to us, and not to the world?" Jesus answered him, "If a man loves me, he will keep my word. My Father will love him, and we will come to him, and make our home with him. He who doesn't love me doesn't keep my words. The word which you hear isn't mine, but the Father's who sent me."

II Thes. 3:6-15 Now we command you, brothers, in the name of our Lord Jesus Christ, that you withdraw yourselves from every brother who walks in rebellion, and not after the tradition which they received from us. For you know how you ought to imitate us. For we didn't behave ourselves rebelliously among you, neither did we eat bread from anyone's hand without paying for it, but in labor and travail worked night and day, that we might not burden any of you; not because we don't have the right, but to make ourselves an example to you, that you should imitate us. For even when we were with you, we commanded you this: "If anyone will not work, neither let him eat." For we hear of some who walk among you in rebellion, who don't work at all, but are busybodies. Now those who are that way, we command and exhort in the Lord Jesus Christ, that with quietness they work, and eat their own bread. But you, brothers, don't be weary in doing well. If any man doesn't obey our word in this letter, note that man, that you have no company with him, to the end that he may be ashamed. Don't count him as an enemy, but admonish him as a brother.

Jer. 11:1-8 The word that came to Jeremiah from Yahweh, saying, Hear the words of this covenant, and speak to the men of Judah, and to the inhabitants of Jerusalem; and say to them, Thus says Yahweh, the God of Israel: Cursed is the man who doesn't hear the words of this covenant, which I commanded your fathers in the day that I brought them forth out of the land of Egypt, out of the iron furnace, saying, Obey my voice, and do them, according to all which I command you: so you shall be my people, and I will be your God; that I may establish the oath which I swore to your fathers, to give them a land flowing with milk and honey, as at this day. Then answered I, and said, Amen, Yahweh. Yahweh said to me, Proclaim all these words in the cities of Judah, and in the streets of Jerusalem, saying, Hear the words of this covenant, and do them. For I earnestly protested to your fathers in the day that I brought them up out of the land of Egypt, even to this day, rising early and protesting, saying, Obey my voice. Yet they didn't obey, nor turn their ear, but walked everyone in the stubbornness of their evil heart: therefore I brought on them all the words of this covenant, which I commanded them to do, but they didn't do them.

Week 22 Day 4   14-Dec

John 14:25-27 "I have said these things to you, while still living with you. But the Counselor, the Holy Spirit, whom the Father will send in my name, he will teach you all things, and will remind you of all that I said to you. Peace I leave with you. My peace I give to you; not as the world gives, give I to you. Don't let your heart be troubled, neither let it be fearful."

II Cor. 1:3-11 Blessed be the God and Father of our Lord Jesus Christ, the Father of mercies and God of all comfort; who comforts us in all our affliction, that we may be able to comfort those who are in any affliction, through the comfort with which we ourselves are comforted by God. For as the sufferings of Christ abound to us, even so our comfort also abounds through Christ. But if we are afflicted, it is for your comfort and salvation. If we are comforted, it is for your comfort, which produces in you the patient enduring of the same sufferings which we also suffer. Our hope for you is steadfast, knowing that, since you are partakers of the sufferings, so also are you of the comfort. For we don't desire to have you uninformed, brothers, concerning our affliction which happened to us in Asia, that we were weighed down exceedingly, beyond our power, so much that we despaired even of life. Yes, we ourselves have had the sentence of death within ourselves, that we should not trust in ourselves, but in God who raises the dead, who delivered us out of so great a death, and does deliver; on whom we have set our hope that he will also still deliver us; you also helping together on our behalf by your supplication; that, for the gift bestowed on us by means of many, thanks may be given by many persons on your behalf.

Ps. 91 He who dwells in the secret place of the Most High will rest in the shadow of the Almighty. I will say of Yahweh, "He is my refuge and my fortress; my God, in whom I trust." For he will deliver you from the snare of the fowler, and from the deadly pestilence. He will cover you with his feathers. Under his wings you will take refuge. His faithfulness is your shield and rampart. You shall not be afraid of the terror by night, nor of the arrow that flies by day; nor of the pestilence that walks in darkness, nor of the destruction that wastes at noonday. A thousand may fall at your side, and ten thousand at your right hand; but it will not come near you. You will only look with your eyes, and see the recompense of the wicked. Because you have made Yahweh your refuge, and the Most High your dwelling place, no evil shall happen to you, neither shall any plague come near your dwelling. For he will put his angels in charge of you, to guard you in all your ways. They will bear you up in their hands, so that you won't dash your foot against a stone. You will tread on the lion and cobra. You will trample the young lion and the serpent underfoot. "Because he has set his love on me, therefore I will deliver him. I will set him on high, because he has known my name. He will call on me, and I will answer him. I will be with him in trouble. I will deliver him, and honor him. I will satisfy him with long life, and show him my salvation."

Week 22 Day 5   14-Jun

John 15:1-4 "I am the true vine, and my Father is the farmer. Every branch in me that doesn't bear fruit, he takes away. Every branch that bears fruit, he prunes, that it may bear more fruit. You are already pruned clean because of the word which I have spoken to you. Remain in me, and I in you. As the branch can't bear fruit by itself, unless it remains in the vine, so neither can you, unless you remain in me."

Rom. 8:28-39 We know that all things work together for good for those who love God, to those who are called according to his purpose. For whom he foreknew, he also predestined to be conformed to the image of his Son, that he might be the firstborn among many brothers. Whom he predestined, those he also called. Whom he called, those he also justified. Whom he justified, those he also glorified. What then shall we say about these things? If God is for us, who can be against us? He who didn't spare his own Son, but delivered him up for us all, how would he not also with him freely give us all things? Who could bring a charge against God's chosen ones? It is God who justifies. Who is he who condemns? It is Christ who died, yes rather, who was raised from the dead, who is at the right hand of God, who also makes intercession for us. Who shall separate us from the love of Christ? Could oppression, or anguish, or persecution, or famine, or nakedness, or peril, or sword? Even as it is written, "For your sake we are killed all day long. We were accounted as sheep for the slaughter." No, in all these things, we are more than conquerors through him who loved us. For I am persuaded, that neither death, nor life, nor angels, nor principalities, nor things present, nor things to come, nor powers, nor height, nor depth, nor any other created thing, will be able to separate us from the love of God, which is in Christ Jesus our Lord.

Jud. 2:1-5 The angel of Yahweh came up from Gilgal to Bochim. He said, "I made you to go up out of Egypt, and have brought you to the land which I swore to your fathers; and I said, 'I will never break my covenant with you: and you shall make no covenant with the inhabitants of this land; you shall break down their altars.' But you have not listened to my voice: why have you done this? Therefore I also said, I will not drive them out from before you; but they shall be in your sides, and their gods shall be a snare to you." It happened, when the angel of Yahweh spoke these words to all the children of Israel, that the people lifted up their voice, and wept. They called the name of that place Bochim: and they sacrificed there to Yahweh.

John 16:5-15 "But now I am going to him who sent me, and none of you asks me, 'Where are you going?' But because I have told you these things, sorrow has filled your heart. Nevertheless I tell you the truth: It is to your advantage that I go away, for if I don't go away, the Counselor won't come to you. But if I go, I will send him to you. When he has come, he will convict the world about sin, about righteousness, and about judgment; about sin, because they don't believe in me; about righteousness, because I am going to my Father, and you won't see me any more; about judgment, because the prince of this world has been judged. I have yet many things to tell you, but you can't bear them now. However when he, the Spirit of truth, has come, he will guide you into all truth, for he will not speak from himself; but whatever he hears, he will speak. He will declare to you things that are coming. He will glorify me, for he will take from what is mine, and will declare it to you. All things whatever the Father has are mine; therefore I said that he takes of mine, and will declare it to you."

Rom. 8:18-27 For I consider that the sufferings of this present time are not worthy to be compared with the glory which will be revealed toward us. For the creation waits with eager expectation for the children of God to be revealed. For the creation was subjected to vanity, not of its own will, but because of him who subjected it, in hope that the creation itself also will be delivered from the bondage of decay into the liberty of the glory of the children of God. For we know that the whole creation groans and travails in pain together until now. Not only so, but ourselves also, who have the first fruits of the Spirit, even we ourselves groan within ourselves, waiting for adoption, the redemption of our body. For we were saved in hope, but hope that is seen is not hope. For who hopes for that which he sees? But if we hope for that which we don't see, we wait for it with patience. In the same way, the Spirit also helps our weaknesses, for we don't know how to pray as we ought. But the Spirit himself makes intercession for us with groanings which can't be uttered. He who searches the hearts knows what is on the Spirit's mind, because he makes intercession for the saints according to God.

Dan. 10:1-19 In the third year of Cyrus king of Persia a thing was revealed to Daniel, whose name was called Belteshazzar; and the thing was true, even a great warfare: and he understood the thing, and had understanding of the vision. In those days I, Daniel, was mourning three whole weeks. I ate no pleasant bread, neither came flesh nor wine into my mouth, neither did I anoint myself at all, until three whole weeks were fulfilled. In the four and twentieth day of the first month, as I was by the side of the great river, which is Hiddekel, I lifted up my eyes, and looked, and behold, a man clothed in linen, whose thighs were adorned with pure gold of Uphaz: his body also was like the beryl, and his face as the appearance of lightning, and his eyes as flaming torches, and his arms and his feet like burnished brass, and the voice of his words like the voice of a multitude. I, Daniel, alone saw the vision; for the men who were with me didn't see the vision; but a great quaking fell on them, and they fled to hide themselves. So I was left alone, and saw this great vision, and there remained no strength in me; for my comeliness was turned in me into corruption, and I retained no strength. Yet heard I the voice of his words; and when I heard the voice of his words, then was I fallen into a deep sleep on my face, with my face toward the ground. Behold, a hand touched me, which set me on my knees and on the palms of my hands. He said to me, Daniel, you man greatly beloved, understand the words that I speak to you, and stand upright; for am I now sent to you. When he had spoken this word to me, I stood trembling. Then he said to me, Don't be afraid, Daniel; for from the first day that you set your heart to understand, and to humble yourself before your God, your words were heard: and I have come for your words' sake. But the prince of the kingdom of Persia withstood me twenty-one days; but, behold, Michael, one of the chief princes, came to help me: and I remained there with the kings of Persia. Now I have come to make you understand what shall happen to your people in the latter days; for the vision is yet for *many* days: and when he had spoken to me according to these words, I set my face toward the ground, and was mute. Behold, one in the likeness of the sons of men touched my lips: then I opened my mouth, and spoke and said to him who stood before me, my lord, by reason of the vision my sorrows are turned on me, and I retain no strength. For how can the servant of this my lord talk with this my lord? for as for me, immediately there remained no strength in me, neither was there breath left in me. Then there touched me again one like the appearance of a man, and he strengthened me. He said, "Greatly beloved man, don't be afraid: peace be to you, be strong, yes, be strong." When he spoke to me, I was strengthened, and said, "Let my lord speak; for you have strengthened me."

Week 22 Day 7 29-Dec

II Cor. 13:5-14 Test your own selves, whether you are in the faith. Test your own selves. Or don't you know as to your own selves, that Jesus Christ is in you?—unless indeed you are disqualified. But I hope that you will know that we aren't disqualified. Now I pray to God that you do no evil; not that we may appear approved, but that you may do that which is honorable, though we are as reprobate. For we can do nothing against the truth, but for the truth. For we rejoice when we are weak and you are strong. And this we also pray for, even your perfecting. For this cause I write these things while absent, that I may not deal sharply when present, according to the authority which the Lord gave me for building up, and not for tearing down. Finally, brothers, rejoice. Be perfected, be comforted, be of the same mind, live in peace, and the God of love and peace will be with you. Greet one another with a holy kiss. All the saints greet you. The grace of the Lord Jesus Christ, the love of God, and the fellowship of the Holy Spirit, be with you all. Amen.

Ps. 119:57-72 Yahweh is my portion. I promised to obey your words. I sought your favor with my whole heart. Be merciful to me according to your word. I considered my ways, and turned my steps to your statutes. I will hurry, and not delay, to obey your commandments. The ropes of the wicked bind me, but I won't forget your law. At midnight I will rise to give thanks to you, because of your righteous ordinances. I am a friend of all those who fear you, of those who observe your precepts. The earth is full of your loving kindness, Yahweh. Teach me your statutes. Do good to your servant, according to your word, Yahweh. Teach me good judgment and knowledge, for I believe in your commandments. Before I was afflicted, I went astray; but now I observe your word. You are good, and do good. Teach me your statutes. The proud have smeared a lie upon me. With my whole heart, I will keep your precepts. Their heart is as callous as the fat, but I delight in your law. It is good for me that I have been afflicted, that I may learn your statutes. The law of your mouth is better to me than thousands of pieces of gold and silver.

Week 23 Day 1 1-Mar

Luke 22:14-20 When the hour had come, he sat down with the twelve apostles. He said to them, "I have earnestly desired to eat this Passover with you before I suffer, for I tell you, I will no longer by any means eat of it until it is fulfilled in the Kingdom of God." He received a cup, and when he had given thanks, he said, "Take this, and share it among yourselves, for I tell you, I will not drink at all again from the fruit of the vine, until the Kingdom of God comes." He took bread, and when he had given thanks, he broke it, and gave to them, saying, "This is my body which is given for you. Do this in memory of me." Likewise, he took the cup after supper, saying, "This cup is the new covenant in my blood, which is poured out for you."

I Cor. 11:17-34 But in giving you this command, I don't praise you, that you come together not for the better but for the worse. For first of all, when you come together in the assembly, I hear that divisions exist among you, and I partly believe it. For there also must be factions among you, that those who are approved may be revealed among you. When therefore you assemble yourselves together, it is not the Lord's supper that you eat. For in your eating each one takes his own supper first. One is hungry, and another is drunken. What, don't you have houses to eat and to drink in? Or do you despise God's assembly, and put them to shame who don't have? What shall I tell you? Shall I praise you? In this I don't praise you. For I received from the Lord that which also I delivered to you, that the Lord Jesus on the night in which he was betrayed took bread. When he had given thanks, he broke it, and said, "Take, eat. This is my body, which is broken for you. Do this in memory of me." In the same way he also took the cup, after supper, saying, "This cup is the new covenant in my blood. Do this, as often as you drink, in memory of me." For as often as you eat this bread and drink this cup, you proclaim the Lord's death until he comes. Therefore whoever eats this bread or drinks the Lord's cup in a way unworthy of the Lord will be guilty of the body and the blood of the Lord. But let a man examine himself, and so let him eat of the bread, and drink of the cup. For he who eats and drinks in an unworthy way eats and drinks judgment to himself, if he doesn't discern the Lord's body. For this cause many among you are weak and sickly, and not a few sleep. For if we discerned ourselves, we wouldn't be judged. But when we are judged, we are punished by the Lord, that we may not be condemned with the world. Therefore, my brothers, when you come together to eat, wait for one another. But if anyone is hungry, let him eat at home, lest your coming together be for judgment. The rest I will set in order whenever I come.

Ex. 12:1-14 Yahweh spoke to Moses and Aaron in the land of Egypt, saying, "This month shall be to you the beginning of months. It shall be the first month of the year to you. Speak to all the congregation of Israel, saying, 'On the tenth day of this month, they shall take to them every man a lamb, according to their fathers' houses, a lamb for a household; and if the household is too little for a lamb, then he and his neighbor next to his house shall take one according to the number of the souls; according to what everyone can eat you shall make your count for the lamb. Your lamb shall be without blemish, a male a year old. You shall take it from the sheep, or from the goats: and you shall keep it until the fourteenth day of the same month; and the whole assembly of the congregation of Israel shall kill it at evening. They shall take some of the blood, and put it on the two doorposts and on the lintel, on the houses in which they shall eat it. They shall eat the flesh in that night, roasted with fire, and unleavened bread. They shall eat it with bitter herbs. Don't eat it raw, nor boiled at all with water, but roasted with fire; with its head, its legs and its inner parts. You shall let nothing of it remain until the morning; but that which remains of it until the morning you shall burn with fire. This is how you shall eat it: with your belt on your waist, your shoes on your feet, and your staff in your hand; and you shall eat it in haste: it is Yahweh's Passover. For I will go through the land of Egypt in that night, and will strike all the firstborn in the land of Egypt, both man and animal. Against all the gods of Egypt I will execute judgments: I am Yahweh. The blood shall be to you for a token on the houses where you are: and when I see the blood, I will pass over you, and there shall no plague be on you to destroy you, when I strike the land of Egypt. This day shall be to you for a memorial, and you shall keep it a feast to Yahweh: throughout your generations you shall keep it a feast by an ordinance forever.'"

Week 23 Day 2   7-Feb

Luke 24:28-35 They drew near to the village, where they were going, and he acted like he would go further. They urged him, saying, "Stay with us, for it is almost evening, and the day is almost over." He went in to stay with them. It happened, that when he had sat down at the table with them, he took the bread and gave thanks. Breaking it, he gave to them. Their eyes were opened, and they recognized him, and he vanished out of their sight. They said one to another, "Weren't our hearts burning within us, while he spoke to us along the way, and while he opened the Scriptures to us?" They rose up that very hour, returned to Jerusalem, and found the eleven gathered together, and those who were with them, saying, "The Lord is risen indeed, and has appeared to Simon!" They related the things that happened along the way, and how he was recognized by them in the breaking of the bread.

Rev. 1:9-20 I John, your brother and partner with you in oppression, Kingdom, and perseverance in Christ Jesus, was on the isle that is called Patmos because of God's Word and the testimony of Jesus Christ. I was in the Spirit on the Lord's day, and I heard behind me a loud voice, like a trumpet saying, "What you see, write in a book and send to the seven assemblies to Ephesus, Smyrna, Pergamum, Thyatira, Sardis, Philadelphia, and to Laodicea." I turned to see the voice that spoke with me. Having turned, I saw seven golden lampstands. And among the lampstands was one like a son of man, clothed with a robe reaching down to his feet, and with a golden sash around his chest. His head and his hair were white as white wool, like snow. His eyes were like a flame of fire. His feet were like burnished brass, as if it had been refined in a furnace. His voice was like the voice of many waters. He had seven stars in his right hand. Out of his mouth proceeded a sharp two-edged sword. His face was like the sun shining at its brightest. When I saw him, I fell at his feet like a dead man. He laid his right hand on me, saying, "Don't be afraid. I am the first and the last, and the Living one. I was dead, and behold, I am alive forevermore. Amen. I have the keys of Death and of Hades. Write therefore the things which you have seen, and the things which are, and the things which will happen hereafter; the mystery of the seven stars which you saw in my right hand, and the seven golden lampstands. The seven stars are the angels of the seven assemblies. The seven lampstands are seven assemblies."

Ge. 28:10-16 Jacob went out from Beersheba, and went toward Haran. He came to a certain place, and stayed there all night, because the sun had set. He took one of the stones of the place, and put it under his head, and lay down in that place to sleep. He dreamed. Behold, a stairway set upon the earth, and its top reached to heaven. Behold, the angels of God ascending and descending on it. Behold, Yahweh stood above it, and said, "I am Yahweh, the God of Abraham your father, and the God of Isaac. The land whereon you lie, to you will I give it, and to your seed. Your seed will be as the dust of the earth, and you will spread abroad to the west, and to the east, and to the north, and to the south. In you and in your seed will all the families of the earth be blessed. Behold, I am with you, and will keep you, wherever you go, and will bring you again into this land. For I will not leave you, until I have done that which I have spoken of to you." Jacob awakened out of his sleep, and he said, "Surely Yahweh is in this place, and I didn't know it."

Week 23 Day 3   18-Sep

Matt. 4:1-11 Then Jesus was led up by the Spirit into the wilderness to be tempted by the devil. When he had fasted forty days and forty nights, he was hungry afterward. The tempter came and said to him, "If you are the Son of God, command that these stones become bread." But he answered, "It is written, 'Man shall not live by bread alone, but by every word that proceeds out of the mouth of God.'" Then the devil took him into the holy city. He set him on the pinnacle of the temple, and said to him, "If you are the Son of God, throw yourself down, for it is written, 'He will put his angels in charge of you.' and, 'On their hands they will bear you up, so that you don't dash your foot against a stone.'" Jesus said to him, "Again, it is written, 'You shall not test the Lord, your God.'" Again, the devil took him to an exceedingly high mountain, and showed him all the kingdoms of the world, and their glory. He said to him, "I will give you all of these things, if you will fall down and worship me." Then Jesus said to him, "Get behind me, Satan! For it is written, 'You shall worship the Lord your God, and you shall serve him only.'" Then the devil left him, and behold, angels came and served him.

Heb. 4:14-5:10 Having then a great high priest, who has passed through the heavens, Jesus, the Son of God, let us hold tightly to our confession. For we don't have a high priest who can't be touched with the feeling of our infirmities, but one who has been in all points tempted like we are, yet without sin. Let us therefore draw near with boldness to the throne of grace, that we may receive mercy, and may find grace for help in time of need. For every high priest, being taken from among men, is appointed for men in things pertaining to God, that he may offer both gifts and sacrifices for sins. The high priest can deal gently with those who are ignorant and going astray, because he himself is also surrounded with weakness. Because of this, he must offer sacrifices for sins for the people, as well as for himself. Nobody takes this honor on himself, but he is called by God, just like Aaron was. So also Christ didn't glorify himself to be made a high priest, but it was he who said to him, "You are my Son. Today I have become your father." As he says also in another place, "You are a priest forever, after the order of Melchizedek." He, in the days of his flesh, having offered up prayers and petitions with strong crying and tears to him who was able to save him from death, and having been heard for his godly fear, though he was a Son, yet learned obedience by the things which he suffered. Having been made perfect, he became to all of those who obey him the author of eternal salvation, named by God a high priest after the order of Melchizedek.

Ge. 3:1-24 Now the serpent was more subtle than any animal of the field which Yahweh God had made. He said to the woman, "Has God really said, 'You shall not eat of any tree of the garden?'" The woman said to the serpent, "Of the fruit of the trees of the garden we may eat, but of the fruit of the tree which is in the middle of the garden, God has said, 'You shall not eat of it, neither shall you touch it, lest you die.'" The serpent said to the woman, "You won't surely die, for God knows that in the day you eat it, your eyes will be opened, and you will be like God, knowing good and evil." When the woman saw that the tree was good for food, and that it was a delight to the eyes, and that the tree was to be desired to make one wise, she took of its fruit, and ate; and she gave some to her husband with her, and he ate. The eyes of both of them were opened, and they knew that they were naked. They sewed fig leaves together, and made themselves aprons. They heard the voice of Yahweh God walking in the garden in the cool of the day, and the man and his wife hid themselves from the presence of Yahweh God among the trees of the garden. Yahweh God called to the man, and said to him, "Where are you?" The man said, "I heard your voice in the garden, and I was afraid, because I was naked; and I hid myself." God said, "Who told you that you were naked? Have you eaten from the tree that I commanded you not to eat from?" The man said, "The woman whom you gave to be with me, she gave me of the tree, and I ate." Yahweh God said to the woman, "What is this you have done?" The woman said, "The serpent deceived me, and I ate." Yahweh God said to the serpent, "Because you have done this, you are cursed above all livestock, and above every animal of the field. On your belly you shall go, and you shall eat dust all the days of your life. I will put enmity between you and the woman, and between your offspring and her offspring. He will bruise your head, and you will bruise his heel." To the woman he said, "I will greatly multiply your pain in childbirth. In pain you will bear children. Your desire will be for your husband, and he will rule over you." To Adam he said, "Because you have listened to your wife's voice, and have eaten of the tree, of which I commanded you, saying, 'You shall not eat of it,' cursed is the ground for your sake. In toil you will eat of it all the days of your life. It will yield thorns and thistles to you; and you will eat the herb of the field. By the sweat of your face will you eat bread until you return to the ground, for out of it you were taken. For you are dust, and to dust you shall return." The man called his wife Eve, because she was the mother of all living. Yahweh God made coats of skins for Adam and for his wife, and clothed them. Yahweh God said, "Behold, the man has become like one of us, knowing good and evil. Now, lest he reach out his hand, and also take of the tree of life, and eat, and live forever..." Therefore Yahweh God sent him out from the garden of Eden, to till the ground from which he was taken. So he drove out the man; and he placed Cherubs at the east of the garden of Eden, and the flame of a sword which turned every way, to guard the way to the tree of life.

Week 23 Day 4   10-Aug

Matt. 16:21-28 From that time, Jesus began to show his disciples that he must go to Jerusalem and suffer many things from the elders, chief priests, and scribes, and be killed, and the third day be raised up. Peter took him aside, and began to rebuke him, saying, "Far be it from you, Lord! This will never be done to you." But he turned, and said to Peter, "Get behind me, Satan! You are a stumbling block to me, for you are not setting your mind on the things of God, but on the things of men." Then Jesus said to his disciples, "If anyone desires to come after me, let him deny himself, and take up his cross, and follow me. For whoever desires to save his life will lose it, and whoever will lose his life for my sake will find it. For what will it profit a man, if he gains the whole world, and forfeits his life? Or what will a man give in exchange for his life? For the Son of Man will come in the glory of his Father with his angels, and then he will render to everyone according to his deeds. Most certainly I tell you, there are some standing here who will in no way taste of death, until they see the Son of Man coming in his Kingdom."

Eph. 6:10-20 Finally, be strong in the Lord, and in the strength of his might. Put on the whole armor of God, that you may be able to stand against the wiles of the devil. For our wrestling is not against flesh and blood, but against the principalities, against the powers, against the world's rulers of the darkness of this age, and against the spiritual forces of wickedness in the heavenly places. Therefore put on the whole armor of God, that you may be able to withstand in the evil day, and, having done all, to stand. Stand therefore, having the utility belt of truth buckled around your waist, and having put on the breastplate of righteousness, and having fitted your feet with the preparation of the Good News of peace; above all, taking up the shield of faith, with which you will be able to quench all the fiery darts of the evil one. And take the helmet of salvation, and the sword of the Spirit, which is the word of God; with all prayer and requests, praying at all times in the Spirit, and being watchful to this end in all perseverance and requests for all the saints: on my behalf, that utterance may be given to me in opening my mouth, to make known with boldness the mystery of the Good News, for which I am an ambassador in chains; that in it I may speak boldly, as I ought to speak.

Ps. 62 My soul rests in God alone. My salvation is from him. He alone is my rock and my salvation, my fortress—I will never be greatly shaken. How long will you assault a man, would all of you throw him down, like a leaning wall, like a tottering fence? They fully intend to throw him down from his lofty place. They delight in lies. They bless with their mouth, but they curse inwardly. Selah. My soul, wait in silence for God alone, for my expectation is from him. He alone is my rock and my salvation, my fortress. I will not be shaken. With God is my salvation and my honor. The rock of my strength, and my refuge, is in God. Trust in him at all times, you people. Pour out your heart before him. God is a refuge for us. Selah. Surely men of low degree are just a breath, and men of high degree are a lie. In the balances they will go up. They are together lighter than a breath. Don't trust in oppression. Don't become vain in robbery. If riches increase, don't set your heart on them. God has spoken once; twice I have heard this, that power belongs to God. Also to you, Lord, belongs loving kindness, for you reward every man according to his work.

Pr 24:12 If you say, "Behold, we didn't know this"; doesn't he who weighs the hearts consider it? He who keeps your soul, doesn't he know it? Shall he not render to every man according to his work?

Week 23 Day 5   18-Feb

Luke 22:39-46 He came out, and went, as his custom was, to the Mount of Olives. His disciples also followed him. When he was at the place, he said to them, "Pray that you don't enter into temptation." He was withdrawn from them about a stone's throw, and he knelt down and prayed, saying, "Father, if you are willing, remove this cup from me. Nevertheless, not my will, but yours, be done." An angel from heaven appeared to him, strengthening him. Being in agony he prayed more earnestly. His sweat became like great drops of blood falling down on the ground. When he rose up from his prayer, he came to the disciples, and found them sleeping because of grief, and said to them, "Why do you sleep? Rise and pray that you may not enter into temptation."

I Pet. 5:8-11 Be sober and self-controlled. Be watchful. Your adversary, the devil, walks around like a roaring lion, seeking whom he may devour. Withstand him steadfast in your faith, knowing that your brothers who are in the world are undergoing the same sufferings. But may the God of all grace, who called you to his eternal glory by Christ Jesus, after you have suffered a little while, perfect, establish, strengthen, and settle you. To him be the glory and the power forever and ever. Amen.

Lam. 3:19-33 Remember my affliction and my misery, the wormwood and the gall. My soul still remembers them, and is bowed down within me. This I recall to my mind; therefore have I hope. It is because of Yahweh's loving kindnesses that we are not consumed, because his compassion doesn't fail. They are new every morning; great is your faithfulness. Yahweh is my portion, says my soul; therefore will I hope in him. Yahweh is good to those who wait for him, to the soul that seeks him. It is good that a man should hope and quietly wait for the salvation of Yahweh. It is good for a man that he bear the yoke in his youth. Let him sit alone and keep silence, because he has laid it on him. Let him put his mouth in the dust, if so be there may be hope. Let him give his cheek to him who strikes him; let him be filled full with reproach. For the Lord will not cast off forever. For though he cause grief, yet he will have compassion according to the multitude of his loving kindnesses. For he does not afflict willingly, nor grieve the children of men.

Week 23 Day 6   27-Sep

Luke 9:57-62 As they went on the way, a certain man said to him, "I want to follow you wherever you go, Lord." Jesus said to him, "The foxes have holes, and the birds of the sky have nests, but the Son of Man has no place to lay his head." He said to another, "Follow me!" But he said, "Lord, allow me first to go and bury my father." But Jesus said to him, "Leave the dead to bury their own dead, but you go and announce the Kingdom of God." Another also said, "I want to follow you, Lord, but first allow me to say good-bye to those who are at my house." But Jesus said to him, "No one, having put his hand to the plow, and looking back, is fit for the Kingdom of God."

Rev. 3:14-22 "To the angel of the assembly in Laodicea write: "The Amen, the Faithful and True Witness, the Head of God's creation, says these things: "I know your works, that you are neither cold nor hot. I wish you were cold or hot. So, because you are lukewarm, and neither hot nor cold, I will vomit you out of my mouth. Because you say, 'I am rich, and have gotten riches, and have need of nothing;' and don't know that you are the wretched one, miserable, poor, blind, and naked; I counsel you to buy from me gold refined by fire, that you may become rich; and white garments, that you may clothe yourself, and that the shame of your nakedness may not be revealed; and eye salve to anoint your eyes, that you may see. As many as I love, I reprove and chasten. Be zealous therefore, and repent. Behold, I stand at the door and knock. If anyone hears my voice and opens the door, then I will come in to him, and will dine with him, and he with me. He who overcomes, I will give to him to sit down with me on my throne, as I also overcame, and sat down with my Father on his throne. He who has an ear, let him hear what the Spirit says to the assemblies.""""

I Ki. 19:15-21 Yahweh said to him, "Go, return on your way to the wilderness of Damascus. When you arrive, you shall anoint Hazael to be king over Syria. You shall anoint Jehu the son of Nimshi to be king over Israel; and you shall anoint Elisha the son of Shaphat of Abel Meholah to be prophet in your place. It shall happen, that he who escapes from the sword of Hazael, Jehu will kill; and he who escapes from the sword of Jehu, Elisha will kill. Yet will I leave seven thousand in Israel, all the knees which have not bowed to Baal, and every mouth which has not kissed him." So he departed there, and found Elisha the son of Shaphat, who was plowing, with twelve yoke of oxen before him, and he with the twelfth: and Elijah passed over to him, and cast his mantle on him. He left the oxen, and ran after Elijah, and said, "Let me please kiss my father and my mother, and then I will follow you." He said to him, "Go back again; for what have I done to you?" He returned from following him, and took the yoke of oxen, and killed them, and boiled their flesh with the instruments of the oxen, and gave to the people, and they ate. Then he arose, and went after Elijah, and served him.

Week 23 Day 7   26-Jun

II Cor. 3:6-18 God made us sufficient as servants of a new covenant; not of the letter, but of the Spirit. For the letter kills, but the Spirit gives life. But if the service of death, written engraved on stones, came with glory, so that the children of Israel could not look steadfastly on the face of Moses for the glory of his face; which was passing away: won't service of the Spirit be with much more glory? For if the service of condemnation has glory, the service of righteousness exceeds much more in glory. For most certainly that which has been made glorious has not been made glorious in this respect, by reason of the glory that surpasses. For if that which passes away was with glory, much more that which remains is in glory. Having therefore such a hope, we use great boldness of speech, and not as Moses, who put a veil on his face, that the children of Israel wouldn't look steadfastly on the end of that which was passing away. But their minds were hardened, for until this very day at the reading of the old covenant the same veil remains, because in Christ it passes away. But to this day, when Moses is read, a veil lies on their heart. But whenever one turns to the Lord, the veil is taken away. Now the Lord is the Spirit and where the Spirit of the Lord is, there is liberty. But we all, with unveiled face beholding as in a mirror the glory of the Lord, are transformed into the same image from glory to glory, even as from the Lord, the Spirit.

Ex. 34:29-35 It happened, when Moses came down from Mount Sinai with the two tablets of the testimony in Moses' hand, when he came down from the mountain, that Moses didn't know that the skin of his face shone by reason of his speaking with him. When Aaron and all the children of Israel saw Moses, behold, the skin of his face shone; and they were afraid to come near him. Moses called to them, and Aaron and all the rulers of the congregation returned to him; and Moses spoke to them. Afterward all the children of Israel came near, and he gave them all of the commandments that Yahweh had spoken with him on Mount Sinai. When Moses was done speaking with them, he put a veil on his face. But when Moses went in before Yahweh to speak with him, he took the veil off, until he came out; and he came out, and spoke to the children of Israel that which he was commanded. The children of Israel saw Moses' face, that the skin of Moses' face shone: and Moses put the veil on his face again, until he went in to speak with him.

Week 24 Day 1   15-Feb

Luke 24:36-49 As they said these things, Jesus himself stood among them, and said to them, "Peace be to you." But they were terrified and filled with fear, and supposed that they had seen a spirit. He said to them, "Why are you troubled? Why do doubts arise in your hearts? See my hands and my feet, that it is truly me. Touch me and see, for a spirit doesn't have flesh and bones, as you see that I have." When he had said this, he showed them his hands and his feet. While they still didn't believe for joy, and wondered, he said to them, "Do you have anything here to eat?" They gave him a piece of a broiled fish and some honeycomb. He took them, and ate in front of them. He said to them, "This is what I told you, while I was still with you, that all things which are written in the law of Moses, the prophets, and the psalms, concerning me must be fulfilled." Then he opened their minds, that they might understand the Scriptures. He said to them, "Thus it is written, and thus it was necessary for the Christ to suffer and to rise from the dead the third day, and that repentance and remission of sins should be preached in his name to all the nations, beginning at Jerusalem. You are witnesses of these things. Behold, I send forth the promise of my Father on you. But wait in the city of Jerusalem until you are clothed with power from on high."

Acts 2:1-4 Now when the day of Pentecost had come, they were all with one accord in one place. Suddenly there came from the sky a sound like the rushing of a mighty wind, and it filled all the house where they were sitting. Tongues like fire appeared and were distributed to them, and one sat on each of them. They were all filled with the Holy Spirit, and began to speak with other languages, as the Spirit gave them the ability to speak.

Acts 2:42-47 They continued steadfastly in the apostles' teaching and fellowship, in the breaking of bread, and prayer. Fear came on every soul, and many wonders and signs were done through the apostles. All who believed were together, and had all things in common. They sold their possessions and goods, and distributed them to all, according as anyone had need. Day by day, continuing steadfastly with one accord in the temple, and breaking bread at home, they took their food with gladness and singleness of heart, praising God, and having favor with all the people. The Lord added to the assembly day by day those who were being saved.

Dan. 12:1-13 "At that time shall Michael stand up, the great prince who stands for the children of your people; and there shall be a time of trouble, such as never was since there was a nation even to that same time: and at that time your people shall be delivered, everyone who shall be found written in the book. Many of those who sleep in the dust of the earth shall awake, some to everlasting life, and some to shame and everlasting contempt. Those who are wise shall shine as the brightness of the expanse; and those who turn many to righteousness as the stars forever and ever. But you, Daniel, shut up the words, and seal the book, even to the time of the end: many shall run back and forth, and knowledge shall be increased." Then I, Daniel, looked, and behold, two others stood, one on the river bank on this side, and the other on the river bank on that side. One said to the man clothed in linen, who was above the waters of the river, How long shall it be to the end of these wonders? I heard the man clothed in linen, who was above the waters of the river, when he held up his right hand and his left hand to heaven, and swore by him who lives forever that it shall be for a time, times, and a half; and when they have made an end of breaking in pieces the power of the holy people, all these things shall be finished. I heard, but I didn't understand: then I said, my lord, what shall be the issue of these things? He said, Go your way, Daniel; for the words are shut up and sealed until the time of the end. Many shall purify themselves, and make themselves white, and be refined; but the wicked shall do wickedly; and none of the wicked shall understand; but those who are wise shall understand. From the time that the continual burnt offering shall be taken away, and the abomination that makes desolate set up, there shall be one thousand two hundred ninety days. Blessed is he who waits, and comes to the one thousand three hundred thirty-five days. But go you your way until the end; for you shall rest, and shall stand in your lot, at the end of the days.

Week 24 Day 2   5-Jan

John 20:19-23 When therefore it was evening, on that day, the first day of the week, and when the doors were locked where the disciples were assembled, for fear of the Jews, Jesus came and stood in the midst, and said to them, "Peace be to you." When he had said this, he showed them his hands and his side. The disciples therefore were glad when they saw the Lord. Jesus therefore said to them again, "Peace be to you. As the Father has sent me, even so I send you." When he had said this, he breathed on them, and said to them, "Receive the Holy Spirit! If you forgive anyone's sins, they have been forgiven them. If you retain anyone's sins, they have been retained."

Rev. 22:12-17 "Behold, I come quickly. My reward is with me, to repay to each man according to his work. I am the Alpha and the Omega, the First and the Last, the Beginning and the End. Blessed are those who do his commandments, that they may have the right to the tree of life, and may enter in by the gates into the city. Outside are the dogs, the sorcerers, the sexually immoral, the murderers, the idolaters, and everyone who loves and practices falsehood. I, Jesus, have sent my angel to testify these things to you for the assemblies. I am the root and the offspring of David; the Bright and Morning Star." The Spirit and the bride say, "Come!" He who hears, let him say, "Come!" He who is thirsty, let him come. He who desires, let him take the water of life freely.

I Chr. 12:14-18 These of the sons of Gad were captains of the army: he who was least was equal to one hundred, and the greatest to one thousand. These are those who went over the Jordan in the first month, when it had overflowed all its banks; and they put to flight all them of the valleys, both toward the east, and toward the west. There came of the children of Benjamin and Judah to the stronghold to David. David went out to meet them, and answered them, "If you have come peaceably to me to help me, my heart shall be knit to you; but if you have come to betray me to my adversaries, since there is no wrong in my hands, may the God of our fathers look thereon, and rebuke it." Then the Spirit came on Amasai, who was chief of the thirty, and he said, "We are yours, David, and on your side, you son of Jesse: peace, peace be to you, and peace be to your helpers; for your God helps you." Then David received them, and made them captains of the band. So David received them and made them leaders of his raiding bands.

Week 24 Day 3   27-Oct

Matt. 28:18-20 Jesus came to them and spoke to them, saying, "All authority has been given to me in heaven and on earth. Go, and make disciples of all nations, baptizing them in the name of the Father and of the Son and of the Holy Spirit, teaching them to observe all things that I commanded you. Behold, I am with you always, even to the end of the age." Amen.

II Cor. 5:11-6:2 Knowing therefore the fear of the Lord, we persuade men, but we are revealed to God; and I hope that we are revealed also in your consciences. For we are not commending ourselves to you again, but speak as giving you occasion of boasting on our behalf, that you may have something to answer those who boast in appearance, and not in heart. For if we are beside ourselves, it is for God. Or if we are of sober mind, it is for you. For the love of Christ constrains us; because we judge thus, that one died for all, therefore all died. He died for all, that those who live should no longer live to themselves, but to him who for their sakes died and rose again. Therefore we know no one after the flesh from now on. Even though we have known Christ after the flesh, yet now we know him so no more. Therefore if anyone is in Christ, he is a new creation. The old things have passed away. Behold, all things have become new. But all things are of God, who reconciled us to himself through Jesus Christ, and gave to us the ministry of reconciliation; namely, that God was in Christ reconciling the world to himself, not reckoning to them their trespasses, and having committed to us the word of reconciliation. We are therefore ambassadors on behalf of Christ, as though God were entreating by us: we beg you on behalf of Christ, be reconciled to God. For him who knew no sin he made to be sin on our behalf; so that in him we might become the righteousness of God. Working together, we entreat also that you not receive the grace of God in vain, for he says, "At an acceptable time I listened to you, in a day of salvation I helped you." Behold, now is the acceptable time. Behold, now is the day of salvation.

Ex. 18:19-23 "Listen now to my voice. I will give you counsel, and God be with you. You represent the people before God, and bring the causes to God. You shall teach them the statutes and the laws, and shall show them the way in which they must walk, and the work that they must do. Moreover you shall provide out of all the people able men, such as fear God: men of truth, hating unjust gain; and place such over them, to be rulers of thousands, rulers of hundreds, rulers of fifties, and rulers of tens. Let them judge the people at all times. It shall be that every great matter they shall bring to you, but every small matter they shall judge themselves. So shall it be easier for you, and they shall share the load with you. If you will do this thing, and God commands you so, then you will be able to endure, and all of these people also will go to their place in peace."

Week 24 Day 4   14-Oct

Luke 8:37-39 All the people of the surrounding country of the Gadarenes asked him to depart from them, for they were very much afraid. He entered into the boat, and returned. But the man from whom the demons had gone out begged him that he might go with him, but Jesus sent him away, saying, "Return to your house, and declare what great things God has done for you." He went his way, proclaiming throughout the whole city what great things Jesus had done for him.

Acts 26:1-23 Agrippa said to Paul, "You may speak for yourself." Then Paul stretched out his hand, and made his defense. "I think myself happy, King Agrippa, that I am to make my defense before you this day concerning all the things that I am accused by the Jews, especially because you are expert in all customs and questions which are among the Jews. Therefore I beg you to hear me patiently. Indeed, all the Jews know my way of life from my youth up, which was from the beginning among my own nation and at Jerusalem; having known me from the first, if they are willing to testify, that after the strictest sect of our religion I lived a Pharisee. Now I stand here to be judged for the hope of the promise made by God to our fathers, which our twelve tribes, earnestly serving night and day, hope to attain. Concerning this hope I am accused by the Jews, King Agrippa! Why is it judged incredible with you, if God does raise the dead? I myself most certainly thought that I ought to do many things contrary to the name of Jesus of Nazareth. This I also did in Jerusalem. I both shut up many of the saints in prisons, having received authority from the chief priests, and when they were put to death I gave my vote against them. Punishing them often in all the synagogues, I tried to make them blaspheme. Being exceedingly enraged against them, I persecuted them even to foreign cities. Whereupon as I traveled to Damascus with the authority and commission from the chief priests, at noon, O king, I saw on the way a light from the sky, brighter than the sun, shining around me and those who traveled with me. When we had all fallen to the earth, I heard a voice saying to me in the Hebrew language, 'Saul, Saul, why are you persecuting me? It is hard for you to kick against the goads.' I said, 'Who are you, Lord?' He said, 'I am Jesus, whom you are persecuting. But arise, and stand on your feet, for I have appeared to you for this purpose: to appoint you a servant and a witness both of the things which you have seen, and of the things which I will reveal to you; delivering you from the people, and from the Gentiles, to whom I send you, to open their eyes, that they may turn from darkness to light and from the power of Satan to God, that they may receive remission of sins and an inheritance among those who are sanctified by faith in me.' Therefore, King Agrippa, I was not disobedient to the heavenly vision, but declared first to them of Damascus, at Jerusalem, and throughout all the country of Judea, and also to the Gentiles, that they should repent and turn to God, doing works worthy of repentance. For this reason the Jews seized me in the temple, and tried to kill me. Having therefore obtained the help that is from God, I stand to this day testifying both to small and great, saying nothing but what the prophets and Moses said would happen, how the Christ must suffer, and how, by the resurrection of the dead, he would be first to proclaim light both to these people and to the Gentiles."

Jon. 1:1-2 Now the word of Yahweh came to Jonah the son of Amittai, saying, "Arise, go to Nineveh, that great city, and preach against it, for their wickedness has come up before me."

Week 24 Day 5   19-Jun

John 21:15-25 So when they had eaten their breakfast, Jesus said to Simon Peter, "Simon, son of Jonah, do you love me more than these?" He said to him, "Yes, Lord; you know that I have affection for you." He said to him, "Feed my lambs." He said to him again a second time, "Simon, son of Jonah, do you love me?" He said to him, "Yes, Lord; you know that I have affection for you." He said to him, "Tend my sheep." He said to him the third time, "Simon, son of Jonah, do you have affection for me?" Peter was grieved because he asked him the third time, "Do you have affection for me?" He said to him, "Lord, you know everything. You know that I have affection for you." Jesus said to him, "Feed my sheep. Most certainly I tell you, when you were young, you dressed yourself, and walked where you wanted to. But when you are old, you will stretch out your hands, and another will dress you, and carry you where you don't want to go." Now he said this, signifying by what kind of death he would glorify God. When he had said this, he said to him, "Follow me." Then Peter, turning around, saw a disciple following. This was the disciple whom Jesus sincerely loved, the one who had also leaned on Jesus' breast at the supper and asked, "Lord, who is going to betray You?" Peter seeing him, said to Jesus, "Lord, what about this man?" Jesus said to him, "If I desire that he stay until I come, what is that to you? You follow me." This saying therefore went out among the brothers, that this disciple wouldn't die. Yet Jesus didn't say to him that he wouldn't die, but, "If I desire that he stay until I come, what is that to you?" This is the disciple who testifies about these things, and wrote these things. We know that his witness is true. There are also many other things which Jesus did, which if they would all be written, I suppose that even the world itself wouldn't have room for the books that would be written.

I Pet. 5:1-7 I exhort the elders among you, as a fellow elder, and a witness of the sufferings of Christ, and who will also share in the glory that will be revealed. Shepherd the flock of God which is among you, exercising the oversight, not under compulsion, but voluntarily, not for dishonest gain, but willingly; neither as lording it over those entrusted to you, but making yourselves examples to the flock. When the chief Shepherd is revealed, you will receive the crown of glory that doesn't fade away. Likewise, you younger ones, be subject to the elder. Yes, all of you clothe yourselves with humility, to subject yourselves to one another; for "God resists the proud, but gives grace to the humble." Humble yourselves therefore under the mighty hand of God, that he may exalt you in due time; casting all your worries on him, because he cares for you.

Ez. 34:1-10 The word of Yahweh came to me, saying, Son of man, prophesy against the shepherds of Israel, prophesy, and tell them, even to the shepherds, Thus says the Lord Yahweh: Woe to the shepherds of Israel who feed themselves! Shouldn't the shepherds feed the sheep? You eat the fat, and you clothe yourself with the wool, you kill the fatlings; but you don't feed the sheep. You haven't strengthened the diseased, neither have you healed that which was sick, neither have you bound up that which was broken, neither have you brought back that which was driven away, neither have you sought that which was lost; but with force and with rigor you have ruled over them. They were scattered, because there was no shepherd; and they became food to all the animals of the field, and were scattered. My sheep wandered through all the mountains, and on every high hill: yes, my sheep were scattered on all the surface of the earth; and there was none who searched or sought. Therefore, you shepherds, hear the word of Yahweh: As I live, says the Lord Yahweh, surely because my sheep became a prey, and my sheep became food to all the animals of the field, because there was no shepherd, neither did my shepherds search for my sheep, but the shepherds fed themselves, and didn't feed my sheep; therefore, you shepherds, hear the word of Yahweh: Thus says the Lord Yahweh: Behold, I am against the shepherds; and I will require my sheep at their hand, and cause them to cease from feeding the sheep; neither shall the shepherds feed themselves any more; and I will deliver my sheep from their mouth, that they may not be food for them.

Week 24 Day 6   16-Apr

Matt. 25:1-13 "Then the Kingdom of Heaven will be like ten virgins, who took their lamps, and went out to meet the bridegroom. Five of them were foolish, and five were wise. Those who were foolish, when they took their lamps, took no oil with them, but the wise took oil in their vessels with their lamps. Now while the bridegroom delayed, they all slumbered and slept. But at midnight there was a cry, 'Behold! The bridegroom is coming! Come out to meet him!' Then all those virgins arose, and trimmed their lamps. The foolish said to the wise, 'Give us some of your oil, for our lamps are going out.' But the wise answered, saying, 'What if there isn't enough for us and you? You go rather to those who sell, and buy for yourselves.' While they went away to buy, the bridegroom came, and those who were ready went in with him to the marriage feast, and the door was shut. Afterward the other virgins also came, saying, 'Lord, Lord, open to us.' But he answered, 'Most certainly I tell you, I don't know you.' Watch therefore, for you don't know the day nor the hour in which the Son of Man is coming."

Jude 17-25 But you, beloved, remember the words which have been spoken before by the apostles of our Lord Jesus Christ. They said to you that "In the last time there will be mockers, walking after their own ungodly lusts." These are they who cause divisions, and are sensual, not having the Spirit. But you, beloved, keep building up yourselves on your most holy faith, praying in the Holy Spirit. Keep yourselves in the love of God, looking for the mercy of our Lord Jesus Christ to eternal life. On some have compassion, making a distinction, and some save, snatching them out of the fire with fear, hating even the clothing stained by the flesh. Now to him who is able to keep them from stumbling, and to present you faultless before the presence of his glory in great joy, to God our Savior, who alone is wise, be glory and majesty, dominion and power, both now and forever. Amen.

Am. 5:18-24 "Woe to you who desire the day of Yahweh! Why do you long for the day of Yahweh? It is darkness, and not light. As if a man fled from a lion, and a bear met him; Or he went into the house and leaned his hand on the wall, and a snake bit him. Won't the day of Yahweh be darkness, and not light? Even very dark, and no brightness in it? I hate, I despise your feasts, and I can't stand your solemn assemblies. Yes, though you offer me your burnt offerings and meal offerings, I will not accept them; neither will I regard the peace offerings of your fat animals. Take away from me the noise of your songs! I will not listen to the music of your harps. But let justice roll on like rivers, and righteousness like a mighty stream."

Week 24 Day 7   3-Jun

Php. 3:12-4:1 Not that I have already obtained, or am already made perfect; but I press on, if it is so that I may take hold of that for which also I was taken hold of by Christ Jesus. Brothers, I don't regard myself as yet having taken hold, but one thing I do. Forgetting the things which are behind, and stretching forward to the things which are before, I press on toward the goal for the prize of the high calling of God in Christ Jesus. Let us therefore, as many as are perfect, think this way. If in anything you think otherwise, God will also reveal that to you. Nevertheless, to the extent that we have already attained, let us walk by the same rule. Let us be of the same mind. Brothers, be imitators together of me, and note those who walk this way, even as you have us for an example. For many walk, of whom I told you often, and now tell you even weeping, as the enemies of the cross of Christ, whose end is destruction, whose god is the belly, and whose glory is in their shame, who think about earthly things. For our citizenship is in heaven, from where we also wait for a Savior, the Lord Jesus Christ; who will change the body of our humiliation to be conformed to the body of his glory, according to the working by which he is able even to subject all things to himself. Therefore, my brothers, beloved and longed for, my joy and crown, so stand firm in the Lord, my beloved.

Ge. 15:1-18 After these things the word of Yahweh came to Abram in a vision, saying, "Don't be afraid, Abram. I am your shield, your exceedingly great reward." Abram said, "Lord Yahweh, what will you give me, since I go childless, and he who will inherit my estate is Eliezer of Damascus?" Abram said, "Behold, to me you have given no seed: and, behold, one born in my house is my heir." Behold, the word of Yahweh came to him, saying, "This man will not be your heir, but he who will come out of your own body will be your heir." Yahweh brought him outside, and said, "Look now toward the sky, and count the stars, if you are able to count them." He said to Abram, "So shall your seed be." He believed in Yahweh; and he reckoned it to him for righteousness. He said to him, "I am Yahweh who brought you out of Ur of the Chaldees, to give you this land to inherit it." He said, "Lord Yahweh, how will I know that I will inherit it?" He said to him, "Bring me a heifer three years old, a female goat three years old, a ram three years old, a turtledove, and a young pigeon." He brought him all of these, and divided them in the middle, and laid each half opposite the other; but he didn't divide the birds. The birds of prey came down on the carcasses, and Abram drove them away. When the sun was going down, a deep sleep fell on Abram. Now terror and great darkness fell on him. He said to Abram, "Know for sure that your seed will live as foreigners in a land that is not theirs, and will serve them. They will afflict them four hundred years. I will also judge that nation, whom they will serve. Afterward they will come out with great wealth, but you will go to your fathers in peace. You will be buried in a good old age. In the fourth generation they will come here again, for the iniquity of the Amorite is not yet full." It came to pass that, when the sun went down, and it was dark, behold, a smoking furnace, and a flaming torch passed between these pieces. In that day Yahweh made a covenant with Abram, saying, "To your seed I have given this land, from the river of Egypt to the great river, the river Euphrates"

Final Thoughts

There is a progression to the Christian life that begins with conversion to Christ, sometimes referred to as a second birth or being born again. Next begins a maturing process as one grows from a spiritual baby hopefully to maturity in Christ. The maturing process usually occurs along with ministry as one learns their gifts and uses them to serve Christ in the church or the world or both. For some there may also be a mission, a work they are specifically called to do in the world. We hope this book will aid in the process of maturity, ministry and perhaps mission as one remains connected to what God is doing in their midst and joins Him in it.

Often after the initial conversion experience one is introduced to basic instructions in the Christian life but then become so immersed in ministry that growth in maturity or Christ-likeness is stunted. This book and the Listening to Jesus program is meant to provide a life-long track to follow for continued growth in maturity and ministry rather than a one-time experience like most programs.

The Listening to Jesus program may be used with one set of readings the first time (or times) through before adding additional readings and used somewhat like a college curriculum:

Level 101	Gospel readings only
Level 201	Gospel readings with Oswald Chambers (O.C.)
Level 301	Gospel readings, O.C. and New Testament readings (N.T.)
Level 401	Gospel readings, O.C., N.T. and Old Testament readings (O.T.)
Level 501	Masters Program (whatever the Master calls you to do)

I've been through the program more than a dozen times and find ever deeper insights each time. I find I am much better able to 'hear' the Lord. This program is not all I use. I read from other parts of scripture, and other spiritual and secular writings, but the 3 daily questions are a constant as I seek to stay connected to what God is allowing in my life so I will understand my place in the world as time passes.

The 3 daily questions help us to abide. You may recall that to abide is to be one with God in purpose, thought and will. The first question helps us understand God's general purposes from scripture. The second question helps us understand what He is thinking by what He is allowing in our lives. The third question allows us to align our wills with his and do what He is calling us to do.

On the next pages I've added a worksheet to work through the times when one struggles with particular issues of life using the elements of tSOAR as well as a personal organization system that I found allows me to be more intentional about doing what I think God wants me to do.

Some of you may live in parts of the world where the Oswald Chambers devotional is not available. If you make us aware of your need along with the preferred language translation we will do our best to see that you receive a copy. Email your request to tSOARMinistries@live.com along with your contact information.

Anxiety, Temptation and Issues of Life

When "the cares of this world, and the deceitfulness of riches, and the lusts of other things entering in, choke the word, and it becomes unfruitful" or problems arise do this:

Time – take time to be alone with Christ.

Discuss with Jesus the truth of your current situation. Write down 1) who or what is being impacted, 2) the implications if nothing changes, 3) how you are being affected emotionally 4) how you helped create the situation, and 5) what truths of scripture apply:

_____

_____

_____

_____

_____

_____

Trust that the Father has allowed it and has a reason for it.

Surrender to (accept) what cannot be changed and trust that also to the Father.

Obey by taking the action(s) you believe God is asking you to take to resolve it:

_____

_____

_____

_____

As you obey you should begin to experience peace as you once again abide in Christ. Take responsibility for damage you may have caused to others and be reconciled to them. List them below and ask their forgiveness.

_____

_____

_____

Personal Organization

This organization system has only one potential flaw: you. The system works, but one must work the system! One of the primary purposes of getting organized is to allow you to clear your mind and use it for what its best at: thinking. It is not great at holding information, keeping track of projects or tasks you need to do. One barrier is that urgent matters often crowd out important ones, so we encourage you to schedule your daily, weekly and quarterly review described below.

Write Everything Down that is an action item that commands your attention. Don't rely on your memory alone. One obvious problem if you don't write everything down is that you might forget it, but that may be the 2nd worse thing. The worst thing might be that you won't forget it, so it keeps recycling through your mind hindering your ability to concentrate. Writing things down get them out of your mind so you can concentrate more completely on matters at hand.

The system has 7 components or files that hold your information:

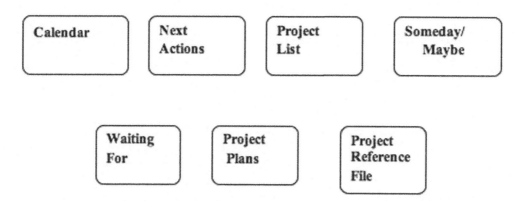

A new action item should be listed in 1 of the 4 files that appear on the top row: Your **Calendar** if the item is associated with a specific date and time. **Next Actions** if it is something that you want to get done soon, but doesn't have to be done on a specific date. **Someday/Maybe** If is not to be done now, but is something you wish to consider doing later. **Project List** if it is a project (something involving multiple steps); add it to your list of active projects then add two Next Actions. 1. Write your **Project Plans** and 2. Prepare a **Project Reference File** to store relevant information.

The **Waiting For** list contains items that you've worked on and done what you can, but requires another person to take action before moving forward. It may be as simple as returning a phone call or email or receiving a report. Having this list means you will not forget it and can follow up as necessary after waiting a sufficient amount of time.

When writing Next Actions and project steps, use 'action' words like list, write, call, etc. versus words like plan, prepare, develop, create, evaluate, etc. which are more difficult for the brain to interpret.

Daily: Write down every new action item that captures your attention in the appropriate file. Review your Calendar and Next Actions. Your daily time with the Lord answering the 3 daily questions may be when you are inspired to add items as a result of the previous day's activities.

When Next Actions that are part of a project are completed, remove it and add the next task from your Project Plans.

Weekly: Review your Calendar and Next Actions to see what is coming up and remove Next Actions that have been completed. Review your Waiting For file to determine if you should follow up on any of the items; if so, add the follow up to your Next Actions or Calendar. Review your Someday/Maybe list to see if any should be started or eliminated. Review your Project List to remind yourself of what you are working on and consider whether they are progressing. If needed, review your Project Plans.

Quarterly: Schedule time quarterly to take time away from your home and office at a park or other place where you can be alone and spend time with the Lord thinking about your life from what is sometimes called 10,000 feet view. Write down what you are trying to accomplish in each area of life (home, work & ministry). List of what each area consists of including the tasks and people.
You may find it useful to categorize using quadrants. On a piece of paper, draw a cross with the vertical line representing time you spend alone at the top and time you spend with others or doing things for others at the bottom. The horizontal line represents time when you are passive or recharging on the left and active or expending energy on the right. Create a separate page for home, work and ministry. Ideally you will have at least one item in each quadrant for each part of your life.

Here is an example of what might be in each quadrant for ministry. The upper left quadrant (alone, passive) might include solitude, journaling, listening prayer, fasting, and silence. The upper right quadrant (alone, active) might include petitioning prayer, worship, and study. The lower left quadrant (others, passive) might include a list of specific people integral to your life and perhaps groupings of people (church congregation for example), as well as corporate worship and fellowship. The lower right quadrant (others, active) would include your personal ministry such as acts of service, teaching, leading worship, and corporate prayer.

Each list should include everything you are doing, whether you think them appropriate or not. Solitude should be included as part of each of the areas of life assuming you are spending time daily answering the 3 daily questions. We should expect the Lord to communicate into every area of our life in our daily time with him. The purpose of creating these lists is for purpose of reviewing them with the Lord so he can speak into your life.

Once you have completed your lists spend time in prayer and ask these questions: **What tasks or relationships need improvement? What tasks or relationships should be eliminated? What tasks or relationships are not now in my life that should be?**

The quadrants can also be useful in your daily reviews to consider what you did in the prior day. Draw a cross and run a mental 'instant replay' of the prior day. List the events of the prior day in the appropriate quadrant and note anything that stands out. It might stimulate thoughts of certain actions to take from the prior day's events or possibly self-revelation.

Made in the USA
Middletown, DE
12 April 2021